EDMUND SPENSER
1900-1936

a reference guide

A
Reference
Guide
to
Literature

Everett Emerson
Editor

EDMUND SPENSER
1900-1936

a reference guide

WILLIAM L. SIPPLE
with the assistance of
Bernard J. Vondersmith

G.K.HALL &CO.

70 LINCOLN STREET, BOSTON, MASS.

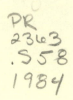
Library of Congress Cataloging in Publication Data

Sipple, William L.
  Edmund Spenser, 1900-1936.

  Includes index.
  1. Spenser, Edmund, 1552?-1599—Bibliography.
I. Vondersmith, Bernard J., 1943-   . II. Title.
Z8830.8.S58 1984 [PR2363] 821'.3   83-10745
ISBN 0-8161-8007-5

This publication is printed on permanent/durable acid-free paper
MANUFACTURED IN THE UNITED STATES OF AMERICA

Contents

The Author

William L. Sipple contributes regularly to the
Modern Humanities Research Association (MHRA) <u>Annual</u>
<u>Bibliography of Language and Literature</u>. He has pub-
lished guides for Audio-Brandon Films on the works and
film adaptations of the plays of Eugene O'Neill and
Tennessee Williams and the stories of John Cheever.
Professor Sipple has delivered papers at national con-
ferences and has published in various journals on
dialectology, pedagogy, and curriculum design. He also
serves as a state-wide evaluator for the Pennsylvania
Humanities Council. At present, Dr. Sipple is professor of English and chair of the English Department at
Waynesburg College. Professor Sipple holds a doctorate
in English from Duquesne University, where he was a
doctoral fellow, and a master of arts degree in English
from Gannon University.

Preface

In general, this reference guide includes all items directly
related to Spenser studies published from 1900 through 1936. The
decisions for including items are grounded in the following criteria.
First, all <u>bona</u> <u>fide</u> critical studies of Spenser are included: mono-
graphs, sections of books, journal articles, critical introductions
to editions of Spenser's works, doctoral dissertations and master's
theses on Spenser, and other studies that treat Spenser in some substantial way. Second, generally excluded from the reference guide
are studies that give only standard information on Spenser (i.e.,
name, dates, lists of works, summary introductions to the works,
etc.) and items that merely mention Spenser in general contexts of
studies of the Renaissance, literary history, and the like. Thus,
excluded are standard encyclopedia entries, introductions to editions
of Spenser's works that are not critical essays, sections of literary
histories that merely place Spenser in his age and mention his works,
journal articles that make only passing reference to Spenser or his
works, general histories of Ireland, studies of the environs of
Kilcolman that do not focus on Spenser, books and articles that
merely mention Spenser's descendants, most reviews of editions of
Spenser's works, notices of publication of editions of Spenser's
works, and all children's books and stories based on <u>The Faerie</u>
<u>Queene</u> and other works. The major difference, then, between this
reference guide and the Carpenter (1923) and Atkinson (1937) bibliographies is the exclusion of these marginal items that the early bibliographers included in their works. The result is a reference guide
for Spenser scholarship from 1900 to 1936 that includes about four-
teen hundred items directly related to Spenser studies. The Selected
Bibliographic Sources is included because of the necessity to re-
examine the Carpenter and Atkinson bibliographies so as to include
as many relevant items as possible.

Since the requisite organization for this reference guide is
chronological with one alphabetized list for each year, the annotations, cross-references, and index help to make the book versatile
and useful. As many items as could be located are annotated and
many of these have rather long annotations because the items are
difficult to locate and such annotations may help scholars determine

exactly what items they need to examine for their own research projects. Also, to a certain extent the trends in twentieth-century Spenser scholarship can be traced through the annotations. Many of the doctoral dissertations and master's theses are not annotated because their titles are enough. Most of the dissertations are published and the published editions are annotated. The dissertations and theses, which are not listed as completely in any other Spenser bibliography, reveal the extent of activity in Spenser scholarship in colleges and universities during the period between 1900 and 1936 and point out the early work of many notable Spenser scholars. For similar reasons many of the individual papers of Edwin Greenlaw's famous and influential "Seminary C" at The Johns Hopkins University are included. Note also that foreign dissertations are included and annotated whenever possible. Overall, the annotations are designed to be informative and nonjudgmental.

Cross-references direct the researcher to reprints, revised editions, and related items. This referencing has been kept to a minimum since from one perspective or another almost all the scholarship ties together. More important, then, for the user is the index. In order to eliminate the need to check several separate lists, this index is a single listing of subjects, works, authors, and persons other than authors treated, and authors and editors of studies and works listed; there are two sublists for The Faerie Queene and one sublist for The Shepheardes Calender. These sublists follow the main entries for The Faerie Queene and The Shepheardes Calender. This arrangement parallels that in the McNeir-Provost bibliography. Note that the spelling of Spenser's works in the annotations is regularized, while that in titles and quotations maintains the individual scholar's preference.

ACKNOWLEDGMENTS

It is a pleasure to thank the many people who have helped through the years of this project to see it to completion. Foremost among them is my Research Associate, Bernard J. Vondersmith. Dr. Vondersmith and I conceived the project in 1976, and during his tenure in the English Department of Indiana State University we worked as coauthors. Career changes, however, required him to take a less active role in the project and ultimately to withdraw from it. He now serves as Assistant to the Commissioner for Higher Education for the state of Maryland. I am indebted to him not only for his significant contribution to the research compiled in this book but also for his permission to complete the project without him. In a very real sense this book is the fruit of his labors as well as of mine.

Also, we are both indebted to Professor Foster Provost for his wise counsel and suggestions for this project, many of which extend back to our dissertations, which were completed under his direction. I am especially grateful to Professor Provost for his careful and thorough reading of this manuscript. We also thank him and Professor Waldo F. McNeir for permission to make references to their bibliography and for allowing us to use it as a model for our Spenser scholarship. I also owe many thanks to my wife Jo-Ann M. Sipple, who spent many tedious hours checking items in bibliographic sources and card catalogs, tracking down elusive items in the dusty corners of the Widener Library, helping to compile the index, and proofreading the manuscript. Waynesburg College deserves recognition for the two Faculty Research Grants I received to support this project. Also, my student research assistants, Suzanne French, William Ryan, and Theresa Kelly were a tremendous help during the summers of 1981 and 1982. I thank Joseph Parizack for his translations of several German articles and dissertations; and special appreciation goes to my typist and proofreader, Dessie Munce.

Without the cooperation of several dedicated librarians and the permission to use special library collections, this project could not have been completed. At Waynesburg College I am grateful to Joan Celento and her assistants for the many interlibrary loan requests they processed for me. In like manner, in the early stages of the project Karen Chittick and the interlibrary loan staff of the Cunningham Memorial Library of Indiana State University were very helpful. I also appreciate the cooperation I received from the research staffs of several libraries, chiefly the Duquesne University Library, the Hillman Library of the University of Pittsburgh, the Carnegie Public Library of Pittsburgh, the Widener and Pusey Libraries of Harvard University, the Sterling Library of Yale University, and the libraries at Johns Hopkins University, Indiana University, and the University of Chicago.

Finally, I thank G.K. Hall editor Janice Meagher and our field editor, Professor Everett Emerson, who made many helpful suggestions and encouraged us to complete the book, and I thank all the many others who helped us in tangible ways to see this project to completion.

Introduction

Edmund Spenser, "the prince of poets in his time," received considerable critical attention during the first third of the twentieth century. This reference guide chronicles Spenserian scholarship through the period 1900-1936 and includes over 1,400 separate items that in some significant way focus on Spenser's works, biography, reputation, or influence. First among the reasons for undertaking this project is the intent to provide scholars and students of Spenser a thorough, useful companion reference volume to the very fine work of Waldo F. McNeir and Fostor Provost, Edmund Spenser, An Annotated Bibliography 1937-1972, Duquesne University Philological Studies, no. 17 (Pittsburgh: Duquesne University Press, 1975). The McNeir-Provost bibliography and this reference guide bring twentieth-century Spenser scholarship into two volumes that are compatible in focus, attitude, and completeness. Indicative of the links between this reference guide and the McNeir-Provost volume are the cross-references "ahead" to reprints of items originally published between 1900 and 1936, but reissued after 1936 and included by McNeir and Provost (format for this referencing is "See McNeir-Provost no. ___").

This early period of twentieth-century Spenser scholarship was initially compiled by two bibliographers: Frederic Ives Carpenter in A Reference Guide to Edmund Spenser (Chicago: University of Chicago Press, 1923); and Dorothy F. Atkinson in Edmund Spenser: A Bibliographical Supplement (Baltimore: Johns Hopkins Press, 1937). Carpenter's and Atkinson's bibliographies served scholars and students well for many years and stand as competent examples of early historical scholarship. However, the scrutiny of more modern researchers reveals that these early bibliographies omit important items of Spenserian scholarship, contain inaccuracies and errors and focus too generally on aspects of the sixteenth century that are only marginally related to Spenser. It is the purpose, then, of this reference guide to update, correct, supplement, and reassess the Carpenter and Atkinson bibliographies and to evaluate and include items from other bibliographical studies of Spenser relevant to the period 1900-1936. The result of this intensive research is a more selective bibliography of early twentieth-century Spenserian scholarship that more accurately reflects Spenser studies during these years.

Early twentieth-century critics pay much attention to the details
of Spenser's biography. While it is certain that Spenser was born
about 1552 and died in 1599, relatively little information on the
poet's life is available, beyond the general accounts of his years
at Merchant Taylors School and Pembroke College, Cambridge, the outline of a few personal relationships, and the fact of his service to
the Earl of Leicester and later to Lord Grey in Ireland. This notable
lack of detail in Spenser's biography leads many researchers to public records and documents in England and Ireland, to church records,
and to genealogies in an attempt to piece together more data on the
poet. Much of this study focuses on identifying the allusions in the
poetic works and speculating on the nature and extent of Spenser's
relationships with contemporaries such as Gabriel Harvey, Sir Philip
Sidney, and Edward Dyer. Others detail Spenser's lineage and line of
descendants, or concern themselves with the very fact of the poet's
existence: a mild controversy exists as to whether "Edmund Spenser"
was or was not a pen name for Francis Bacon. Researchers also assess
Spenser's involvement in contemporary affairs: the politics of
Elizabeth's court and the subjugation of the Irish. While these
biographical studies have clarified much about the poet's life and
his relationship to his age, still relatively little is known for
certain; note that these kinds of studies, while decidedly fewer in
number as the century progresses, still occupy scholars' efforts (see
McNeir Provost, nos. 118-240).

What stand clear, though, are Spenser's works. Much of the poet
is revealed through the works, and appropriately, the bulk of schol-
arly attention is on the works themselves. Since this reference
guide is directed not only to Spenser scholars but also to persons
relatively unfamiliar with Spenser scholarship, it is appropriate to
present an overview of the works and the chief trends in early
twentieth-century criticism on them. The discussion treats the minor
works first,[1] roughly in chronological order of publication, and then
The Faerie Queene.

MINOR WORKS

The Shepheardes Calender

Spenser's earliest important publication, The Shepheardes Calender
(1579), enters the literary world cloaked in mystery, for besides al-
luding to many contemporary persons and events, Spenser signs his series of pastoral eclogues with the pseudonym Imeritô. To add to the
secrecy, one E.K. authors a commentary on the poem and dubs Imeritô
"the new poet." Unravelling this web of allusions and secrecy concerned many critics of the early part of the century, for much of the
scholarship on The Shepheardes Calender from 1900 to 1936 identifies
allusions, speculates on the identity of E.K., and addresses the significance of E.K.'s glosses to the eclogues of the Calender.

The twelve eclogues, structured as a calendar with one eclogue
for each month, are shaped as dialogues among shepherds, except for
"January" and "December," which are complaints of Colin Clout, the
central figure and author of the poem. Colin's disappointing love
relationship with Rosalinde threads through The Shepheardes Calender,
giving the separate eclogues a kind of dramatic cohesiveness and a
central thematic focus, further enhanced by the four-season motif
running through the poem. Colin's association with Hobbinol also
expands in the poem: from a mere companion in the early eclogues
Hobbinol becomes Colin's trusted advisor and confidant in the end.
The Shepheardes Calender touches upon other themes in its individual
eclogues, broadly delineated by E.K.'s division of the eclogues into
plaintive, recreative, and moral types. In his "Arguement" for the
poem, E.K. says, "For eyther they be plaintive, as the first, the
sixth, the eleventh, and the twelfth; or recreative, such as al those
be which containe matter of love, or commendation of special personages; or moral, which for the most part be mixed with some satyrical
bitterness: namely the second, of reverence dewe to old age, the
fift, of coloured deceipt, the seventh and ninth, of dissolute shepheardes and pastours, the tenth, of contempt of poetries and pleasaunt
wits." Contemporary Spenserian scholars pay considerable attention
to the thematic aspects of The Shepheardes Calender, moving generally
from commentaries on specific parts of the poem and identifications
of individual persons and events, to studies of the overall unity and
structure of the Calender.

As a collection of eclogues, The Shepheardes Calender follows in
the main tradition of the pastoral, influenced chiefly by Theocritus,
Virgil, Baptista Mantuanus, and Clément Marot. Theocritus establishes
the general characteristics of the pastoral genre with his Idyls
(third century B.C.): idyllic setting; dramatic situations involv-
ing simple peasant types, generally shepherds, who meet to sing songs
and debate; their talk, usually a low dialect, leads to precise observations on the beauty of the world. Studies of Spenser's sources
and influences comprise a significant part of the commentary on The
Shepheardes Calender during the period 1900-1936. Theocritus's influence on Spenser is evident in the singing match of "August"
(Theocritus's fifth idyl), and in Colin's dejected attitude
(Theocritus's third idyl), besides in the general aspects of the
pastoral situation in the poem. Moschus and Bion, successors of
Theocritus, contribute to the early tradition, and Bion, especially,
should be noted for the parallels between his fourth idyl and
Spenser's "March" eclogue. Later in the tradition, Virgil's ten
Eclogues (37 B.C.) move the pastoral into the realm of the personal
and the political by making the eclogue a vehicle for slightly veiled
personal interests or themes of national import. Spenser's use of
the pastoral eclogue for allegorical purposes owes something to
Virgil; for example, relationships exist between Spenser's "June"
eclogue and Virgil's first and between the "August" eclogue and
Virgil's third.

Petrarch and Boccaccio receive the Virgilian tradition in the
fourteenth century, but neither significantly influences Spenser's
Calender. In the sixteenth century Mantuanus employs an allegorical
pastoral that closely parallels Spenser's eclogues. Noted for their
ecclesiastical satire, Mantuanus's Eclogues (ca. 1468) relate closely
to the religious satire of the "July" and "September" eclogues
(Mantuanus, VII and VIII); other parallels exist between Spenser's
complaint over the hard lot of the poet in the "October" eclogue and
Mantuanus's fifth eclogue, and between Mantuanus's eclogues and
Spenser's dirge in "November." More important for the "November"
eclogue, however, is the Complaincte de ma Dame Loyse de Savoye of
Clément Marot, poet in the court of Margaret de Valois. The shepherds of Marot's Complaincte and Spenser's Calender bear many of the
same names and engage in very similar activities, with Marot's influence most evident in the "December" eclogue, which follows the
Eglogue au Roy soubs les noms de Pan et Robin (1539) in plan, attitude, and detail. By Spenser's time, then, there exists an extensive
pastoral literature, which critics relate variously to Spenser, frequently through Chaucer. Most agree that the calendar framework,
however, is original with Spenser, even though the linking together
of eclogues with a romantic theme was anticipated by Boccaccio,
Sannazaro, and, in a sense, Marot. Also, scholars point to Spenser's
original use of fables within the pastoral eclogue, as in "February"
with "The Oak and the Briar" and in "May" with "The Fox and the Kid"
fables.

Complaints

Twelve years after the publication of The Shepheardes Calender
and one year after the successful public reception of three books of
The Faerie Queene, William Ponsonbie published the Complaints, Containing Sundrie Small Poems of the Worlds Vanitie (1591), a collection of Spenser's short poems which Ponsonbie claims have "bene
diverslie imbeziled and purloyned from him [Spenser], since his
departure over sea." These poems of uneven quality record, in parallel
with The Shepheardes Calender, Spenser's development as a poet, for
some of the Complaints date before 1580, even though Spenser probably
made revisions prior to publication. While many scholars have debated
the dating of composition and proper ordering of these poems, it is
fairly certain that the Visions and the Ruines of Rome date from
Spenser's university days; that Virgil's Gnat, Prosopopoia: or
Mother Hubberds Tale, and The Teares of the Muses are contemporary
with The Shepheardes Calender and the beginning of The Faerie Queene;
and that The Ruines of Time and Muiopotmos: or The Fate of the
Butterflie date from shortly before the publication of the collection
and needed no revision for inclusion in the volume. Even though the
impression given by Ponsonbie's introductory note leads some scholars
to believe that he collected these poems from Spenser and arranged
the volume without Spenser's assistance or input, critics generally
discredit this view and maintain that Spenser was too careful a poet
to leave the arrangement of his poetry to his printer. Many, however,

debate the degree of Spenser's involvement with Ponsonbie. More
abundant, though, in the early twentieth-century criticism on the
Complaints are studies of themes and techniques in the poems, showing how Spenser's work here, as in The Shepheardes Calender, introduces his mature poetry.

   Ponsonbie accurately characterizes this volume of poems as all
containing "like matter of argument in them, being all complaints and
meditations of the worlds vanitie, verie grave and profitable." The
Complaints variously probe aspects of the pervasive Elizabethan theme
of the danger of placing too much stock in impermanent earthly glory.
The Elizabethans, like their ancestors in the Middle Ages, look to a
spiritual world for permanence and place considerable faith in the
permanance of poetry. Several commentators note that precedent exists for this sort of volume of poems in Jonker Jon Van der Noot's
Theatre for Worldlings (1569). Spenser's first published poems
(translations) are contained in the Theatre for Worldlings.

   Other analogues to Spenser's Complaints include Boccaccio's
De Casibus Virorum Illustrium, Lydgate's Fall of Princes, Chaucer's
Monk's Tale, and in the Renaissance the Mirror for Magistrates.
Googe's translation of Palingenius's Zodiake of Life and Gascoigne's
Droome of Doomes Day also parallel thematic aspects of the Complaints.
In general, then, the Complaints reflect Spenser's waning youthful
idealism and indicate his mature dissatisfaction with the world.
The bulk of the scholarship on the individual poems concerns Spenser's
varied exploration of the themes of the world's vanity.

   The first poem in the volume, the Ruines of Time, a verse commem-
orating the Dudleys, establishes the tone for the Complaints. Par-
tially an English rendition of Du Bellay's Antiquitez de Rome (1558),
the Ruines of Time is a lament on the decay of earthly glory expressed
through the spirit of the ancient city of Verulam, a once-glorious
city that stood on the present-day sight of St. Albans. The initial
lament introduces a history of the Dudley family, which focuses on
Sidney and comments on fame and the immortality that a poet can
achieve through his poetry. Spenser concludes the poem with two
series of visions that, in a sense, provide a hopeful conclusion to
the lamentation of the first parts. Finally, in the concluding
stanza of the envoy, Spenser returns to the dedication of the poem
to Lady Mary, the Countess of Pembroke and sister of Philip Sidney,
hoping that "this moniment of his last praise" consoles and inspires
her with heavenly thoughts that rise above the "drosse of sinful
worlds desire." Generally, the little critical commentary there is
on the Ruines of Time focuses on Spenser's theme of fame and poetic
immortality.

   Similar in theme to the Ruines of Time, Teares of the Muses,
second in the volume, conveys the attitude that the "mightie peeres"
no longer care about the immortality poetry affords the poet; this
universal barbarity destroys the accomplishments and import of the

muses and, thus, each in turn laments the present degenerate situation, recalls a more glorious past when poetry was respected, and finally weeps tragically. Spenser's commentators frequently question the date of this poem, for this assessment of the indifference toward the arts and preponderance of universal ignorance seem incongruous in light of the magnificent Elizabethan culture of 1591. If Teares of the Muses dates as early as 1579 or 1580, its critique of sixteenth-century culture seems to have more justification, for the poem would then antedate many of the writers who attained prominence in the 1580s: Sidney, Marlowe, and Greene. Critics suggest, then, that Spenser's theme reveals something of the attitude of the Pléiade, the group of French poets, among them Ronsard and Du Bellay, who regenerated French literature in the mid-sixteenth century. The theme of Teares of the Muses resembles that of Du Bellay's La Déffence et Illustration de la Langue francoyse (1549), which also treats the theme of poetry and its power to create immortality for the poet. Spenser, like Du Bellay, also makes a distinction between the virtuous poet and the ignorant rhymer. Early in the twentieth century, as with the commentary on The Shepheardes Calender, critics interpret Teares of the Muses largely in historical and topical terms, finding the date crucial to understanding Spenser's theme and allusions. As the century progresses, however, scholars pay more attention to larger thematic aspects of the poem, generally agreeing that while a tone of pathos dominates Teares of the Muses, the thematic and structural elements of the poem express Spenser's frustrated hope for a world regenerated by the power of poetry: poetry no longer affects men as it used to, and the muses as Spenser conceived them "Walk through the world of euery one reuiled."

Third in the Complaints comes Spenser's adaptation of the pseudo-Virgilian Culex, Virgil's Gnat, dedicated to Leicester and generally believed to date from the later years of Spenser's association with Robert Dudley, 1577-1580. As the dedicatory sonnet implies, Spenser apparently suffered some wrong because of Leicester, the nature of which eludes critics throughout the century. Early commentators read Virgil's Gnat as a warning to Leicester against the dangers of the proposed marriage of Elizabeth and the Duc d'Alençon. However, nowhere in the poem does Spenser make any direct reference to justify a topical interpretation. Other commentators who compare and contrast Spenser's spirited poem with the Culex conclude that Spenser enlarges only the descriptive passages of the original "epyllion," or little epic, mainly in the beginning, and that he alters the original's hexameters to ottava rima, a form which allows for the freer, more relaxed movement of Spenser's style.

Prosopopoia: Or Mother Hubberds Tale, from the same period as Virgil's Gnat (1577-1580), decries the evils of society in a range of satiric comment similar to that in The Shepheardes Calender. Spenser's one fully satiric poem, Mother Hubberds Tale emulates the Roman de Renard tales (translated into English by Caxton in 1481 and by Gaultier in 1550) in both the details of its setting and its two

conniving characters, the Fox and the Ape; the breadth and movement
of Spenser's satire in Mother Hubberds Tale recalls Boccaccio's
Decameron and, of course, Chaucer's Canterbury Tales. In the poem
Spenser adeptly manipulates his Ape and Fox through a series of incongruous events on all levels of society with the same flair and
ease that he displays in managing the diverse world of The Faerie
Queene. In the narrative old Mother Hubberd consoles the poet with
a tale of a Fox and Ape, who, dissatisfied with their low estate,
seek adventure in a foreign land. From their common beginnings,
they soon rise to the rank of clergy through their disguises and
then move on to court and the decadent life among the nobility,
which affords Spenser the opportunity to comment on the intrigues
and pettiness of court life, as well as on the major ills of society.
Because of the scope of Spenser's satire in Mother Hubberds Tale,
critics interpret the poem as a commentary on various controversies
of the sixteenth century in much the same vein as the topical passages of The Shepheardes Calender. On a more general level of criticism, Spenserians note more universal themes in the poem: the
transitoriness of earthly glory, the corruption that often accom-
panies power, the decay of the mutable world in contrast to the
eternal glories of the world of permanence. Other writers on Mother
Hubberds Tale note Spenser's skillful handling of various genres in
constructing this satire; the états du monde form and the beast-
fable stand out in this regard.

The Ruines of Rome, the next poem after Mother Hubberds Tale in
the Complaints, is generally considered an exercise from Spenser's
university days. In his series of sonnets in the English form (rhymed
abab cdcd efef gg) Spenser translates a main section of Du Bellay's
Antiquitez de Rome, which corresponds to his adaptations of Du Bellay
in the Ruines of Time and The Visions of Bellay. What little critical attention the Ruines of Rome receives focuses on the quality of
Spenser's translations, concluding that while Spenser's adaptation is
resourceful and apt at times, overall it is inaccurate and displays
little knowledge of French.

Muiopotmos, or the Fate of the Butterflie (1590), a mature piece
often considered to be the most sophisticated of the Complaints, relates the story of how Aragnoll entraps and murders the unsuspecting
Clarion, the most beautiful "of all the race of silver-winged flies."
This beautiful lyric, full of glowing description and classical allusion, seems at times mock-heroic because of the epic preparations
Clarion and Aragnoll make for battle; yet, the poem lacks the usual
light tone and humor common to the mock-heroic, and suggests that
here, as in most of his other poems, Spenser presents an allegory.
Critics variously interpret Muiopotmos as a topical allegory of some
political controversy between two powerful figure of Elizabeth's
court, as a delightful narrative with little secondary significance,
as a mock-heroic poem, as a parody of The Faerie Queene, as an allegory on the fate of excellence in a corrupt world, and as an allegory
of man's futile search for happiness while struggling with mutability.

Also, throughout the century commentators debate the genre to which
Muiopotmos belongs, a matter often closely related to the study of
the poem's meaning, and assess the degree of Chaucerian influence
evident in the poem. At the beginning of the century three views
of Muiopotmos prevail: (1) Clarion represents Spenser and the poem
is largely a biographical allegory; (2) the poem is an allegory of
the Raleigh--Essex tension, the Burghley--Leicester antagonism, the
Oxford--Sidney feud, or some other political problem close to Elizabeth's court; (3) Clarion, unconscious of the force of death imping-
ing on his carefree existence, simply represents youth and joy.

     Spenser concludes the Complaints with a series of visions,
Visions of the Worlds Vanitie, The Visions of Bellay, and The Visions
of Petrarch, all short series of sonnets in Spenser's own form (abab
bcbc cdcd ee) that date early in his career. Only the Visions of the
Worlds Vanitie is original with Spenser; the others are adapted from
Du Bellay and Petrarch: The Visions of Bellay is a translation of
the Songe at the conclusion of Du Bellay's Antiquitez de Rome and
The Visions of Petrarch is ultimately a translation of Petrarch's
canzone, Rime no. 323. Commentators find more immediate links,
though, between Marot's "Des Visions de Pétrarch" and Spenser's
Visions of Petrarch. The little critical attention directed to the
Visions centers on the accuracy and innovativeness of Spenser's translations and adaptations. In the Visions Spenser probes the theme of
pride, and like all the Complaints, the Visions express the results
of man's vanity.

Daphnaida, Colin Clouts Come Home Againe, Astrophel

     In the last decade of the sixteenth century the "new poet" of
The Shepheardes Calender gains increasing recognition and reputation
among his contemporaries with the publication of Daphnaida (1591), an
elegy requested for the death of a woman Spenser never met, the
daughter of Henry Lord Howard, Colin Clouts Come Home Againe (1595),
a Virgilian pastoral inspired by Spenser's 1589 trip to London with
Raleigh, and Astrophel (1595), a pastoral elegy on the death of
Philip Sidney that serves as an introduction to several obituary
poems in Sidney's honor included in the volume. These poems and
Book VI of The Faerie Queene (1596) represent Spenser's last large
scale use of the pastoral; the Amoretti, Epithalamion, and the Fowre
Hymnes include only pastoral elements.

     Dedicated to Lady Helena, Marquesse of Northampton, Daphnaida
laments the death of eighteen-year-old Douglas Howard, daughter of
Lord Howard and wife to Arthur Gorges, Raleigh's friend whom Spenser
remembers in Colin Clouts Come Home Againe as "sad Alcyon." In his
elegy for Daphne, Spenser sustains a haunting emotional tone, due in
part to his free use of rhetorical devices and his alteration of the
rhyme royal stanza and in part to his improvisation on Chaucer's
elegiac vision, the Book of the Duchess. Evaluation of Spenser's
use of Chaucer's poem as a model is the central issue of critical

Introduction

studies of Daphnaida. Spenser, however, enlarges his elegy with a
seven-stanza lament that becomes progressively more pessimistic,
with no attempt at a passage of solace which would correspond to
Chaucer's abrupt, but hopeful conclusion. Critics early in the century tend to find Daphnaida somewhat original as a "love-vision-
elegy," while later critics consider it a lackluster elegy or an
excessively passionate lyrical complaint.

A much more accomplished poem than Daphnaida, Colin Clouts Come
Home Againe serves poetic and didactic ends similar to those of The
Shepheardes Caldender. Within the pastoral setting, Colin Clout recalls his recent journey to a distant land (Spenser's 1589 trip to
London) and his visit to the court of Cynthia. Colin's dismay and
bitterness over the corrupt life at court set the tone for Spenser's
criticism of complex court intrigues and immorality in court life.
Nevertheless, Colin's excitement over his competition at court with
the Shepherd of the Ocean, his descriptions of the ladies and courtiers at Cynthia's court, and his praise for the great Queen herself
reveal his devotion to Elizabeth and her rule. Colin's observations
on love at court distinguish base from ideal love, views of love that
scholars find fully developed in Spenser's later poems and in The
Faerie Queene. Also, scholars praise Colin Clouts Come Home Againe
for Spenser's expertise in subtly unifying numerous and diverse top-
ics within a pastoral frame that is neither overly obtrusive nor too
restrictive; it affords Spenser the opportunity for bluntness through
Colin's humble shepherd's pose, the freedom to satirize with the
directness of Mother Hubberds Tale, and the poetic flexibility for
lyrical rhapsody. Colin Clouts Come Home Againe stands not only as
the longest single eclogue in the language, but also as a summation
of Spenser's mastery of the genre passed down to him from Theocritus,
Virgil, Mantuanus, and Marot.

No discernible trend emerges in the early criticism of Colin
Clouts Come Home Againe: for half of the century the tight unity of
the poem goes unrecognized, while commentators regard the poem mainly
as a loosely autobiographical pastoral. They attempt to uncover in
it many allusions to poets and court personalities, historical situations and other topical matters, with the attitude that the poem lacks
overall unity. Concurrent with this criticism runs commentary on the
nature of the pastoral itself, on Spenser's place in the pastoral tradition, and on the sources for Spenser's poem and the chief influences
on it. As critics of the early part of the century move toward inter-
pretations of Colin Clouts Come Home Againe that treat more universal
themes and the unity of the poem, they emphasize several aspects of
the poem: the centrality of Spenser's relationship with Raleigh in
the poem, Spenser's disdain for courtly love and affirmation of married love, Spenser's interest in Ireland as a source of inspiration
for his poetry, and a general sense that Spenser's personal power
and influence as a poet are growing.

Published in the same volume with <u>Colin Clouts Come Home Againe</u>, <u>Astrophel</u> laments the death of Sir Philip Sidney and introduces a series of elegies for Sidney by Lodowich Bryskett, Matthew Royden, and Sir Walter Raleigh, whose poems often reach more genuine emotional peaks than Spenser's own. <u>Astrophel</u> concludes with the introduction of Clorinda, Astrophel's sister, who sings the first lamentation. Spenser's commentators regard the <u>Doleful Lay of Clorinda</u>, purported to be written by Sidney's sister, the Countess of Pembroke, actually to be Spenser's own dramatic beginning of the succession of real mourners, who honor Sidney with their own elegies. Commentators link Spenser's <u>Astrophel</u> to Bion's <u>Lament for Adonis</u>, mainly because of the parallel hunting sequences, to Ronsard's <u>Adonis</u>, because of the love theme, and to Spenser's lament for Dido in the "November" eclogue of <u>The Shepheardes Calender</u> and to <u>Daphnaida</u>. Critics early in the century focus on Spenser's indebtedness to Bion and Ronsard for models for <u>Astrophel</u>. Later critics find thematic unity in the poem and generally consider the <u>Doleful Lay of Clorinda</u> to be an integral part of <u>Astrophel</u>'s total structure. Finally, Spenser's treatments of love in <u>Astrophel</u> and in <u>Colin Clouts Come Home Againe</u> contrast with his more positive and happy treatments of love in the <u>Amoretti</u> and <u>Epithalamion</u>.

<u>Amoretti</u>, <u>Epithalamion</u>, <u>Prothalamion</u>

Published together in 1595, the <u>Amoretti</u> and <u>Epithalamion</u> celebrate Spenser's attitudes on the confident and joyous love of courtship and marriage, and apparently recollect his courtship and marriage of his second wife, Elizabeth Boyle. Critics find few facts to substantiate the correlation between the poetic accounts and the actual events, yet the two works clearly embody autobiographical allusions and reveal an emotional intensity that strongly suggests personal involvement. Many scholars early in the century focus their attention on identifying the lady of the sonnets and marriage song; today few disagree that she is Elizabeth Boyle. The more important link between the <u>Amoretti</u> and <u>Epithalamion</u> is the love theme, suggesting that the marriage ode naturally and logically completes the sequence of sonnets. Circumstantial evidence supports this: Spenser's printer gives each sonnet and each stanza of the <u>Epithalamion</u> a separate page, running the same border decoration along the top and bottom of each page throughout, indicating that the poems are more than companion pieces. Also, the four anacreontic verses about Cupid and Venus, which Spenser places between the <u>Amoretti</u> and the <u>Epithalamion</u>, can serve as a bridge between the sonnet sequence and the marriage song. Scholars in the latter part of the twentieth century substantiate the links between the poems, supporting early critics' suggestions that the poems are indeed one unified work.

Appearing at the end of the sixteenth century in the rush of English sonnet sequences, the eighty-eight sonnets of Spenser's <u>Amoretti</u> employ the conventional theme of the lover vying for the affections of a beautiful woman. Sidney's story of passionate and unrequired love in <u>Astrophel and Stella</u> (1591) inspired his contemporaries to write their own versions of the theme. Immediately preceding Spenser's <u>Amoretti</u>, Constable's <u>Diana</u> (1592), Giles Fletcher's <u>Licia</u> (1593), and Drayton's <u>Idea's Mirror</u> (1594) forward this dictinctive tradition of love poetry, which has roots in the "<u>dolce stil nuovo</u>" poetry of Dante's sonnets to Beatrice and in Petrarch's poems to Laura. Critics point out, however, that while Spenser incorporates the well-established conventions into his sonnets, he achieves uniqueness in that he subtly makes jest of these stock Petrarchan reactions and images, exposing their limitations and inappropriateness for his expression of love. The love of the <u>Amoretti</u>, unlike the futile relationships depicted in other sequences of the day, moves consistently from chastity to the happy promise of married love, which is appropriately celebrated in the <u>Epithalamion</u>. A genuine warmth and sincerity permeates the "little loves" that pay tribute not only to the lady but also to the love itself.

Much of the early commentary on the <u>Amoretti</u> focuses on the sources and influences relevant to Spenser's conception of love: mainly, critics question the degree of Petrarchan and Platonic influence on Spenser. For three decades scholars favor Petrarchan influences, pointing to the poetry of the Pléiade (notably Desportes's <u>Cléonce</u>, <u>Les Amours d'Hypolyte</u>, and <u>Diane</u>) as likely sources. During the 1930s, however, critics discuss Spenser's theme of chaste love and tend to find more Platonic influences in the sequence. This concern for sources gradually gives way to discussions of the unity among the sonnets and of the unity between the <u>Amoretti</u> and <u>Epithalamion</u>. Also, early twentieth-century scholars comment on Spenser's inventiveness in the sonnet form, concluding that the interlocking <u>abab</u> <u>bcbc</u> <u>cdcd</u> <u>ee</u> rhyme scheme is original with Spenser, but that several Scottish poets independently developed the form at about the same time.

Frequently praised as Spenser's finest and most original lyrical poem, the <u>Epithalamion</u> sparks new life into a literary genre that extends back to Psalm forty-four, the Book of Canticles, Hesiod's <u>Shield of Herakles</u>, and Homer's <u>Iliad</u>, Book 18. Scholars generally agree that the <u>Epithalamion</u>, translating "on the marriage bed" or "at the nuptual chamber," pays tribute to Elizabeth Boyle and Spenser's marriage to her on June 11, 1594, near Kilcolman, Ireland. In form the poem follows the <u>canzone</u> of Dante and Petrarch; Spenser, however, enlarges the typical pattern of five or six long stanzas followed by a five to seven line <u>tornata</u> to a much more generous format of twenty-three long stanzas (seventeen to nineteen lines each) with the traditional <u>tornata</u>. Unlike most of his contemporaries who wrote epithalamia to celebrate aristocratic marriages in imitation of classical epic epithalamia (Catullus 64, Theocritus 18), which sing of the loves of gods and heroes with all of Olympus in attendance, Spenser follows in the tradition of the lyric epithalamia (Catullus 61, 62), which is characterized by its focus on human marriages and its use of a refrain. Spenser writes of his own bride and wedding, makes the bridegroom the speaker in the poem, and mixes details of

Irish geography and English folk customs with the typical mythological
allusions. As a result, Spenser maintains an emotional tone and personal involvement throughout his Epithalamion as he does in the
Amoretti. Critics throughout the century recognize the Epithalamion
as an exquisite love poem, trace the classical and more recent sources
of Spenser's poem, enumerate and evaluate borrowings, and list the
various love motifs in it. It is not until mid-century that Spenserians begin to recognize the structural functions of the love theme and
to demonstrate the close links between the Amoretti and Epithalamion.
In the first two decades of the century critics tend to focus on
Spenser's use and adaptation of classical sources; in the 1930s
their attention centers on Spenser's debt to the Pléiade, especially
to Du Bellay and Marc-Claude de Buttet, to whom Spenser owes more
than to Catullus.

By Spenser's time betrothal celebrations were common practice in
Elizabethan England, often marked by poems, pageants, masques, and
minstrels. With the Prothalamion (1596) Spenser creates a genre
specifically for these celebrations, in this instance the double
betrothal and marriage of the daughters of Edward Somerset, Earl of
Worcester. The poem commemorates their ceremonial visit to Essex
House a short time before the wedding. The bridal party probably
travelled up to Essex House from Greenwich by barge on the Thames,
floating with the tide and accompanied by numerous smaller boats.
In the poem the poet-speaker recreates this scene with the two brides
depicted as mythical swans. The poet-speaker contrasts his woes and
defeats with the procreative hopes of the marriages. When Essex
appears to greet the bridal parties, the poet resolves his conflict-
ing moods by recalling his own happy days at Essex House (formerly
Leicester House) and the poem ends with a tribute to England and
praise for Elizabeth. Critics suggest that for the three central
motifs of the Prothalamion, the journey of the swans, the marriage
of the rivers, and the description of the shore-line locales, Spenser
draws on the tradition of river poems and such works as Leland's
Cygnea Cantio (1545), Camden's fragmentary De Connubio Tamis et Isis
(1586), and Vallan's A Tale of Two Swans, in addition to using various epithalamic conventions and the devices of the encomium (allegory, rhetorical elaboration, veiled references through pun and
anagram, heraldic allusions). For well over half a century critics
view the Prothalamion only as a carefully crafted set-piece; in the
latter part of the century critics discover more universal themes in
the poem.

Fowre Hymnes

Published shortly after the Prothalamion in 1596, the Fowre Hymnes
sing praise to various divinities, mythic and Christian, in the
Platonic language generally associated in the Renaissance with love
and beauty. Platonic in tone, yet affirming Spenser's strong Christian commitment, the Fowre Hymnes further reveal Spenser's concept of
love as a powerful harmonizing force in the order of the universe, a

theme that at least by implication runs through Spenser's earlier love poetry. The first pair of hymns, An Hymne in Honour of Love, dedicated to Cupid, and An Hymne in Honour of Beautie, addressed to Venus, honor erotic love (eros) and feminine beauty. In contrast, the second pair, An Hymne of Heavenly Love and An Hymne of Heavenly Beautie, praise Christ and God himself, respectively, and move "from this base world unto thy heavens hight" to sing "a heavenly hymne" unto the "God of Love, high heavens king" and reveal "some little beames to mortall eyes below / Of that immortall Beautie." The two earthly hymns draw on the tradition that extends from the Platonic dialogues, mainly the Symposium and the Phaedrus, which came to Spenser most likely through such works of the Florentine Academy as Ficino's Commentary (1469) on the Symposium, Bruno's De gl'heroici furori (1585), Benivieni's Canzone delle Amore celeste et divino (1500), and Pico's Commentary (1500) on Benivieni's Canzone, as well as works such as Hoby's translation (1561) of Castiglione's Il Cortegiano and the tradition of love poetry that extends from Dante and Petrarch. Recent Spenserians minimize Spenser's actual accept- ance of Platonism, even though critics throughout the century regu- larly assign Platonic sources to Spenser's ideas. The distinct Christian tenor of the hymns honoring heavenly love and beauty suggests that Spenser rejects Neoplatonism and affirms the Christian view in these, his final poetic works.

One critical problem with dating the composition of the Fowre Hymnes concerns scholars throughout the century; it stems from Spenser's comments in the dedication of the Fowre Hymnes where he suggests that the first two hymns date from his youth and that the second pair are later redactions. Because of the ambiguity of Spenser's comments, critics debate two positions: that all four hymns date late in Spenser's career with the dedication providing a fictive occasion for what is actually one unified work; and that the two pairs of hymns are separate works with the latter two serv- ing as revisions of youthful poems and indicating a shift in Spenser's viewpoint. Most recent scholars consider the Fowre Hymnes a single unified work that dates late in Spenser's career, an opinion due largely to the discovery that Spenser's interests in Neoplatonism are most evident in his later poetry. A closely related area of scholar- ship on the Fowre Hymnes centers on the balance of Platonic philosophy with Christian theology in the hymns; the identification of appropri- ate sources is part of these discussions. Early in the century critics generally find strong Platonic influence in the hymns, while later commentators emphasize other models for the hymns such as Calvin's Institutes (1559). After mid-century, as with the criticism on Spenser's other works, commentators focus on more universal themes rather than on source study. In summary, the chief views of the Fowre Hymnes during the 1900-1936 period are these: (1) Platonic influences in Spenser's works divide into two types: that character- ized by The Shepheardes Calender and Book I of The Faerie Queene, and that found in Book IV of The Faerie Queene, the Amoretti, and the Fowre Hymnes; (2) Christian imagery merely "clothes" Neoplatonic

doctrine in the hymns; (3) the hymns synthesize an essentially
Calvinistic point of view with Platonic mysticism; (4) the hymns
represent the secular and divine traditions in Renaissance poetry;
and (5) the Fowre Hymnes illustrate the course of spiritual development of the sensitive man and present a treatise on the mystical life.

PROSE WORKS

Spenser's prose works number only five--two essays and three
letters. The essays result from Spenser's term as personal secretary
to Arthur Lord Grey, the Queen's Deputy to Ireland from 1580 to 1582.
One essay, an unfamiliar Brief Note of Ireland, officially reports the
Tyrone rebellion to the Queen and receives no notable critical attention throughout the twentieth century. The other, however, A Veue of
the Present State of Ireland (1594-1597, published 1633), attracts
considerable attention as a historical-political treatise on Grey's
affairs in Ireland and as an insight into Spenser's personal political acumen. The letters include the one to Walter Raleigh that sets
forth the purpose and method of The Faerie Queene and two early ones
to Gabriel Harvey that provide insight into Spenser's poetic experimentation and literary friendships. Discussion of the Veue is first,
followed by discussion of the Spenser-Harvey correspondence; the letter to Raleigh is treated with The Faerie Queene.

Originally published in Sir James Ware's Historie of Ireland,
collected by Three Learned Authors (1633), A Veue of the Present
State of Ireland stands as perhaps the only extant report of the
Irish uprisings from an Elizabethan viewpoint, for the work maintains
Lord Grey's attitude and perspective throughout with Spenser faith-
fully defending his patron's policies and decisions. A Veue of the
Present State of Ireland takes the form of an expository dialogue
between Irenaeus, who represents Spenser, and his friend, Eudoxus,
who keeps the discussion moving with his probing questions and pro-
vocative remarks. As a dialogue, A Veue of the Present State of
Ireland compares to Raleigh's Perogative [sic] of Parliament in
England Proved in a Dialogue between a Counsellour of State and a
Justice of the Peace (1628) and Buchanan's Dialogue concerning the
Rights of the Crown of Scotland (ca. 1582). In the Veue Spenser
gives the impression of travelling with Grey and witnessing many
events first-hand, such as the siege of Fort de Oro on the shore of
Smerwick Bay. Spenser vividly relates the merciless two-day siege
and forced surrender of the Spanish forces at the fort, who came to
the aid of the Desmond rebels, and then calmly explains how Grey
massacred nearly six hundred men, hanged the non-combatants, including the women, and separated special Irish and English captives for
torture before hanging, sparing only the leaders for ransom. From
one such encounter to another Spenser follows Grey around Ireland as
he hangs rebels, cuts ears off purveyors, and burns crops, for famine
and force were his chief methods of subjugating the rebels. Besides
the account of Grey's tactics, the Veue includes lovely descriptions

of the Irish countryside, digressions on aspects of Irish history, and commentaries on the nature of government and the kinds of laws that best control a people.

Throughout the century scholars look to <u>A Veue of the Present State of Ireland</u> for insights into Spenser's political stance. Early in the century critics regard Spenser as a particularly adept exponent of governmental policy, whose stern measures for controlling the Irish reflect some original rethinking of various continental political theories, especially Machiavelli's <u>Il Principe</u> and Bodin's <u>Methodus ad facilem historiarum cognitionem</u>. More recently, critics focus less on the harsh controls and more on the general nature of the <u>Veue</u> as a progressive piece of Elizabethan statecraft. In the <u>Veue</u> Spenser reveals an in-depth understanding of Irish tribal customs, showing them to be ineffective in maintaining peace. Some critics regard Grey's severe measures as the means to replace these tribal customs with a government that would bring peace and justice to Ireland. In general, critics find Spenser's attitude in <u>A Veue of the Present State of Ireland</u> to be that of a loyal Englishman whose government's official policy was imperialism.

As with <u>A Veue of the Present State of Ireland</u>, critics probe Spenser's two letters of 1580 to Gabriel Harvey for insights into his personal relationships and attitudes. The letters suggest something of the young writer's enthusiasm for poetic experimentation, give a list of projected projects, and mention literary and court notables with whom Spenser probably associated. Spenser's letters were published with three of Harvey's in two booklets: <u>Three Proper, and Wittie, familiar Letters: lately passed between two Universitie men: touching the Earthquake in April last, and our English reformed Versifying, With a Preface of a Wellwisher to them both</u>, and <u>The Other, very commendable Letters, of the same mens writing: both touching the foresaid Artificiall Versifying, and certain other Particulars: More lately delivered unto the Printer</u>. Critics generally find the letters interesting because they call attention to Spenser's experimentation with classical meters in English poetry and they link Spenser with a literary group, the Areopagus, whose founders were purported to be Philip Sidney and Edward Dyer, with Fulke Greville among the members. Many critics point out that the letters do not extensively describe Spenser's friendship with Sidney, nor do they affirm the actual existence of the Areopagus as an organized group; Spenser may have exaggerated both. Also, the actual importance of the quantitative verse experiments is questionable because Spenser never uses the form in his major poetry. This century's commentary on the letters focuses mainly on the nature of Spenser's friendships with the notable writers of his day and on the actual existence of the Areopagus, concluding on the latter that whether it existed or not the writers of the Areopagus do shape the "new poetry" of the sixteenth century as they had intended. Other scholars study the influence that Spenser's contemporaries had on his poetry, the extent of the influence of the Pléiade on English poetry, and the nature and import of the quantitative verse experiments.

The Faerie Queene

    Chief among Spenser's works and the crowning achievement of his
poetic career, The Faerie Queene, along with the Letter to Raleigh
and the Cantos of Mutabilitie, receives considerable critical attention throughout the twentieth century and is the best known of the
poet's works. Spenser first mentions The Faerie Queene in his 1580
letter to Gabriel Harvey. The first three books of The Faerie Queene
were published in 1590. By the time of Spenser's Letter to Walter
Raleigh he had completed a quarter of his proposed poem and planned
to finish it in the near future. The second three books were published in 1596, with the first three in slightly revised form;
scholars generally agree that Spenser had completed these books by
1594 as suggested by references in the Amoretti. The six completed
books of The Faerie Queene and the Cantos of Mutabilitie were published together in 1609.

    Several Spenserians throughout the century have writen commen-
taries on the scholarship directed to The Faerie Queene; these deserve
mention because they are full and useful studies that provide excel-
lent insight into the general movements in Spenser studies and the
trends in Faerie Queene criticism. First, Herbert Ellsworth Cory's
The Critics of Edmund Spenser (1911.8) stands as a major early study
of Spenser scholarship. Cory traces the criticism from Harvey to
Edward Dowden, noting Dryden as the father of Faerie Queene criticism
because of his sober explorations into the poem's verse form, allegory, and general structure, and pointing out the significance of
eighteenth-century criticism and the weaknesses of the "art for art's
sake" critics of the nineteenth century. Covering some of the same
material as Cory, Jewel Wurtsbaugh in Two Centuries of Spenserian
Scholarship (1609-1805) (1936.53) completes the consideration of pre-
twentieth-century scholarship, while emphasizing in her work the editions of Spenser published between 1609 and 1805 and the improvement
of Spenser's text up to and including the Variorum of 1805. Four
other scholars study the criticism of The Faerie Queene published during the twentieth century, providing histories of the criticism from
varying perspectives. These studies are Chung Wen Shih, "The Criticism
of The Faerie Queene," Ph.D. dissertation, Duke University, 1955;
William R. Mueller, Spenser's Critics: Changing Currents in Literary
Taste, Syracuse: Syracuse University Press, 1959; Bernard J.
Vondersmith, "A History of the Criticism of The Faerie Queene,
1910-1947," Ph.D. dissertation, Duquesne University, 1971; and
Carolyn Burgholzer, R.S.M., "Edmund Spenser's The Faerie Queene:
A History of Criticism 1948-1968," Ph.D. dissertation, Duquesne
University, 1970. Shih includes studies from the eighteenth century
onward and focuses mainly on the structure, allegory, and poetical
qualities of The Faerie Queene, selecting representative pieces of
scholarship. Mueller's work is an anthology of essays and excerpts
from writers extending from John Hughes to W.B.C. Watkins, with an
introduction that surveys twentieth-century scholarship generally.
Much more inclusive and thorough are the histories of criticism on

The Faerie Queene by Vondersmith and Burgholzer. Finally, one other
essay provides valuable insight into the trends in Faerie Queene
scholarship: Foster Provost's "Treatments of Theme and Allegory in
Twentieth-Century Criticism of The Faerie Queene," in Contemporary
Thought on Edmund Spenser, edited by Richard C. Frushell and
Bernard J. Vondersmith (Carbondale: Southern Illinois University
Press; London: Feffer & Simons, 1975), pp. 1-40. Provost identifies
the major treatments of theme and allegory in Faerie Queene criticism,
giving us a useful frame of reference for other types of studies of
The Faerie Queene.

The major trends in the criticism of The Faerie Queene for the
1900-1936 period fall into five main areas of study. Calling on
evidence from Spenser's educational background and friendships, from
the Letter to Raleigh, from his minor works, from The Faerie Queene
itself, and from commentators on the poem from the seventeenth,
eighteenth, and nineteenth centuries, critics in the early twentieth
century debate, argue, and compromise in these areas: (1) the philosophical and literary sources for The Faerie Queene; (2) the elements of Spenser's style (diction, grammar, figurative language,
narrative technique, stanzaic form); (3) the whole of The Faerie
Queene and its structure; (4) the historical allegory of the poem;
and (5) the influence of The Faerie Queene on poets of the last three
centuries (Shakespeare, Jonson, Milton, Thomson, Wordsworth, Keats).
These critics reveal new aspects of this multifaceted poem, clear up
misunderstandings and confusions, and justify Milton's acclaim of
Spenser and The Faerie Queene.

In the Letter to Walter Raleigh Spenser announces, or at least
implies, his indebtedness to classical, continental, and English
authors. Many of his own claims went unexamined until the early
twentieth century. With regard to Spenser's use of classical sources,
scholars analyze Spenser's reliance on Aristotelian and Platonic ideas
in The Faerie Queene, focus on his use of Lucretius and Virgil, and
consider a number of other classical authors as sources. Other critics assess Spenser's debts to Italian poets of medieval and Renaissance times. A few commentators look to Dante, Boccaccio, and Boiardo
for influence, while others rightly emphasize the comic Ariosto and
the more serious Tasso for elements of style, structure, character,
narrative, and allegory. Studies of Spenser's adaptation of and use
of British materials consider the relationship between the structure
of The Faerie Queene and English fairy mythology, Spenser's fairy
lore as represented in the mythological and legendary materials which
surround Arthur and Gloriana, and the possible influence of Arthurian
romance on The Faerie Queene. Perhaps the most significant trend in
Faerie Queene criticism in the first half of this century is the movement away from concentration on isolated subjects in the poem (e.g.,
its sources and its style), to critical concern for the entire poem,
for the interworkings of its multiple elements, and for its structure.
Some critics before and during this period ignore or deny the possibility of structure in The Faerie Queene, but the majority move

consistently toward considerations of the poem that posit structural
and philosophical harmony in The Faerie Queene and account for the
place of the Mutabilitie Cantos in The Faerie Queene as we have it.
Finally, several critics study Spenser's historical and political
allegory in The Faerie Queene, laying the foundation for studies of
the second half of the century that fully recognize the unity of
structure and allegory in The Faerie Queene and that demonstrate
Milton's praise for Spenser as "a better teacher than Scotus or
Aquinas."

LANGUAGE, PROSODY, IMAGERY IN SPENSER'S WORKS

A significant part of early twentieth-century criticism on
Spenser's works examines poetic techniques and how Spenser uses and
adapts them to his various purposes in the individual works. There
is a significant number of these studies and, thus, they constitute
a trend in the scholarship. Three aspects of technique--language,
prosody, and imagery--deserve attention since studies of these apply
in general to Spenser's works. Studies of Spenser's language include,
for example, poetic diction, rhetorical devices, and linguistic features. Critics set these matters in perspective by reference to
Renaissance theories that discriminate a literary style and language
from the idiom of everyday speech. The second main area of technique--
prosody--includes criticism that pertains to versification, rhyme
schemes, and stanza forms. Finally, the criticism of Spenser's imagery looks at the poet's technique of forming and employing images
and the sources for specific images. In the scholarship of the twentieth century a general trend emerges in the criticism on Spenser's
poetic techniques: studies of specific techniques, influences, and
sources dominate early in the century, while more recent studies
treat these matters as corollaries of larger thematic aspects of
the works.

The language of Spenser's poetry, in effect, synthesizes elements
from two main traditions, one which extends back to Chaucer and Malory,
characterized by an archaic style, and one that reaches back to
Aristotle through the Pléiade, the Italian writers Tasso, Minturno,
Vida, and Dante, and the Roman poet Horace, characterized by an ele-
vated style, the use of language innovations and common language, and
the controls of the laws of decorum. Through comparative studies of
Spenser's language and these sources, commentators show that in his
poetry Spenser adapts a vernacular that is both inventive and deco-
rous. The innovations in Spenser's language include alterations in
pronunciation, new vocabulary, and rhetorically sophisticated syntax.
Since these variations in language cause some eighteenth and
nineteenth-century commentators to conclude that Spenser's poetic
diction is ineffective, critics early in this century defend Spenser's
practices in general, while debating specific aspects of them, such
as Spenser's use of archaisms and the significance of his sources and
models. This debate leads to many discussions of Spenser's use of
idioms, dialects, and archaic language.

Introduction

Spenser's prosody, often noted for its experimental and versatile qualities, blends easily with the diction of the poems to effect a harmony of thought and sound. The Shepheardes Calender, for example, displays thirteen different verse forms of which at least ten were either original or distinctly adapted by Spenser. Critics also note Spenser's inventive rhyme scheme for the Amoretti, the adaptation of the canzone for the Epithalamion and the Prothalamion, and, of course, the original stanza form for The Faerie Queene. With closer examination several commentators point out the continual experimentation with rhyme schemes and stanza patterns in Spenser's poetry: note, for example, the six-line stanza of three rhymes of the "October" eclogue and the eight-line stanza of two rhymes of the "June" eclogue of The Shepheardes Calender, the variation of rhyme royal in Daphnaida, and the couplet variations of Mother Hubberds Tale. Other studies emphasize the musical qualities of Spenser's language.

Finally, many critics regard Spenser's use of imagery as a major contribution to his effectiveness as a poet, focusing on two closely related aspects: the manner in which the images function in the individual poems and the sources from which Spenser derives his images. Early in the century attention centers on the relationship between individual images and well known paintings, showing how Spenser re-creates or adapts visual art in his poetry. Typical of this type of study is one critic's linking of Spenser's maiden queen of the "April" eclogue of The Shepheardes Calender with Botticelli's Primavera. Other critics find sources for Spenser's imagery in descriptive works on rivers, astrological sources, and conventional iconography. Overall, Spenserians agree that Spenser's use of language, prosody, and imagery ultimately serves his larger, thematic purposes in both the minor works and The Faerie Queene.

Note
1. For a fuller discussion of the minor works, see W. L. Sipple, "A History of the Twentieth-Century Criticism of Edmund Spenser's Minor Works," Ph.D. diss., Duquesne University, 1974.

Writings by Edmund Spenser

Amoretti (1595)

Astrophel (1595)

Colin Clouts Come Home Againe (1595)

Complaints (1591)

Daphnaida (1591)

Epithalamion (1595)

Fowre Hymnes (1596)

The Faerie Queene (1590; 1596)

An Hymne in Honour of Beautie (1596)

An Hymne in Honour of Love (1596)

An Hymne of Heavenly Beautie (1596)

An Hymne of Heavenly Love (1596)

The Lay of Clorinda (1595)

A Letter of the Authors . . . To . . . Sir Walter Raleigh (1589)

Prosopopoia, or Mother Hubberds Tale (pub. 1591)

Muiopotmos, or The Fate of The Butterfly (pub. 1591)

Prothalamion (1596)

Ruines of Rome (pub. 1591)

The Ruines of Time (pub. 1591)

The Shepheardes Calender (1579)

A Theatre for Worldlings (1569)

The Teares of the Muses (pub. 1591)

The Visions of Bellay (pub. 1591)

Virgils Gnat (pub. 1591)

A Veue of the Present State of Ireland (pub. 1633)

The Visions of Petrarch (pub. 1591)

Visions of the Worlds Vanitie (pub. 1591)

Selected Bibliographic Sources

ATKINSON, DOROTHY F. Edmund Spenser: A Bibliographic Supplement.
   Baltimore: Johns Hopkins Press, 1937.

BURGHOLZER, CAROLYN, R.S.M. "Edmund Spenser's The Faerie Queene:
   A History of Criticism 1948-1968." Ph.D. diss., Duquesne
   University, 1970.

CARPENTER, FREDERIC IVES. A Reference Guide to Edmund Spenser.
   Chicago: University of Chicago Press, 1923.

CORY, HERBERT ELLSWORTH. The Critics of Edmund Spenser. University
   of California Publications in Modern Philology, vol. 2.
   Berkeley: University of California Press, 1911.

Doctoral Dissertations Accepted By American Universities

Essay and General Literature Index

FLAGG, CHARLES A. A List of American Doctoral Dissertations Printed
   in 1912. Washington, D.C.: Government Printing Office, 1913.

GLEESON (KEANEY), WINIFRED. "Annotated Bibliography on Literary
   Relations Between Edmund Spenser and English Authors Following
   John Milton." Master's thesis, Duquesne University, 1966.

JACOBS, KATHARINE. A List of Doctoral Dissertations Printed in 1918.
   Washington, D.C.: Government Printing Office, 1921.

JONES, MABLE LAVERNE. "Recent Interest in Edmund Spenser (1910-1930)."
   Master's thesis, University of Oklahoma, 1930.

MacNAIR, MARY WILSON. A List of American Doctoral Dissertations
   Printed in 1926. Washington, D.C.: Government Printing Office,
   1928.

McNEIR, WALDO F., and FOSTER PROVOST. Edmund Spenser, An Annotated
    Bibliography 1937-1972. Duquesne University Philological Series,
    no. 17. Pittsburgh: Duquesne University Press, 1975.

Modern Humanities Research Association Annual Bibliography

Modern Language Association Annual Bibliography

MUELLER, WILLIAM R. Spenser's Critics: Changing Currents in
    Literary Taste. Syracuse: Syracuse University Press, 1959.

PARROTT, ALICE. "A Critical Bibliography of Spenser from 1923-1928."
    SP 25 (1928):468-90.

PROVOST, FOSTER. "Treatments of Theme and Allegory in Twentieth-
    Century Criticism of The Faerie Queene." In Contemporary Thought
    on Edmund Spenser. Edited by Richard C. Frushell and Bernard J.
    Vondersmith. Carbondale: Southern Illinois University Press;
    London: Feffer & Simons, 1975, pp. 1-40.

SHIH, CHUNG WEN. "The Criticism of The Faerie Queene." Ph.D. diss.,
    Duke University, 1955.

SIPPLE, WILLIAM L. "A History of the Twentieth-Century Criticism of
    Edmund Spenser's Minor Works." Ph.D. diss., Duquesne University,
    1974.

STEPHENS, ALIDA M. A List of American Doctoral Dissertations Printed
    in 1913. Washington, D.C.: Government Printing Office, 1914.

STEPHENS, ROBERT F. A Checklist of Master's Theses on Edmund Spenser.
    Mimeographed. Bibliographical Society of Virginia, 1950.

Studies in Philology, Annual Bibliography, "Literature of the
    Renaissance."

Van PATTEN, NATHAN. An Index to Bibliographies and Bibliographical
    Contributions Relating to the Work of American and British Authors,
    1923-32. Stanford: Stanford University Press; Oxford: Oxford
    University Press, 1934.

VONDERSMITH, BERNARD J. "A History of the Criticism of The Faerie
    Queene, 1910-1947." Ph.D. diss., Duquesne University, 1970.

WURTSBAUGH, JEWEL. Two Centuries of Spenserian Scholarship, 1609-
    1805. Baltimore: Johns Hopkins Press, 1936.

WYLLIE, J.C., and R.W. CHURCH. A Spenser Bibliography for 1928-30.
    Mimeographed. Charlottesville: University of Virginia Library,
    1931; revised 1932.

Selected Bibliographic Sources

<u>The Year's Works in English Studies</u>.

ZIMMERMAN, DOROTHY WAYNE. "Romantic Criticism of Edmund Spenser."
    Ph.D. diss., University of Illinois, 1957.

Abbreviations

AL   American Literature

Archiv   Archiv für das Studium der Neuren Sprachen und Literaturen

Atkinson, 1937   Atkinson, Dorothy F. Edmund Spenser: A Bibliographic Supplement. Baltimore: Johns Hopkins Press, 1937.

ContempR   Contemporary Review

CW   Classical Weekly

E & S   Essays and Studies by Members of the English Association

EHR   English Historical Review

ELH   Journal of English Literary History

ES   English Studies

JAF   Journal of American Folklore

JCHAS   Journal of the Cork Historical and Archaeological Society

JEGP   Journal of English and Germanic Philology

JRSAI   Journal of the Royal Society of Antiquaries of Ireland

McNeir-Provost   McNeir, Waldo F., and Foster Provost. Edmund Spenser, An Annotated Bibliography 1937-1972. Duquesne University Philological Series, no. 17. Pittsburgh: Duquesne University Press, 1975.

MLN   Modern Language Notes

MLQ	Modern Language Quarterly
MLR	Modern Language Review
MP	Modern Philology
NQ	Notes and Queries
NYTBR	New York Times Book Review
PBA	Proceedings of the British Academy
PMLA	Publications of the Modern Language Association
PQ	Philological Quarterly
QR	Quarterly Review
RES	Review of English Studies
RLC	Revue de littérature comparée
SatR	Saturday Review of Literature
SJW	Shakespeare-Jahrbuch (Weimar)
SP	Studies in Philology
SR	Sewanee Review
Stephens, 1950	Stephens, Robert F. A Checklist of Master's Theses on Edmund Spenser. Mimeographed. Bibliographical Society of Virginia, 1950.
TLS	Times Literary Supplement

Writings about Edmund Spenser, 1900-1936

<u>1900</u>

*1   ABBATT, THOMAS K., ed. <u>Catalogue of the Manuscripts in the Library of Trinity College, Dublin</u>. Dublin: Hodges, Figgis; London: Longmans, Green.
      Cited in Atkinson, 1937; library holds manuscript of <u>A Veue of the Present State of Ireland</u>.

2   CARPENTER, W. BOYD. "Edmund Spenser." In <u>The Religious Spirit of the Poets</u>. London: Isbister, pp. 60-80.
      Spenser a moral and spiritual teacher who teaches without appearing to. Using Queen Elizabeth as his symbol of truth, right, and liberty, he created in <u>The Faerie Queene</u>, a pageantry of the chivalry of old days full of the spirit of his own times. Analyzes <u>The Faerie Queene</u> in terms of four themes: truth, freedom, self-control, and single-mindedness. Reprinted: 1901.4.

3   CLARK, J. SCOTT. "Spenser, 1152(?)-1599." In <u>A Study of English and American Poets: A Laboratory Method</u>. New York: Charles Scribner's Sons, pp. 38-88.
      Part of a handbook intended to assist students in determining the "particular and distinctive features of a writer's style." Following a brief biographical sketch and a bibliography of criticism, discusses Spenser under ten different headings: Rich imagination--Idealism; Incongruity--Artificiality; Exquisite Melody; Perception of Beauty--Sensitiveness; Moral Elevation--Manliness; Reverence for Womanhood; Diffuseness--Obscurity; Verbal License; Flattery--Adulation; Pictorial Power. Each section includes selected quotations from critics listed the the brief bibliography and three illustrations from Spenser's works. Reprinted: 1907.5; 1909.6; 1917.4.

4   EATON, H.A. "The Pastoral Idea in English Poetry in the Sixteenth Century." Ph.D. diss., Harvard University, paper VI, paper IX, passim.
      Series of separate papers on pastoral intended as base for a history of pastoral tradition, Paper VI, "Spenser's 'Shepherds'

1

Calendar,'" summarizes nineteenth-century attitudes and presents
overview of poem. Concludes that Spenser's chief contributions
to pastoral verse "were variety of metrical structure and genius;"
that all other aspects of poem were not original with Spenser,
that religious commentary is inconsistent, and that while The
Shepheardes Calender stands as "finest lyric expression in English literature up to then," its influence has been "considerably
overstated." Paper IX, "The Pastoral Eclogue Between 1579 and
1603," discusses influence of Spenser, mainly on Drayton's Idea
or the Shepherd's Garland and Davidson's Poetical Rhapsody.

5   EINSTEIN, LEWIS. "A Notice of Spenser." Athenaeum 2:57.
         Quotes contemporary notices of Edmund Spenser in Harleian
Manuscript 4107. "He would seem from the above cited manuscript
to have drawn the pay of a register or clerk of the chancery at
the same time he held the secretaryship, a deputy allowed him."
Manuscript dates from 1581.

6   FLETCHER, JEFFERSON B. "Spenser and 'E.K.'" MLN 15:165-66.
         Collaboration of Spenser and E.K. on glosses to The Shep-
heardes Calender for short time before Spenser's continental
journey. Accounts for both insights and blunders in glosses.

7   GREENSLET, FERRIS. Joseph Glanville, A Study in English
     Thought and Letters of the Seventeenth Century. New York:
     Columbia University Press, pp. 10, 23, 41, 172.
         Influence of Symposium and/or works by Benevieni on Fowre
Hymnes. Spenser's influence on Henry More.

8   HOPE, CONSTANCE. "Alma. A Study from Spenser." Month 96:
     384-91.
         Praises Spenser's distinctive picturing of the will and
the ruling love of man in Alma and the House of Temperance.
Summarizes the action of The Faerie Queene II.ix and xi.

9   HUNT, THEODORE. "Edmund Spenser and the English Reformation."
     Bibliotheca Sacra 57:39-53.
         Develops discussion of Spenser's rejection of paganism
(i.e., "opposition to all Christian systems and faiths"), his
support of Protestantism (illustrated with themes of The Faerie
Queene, Complaints, and The Shepheardes Calender), and his modified Anglicanism, a "rational and moderate position, midway between the extremes of a bigoted Puritanism and an equally bigoted
Anglicanism." Notes Spenser's rejection of Calvinism because of
its intolerance and extremes, and his anti-Catholic sentiments.

10   KOEPPEL, E. "Ueber Die Echtheit der Edmund Spenser Zuge-
     schriebenen 'Vision of Petrarch' and 'Visions of Bellay.'"
     Englische Studien 27:100-11.
         Suggests that Spenser only altered earlier versions of
poems (change from blank verse to rhymed sonnet form) for

Complaints volume (1591), having published poems in Theatre of
Worldlings (1569). Enlarges earlier study: Englische Studien
15 (1891):74-111.

11   MOORE, COURTENAY. "Mourne Abbey and Barrett's Castle or
     Castlemore, Co. Cork." JCHAS 6:210-14.
        Notes that Spenser fled Ireland in 1598, same year
     Kilcolman burned.

12   OSGOOD, CHARLES GROSVENOR. The Classical Mythology of
     Milton's English Poems. Edited by Albert S. Cook. Yale
     Studies in English, 8. New Haven: Yale University Press;
     London: Oxford University Press, 112 pp.
        Cites Spenser among many sources for some of Milton's
     mythological characters: Adonis, Geryon, Horror, Sea Gods.

*13 PATON, LUCY ALLEN. "Morgain la Fée, a Study in the Fairy
     Mythology of the Middle Ages." Ph.D. diss., Radcliffe
     College.
        For published edition, see 1903.26.

14   SARRAZIN, GREGOR. "Neue italienische Skizzen zu Shakespeare."
     SJW 36:95-108.
        Mentions Spenser's botanical knowledge, evident in
     Muiopotmos, Virgils Gnat, and The Shepheardes Calender.

15   WARREN, KATE M., ed. Introduction to The Faerie Queene Book
     V. Westminster: Archibald Constable & Co., pp. vii-xxxviii.
        Unlike any of the other books, Book V characterized by sim-
     plicity of allegory, absence of color and ornament, a business-
     like tone, and even level of verse. Spenser not only pictures
     the virtue of Justice but also defends before the world the char-
     acter of Lord Grey de Wilton, whom he figures forth as Artegall.
     Spenser's narrow conception of Justice as an avenger is relieved
     by the meeting of Radigund, and the character of Britomart. In-
     cludes synopsis of Book V and identification of historical char-
     acters. Fifth of six volumes published 1897-1900. For edition
     of Book VI, see 1900.16.

16   _____. Introduction to The Faerie Queene Book VI.
     Westminster: Archibald Constable & Co., pp. vii-xxxii.
        Book VI characterized by simplicity of idea and execution,
     the simplicity caused by Spenser's personal happiness with his
     love. Sir Calidore's inability to bridle the Blatant Beast for
     all time indicates Spenser's acquisition of "one of the hardest
     truths that the lover of the ideal has to learn in this life--
     the enormous strength of evil in the world, of cruelty, hypocrisy,
     injustice, falsehood, jealousy, malice, and all the rest; and how
     infinitely small is the headway that any single man or woman can
     make against it." The great enemies of courtesy are calumny,
     slander, evil-speaking, and back biting; its fruits are

sincerity, courage, pity, long-suffering, faithfulness, gentle-
ness, helpfulness and honor. The three chief warriors for courtesy in Book VI are Calidore, Calepine, and Arthur, whose
adventures are "a means of illustrating the practice of Courtesy." Includes synopsis of Book VI. Last of six volumes published 1897-1900. For edition of Book V, see 1900.15.

17   WINSTANLEY, LILIAN. "Spenser and Puritanism." MLQ (London)
     3:6-16, 103-10.
          Treats both The Faerie Queene and the minor poems. Con-
     cludes that "Spenser's religious position . . . shows a state of
     transition. He is intensely Puritan, yet in him Puritanism is
     undeveloped, and from some of its aspects he is wholly . . .
     free. He embraced the Reformation on its extremist side . . .
     but he loved the poetry and beauty of the Catholic worship."

                              1901

1   BARRY, E. "Records of the Barrys, Chapter III." JCHAS 7:
     65-80.
          Notes marriage of Silvanus Spenser to Ellis Nagle, daughter
     of David Nagle of Moneanimney, and their two sons, Edmond and
     William.

2   BEERS, HENRY AUGUSTUS. A History of English Romanticism in
     the Nineteenth Century. New York: Henry Holt & Co., pp. 3,
     4, 93, 107, 120-22, 329.
          Considers Spenser as an influence on Scott, Hunt, and Keats.

3   BOMPAS, G.C. "Edmund 'Spenser's' Poems." Baconiana, n.s. 9:
     71-77.
          Using biographical data and internal evidence, argues that
     Edmund Spenser is true author of The Faerie Queene and other
     poems bearing his name: "No fact has been adduced controverting
     or casting suspicion upon Spenser's authorship."

4   CARPENTER, W. BOYD. "Edmund Spenser." In The Religious
     Spirit of the Poets. New York: Thomas Y. Crowell, pp. 60-80.
          Reprint of 1900.2.

5   COLLINS, JOHN CHURTON. Ephemera Critica: or Plain Truths
     about Current Literature. London: Archibald Constable & Co.,
     pp. 112-13, 120-21, 280.
          Responds to Edmund Gosse's charges that Book II of The
     Faerie Queene is loose and incoherent, that Spenser was unaf-
     fected by Greek or Latin ideas, and that Milton was only slightly
     subjected to the influence of Spenser. Reprinted: 1902.10.

6   CRAWFORD, CHARLES. "Edmund Spenser"; "Locrine"; and "Selimus."
     NQ 106:61-63, 101-3, 142-44, 203-5, 261-63, 324-25, 384-86.

Concludes on basis of borrowings or parallels from Spenser's works that Christopher Marlowe, not Robert Greene, wrote <u>Selimus</u>, that <u>Selimus</u> is Marlowe's first play and was immediately followed by <u>The First Part of Tamburlaine</u>. Suggests that Greene may have written <u>Locrine</u>. For related studies, see 1905.16; 1913.17; 1916.14. Reprinted: 1906.6.

*7 CUNNINGHAM, GRANVILLE C. <u>The Strange Case of Francis Tidir</u>. London: [publisher not located], pp. 47-54.
   Cited in 1923.6, which notes Cunningham's Baconian conjectures.

8 CUTTELL, JOHN. "The Poetic 'Pléiades': V. Spenser's <u>Faerie Queene</u>." <u>Great Thoughts</u>, 4th ser. 8:283-84.
   Discusses the circumstances under which the poem was written, "the character of the scenery in the midst of which it was mostly written," and Raleigh's reaction to the poem and encouragement in publication. Comments briefly on Spenser's massive learned lore shaped by his prolific imagination; his lively and picturesque narration; his striking similes, proverbs, and his strong moral and religious tone.

9 de VERE, AUBREY. "Lucretius and Spenser." <u>Great Thoughts</u>, 4th ser. 8:219.
   For Spenser, "all phenomena received their interpretation from above; for Lucretius, it came from below."

10 GALLUP, ELIZABETH WELLS. "The Bilateral Cipher of Francis Bacon." Baconiana, n.s. 9:77-84.
   Finds clues to link Bacon's cipher writings and <u>The Shepheardes Calender</u>.

11 GREENOUGH, JAMES BRADSTREET, and GEORGE LYMAN KITTREDGE. <u>Words and Their Ways in English Speech</u>. New York and London: Macmillan, pp. 118, 295, 354, 375.
   Discusses in context of general study of language Spenser's archaisms, his alterations of meanings of words, and his creation of new words. Reprinted: 1902.16; 1906.11; 1908.17; 1911.18; 1914.6; 1920.11; 1926.19; 1929.19; 1931.21; 1933.27; 1935.29; 1937; 1953.

12 THE GROLIER CLUB. <u>Catalogue of an Exhibition of Selected Works of the Poets Laureate of England</u>. New York: Grolier Club, p. 7.
   Lists Spenser among "the Volunteer Laureates."

*13 HEISE, WILHELM. "Die Gleichnisse in Edmund Spensers <u>Faerie Queene</u> und ihre Vorbilder." Ph.D. diss., Kaiser-Wilhelms-Universität, 1901.
   For published edition, see 1902.19.

14   HUNTER, MARGARET. "Some of Spenser's Women." Twentieth
      Century (London) 3:198-212.
           In Book II of The Faerie Queene Medina, Belphoebe, and
      Alma illustrate three types of womanhood.

15   HYDE, DOUGLAS. A Literary History of Ireland. From Earliest
      Times to the Present Day. London: T. Fisher Unwin,
      pp. 493-96.
           Notes Spenser's unfair and ill-informed view of Irish bards
      in context of discussion showing importance of these Irish poets.
      Originally published: 1892. Reprinted: 1899; 1901; 1903.17;
      1910.12; 1920.13; London: Benn; New York: Barnes & Noble, 1967.

16   JONES, WALTER A. "Doneraile and Vicinity." JCHAS 7:238-42.
           Presents brief biography of poet with emphasis on works
      written at Kilcolman Castle.

17   KOEPPEL, E. "Spenser's Florimel und die Britomartis Sage des
      Antoninus Liberalis." Archiv für das Studium der neuern
      Sprachen und Litteraturen 107:394-96.
           Considers Ariosto and Antonius Liberalis as possible influ-
      ences on the Florimell plot in Book III of The Faerie Queene.

18   McKERROW, R.B. "Classical Metres in Elizabethan Verse."
      MLQ (London) 4:172-80.
           Defines and contrasts verse written according to stress and
      that written according to quantity; thus reviews the sixteenth-
      century experiments with quantitative verse in England, mention-
      ing More, Ascham, Drant, Harvey, and especially Sidney and Dyer.
      Concludes: "I do not think they had any precise idea of what
      they were aiming at." Notes that "Spenser seems to have taken
      the matter up even less seriously than his friends."

19   MacLIR, MANANAAN. "Spenser as High Sheriff of Cork County."
      JCHAS 7:249-50.
           Reproduces "Letter to Make Edmond Spenser Sheriff of County
      Cork" dated 30 September 1598, from Harl. MS 286, p. 272; and
      Index to Spenser's grant of lands from Calendar to the Fiants of
      Elizabeth, dated 20 October 1590.

*20   MEREDITH, GEORGE. "The Poetry of Spenser." In Poems.
      New York: Scribner's, pp. 27+.
           Cited in 1923.6. Reprint of London: J.W. Parker, 1851,
      1898; New York: Scribner's, 1898, 1899. Reprinted: National
      Union Catalogue lists numerous reprints.

21   MOULTON, CHARLES WELLS, ed. The Library of Literary Criticism
      of English and American Authors. Vol. 1. Buffalo: Moulton
      Publishing Co., 368-400.
           Provides brief biographical listing and collection of more
      than 170 excerpts of statements and poems on Spenser and his

works by various editors, essayists, and poets from late sixteenth to late nineteenth centuries. Reprinted: Buffalo:
Peter Smith, 1959; New York: F. Ungar Publishing Co., 1966.

22   ROLFE, WILLIAM [JAMES]. A Life of William Shakespeare.
     Boston: L.C. Page & Co., pp. 521-22.
          Identifies Aëtion of Colin Clouts Come Home Againe as
     William Shakespeare. Reprinted: 1904.34.

23   WESTROPP, T[HOMAS] J. "The Name 'Buttevant.'" JRSAI 31:87.
          Name derived from Barrys' war cry "Boutez en avant";
     mentions Spenser's use in The Faerie Queene.

24   WOODWARD, PARKER. "Edmund Spenser's Poems." Baconiana,
     n.s. 9:21-26.
          Suggests that Bacon "published the 'Shepherd's Calendar'
     anonymously, that subsequently being fearful of discovery he
     induced Spenser to let him use his name, Spenser being rewarded
     by the apointment in Ireland procured for him." See also
     1901.25.

25   _____. "The Poems Ascribed to Spenser." Baconiana, n.s. 9:
     117-28, 177-85.
          Supports theory that Bacon "by consent used the name of a
     certain Edmund Spenser as the ostensible author of these poems."
     Examines traditional attitudes, Harvey connections, printing and
     publishing inferences, dedications, theory of Spenser's disap-
     pointment, references and allusions in works, poet's profession
     as lawyer, humor in works, and parallels in works by Bacon,
     Spenser, and Shakespeare to support view. For a related study,
     see 1901.24.

1902

1   ANON. "Astarte." "Faerie Queene: Supplement to." NQ
     105:28.
          Queries existence of manuscript supplement to The Faerie
     Queene in public library at Cambridge.

2   ANON. "The Elizabethan Lyric." QR 196:438-61.
          Spenser mentioned in discussion of development of lyric
     poetry.

3   ANON. "Giordano Bruno in England." QR 196:483-508.
          Bruno and Spenser drew from same sources of Neoplantonism.
     Cites echoes and parallels of Bruno's Spaccio in The Faerie
     Queene but notes that Bruno's naturalistic ethical ideal is a
     corrective to medieval and chivalric ideal in The Faerie Queene.

4   BARROW, SARAH FIELD. "Studies in the Language of Spenser, with Special Attention to the Etymological Attempts." Master's thesis, University of Chicago, 48 pp.
    Examines Spenser's language from linguistic and literary points of view to show that Spenser conceived of language "as an evolutionary product susceptible of analysis and readjustment of parts even within the limits of the word" and that Spenser's etymological and other linguistic experiments support his literary ends.

5   BEALE, DOROTHEA. "Britomart, of Spenser's Ideal of Woman." In Literary Studies of Poems, New and Old. London: George Bell & Sons, pp. 25-51.
    Summarizes plot of Books III-V of The Faerie Queene. Concludes with twelve teachings of Spenser on the nature of the ideal woman.

6   BOND, R. WARWICK. The Complete Works of John Lyly. Vol. 1. Oxford: Clarendon Press, p. 62.
    Identifies "Pleasant Willy" (Teares of the Muses) as Lily: "Spenser's lines are put into the mouth of the Muse of Comedy, and are far more appropriate to Lyly, with his reputation for wit and learning and plays free from ribaldry, than to the yet obscure Shakespeare or any other dramatist of this time." Notes influence of Spenser's allegory on Lyly.

*7 BOTTA, ANNE C. LYNCH. Handbook of Universal Literature. Boston: Houghton Mifflin Co., pp. 481-82.
    Reprint of 1860, 1861, 1885 editions. Reprinted: 1922.3. For revised edition, see 1923.4.

8   BUTTERWORTH, WALTER. "Symbol and Allegory in Spenser." Manchester Quarterly 21:229-43.
    Writing in tradition of continental and English allegory, Spenser attempted an allegory of "man perfecting all his faculties in the fight on earth for heaven, or the struggle of the human soul toward light and emancipation." The Faerie Queene represents Spenser, "the very man, his thoughts, his aspirations, his deep convictions," and presents themes of ideal Elizabethan manliness and sacred womanhood.

9   CELER. "Tedula, A Bird." NQ 107:433.
    Correct name for bird is "trochilus" (Pliny, book VIII, c. 25). For related comments, see 1902.22-23, 27, 29.

10 COLLINS, JOHN CHURTON. Ephemera Critica: Or Plain Truths About Current Literature. New York: E.P. Dutton & Co.; Westminster: Archibald Constable & Co., pp. 112-13, 120-21, 280.
    Reprint of 1901.5.

11   COX, RICHARD. "Regnum Corcagiense; or, A Description of the
     Kingdom of Cork." Edited by Robert Day. JCHAS 8:156-79.
         Mentions Spenser's estate on the Mulla where he composed
     The Faerie Queene.

12   DUNLOP, ROBERT. "Map of 'Ireland from 1541-1653,' with
     Descriptive Text." In Historical Atlas of Modern Europe.
     Edited by Reginald L. Poole. Oxford: Clarendon Press,
     no. xxxi.
         Relevant for A Veue of the Present State of Ireland.

13   DURNING-LAWRENCE, E.J. "To the Editors of Baconiana."
     Baconiana, n.s. 10:98-100.
         Cites Spenser, among others, in defense of fellow Baconian.

14   EINSTEIN, LEWIS. The Italian Renaissance in England. New
     York: Columbia University Press, pp. 336-46, 348-59, passim.
         Italian influence on Spenser "has often been exaggerated,
     especially by continental critics, who looking at the surface
     rather than the spirit, have seen reflected in the poem [The
     Faerie Queene] the art and beauty of the Italian Renaissance."
     While Spenser made use of characters suggested by Ariosto and
     descriptions from Tasso, spirit of The Faerie Queene differs
     greatly from Italian romantic epic: "Its austerity inclined
     rather to the Platonism of Petrarch than the easy self-indulgence
     of Ariosto, or the high-colored seriousness of Tasso." Concludes
     that "the Italian literary influence can be traced in Spenser in
     outward form rather than in inward spirit." Discusses Spenser's
     Petrarchanisms and knowledge of Italian Platonism; notes influ-
     ence on Fowre Hymnes.

15   FITZGERALD, WALTER. "New Abbey of Kilcullen." Journal of
     the County Kildare Archaeological Society 3:301-17.
         Mentions Spenser's lease dated 24 August 1582.

16   GREENOUGH, JAMES BRADSTREET, and GEORGE LYMAN KITTREDGE.
     Words and Their Ways in English Speech. New York and London:
     Macmillan, pp. 118, 295, 354, 375.
         Reprint of 1901.11.

*17 HAZLITT, WILLIAM CAREW. Shakespear. London: B. Quaritch,
     pp. 52, 288.
         Notes allusions in Colin Clouts Come Home Againe and Teares
     of the Muses. Revised and reprinted: 1902.18; 1908.21; 1912.21.

*18 _____. Shakespear, Himself and His Works, A Study from New
     Points of View. London: B. Quaritch.
         Revised edition of 1902.17. Reprinted: 1908.21; 1912.21.

19   HEISE, WILHELM. Die Gleichnisse in Edmund Spensers "Faerie
     Queene" und ihre Vorbilder. Konigsee: Selmar von Ende, 181 pp.

Part 1 lists 389 similes from The Faerie Queene in two
major categories: images of the world of nature and images of
human affairs. Part 2 lists examples of the classical, Italian,
and English models for the 389 similes. Published version of
1901.13.

20   JUSSERAND, J.J. "Spenser's 'Visions of Petrarch.'"
     Athenaeum, no. 3889 (10 May), pp. 595-96.
         Maintains that Spenser followed Marot's "Des Visions de
Pétrarque," not Petrarch's "Canzone." Counters assumption that
Spenser knew Italian at an early age.

21   KREB, VALENTIN, ed. Introduction to The Valient Welshman,
     by R.A. Gent. Erlangen and Leipzig: A. Deichert'sche
     Verlagsbuche, pp. xlii-xlv.
         Includes comments on The Faerie Queene as one source for
The Valiant Welshman.

22   L., H.P. "Tedula, A Bird." NQ 107:389.
         Defines "tedula" as squeamish (in Visions of the World's
Vanitie). For related comments, see 1902.9, 23, 27, 29.

23   _____. "Tedula, A Bird." NQ 107:516-17.
         Adds reference in Herodotus, II, 68. For related
comments, see 1902.9, 22, 27, 29.

24   MACARTHUR, JOHN R. "The Influence of Huon of Burdeaux upon
     The Faerie Queene." JEGP 4:215-238.
         Refutes view that Spenser took from Huon of Burdeaux "the
main outlines and characters of this fairy world." Suggests
that influence of Huon shows itself in details of The Faerie
Queene rather than in main outline of the story.

25   REEVES, W.P. "The Gardens of Adonis." MLN 17:16.
         Corrects writer in New Shakespeareana who states that
first mention of Adonis's Gardens is at III.vi.39 of The Faerie
Queene and challenges writer's claim of a "discovery" of parallel allusion in Shakespeare's I Henry VI, I.vi.6.

26   SAINTSBURY, GEORGE. A History of Criticism and Literary
     Taste in Europe from the Earliest Texts to the Present Day.
     Vol. 2, From the Renaissance to the Decline of Eighteenth
     Century Orthodoxy. Edinburgh and London: W. Blackwood & Sons,
     pp. 165-69.
         Discusses Spenser-Harvey correspondence within the context
of Renaissance poetic theory, with emphasis on classical meters
in English poetry.

27   STRONG, H.A. "Tedula, A Bird." NQ 107:516.
         Suggests "titula," meaning a little tit. For related
comments, see 1902.9, 22-23, 29.

28   Van DAM, BASTIAN A.P., and CORNELIUS STOFFEL. Chapters on
      English Printing, Prosody, and Pronunciation (1550-1700).
      Anglistische Forschungen herausgegeben von Johannes Hoops,
      no. 9. Heidelberg: Carl Winter's Universitätsbuchhandlung,
      pp. 7-9, 40-41, 66, 76-79.
           Cites examples of printing-house tamperings with Spenser's
      text which alter rhymes or add extra syllables.

29   WARD, C.S. "Tedula, A Bird." NQ 107:516.
           Asks meaning of "edula." For related comments, see
      1902.9, 22-23, 27.

*30   WEELER, PHILIP. "Josuah Sylvesters Englische Übersetzungen
      der Religiösen Epen des DuBartas." Ph.D. diss., University
      of Tübingen.
           Cited in Atkinson, 1937.

31   WHEELER, ETHEL. "The Fairylands of the Poets: II. The
      Fairyland of Imagination." Great Thoughts, 4th ser., 9:75-76.
           "The Faery Queen combines into a perfect harmony the two
      dissevered and generally antagonistic characteristics of the
      Renaissance--its moral aspiration and its physical beauty."

32   WILLIAMS, A.J. Baconiana, n.s. 10:54-55.
           Notes that unique depiction of Elizabeth and Leicester on
      title page of 1611 folio of The Shepheardes Calender serves as
      clue to Bacon's connection with work and his relationship as son
      to Queen and Leicester.

                                1903

1   ALDEN, RAYMOND M. English Verse. Specimens Illustrating Its
      Principles and History. New York: Henry Holt & Co.,
      pp. 103-9, passim.
           Discusses and illustrates Spenser's metrics and verse
      forms, including Spenserian stanza and imitators' uses of it.
      Reprinted: 1931.1.

2   ANON. "The Poet's Poet." Academy (London) 65:248-49.
           Comments on Spenser's diction: archaisms are minimal; his
      lyrics convey subtlety of emotion.

3   BEACH, JOSEPH WARREN. "A Sonnet of Watson and a Stanza of
      Spenser." MLN 18:218-20.
           Suggests that Watson borrowed lines 5-10 in Sonnet 51 of
      his Tears of Fancie from The Faerie Queene II.vi.13.1-6.

4   BOAS, Mrs. FREDERICK (HENRIETTA O'BRIEN). In Shakespeare's
      England. London: James Nisbet & Co.; New York: J. Pott,
      pp. 232-53.

General, simplified overview of Spenser and his works including identifications in allegory. Reprinted 1904.4.

5   BROADUS, EDMUND KEMPER. "The Red Cross Knight and Lybeaus
    Desconus." MLN 18:202-4.
       Points out Lybeaus Desconus as parallel to story of Red
    Cross Knight which is closer than story of Gareth and Linet in
    Malory's Morte D'Arthur, usually assigned as the closest
    parallel.

6   DAY, ROBERT. "Cooke's Memoirs of Youghal, 1749." JCHAS 9:
    34-63, 105-17.
       Mentions John Spencer.

7   ____. "Notes on Youghal." JRSAI 33:325.
       Notes Spenser's residence in "old castle of Kilcoran [sic],"
    where he wrote Amoretti, 75.

8   ERSKINE, JOHN. The Elizabethan Lyric. New York: Columbia
    University Press, pp. 107-16, 153-58, 176-82, 189-96, 302.
       General introduction to development of lyric. Examines
    careful construction of lyrics in The Shepheardes Calender to
    show how "the emotional state of the poet's mind undergoes a
    natural change" from inarticulate grief to resolute action.
    Considers Amoretti more distinctive as a series than as indi-
    vidual sonnets; it is "the truest sequence of the decade. There
    is progression in the story and in the poet's moods, from the
    beginning to the end, and each sonnet has its inevitable place."
    Amoretti falls into two parts of sixty-one and twenty-two sonnets
    each: "the first deals with the unsuccessful wooing of the poet;
    in the second the lady accepts him, and the days of their be-
    trothal are described." Epithalamion concludes the series and
    parallels Amoretti in structure--"the sonnet serving as the lyric
    unit in the one case, the stanza in the other." Comments on
    Spenser's sources and forms used in Daphnaida, Complaints,
    Astrophel, Prothalamion, and on Neoplatonism in the structure
    of Fowre Hymnes. Reprinted: 1905.7; 1916.5; 1931.15.

9   FLEMING, HORACE T. "Some Notes on the Tynte Family."
    JCHAS 9:156-57.
       Notes Elizabeth Boyle as Robert Tynte's second wife.

10 FLETCHER, J[EFFERSON]. B. "Mr. Sidney Lee and Spenser's
    Amoretti." MLN 18:111-13.
       Rejects Lee's comment that the "Idea" of Sonnet 87 is a
    key to knowing to whom Spenser is addressing his sequence.

11 GALIMBERTI, ALICE. "L'Ariosto inglese." Nuova antologia di
    lettere, scienze ed arti, 4th ser. 106:407-18.
       Discusses Spenser's greatness, emphasizing The Faerie
    Queene, Spenser's development as a poet, and Italian influences
    on Spenser.

*12   GARNETT, RICHARD, and EDMUND GOSSE. English Literature An
      Illustrated Record. From the Age of Henry VIII to the Age of
      Milton. Vol. 2. London: W. Heinemann.
         For annotation, see 1904.12.

 13   GAYLEY, CHARLES MILLS. Representative English Comedies. From
      the Beginnings to Shakespeare. New York: Macmillan Co.,
      778 pp., passim.
         Compares Spenser and Lyly to show that Lyly's works embody
      same influences as Spenser's. Identifies "Pleasing Alcon"
      (Teares of the Muses) as "an allusion to Lodge's authorship of
      that character in the Looking-Glasse for "nearly all the speeches
      of Alcon are distinctively the work of Lodge." Reprinted: New
      York: AMS Press, 1969.

 14   GREG, WALTER WILSON. Catalogue of Books Presented by Edward
      Capell to Trinity College, Cambridge. Cambridge: Cambridge
      University Press, pp. 144-50.
         Describes early editions of Spenser, including 1611 and
      1617 editions.

*15   HARRISON, JOHN S. "Platonism in English Poetry of the Six-
      teenth and Seventeenth Centuries." Ph.D. diss., Columbia
      University. For published edition, see 1903.16.

 16   _____. Platonism in English Poetry of the Sixteenth and
      Seventeenth Centuries. New York: Macmillan Co., 235 pp.
         Discusses Christian discipline and Platonic idealism
      blended in Book I of The Faerie Queene. Book II based on
      Platonic conception of temperance as "the necessary condition
      for the presence of any virtue in the soul." Platonism as sys-
      tem of ethics disappears in The Faerie Queene after Book II but
      colors thinking of remaining books.
         Considers Fowre Hymnes "most comprehensive exposition of
      love in light of Platonic theory" in English. Explains Spenser's
      reconciliation of Platonic love ("a desire of birth in absolute
      beauty") with Christian love in two "heavenly" hymns; discusses
      earthly love ("unrequited passion" of Petrarchan lover) in Hymne
      in Honour of Love and Hymne in Honour of Beautie. Notes presence
      of Spenser's creative power of love in Colin Clouts Come Home
      Againe. Published version of 1903.15. Reprinted: 1919.7;
      Russell & Russell, 1965.

 17   HYDE, DOUGLAS. A Literary History of Ireland. From Earliest
      Times to the Present Day. London: T. Fisher Unwin, pp. 493-96.
         Reprint of 1901.15.

 18   JUSSERAND, JEAN A.A. JULES. "Edmond Spenser." Revue de
      Paris (May), pp. 58-95.
         General introduction to Spenser and his works. Partial
      reprint of 1896 edition of Histoire littéraire du peuple Anglais;
      see 1904.21.

19   LENZ, LUDWIG. <u>Wielands Verhältnis zu Edmund Spenser, Pope und
      Swift</u>. Wissenschaftliche Beilage zum Programm des Koniglichen
      Gymnasiums zu Hersfeld. Hersfeld: Druck von Ludwig Funks
      Buchdruckerei, 12 pp.
            General introduction to Spenser and <u>The Faerie Queene</u>.

20   McINTYRE, J. LEWIS. <u>Giordano Bruno</u>. London: Macmillan & Co.,
      p. 33.
            Notes possible influence of Bruno's <u>Spaccio</u> on <u>Mutabilitie
      Cantos</u>.

21   MAIBERGER, MAX. "Studien über den Einfluss Frankreichs auf
      die Elisabethanische Literatur. Erster Teil: Die Lyrik in
      der zweiten Hälfte des xvi Jahrhunderts." Ph.D. diss., Uni-
      versity of Munich.
            For published edition, see 1903.22.

22   _____. <u>Studien über den Einfluss Frankreichs auf die
      Elisabethanische Literatur. Erster Teil: Die Lyrik in der
      zweiten Hälfte des xvi Jahrhunderts</u>. Frankfurt: Gebrüder
      Knauer, pp. 20-21, 50-54.
            Discusses Complaints and <u>The Shepheardes Calender</u> in gen-
      eral evolution of sixteenth-century lyric poetry; stresses con-
      tinental sources,

23   OEHNINGER, LUDWIG. "Edm. Spenser's Faerie Queene." In
      "Die Verbreitung der Königssagen der Historia Regum
      Brittanniae von Geoffrey of Monmouth in der poetischen
      elisabethanischen Literatur." Ph.D. thesis, Ludwigs-
      Maximilian-Universität, Munich, pp. 98-101.
            Briefly discusses Spenser's use of Geoffrey in <u>The Faerie
      Queene</u>, II.9. For published edition, see 1903.24.

24   _____. "Edm. Spenser's Faerie Queene." In <u>Die Verbreitung
      der Königssagen der Historia Regum Brittanniae von Geoffrey
      of Monmouth in der poetischen elisabethanischen Literatur</u>.
      Munich: Messhett & Hissiger, pp. 98-100.
            Published version of 1903.23.

25   ORPEN, GODDARD H. "Place Where Dermot M'Morrough Embarked
      When Driven from Ireland in 1166." <u>JRSAI</u> 33:418-19.
            Notes Elizabeth Spenser's residence at Kilcoran, her mar-
      riages to Spenser, Seckerstone, and Tynte.

26   PATON, LUCY ALLEN. <u>Studies in the Fairy Mythology of
      Arthurian Romance</u>. Radcliffe College Monographs, no. 13.
      Boston: Ginn & Co., pp. 29, 271.
            Mentions Spenser in two footnotes. Published and revised
      edition of 1900.13. Revised: ed. Roger Sherman Loomis (New
      York: Burt Franklin, 1960).

*27   PERRETT, WILFRED. "The Story of King Lear from Geoffrey of
      Monmouth to Shakespeare." Ph.D. diss., University of Jena.
          For published editions, see 1903.28; 1904.32.

*28   _____. The Story of King Lear from Geoffrey of Monmouth to
      Shakespeare. Weimer: K. Wagner Sohn, 33 pp.
          Published version of 1903.27. For annotation, see 1904.32.

 29   READ, WILLIAM A. "Keats and Spenser." MLN 18:204-6.
          Shows Spenserian influence on Keats's poetry, especially
      in vocabulary, meter, stanza patterns, and chivalric theme.

 30   [THOMPSON, FRANCIS.] "The Poet's Poet." The Academy and
      Literature 65:248-49.
          Spenser planned The Faerie Queene "on a scale beyond his
      physical power of endurance." Later books of poem fail in power
      and Spenserian stanza becomes "a very wearisome and cumbrous
      narrative form." Spenser, nonetheless, was a supreme lyric poet,
      allured by tradition and example to exhaust himself in narrative
      poetry; he found his true calling in the shorter poems of his
      closing years. For abridged version, see 1913.38; 1925.33.

*31   TRENT, WILLIAM P., ed. Introduction to The Complete Works of
      Edmund Spenser. New York: Thomas P. Crowell & Co.
          Reprinted: 1910.30.

 32   WESTROPP, THOMAS J. "Notes on Askeaton, County of Limerick."
      JRSAI 33:153-74.
          Mentions Spenser as undertaker, that is, an English land-
      lord of land found by Irish peasants.

 33   _____. "Temple-na-Caille and the Churches near Kilkeedy,
      County Limerick." JRSAI 33:297.
          Notes on Kilcolman.

 34   WHITAKER, LEMUEL. "Michael Drayton as a Dramatist." PMLA 18:
      378-411.
          Briefly discusses Drayton as a Spenserian.

                              1904

 *1   AMES, PERCY W. "Spenser." Transactions of the Royal Society
      of Literature 25:91-125.
          Cited in 1923.6.

  2   BENCHOFF, HOWARD J. "The Political Element in Spenser's
      Poetry." Master's thesis, Columbia University, 40 pp.
          On political allegory of The Faerie Queene.

*3   BERKELEY, FRANCES C.   "The Relation of Spenser's <u>Faerie Queene</u>
     to the <u>Arcadia</u> of Sir Philip Sidney." Master's thesis,
     Columbia University.
          Cited in Stephens, 1950.

4   BOAS, Mrs. FREDERICK. <u>In Shakespeare's England</u>. London:
     James Nisbet & Co.; New York: J. Pott, pp. 232-53.
          Reprint of 1903.4.

5   BRADLEY, HENRY. <u>The Making of English</u>. London: Macmillan &
     Co.; New York: St. Martin's Press, pp. 126-27, 227-29.
          Spenser's compounds are relatively few, but "the exceeding
     felicity" of them makes "an impression that has led many to sup-
     pose that they are peculiarly characteristic of his style."
     Spenser's language, his own artificial dialect created from
     archaic and provincial speech and his invention, "was the only
     fitting vehicle for his tone of thought and feeling."

6   BUCK, P[HILO] M., Jr. "New Facts Concerning the Life of
     Edmund Spenser." <u>MLN</u> 19:237-38.
          Presents documents to substantiate Spenser's presence in
     Ireland during 1583-84.

7   BUTLER, T.C. "Spenser and Shakespeare." <u>NQ</u> 109:204.
          Finds parallel names in <u>The Shepheardes Calender</u> and <u>As You
     Like It</u>: Rosalind, Colin, William.

8   CANNING, ALBERT S.G. "Spenser and Raleigh." In <u>Literary
     Influence in British History: A Historical Sketch</u>. Rev. ed.
     London: T.F. Unwin, pp. 49-56.
          A strongly partisan Spenser overlooked ill treatment that
     Irish received, saw their poets and clergymen as chief foes to
     England, and, despite his knowledge of Ireland and his admiration
     of its scenery, was ruled by his anxiety to see that country
     under Protestant dominion. Original edition: London: W.H.
     Allen, 1889.

9   CORBETT, FREDERICK St. JOHN. <u>A History of British Poetry,
     from the Earliest Times to the Beginning of the Twentieth
     Century</u>. London: Gay & Bird, pp. 94-103, 624.
          General introduction to works; lists Spenser as first
     poet-laureate (1591-1599).

10   ELTON, OLIVER. "Literary Fame: A Renaissance Study." <u>Otia
     Merseiana</u> 4:24-52.
          Traces development of two conflicting notions of fame popu-
     lar in English Renaissance literature. Examines <u>Complaints</u> and
     considers <u>The Ruines of Time</u> "the first and, but for Shakspere
     [sic], maybe the loftiest expression in our poetry of the pecul-
     iar kind of hope we are chronicling." Poems in <u>Complaints</u> vol-
     ume treat theme of Fame-in-combat-with-Time.

11   FLOOD, WILLIAM H. GRATTAN. "Enniscorthy in the Thirteenth
      Century--Who Built the Castle?" JRSAI 34:380-83.
          Notes Spenser's lease of castle dated 6 December 1581.
      For related commentary, see 1905.11.

12   GARNETT, RICHARD, and EDMUND GOSSE. English Literature An
      Illustrated Record. From the Age of Henry VIII to the Age of
      Milton. Vol. 2. New York: Macmillan Co., pp. 109-30.
          Mainly a biography with references to Spenser's works and
      many illustrations. Reprint of 1903.12. Reprinted: 1905.13;
      1906.10; 1908.16; 1923.12; 1926.17; 1931.18; 1935.24.

13   GLASENAPP, GUSTAV. "Edmund Spenser und die Bartholomaeus-
      Kircke zu Smithfield." Archiv 112:392-94.
          Proves Spenser's relationship to St. Bartholomew's Church
      in Smithfield, the Church of his youth destroyed by fire. In-
      scription in Church links Elizabeth Scudamore with character
      Scudamour in The Faerie Queene. Notes that "Be not too bold" in
      House of Busyrane (Book III) is pun on family name of Agnes
      Tewbold, buried at this church.

14   ____. "Zur Vorgeschichte der Allegorie in Edmund Spensers
      Faerie Queene." Ph.D. diss., University of Berlin.
          For published edition, see 1904.15.

15   ____. Zur Vorgeschichte der Allegorie in Edmund Spensers
      "Faerie Queene". Berlin: G. Schade, 65 pp.
          Categorizes moral allegory before Spenser as pure, academic,
      and political. Considers courtly allegory before Spenser. Ana-
      lyzes various types of allegory in The Faerie Queene. Concludes
      that Spenser used all extant allegory available to him. Pub-
      lished version of 1904.14.

*16   GREENLAW, EDWIN A. "The Avowing of Arthur, A Study in
      Medieval Fiction." Ph.D. diss., Harvard University.
          Cited in Atkinson, 1937. Also listed at Harvard: "The
      Influence of Machiavelli on Spenser."

17   GWYNN, STEPHEN LUCIUS. The Masters of English Literature.
      New York and London: Macmillan, pp. 21-40.
          Presents general, somewhat negative assessment of Spenser.

*18   HUME, THEODORE W. "The Faerie Queene--A Religious Romance."
      Homiletic Review 48:98-102.
          Cited in 1923.6.

19   JOHNSON, CHARLES F. Forms of English Poetry. New York:
      American Book Co., pp. 149-52.
          Considers Epithalamion un-Pindaric in form; Spenser influ-
      enced by Latin and Italian models.

20   JOYCE, P.W. "Canon Courtenay Moore's Paper on 'Spenser's
      Knowledge of the Neighbourhood of Mitchelstown.'" JCHAS 10:
      133-34.
          Addenda to and correction of Moore (1904.30). Questions
      identity of "Stony Aubrian." Notes Spenser's exceptionally accu-
      rate Irish descriptions. For other studies of rivers, see
      1912.15; 1916.6.

*21   JUSSERAND, JEAN A.A. JULES. Histoire littéraire du peuple
      Anglais. Paris: Firmin-Didot.
          Reprint of 1894, 1896 editions. Partially reprinted:
      1903.18. Translated: A Literary History of the English People,
      From the Origins to the Renaissance (London: T.F. Unwin, 1895,
      1906-1909, 1925-1926; New York: Putnam, 1895-1909, 1909-1914).
      For revised edition, see 1926.25.

22   KINDON, J. "Byron versus Spenser." International Journal of
      Ethics 14:362-77.
          Contrasts Spenser and Byron in terms of ideals, aims,
      methods and views of art. Byron rejects moral rule and civil
      order; in Spenser, moral and spiritual truths triumph.

23   KUHNS, OSCAR. Dante and the English Poets from Chaucer to
      Tennyson. New York: Henry Holt & Co., pp. 58-70.
          Concludes that Spenser never consciously imitated Dante or
      had read his works.

*24   LAWSON, CHARLES F. "The Allegory of The Faerie Queene."
      Master's thesis, Columbia University.
          Cited in Stephens, 1950.

25   LEE, SIDNEY. "Elizabethan Plagiarism." TLS, June 24, p. 197.
          Notes that Amoretti 81 is almost a literal translation of
      Tasso's Rime 1585, iii.

26   _____, ed. Introduction to Elizabethan Sonnets. An English
      Garner. Vol. 2. New York: E.P. Dutton & Co.; Westminster:
      Archibald Constable & Co., pp. xxiv-xxxvii, lxxxv-xcix, passim.
          Finds Amoretti highly conventional, original in its metrics,
      strongly influenced by continental poets. Spenser (and Sidney)
      "to a large extent handled the sonnet as a poetic instrument
      whereon to repeat in [their] mother-tongue what [they] regarded
      as the finest and most serious examples of poetic feeling and
      diction in Italy and France."

27   LEE, SIDNEY. Great Englishmen of the Sixteenth Century.
      New York: Charles Scribner's Sons; London: A. Constable &
      Co., pp. 155-213.
          Mainly gives account of Spenser's life and general intro-
      duction to his works. Reprinted: 1907.18; 1925.15.

*28   MAXWELL, ANNIE A. "A Glossary of the Non-Classical Names of
       Spenser." Ph.D. diss., Cornell University, 95 pp.
           Cited in 1923.6.

*29   MELE, EUGENIO. Fanfulla della Domenica (Rome) year 26, no. 34
       (21 August).
           Cited in 1923.6. Notes Spenser's and Francisco de la
       Torre's borrowings from Tasso (Amoretti, 81).

 30   MOORE, COURTENAY. "Spenser's Knowledge of the Neighbourhood
       of Mitchelstown." JCHAS 10:31-33.
           Notes accuracy of Spenser's descriptions, his precise use
       of Irish rivers and places, and the "Spenser oak" at Renny
       House, Ballyhooly. For other studies of rivers, see 1904.20;
       1912.15; 1916.6.

*31   O'DONOGHUE, F., ed. British Museum Catalogue of Engraved
       Portraits. Vol. 4. London: British Museum Publications,
       pp. 166-67.
           Cited in Atkinson, 1937. Lists seventeen Spenser portraits.

 32   PERRETT, WILFRED. The Story of King Lear from Geoffrey of
       Monmouth to Shakespeare. Palaestra, Untersuchungen und Texte
       aus der deutschen und englischen Philologie, edited by Alois
       Brandl, Gustav Roethe, and Erich Schmidt, vol. 25. Berlin:
       Mayer & Muller, pp. 90-92.
           Spenser's story of Lear too compendious and too independent
       for definite assignment of source, though Holinshed seems most
       likely. Reprint of 1903.28.

 33   READE, COMPTON. Memorials of Old Herefordshire. London:
       Bemrose & Sons, p. 176.
           Notes Spenser's immortalizing of Sir John Scudamore in The
       Faerie Queene.

 34   ROLFE, WILLIAM [JAMES]. A Life of William Shakespeare.
       Boston: L.C. Page & Co., pp. 521-22.
           Reprint of 1901.22.

 35   SCHELLING, FELIX E. The Queen's Progress and Other Eliza-
       bethan Sketches. Boston and New York: Houghton Mifflin &
       Co., pp. 94-100 passim.
           Views Areopagus as loosely organized writers' group with
       Spenser more concerned with his own work than with the group.
       Reviews Spenser-Harvey correspondence.

 36   SMITH, G. GREGORY, ed. Introduction to Elizabethan Critical
       Essays. Oxford: Clarendon Press, pp. xxxiv-xxxv, xlii, xlix,
       lxxxi, xc, passim.
           Develops overview of Elizabethan critical theory; comments
       on Spenser's use of classical ideas, his attitude on decorum, his

prosody and sources. Comments on Spenser-Harvey correspondence
and E.K.'s glosses to The Shepheardes Calender (glosses reprinted
in volume.)

37   TOWNSHEND, DOROTHEA. The Life and Letters of the Greal Earl
of Cork. London: Duckworth; New York: E.P. Dutton & Co.,
pp. 8, 13, passim.
     Speculates that Spenser met Elizabeth Boyle either at
Ballynetra or at Lisfinnon Castle and that he died in poverty.

38   WENDELL, BARRETT. The Temper of the Seventeenth Century in
English Literature. Clark Lectures Given at Trinity College,
Cambridge in the Year 1902-1903. New York: Charles
Scribner's Sons, pp. 25-29, 104, 107-112, 128-35, 150-53,
288-90.
     Praises the beauty and individuality of Spenser's language
and notes poet's influence on William Brown, Giles Fletcher, and
George Wither. Reprinted: Freeport, N.Y.: Books for Libraries
Press, 1967.

1905

1   ANON. "Pedigree of the Poet Spenser's Family." JCHAS 10:196.
     Reprint of pedigree contributed to The Patrician for Jan-
uary 1848. For other studies of pedigree, see 1906.8; 1909.10.

2   BARBER, CORA LIVINGSTON. "Spenser's Influence on William
Browne." Master's thesis, Columbia University, 30 pp.
     Finds Spenser to be chief influence on Browne's poetry.

3   BERRY, HENRY F. "Sheriffs of County Cork." JRSAI 35:49-52.
     Notes Robert Tynte as third husband of Elizabeth Boyle.

*4   BROWN, PETER FRANKLIN. "The Influence of Edmund Spenser on the
British Romantic Poets, 1800-1840." Master's thesis, University of Chicago, 47 pp.
     Cited in Stephens, 1950.

5   CLARK, ANDREW. "Dr. Plume's Pocket-Book." Essex Review 14:
9-20.
     Notes in MS Plume No. 25 a comment on The Faerie Queene,
identifying Fidessa as Elizabeth [sic] and Duessa as Mary Queen
of Scots.

6   DUNLOP, ROBERT. "Sixteenth-Century Maps of Ireland." EHR 20:
309-37.
     Catalog of printed maps and maps in manuscript in the
British Museum, Public Record Office, Library of Trinity College,
and elsewhere.

7   ERSKINE, JOHN. The Elizabethan Lyric. New York: Columbia
    University Press, pp. 107-16, 153-58, 176-82, 189-96, 302.
        Reprint of 1903.8.

8   FALKINER, C. LITTON. "Spenser in Ireland." Edinburgh Review
    201:164-88.
        Discusses strong influence of Ireland on imagery, allusions,
    and "actual texture" of Spenser's poetry, especially The Faerie
    Queene, Colin Clouts Come Home Againe, and Epithalamion. Indi-
    cates that A Veue of the Present State of Ireland reflects
    Spenser's official attitude.

9   FITZMAURICE-KELLY, JAMES. "Note on Three Sonnets." Revue
    hispanique 13:257-60.
        Notes that Amoretti, 81, and Francisco de la Torre's Obras
    del Bachiller, 23, have common source in Tasso and that both
    Spenser and Francisco de la Torre borrowed from Tasso, not from
    each other.

*10 FLETCHER, JEFFERSON B. "Spenser, The Cosmopolitan Poet."
    English Graduate Record, Columbia University, October,
    pp. 65-80.
        Cited in 1923.6. Comments on Spenser's Platonism and on
    sources for parts of The Shepheardes Calender.

11 FLOOD, WILLIAM H. GRATTAN. "Enniscorthy Castle." JRSAI 35:
    177-78.
        Notes that Spenser conveyed his twenty-one year lease on
    castle to Richard Synnott of Ballybrennan three days after he
    acquired it on 6 December 1581. For related commentary, see
    1904.11.

*12 FOX, A.W. "Edmund Spenser and the Poet's Poet." Transactions
    of the Burnley Literary and Scientific Club 20-21:97-101.
        Cited in 1923.6.

13 GARNETT, RICHARD, and EDMUND GOSSE. English Literature An
    Illustrated Record. From the Age of Henry VIII to the Age of
    Milton. Vol. 2. New York: Macmillan Co., pp. 109-30.
        Reprint of 1904.12.

14 GREENLAW, EDWIN. "The Sources of Spenser's 'Mother Hubberd's
    Tale.'" MP 2:411-32.
        Rejects Grosart's theory that The Moral Philosophic of Doni,
    englished out of Italian by Thomas North (pub. 1570 in London) is
    source for Mother Hubberds Tale. Identifies two more apparently
    influential sources for poem: the Decameron and, for the over-
    all plan of the tale, the Fox and Ape story, the medieval Renard
    story-cycles.

15 GREG, WALTER W. Pastoral Poetry and Pastoral Drama. A Liter-
    ary Inquiry, with Special Reference to the Pre-Restoration
    Stage in England. London: A.H. Bullen, pp. 82-154, passim.
        Discusses Spenser's works within pastoral tradition. The
    Shepheardes Calender, of prime historical importance, combines
    traditional pastoral elements (from Theocritus, Bion, through
    Marot) with native inspiration in innovative calendar framework,
    which unifies themes of individual eclogues in season-year motif.
    Defends Spenser's language (archaisms and dialect) as artistic
    device to naturalize characters. Notes extensive Chaucerian in-
    fluence on poem. Regards Colin Clouts Come Home Againe as "long-
    est and most elaborate eclogue ever written" and a significant
    step in development of Spenser's poetic diction. Cites similar-
    ity of themes in parts of The Shepheardes Calender, Colin Clouts
    Come Home Againe, and Mother Hubberds Tale. Discusses imitations
    of The Shepheardes Calender. Reprinted: 1906.2.

16 KOEPPEL, E. "'Locrine' und 'Selimus.'" SJW 41:193-99.
        Notes that Selimus contains a considerable number of
    "plagiarisms" from Spenser and that it conforms almost literally
    to the Locrine. Concludes that the author of Selimus could have
    as easily drawn Spenser references from Locrine as from The
    Faerie Queene itself. Rejects Crawford's view (1901.6) that
    Selimus is Marlowe's first drama and Greene wrote Locrine. Con-
    cludes that Selimus is indebted to Locrine and that insufficient
    evidence exists to prove authorship of works. For related com-
    mentaries, see 1901.6; 1906.6; 1913.17; 1916.14.

17 KRANS, HORATIO S. "Sidney Lee's Great Englishmen of the Six-
    teenth Century." Current Literature 38:435-39.
        Comments on Lee's book (1904.27); includes Kinnoul portrait
    of Spenser.

18 LEE, SIDNEY. "The Elizabethan Age of English Literature."
    In Cambridge Modern History. Edited by A.W. Ward, G.W.
    Prothero, and Stanley Leathers. Vol. 3. Cambridge:
    Cambridge University Press; New York: Macmillan Co.,
    pp. 364-421.
        Places Spenser and his works in literary history of age.
    Reprinted: 1934.37.

19 MOORMAN, FREDERIC W. "Spenser." In The Interpretation of
    Nature in English Poetry from "Beowulf" to Shakespeare.
    Edited by Alois Brandl, Ernst Martin, and Erich Schmidt.
    Quellen und Forschungen zur Sprachund Culturgeschichte der
    Germanischen Völker, 95. Strassburg: Karl J. Trübner,
    pp. 177-90.
        "In his delineation of the natural world Spenser is under
    the sway of both native and foreign influences." He is "the
    lineal descendant of Chaucer and the medieval school of English
    poetry" and "he came profoundly under the influence of Ariosto

and of other Italians, and through them under that of the Greek poets."

20　MORE, PAUL ELMER. "Elizabethan Sonnets." In Shelburne
　　Essays. 2d ser. New York: Houghton Mifflin Co.; Cambridge,
　　Mass.: Riverside Press, pp. 1-19.
　　　　Distinguishes between Platonic and Petrarchan influences
　　on sonneteers. Finds evidence in Amoretti of the "idealism of
　　the Petrarchist at its best, the hope that his love shall some-
　　how survive mortality and mingle with eternal things."

21　MUSTARD, WILFRED P. "Note on Spenser, F.Q., v. 5, 24."
　　MLN 20:127.
　　　　In Spenser's story of Hercules, Iole plays the part usually
　　assigned to Omphale. This bit of Italianate mythology probably
　　came to Spenser through Tasso.

*22　RIEDNER, WILHELM. "Spensers Belesenheit." Ph.D. diss.,
　　Ludwig-Maximilians-Universität, Munich.
　　　　For published and enlarged editions, see 1906.19; 1908.31.

23　S., H.K. St. J. "Spenser's Epithalamion." NQ 110:246-47.
　　　　Analyzes verse form, rhyme schemes of poem.

24　SCHRÖER, ARROLD. "Zu Spenser im Wandel der Zeiten." Die
　　Neueren Sprachen 13:449-60.
　　　　Notes how Spenser's reputation was kept alive through imi-
　　tations and how recent works of criticism prevent Spenser from
　　being an unknown poet.

25　SMITH, G.C. MOORE, ed. Introduction to Pedantius, A Latin
　　Comedy Acted in Trinity College, Cambridge. Materialien zur
　　Kunde des älteren Englischen Dramas, 8. Louvain:
　　A. Uystpruyst, pp. xxvii, xxxiii, xxxvi-xl, passim.
　　　　Comments on friendship between Gabriel Harvey and Spenser
　　and on formation of Areopagus. Pedantius, acted around 1580,
　　satirizes Harvey; Leonidas, student of Pedantius, represents
　　Spenser.

26　WHITE, JAMES GROVE. Historical and Topographical Notes, Etc.
　　on Buttevant, Castletownroche, Doneraile, Mallow, and Places
　　in their Vicinity. Vol. 1. Cork: Guy & Co., pp. 57, 101,
　　301, 353, passim.
　　　　Notes on Spenser's family, lineage, marriage, and on
　　Kilcolman Castle, Bregoge river, and Abbey of Buttevant. For
　　Volume 2, see 1911.41.

27　WOODBERRY, GEORGE E. "Spenser." In The Torch: Eight Lec-
　　tures on Race Power in Literature. London and New York:
　　McClure, Phillips & Co., pp. 113-36.
　　　　The Faerie Queene reflects and embodies "a climax in the
　　spiritual life of humanity to which imagination gives form,

23

beauty, and passion." Fundamental conceptions in poem are "life
as quest, with an atmosphere of danger and mystery, presided over
by great principles such as wisdom, grace, chastity, so clad in
loveliness to the moral sense that they seem like secondary forms
of Divine being." Spenser blended the tradition of chivalry and
worship of beauty in new worship of womanhood. In addition,
Spenser debates for six books the question, what is a Christian
soul, perfected in human experience? Concludes that knights of
The Faerie Queene represent "Renaissance courtier Christian-
ized. . . . the final spiritualization of the long result of
chivalry as the ideal of manly life." Reprinted: 1906.24;
1912.43; 1920.29; Freeport, N.Y.: Books for Libraries Press,
1969; Folcroft, Pa.: Folcroft Reprint Co., 1971.

*28   ZANDER, FRIEDRICH. "Stephen Hawes' Passetyme of Pleasure
       verglichen mit Edmund Spenser's Faerie Queene unter
       Berücksichtigung der allegorischen Dichtung in England:
       Ein Beitrag zur Quellenfrage der Faerie Queene." Ph.D. diss.,
       University of Rostock.
            Cited in Lawrence F. McNamee, Dissertations in English and
       American Literature (New York and London: R.R. Bowker Co., 1968),
       p. 184. For published edition, see 1905.29.

29   _____. Stephen Hawes' "Passetyme of Pleasure" verglichen mit
       Edmund Spenser's "Faerie Queene" unter Berücksichtigung der
       allegorischen Dichtung in England: Ein Beitrag zur
       Quellenfrage der "Faerie Queene." Rostock: Carl Hinstorffs
       Buchruckerei, 114 pp.
            Establishes hypothesis that Spenser is influenced in The
       Faerie Queene by Hawes' Passetyme of Pleasure. Compares two
       texts, and concludes that Hawes' work is a direct source for
       The Faerie Queene from which Spenser drew freely. Published
       version of 1905.28.

                                   1906

1   ANON. A.L.A. Portrait Index. Washington, D.C.: Government
       Printing Office, p. 1372.
            Lists about twenty-five references, mainly to Althorp and
       Earl of Kinnoul portraits.

2   BERRY, HENRY F. "The English Settlement in Mallow under the
       Jephson Family." JCHAS 12:1-26.
            Mentions Spenser's friendship with Sir Thomas Norreys, one
       of distinguished group who heard Spenser unfold plan of The Faerie
       Queene at Dublin residence of Lodowick Bryskett. Spenser carried
       letters for Norreys to Privy Council in England and visited
       Mallow in a judicial capacity on at least two occasions.

3   BORGHESI, PETER. <u>Petrarch and His Influence on English</u>
     <u>Literature</u>. Bologna: Nicholas Zanichelli, 135 pp., passim.
          "Can scarcely" call Spenser a Petrarchist, yet there is
     influence in the <u>Amoretti</u>. Faults Spenser for intellectualizing
     "his emotion so much that it is emotion no longer," thus reducing
     the effectiveness of the sonnets.

4   BUCK, P[HILO] M., Jr. "Notes on the <u>Shepherd's Calendar</u>, and
     Other Matters Concerning the Life of Edmund Spenser." <u>MLN</u>
     21:80-84.
          Evidence in <u>The Shepheardes Calender</u> and Spenser-Harvey
     correspondence dates Spenser's acquaintance with Sidney earlier
     than 1576, locates composition of <u>The Shepheardes Calender</u> at
     Sidney's home (Penhurst in Kent), and reveals slight influence
     of Spenser's northern journey in poem.

5   CARGILL, ALEXANDER. "An Old-Time Irish Secretary."
     <u>Westminster Review</u> 165:249-54.
          Comments on Spenser's knowledge of Irish affairs as ex-
     pressed in <u>A Veue of the Present State of Ireland</u>, "probably the
     first really authoritative work bearing on the subject ever
     printed."

6   CRAWFORD, CHARLES. "Edmund Spenser, 'Selimus,' and 'Locrine.'"
     In <u>Collecteana</u>. 1st ser. Stratford-on-Avon: Shakespeare
     Head Press, pp. 47-100.
          Reprint of 1901.6. For other studies, see 1905.16;
     1913.17; 1916.14.

*7   DASENT, J.R., ed. <u>Acts of the Privy Council of England</u>.
     n.s. London: Stationery Office, 31, p. 251.
          Cited in Atkinson, 1937: "A letter to Sir George Carew
     from the Lords of the Privy Council dated '29 Mar. 1601 at
     Whitehall,' asking favor and assistance for Spenser's widow and
     children in recovering things which should be theirs."

8   DEVEREUX, W. "Re Spencer Pedigree." <u>JCHAS</u> 12:50-51, 152-53.
          Notes link between Spenser and Sherlock: Joseph Sherlock
     married Alicia Burne, daughter of James Burne and Rosamund
     Spencer. Also notes Spenser's descendants. For other studies
     of pedigree, see 1905.1; 1909.10.

*9   DRYDEN, ALICE, ed. <u>Memorials of Old Wiltshire</u>. London:
     Bemrose & Sons, p. 157.
          Notes Spenser's presence at Wilton due to Sidney's intro-
     duction. Cited in Atkinson, 1937.

10   GARNETT, RICHARD, and EDMUND GOSSE. <u>English Literature An</u>
     <u>Illustrated Record</u>. <u>From the Age of Henry VIII to the Age</u>
     <u>of Milton</u>. Vol. 2. New York: Macmillan Co., pp. 109-30.
          Reprint of 1904.12.

11   GREENOUGH, JAMES BRADSTREET, and GEORGE LYMAN KITTREDGE.
      Words and Their Ways in English Speech. New York and London:
      Macmillan, pp. 118, 295, 354, 375.
          Reprint of 1901.11.

12   GREG, WALTER W. Pastoral Poetry and Pastoral Drama. A
      Literary Inquiry, with Special Reference to the Pre-Restoration
      Stage in England. London: A.H. Bullen, pp. 84-154, passim.
          Reprint of 1905.15.

13   JUSSERAND, J.J. "Spenser's 'Twelve Private Morall Vertues
      as Aristotle Hath Devised.'" MP 3:373-83.
          Challenges the notion that Aristotle is the groundwork of
      The Faerie Queene: "Aristotle draws nowhere any dogmatic list
      of virtues. . . . Temperance . . . is the only one of Spenser's
      six virtues truly and plainly corresponding to one of Aristotle's."
      Concludes that Spenser borrowed from Aristotle, but borrowed as
      much from such moderns as Piccolomini and Bryskett. For comments
      on this study, see 1918.9.

*14   KERLIN, ROBERT T. "Theocritus in English Literature." Ph.D.
      diss., Yale University.
          For published edition, see 1910.13.

15   KOEPPEL, E. "Edmund Spenser." In Ben Jonson's Wirkung auf
      zeitgenössische Dramatiker und andere Studien zur inneren
      Geschichte des englischen Drama. Anglistische Forschungen
      Herausgegeben von Dr. Johannes Hoops, no. 20. Heidelberg:
      Carl Winter's Universitätsbuchhandlung, pp. 80-93.
          Spenser's The Faerie Queene an early influence on English
      drama shortly after the first three books were published in 1590.
      Shows similarities between language of Spenser and some language
      in dramatic works of Marlowe, Peele, Chapman, John Fletcher,
      Heywood, Massinger, Dekker, and Johnson.

16   LEWIS, CHARLTON M. The Principles of English Verse. New
      York: Henry Holt & Co., pp. 83-84.
          Cites the first stanza of The Faerie Queene as an example
      of the rimed pentameter stanza which is marked by a substantial
      pause at its end. Reprinted: 1907.19; 1929.30.

17   LONG, PERCY W. "Courtly Love in the Reign of Queen Elizabeth."
      Ph.D. diss., Harvard University, pp. 58-60, 185-89, passim.
          Develops detailed discussion of conventions of courtly
      love based on literature of sixteenth century, including
      Amoretti, Daphnaida, Colin Clouts Come Home Againe, and
      Epithalamion. Suggests Lady Carey is lady of Amoretti.

18   ____. "Spenser's Dating of 'Colin Clout.'" Nation 83:368-69.
          Attempts to solve problem of dates for Colin Clouts Come
      Home Againe (Kilcolman, 27 December 1591) and Daphnaida (London,

26

1 January 1591) by suggesting that Spenser was in London the
entire time and used the Kilcolman location as a literary device.

19   RIEDNER, WILHELM.   Spensers Belesenheit.   Naumburg: Lippert &
          Co., 40 pp.
          Demonstrates how Spenser carried his close reading of Bible
and Homer to The Faerie Queene. Published version of 1905.22.
For enlarged edition, see 1908.31.

20   SCRIBNER, DORA ANNA. "The History of Spenser's Literary
          Reputation." Master's diss., University of Chicago, 115 pp.
          Studies Spenser's literary reputation from 1579 to 1906.
Concludes that Spenser has always been regarded a great poet,
but never enjoyed as much popularity as in his own day, and
never received much attention from non-English speaking world.

21   SHELLEY, HENRY C.   Literary By-Paths in Old England.   Boston:
          Little, Brown, & Co., pp. 1-55.
          Biographical account of Spenser and his family, with em-
phasis on various places he lived and probably visited. Illus-
trations. Accepts the Dublin portrait of Spenser as authentic:
an exact replica is in collection of Earl Spencer at Althorp
with note on back referring to another portrait destroyed at
Kilcolman. Reprinted: 1907.29.

22   SMITH, G.C. MOORE, ed.   Introduction to Victoria, A Latin
          Comedy, by Abraham Fraunce. Materialien zur Kunde des
          alteren Englischen Dramas, vol. 14. Louvain: A. Uystpruyst;
          London: David Nutt, passim.
          Suggests that Fraunce may have known Spenser, notes
Fraunce's borrowings from and regard for The Shepheardes Calender.
Identifies Corydon in Colin Clouts Come Home Againe with Fraunce.

23   TUCKWELL, WILLIAM.   Spenser.   London: George Bell & Sons,
          85 pp.
          Overall introduction to Spenser with chapters on "Life of
Spenser," "Minor Works," "The 'Fairy Queene,'" "The Spenserian
Secret," and "Bibliography." Comments mainly on use of pastoral
and political satire in The Shepheardes Calender and Colin Clouts
Come Home Againe. Generally a negative view of The Faerie Queene;
it does not measure up to other epics and/or romances. Poem
lacks consistency of plot and allegory is overly obscure:
"Allegory there is, indeed, abundantly, and that perhaps the
finest element in the poem; but as regards the moral virtues
this much is kept up, that the conceit of each Book is indicated
in its first page, and recalled in its last: all between is an
exercise ground for the poet's genius, on which the stores of his
vast reading and bursting fancy careen without a system and without a check." Concludes that poem lacks subject, hero, an argument, and plot, and abounds with incongruities and anachronisms.
Summarizes religious and political allegory of The Faerie Queene.

Considers Spenser to be most successful in his imagery (especially his "picture-writing in his allegorical impersonations,
new to our literature"), similes, diction (softness of diction
due to borrowings from French, use of "vulgar terms" when appropriate, limited use of archaisms), and the melody and music of
his verse. Reprinted: Folcroft, Pa.: Folcroft Press, 1970.

24   WOODBERRY, GEORGE E. "Spenser." In The Torch: Eight Lectures
      on Race Power in Literature. New York: McClure, Phillips &
      Co., pp. 113-36.
          Reprint of 1905.27.

25   ZOCCO, IRENE. Petrarchismo e Petrarchisti in Inghilterra.
      Palermo: G. Pedone Lauriel--Editore, pp. 89-95.
          Considers Spenser in context of development of sonnet.
      Concludes that Spenser bases some sonnets on real experiences
      and emotions. Notes Petrarchan influences on Amoretti, but
      stresses Spenser's originality in using conventions and in his
      conception of the woman.

                                  1907

1   ANON. "The First Earl of Lytton." QR 206:435-56.
          Had Robert Lytton been born before the reign of James he
      would have been a "son" of Spenser, because both were practical
      visionaries.

2   ANON. "The Pléiade and the Elizabethans." Edinburgh Review
      205:353-79.
          In general discussion of Pléiade links Spenser to individual
      writers, mainly to Ronsard.

3   BUCK, PHILO M., Jr. "ADD. MS. 34064 and Spenser's Ruins of
      Time and Mother Hubberd's Tale." MLN 22:41-46.
          Variant readings of the poems.

4   CLARK, ANDREW, ed. The Shirburn Ballads, 1585-1616. Oxford:
      Clarendon Press, p. 351.
          Identifies "Pleasant Willy" (Teares of the Muses) as Richard
      Tarlton, not Sidney, on basis of Tarlton being Elizabeth's favor-
      ite jester, singer of ballad-dramas, and comedian.

5   CLARK, J. SCOTT. "Spenser, 1552(?)-1599." In A Study of
      English and American Poets: A Laboratory Method. New York:
      Charles Scribner's Sons, pp. 38-88.
          Reprint of 1900.3.

*6   COLE, GEORGE W. Catalogue of Books . . . of the Library of
      Elihu D. Church. New York: Dodd, Mead, Co.; Cambridge:
      Cambridge University Press.

Lists early editions of Spenser. Reprinted: 1909.7;
New York: Redax Microprint, 1940, 1956; New York: P. Smith,
1951.

7   COOK, ALBERT S. "Spenser F.Q. I. i. 1. 6." MLN 22:208-9.
        Notices that Spenser translates Virgil in The Faerie Queene
I.i.1.6 and contrasts Spenser's translation to those of Phaer,
Googe, Stanyhurst, DuBartas, Harington, Milton, Dryden, Caxton,
Chaucer, Fairfax, and Shakespeare.

8   _____. "Spenser, F.Q. 1. Int. 3. 5." MLN 22:209.
        Suggests Spenser's influence on a line in Jonson.

9   CUNINGHAM, GRANVILLE C. "Bacon and Edmund Spenser."
     Baconiana, n.s. 5:153-77.
        Presents evidence to suggest that Bacon used name of
"Spenser" as a mask, based on Bacon's cipher story. Evidence
includes comments on the erroneous 1510 birth date of Spenser,
lack of biographical knowledge of Spenser, lack of praise or
comment on Spenser by Jonson (versus his extreme commentary on
Bacon), lack of correspondence from court ladies whom Spenser
honored in his poems, and the close parallels between Bacon's
life and biographical details of The Shepheardes Calender (contends Colin could easily be Bacon and Rosalinde Marguerite de
Valois).

10   DOWDEN, ERNEST. "Elizabethan Psychology." Atlantic Monthly
     100:388-99.
        An interpretation of the House of Temperance (The Faerie
Queene II.ix.22) based on Bartholomew Anglicus. The triangle of
the Castle of Alma is the vegetative soul, the quadrate the sen-
sible soul, and the circle the rational soul. The triangle and
the quadrate add up to seven, which sums up the corporeal part
of man. The rational soul, with its two faculties of understanding and will, raises the number to nine.

11   ELTON, OLIVER. Modern Studies. London: E. Arnold, pp. 66-
     77, passim.
        Treats Spenser in various of these collected essays and
concentrates on The Faerie Queene in "Colour and Imagery in
Spenser," pp. 66-77. Though Spenser borrows more than 150
images and similes from Ariosto and Tasso, shadowy images are
his own. Enumerates classes for most of Spenser's images:
light mingled with darkness, sea-tempest and rapine, animal
combat and the chase. Reprinted: Freeport, N.Y.: Books for
Libraries Press, 1967.

12   FLETCHER, JEFFERSON B. "'Widdowes Daughter of the Glenne.'"
     MLN 22:63.
        Use of "glenne" in The Shepheardes Calender, "April"
(line 26), apparently misunderstood by E.K., but intended by

Spenser to compliment his mistress Rosalind in conventionally
Petrarchan manner.

13   FLETCHER, PRISCILLA. "A Study of English Blank Verse, 1582-
     1632." Colorado College Publications, Language 2:41-65.
        Notes Spenser's imitation of Chaucer.

14   GOLLANCZ, I. "Spenseriana." PBA 3:99-105.
        Reports possession of Spenser's personal copy of The Faerie
     Queene, verified by marginalia and variant version of Amoretti, 1,
     inscribed for presentation to Elizabeth Boyle. Claims as Spenser
     holograph an indictment against Lord Roche, dated 12 October 1589.
     Reports finding of Harvey's gift book of The Shepheardes Calender,
     which helps date poem and interpret tale of "Wolf and Lamb"--
     tale may "refer to the history of Thomas Watson, the Romish
     bishop of Lincoln, who in January 1578-9 was committed to the
     keeping of the Bishop of Rochester, and caused difficulties."
     Notes that Harvey's book was inscribed with "Ex dono Edmundi
     Spenseri, Episcopi Roffensis Secretarii, 1578."

15   HERFORD, C.H., ed. Introduction to Shepheards Calendar,
     Containing Twelve Eclogues Proportionable to the Twelve Months.
     London and New York: Macmillan & Co., pp. i-lxxiii.
        Comments on Spenser's biography, poetry, and details of
     The Shepheardes Calender: conventions, pastoral tradition,
     language, allegory, glosses, and identification of E.K. as
     Edward Kirke. Considers poem a summation of pastoral tradition
     to date. Presents detailed analysis of dialect, archaisms, and
     grammar of poem. Reprinted: 1914.8.

16   HICKEY, E. "Catholicity in Spenser." American Catholic
     Quarterly Review 32:490-502.
        Concludes from an examination of Book I of The Faerie Queene
     that in some ways Catholicity is integral to Spenser's thought
     and that on certain points his teaching is definitely Catholic.

*17 KITE, EDWARD. "Wilton House, and its Literary Associations."
     Wiltshire Notes and Queries 58 (June):436, 439.
        Cited in Atkinson, 1937.

18   LEE, SIDNEY. Great Englishmen of the Sixteenth Century.
     New York and London: Nelson, pp. 155-213.
        Reprint of 1904.27.

19   LEWIS, CHARLTON M. The Principles of English Verse. New
     York: Henry Holt & Co., pp. 83-84.
        Reprint of 1906.16.

20   LOFTIE, WILLIAM J. "Edmund Spenser of Penhurst." In Poet's
     Country. Edited by Andrew Long. London: T.C. and E.C. Jack,
     pp. 313-24.

Notes that Spenser probably visited Sidney at Penhurst, which influenced descriptions in The Shepheardes Calender and in The Faerie Queene.

21 LONG, PERCY W. "A Name for Spenser's Rosalind." PMLA 22: Proceedings xiv.
   Abstract of paper which identifies Rosalind (The Shepheardes Calender) as Elizabeth North (code name: Eliza Nord), daughter of Thomas North. Rosalind's faithlessness ("June" eclogue) presented in same month that Elizabeth married (June 1579). For related study, see 1908.27.

22 MAYNADIER, HOWARD. "Spenser." In The Arthur of the English Poets. Boston and New York: Houghton, Mifflin & Co.; Cambridge, Mass.: Riverside Press, pp. 257-77.
   Though influenced by many, Spenser knew Arthurian legends best through Malory. Only Book I strongly reminiscent of any famous Arthurian quest. Other reminiscences include names, castles, and monsters. Spenser remains faithful to old romantic tone while he represents the change from the medieval spirit to the modern. Reprinted: 1935.48; N.Y.: Haskell House, 1966; New York: Johnson Reprint Co., 1969.

23 MORTON, EDWARD PAYSON. "The Spenserian Stanza before 1700." MP 4:639-54.
   Cites the "Mirrour for Magistrates" as a forerunner of the Spenserian stanza, notes that few of Spenser's contemporaries used the stanza, considers some of the Spenserian poems or imitations which appeared in forty-seven of the years between 1590 and 1698, notes Dryden's acknowledgement of his debt to Spenser for the alexandrine, and concludes that Spenser's influence before 1700 was constant and profound.

24 MORYSON, FYNES. Itinerary, 1617. Vol. 2. Printed by John Beale, 1617. Reprinted: Glasgow: James Maclehose & Sons, p. 173.
   Of biographical interest; notes undertakers' disposal of lands in Ireland.

25 POTT, CONSTANCE M. "Francis St. Alban and His 'Fair Lady.'" Baconiana, n.s. 5:178-96.
   Suggests that new philosophy of Renaissance literature, "allegories of the marriage of Truth and Beauty," comes from Mr. Francis Bacon's Speech in Praise of the Queen. Spenser's works embodying this philosophy include Amoretti, Epithalamion, Fowre Hymnes, The Faerie Queene. Concludes that the "Sovereign Mistress" of Francis St. Alban, "Truth, spiritual and material," parallels Gloriana of The Faerie Queene, Sapience of Fowre Hymnes, and "Queen" of Amoretti; all "re-echo the Song of Solomon and the Convito of Dante through the voice of Francis St. Alban."

26   SCHOENEICH, GEORG. "Der Literarische Einfluss Spensers auf Marlowe." Ph.D. diss., Friedrichs-Universität, Halle-Wittenberg.
        For published edition, see 1907.27.

27   _____. Der Literarische Einfluss Spensers auf Marlowe. Halle: Hohmann, 102 pp.
        Considers parallels between The Faerie Queene and Tamburlaine; notes parallels between The Faerie Queene and Dr. Faustus, The Jew of Malta, The Massacre at Paris, and Edward II. Published version of 1907.26.

*28   SCHROEDER, KURT. "Platonismus in der Englischen Renaissance vor und bei Lyly." Ph.D. diss., University of Berlin.
        Cited in 1923.6. For related study, see 1920.23.

29   SHELLEY, HENRY C. Literary By-Paths in Old England. Boston: Little, Brown, & Co., pp. 1-55.
        Reprint of 1906.21.

30   SMITH, G.C. MOORE. "Spenser, 'Shepherd's Calendar,' 'November.'" MLR 2:346-47.
        Identifies Dido in "November" as Ambrosia Sidney, Leicester's neice and Philip Sidney's sister, who died 22 February 1574-75.

*31   STEBBING, WILLIAM. The Poets: Geoffrey Chaucer to Alfred Tennyson: Impressions. London and New York: Henry Froude; Oxford: Oxford University Press.
        Cited in 1923.6. Reprinted: 1910.28; 1913.36.

32   TUCKER, THOMAS G. The Foreign Debt of English Literature. London: George Bell & Sons, 257 pp., passim.
        Notes classical, continental, and other sources for Spenser, in context of general discussion of foreign influences on English literature.

33   WINSTANLEY, LILIAN, ed. Introduction to The Fowre Hymnes. Cambridge: Cambridge University Press, 151 pp.
        Thorough introduction to Platonism in Spenser's works (72 pages). Finds "two main periods of Platonic influence, one early (Shepheards Calender and Faerie Queene, Book I) which consists of Platonism pure and simple and the other later (Faerie Queene, Book VII and Amoretti) in which Platonism is largely tinged with Neo-Platonism." First two hymns, which are erotic, fall under early influence; latter two are basically Neoplatonic in mentality. Considers latter two hymns separate from first two and sees them as corrections or retractions of early humns. Believes Spenser was particularly attuned to understand Platonism and it served as a balance for his Puritanism. Phaedrus and Symposium are sources for Spenser's ideas of love and beauty.

Discusses influence of Ficino and Bruno on Fowre Hymnes: builds
discussion on assumption that Spenser read Ficino's commentary
on the Symposium in Commentarium in Convivium and Bruno's erotic
treatise De gl'heroici furosi. Demonstrates influence with
parallel passages. Notes similar influence in The Faerie Queene,
Amoretti, Epithalamion, Colin Clouts Come Home Againe, and Teares
of the Muses.

34   WOODWARD, PARKER. "Immerito." In Euphues the Peripatician.
     London: Gay & Bird, pp. 25-53.
          Bacon bought the use of Spenser's name and wrote the works
     attributed to Spenser.

35   YARDLEY, E. "Spenser's Faerie Queene." NQ 116:105-106.
          Points out some of the many mistakes Spenser makes in
     using his otherwise extensive classical learning.

                              1908

*1   ANON. Catalogue of MSS in the Library of Gonville and Caius
     College, Cambridge. Vol. 1. Cambridge: Cambridge University
     Press, p. 217, no. 188.
          Cited in 1923.6; notes sixteenth-century manuscript of
     A Veue of the Present State of Ireland.

*2   ANON. Catalogue of MSS in the Library of Gonville and Caius
     College, Cambridge. Vol. 2. Cambridge: Cambridge University
     Press, p. 627, no. 595.
          Cited in 1923.6; notes a manuscript translation of The
     Shepheardes Calender into Latin hexameter verse by John Dove,
     which differs from copy in the British Museum.

*3   ASHTON, HARRY. "DuBartas en Angleterre." Ph.D. diss.,
     University of Paris.
          Cited in Atkinson, 1937.

 4   AYRES, HARRY MORGAN. "The Faerie Queene and Amis and Amiloun."
     MLN 23:177-80.
          Spenser incorporates in the Amyas-Aemylia story (Book IV
     of The Faerie Queene) parts of the romance of Amis and Amiloun.

 5   BAYNE, THOMAS. "'Well of English Undefyled.'" NQ 117:267-68.
          Points out a typical instance of the misquotation of
     Spenser's tribute to Chaucer in The Faerie Queene, IV.ii.32.8.

 6   BLACHISTON, H.E.D. "Name Puzzle in Early Spenser." NQ 117:
     114.
          Suggests Lovegood or Lovegod as the name of the author of
     the puzzle queried in 1908.8.

7   BOND, R. WARWICK. "Ariosto." QR 208:125-54.
          Though Tasso contributed much to Spenser's moral scheme,
     The Faerie Queene resembles more than the purely romantic method
     of Ariosto. Spenser lags behind Ariosto in unity and management,
     but his discipleship is nonetheless evident in his borrowing of
     techniques of prophecy, magic, and allegory.

8   BOYS, H. WARD. "Name-Puzzle in Early Spenser." NQ 117:48.
          Queries solution to Latin name-puzzle inscribed on a fly-
     leaf of personally owned 1617 edition of Spenser's works. For
     response, see 1908.6.

9   BUCK, PHILO M., Jr. "Spenser's Lost Poems." PMLA 23:80-99.
          Speculates that most of the lost works were satires, sup-
     pressed in 1580, and were of minimal value. Examines Complaints
     to show Spenser's dislike of Burghley. Interprets Ape and Lion
     of Mother Hubberds Tale to be Burghley and Leicester, respectively.
     Most of "lost" works were published in 1591 with new titles:
     Teares of the Muses, Visions of the World's Vanitie, The Ruines
     of Time.

10   COURTHOPE, WILLIAM J. "The Poetry of Spenser." In The
     Cambridge History of English Literature. Edited by A.W. Ward
     and A.R. Waller. Vol. 3. Cambridge: Cambridge University
     Press, pp. 211-46.
          Discusses Spenser's works and his notable achievement as
     poet. Reprinted: 1932.16.

11   CUNINGHAM, GRANVILLE C. "Bacon and Edmund Spenser."
     Baconiana, 3d ser. 6:134-35.
          Bacon, as author of The Faerie Queene, wrote the account of
     his birth to Queen Elizabeth and Leicester in I.ix of that poem.

12   DAVIS, WILLIAM HAWLEY. "Castiglione and Spenser, A Study in
     Comparative Literature." Master's thesis, Columbia University,
     27 pp.
          Discusses Spenser's apparent knowledge of The Courtier and
     shows that Castiglione's model for the ideal courtier probably
     influenced Spenser's conception of Sir Calidore (The Faerie
     Queene, IV) and the courtier in Mother Hubberds Tale, lines
     710-93.

13   De SELINCOURT, HUGH. "Ralegh and Spenser." In Great Ralegh.
     New York: G.P. Putnam's Sons; London: Methuen, pp. 106-13.
          Raleigh's stay in Ireland gave Spenser an outlet for his
     melancholy and dreams, and Raleigh inspired Spenser with new
     life.

14   DODGE, R.E. NEIL. "The Well of Life and the Tree of Life."
     MP 6:191-96.

Concludes that in The Faerie Queene I.ix the Well of Life represents Baptism and the Tree of Life represents the Last Supper.

*15   ENGEL, HUBERT. "Spenser's Relativsatz." Ph.D. diss., University of Berlin.
Cited in 1923.6.

16   GARNETT, RICHARD, and EDMUND GOSSE. English Literature An Illustrated Record. From the Age of Henry VIII to the Age of Milton. Vol. 2. New York: Macmillan Co., pp. 109-30.
Reprint of 1904.12.

17   GREENOUGH, JAMES BRADSTREET, and GEORGE LYMAN KITTREDGE. Words and Their Ways in English Speech. New York and London: Macmillan, pp. 118, 295, 354, 375.
Reprint of 1901.11.

18   GREENWOOD, G[RANVILLE] G. The Shakespeare Problem Restated. London and New York: John Lane, Bodley Head, 588 pp., passim.
Shakespeare allusions: "Pleasant Willy" (Teares of the Muses) and Aëtion (Colin Clouts Come Home Againe). Notes differences in Spenser's and Shakespeare's conceptions of "nature." Comments on Spenser's autograph. Reprint: Westport, Conn.: Greenwood Press, 1970.

*19   HARPER, CARRIE A. "The Sources of the British Chronicle History in Spenser's Faerie Queene." Ph.D. diss., Bryn Mawr College.
For published edition, see 1910.9.

20   HAYES, JOHN R. "Poets of Country Life: Spenser." Book News Monthly 26:913-17.
Names Spenser the first poet of English shepherd life and discusses The Shepheardes Calender briefly.

*21   HAZLITT, WILLIAM CAREW. Shakespear, Himself and His Works, A Study from New Points of View. London: B. Quaritch.
Reprint of 1902.18.

22   HINCHMAN, WALTER S., and FRANCIS B. GUMMERE. "Edmund Spenser." In Lives of Great English Writers: From Chaucer to Browning. Boston and New York: Houghton Mifflin Co., pp. 44-55.
Brief biography of the poet and survey of his works. Reprinted: 1970.

23   KASTNER, L.E. "Spenser's 'Amoretti' and Desportes." MLR 4: 65-69.
Notes much silent borrowing from Desportes' Cleonice (1583) and other works, which, in part, accounts for Spenser's tone of artificiality in the sequence; sees little borrowing from Ronsard and Du Bellay.

24   KERR, W.A.R. "The Pléiade and Platonism." MP 5:407-21.
         Study of Platonism in poetry of Ronsard, Du Bellay, and
     others. No mention of Spenser.

25   LEE, SIDNEY. "The Elizabethan Sonnet." In The Cambridge
     History of English Literature. Edited by A.W. Ward and A.R.
     Waller. Vol. 3. Cambridge: Cambridge University Press,
     pp. 247-72.
         Emphasizes sources for Amoretti (Ronsard and Desportes,
     mainly). Reprinted: 1932.42.

26   LONG, PERCY W. "Spenser and Lady Carey." MLR 3:257-67.
         Contends that Epithalamion addresses Elizabeth Boyle, while
     Amoretti honors Lady Carey, Spenser's court mistress; however,
     love expressed in Amoretti is chaste and approved by the Queen.

27   _____. "Spenser's Rosalind." Anglia 31:72-104.
         Suggests that Rosalind of The Shepheardes Calender refers
     to Elizabeth North, daughter of Thomas North, whom Spenser prob-
     ably knew. Name also fits anagram and allusions in poem are
     relative to Elizabeth North's circumstances. Rejects earlier
     identifications of Rosalind and illustrates that dialect of The
     Shepheardes Calender is not peculiarly Lancastrian. For related
     study, see 1907.21.

28   MUNRO, JOHN. "Spenser Allusions." NQ 118:121.
         Lists nineteen allusions between 1637 and 1709 to Spenser's
     exile at Kilcolman.

29   MUSTARD, WILFRED P. "Virgil's Georgics and the British Poets."
     American Journal of Philology 29:1-32.
         Allusion to Georgics in The Shepheardes Calender, "October,"
     lines 55-60.

30   NADAL, THOMAS WILLIAM. "Spenser's Daphnaida and Chaucer's
     Book of the Duchess." PMLA 23:646-61.
         Shows that in Daphnaida Spenser imitates Chaucer's Duchess
     "in general form and outline, in manner of treatment, and in
     style and subject matter"; he has taken "certain stanzas almost
     entire, has borrowed from it whole sections of eulogistic ideas
     and elegaic conceits, and has adopted Chaucer's phraseology it-
     self, with a freedom at once both striking and convincing."
     For related studies, see 1909.29; 1910.18.

31   RIEDNER, WILHELM. Spensers Belesenheit. I Teil: Die Bibel
     und das Klassische Altertum. Leipzig: A. Deichert, 131 pp.
         Expands 1906.19 to include forty-nine classical authors in
     addition to Homer.

32   SAINTSBURY, GEORGE. A History of English Prosody. From the
     Origins to Spenser. Vol. 1. London: Macmillan & Co.,
     pp. 350-69.

Considers Spenser an original poet, one who is "staunch to true English prosody in measure and rhyme." Illustrates with variety of examples from The Shepheardes Calender and other minor poems. Reprinted: 1923.39.

*33   SCHRAMM, R. "Spensers Naturschilderungen." Ph.D. diss., University of Leipzig.
        For published edition, see 1908.34.

34   _____. Spensers Naturschilderungen. Leipzig: Dr. Seele & Co., 96 pp.
        Considers Spenser's subjective, objective, and learned portrayal of nature, and similes derived from nature. Concludes that Spenser's portrayal of nature is descended from Italian and classical literature but transmitted through his personal experience with nature in England and Ireland. Published version of 1908.33.

35   SYMTHE-PALMER, A. The Ideal of a Gentleman. London: George Routledge & Sons; New York: E.P. Dutton, pp. 6, 316, 391, 427.
        Quotes from The Faerie Queene, Fowre Hymnes, Mother Hubberds Tale, and A Veue of the Present State of Ireland to illustrate qualities of gentleman.

*36   UPHAM, ALFRED HORATIO. "The French Influence in English Literature from the Accession of Elizabeth to the Restoration." Ph.D. diss., Columbia University.
        For published edition, see 1908.37.

37   _____. The French Influence in English Literature. From the Accession of Elizabeth to the Restoration. New York: Columbia University Press, pp. 25-90, passim.
        Suggests that Spenser-Harvey correspondence verifies existence of Areopagus group, which included Spenser, Harvey, Sidney, Dyer, Greville, and later Daniel and Fraunce. Presents evidence for strong unity of group, Spenser-Sidney friendship, and Italian models for Areopagus structure, although Pléiade was similar also. French influence on Spenser chiefly from DuBellay, seen in The Visions of Petrarch, The Visions of Bellay, Ruines of Time, and Visions of the Worlds Vanitie. Marot's influence on "November" and "December" of The Shepheardes Calender. Notes parallels between Du Bartas' Semaines and The Faerie Queene, notably with Spenser's House of Alma (II.ix); also parallels among House of Alma, Sylvester's Du Bartas, and Phineas Fletcher's Purple Island. Inspiration for Amoretti more Italian than French. Published version of 1908.36. Reprinted: 1911.39; New York: Octagon Books, 1965.

37

1909

1   ADDLESHAW, PERCY. Sir Philip Sidney. London: Methuen;
    New York: Putnam's, pp. 259-71, passim.
        Notes that A Veue of the Present State of Ireland is ex-
    treme and inaccurate in describing Ireland: Spenser's "supposed
    conversation between Eudoxus and Irenaeus" misrepresents the
    Irish. Spenser's view of Ireland shared in general by Sidney.
    Considers Areopagus a formally organized group and Spenser and
    Sidney friends, but not close: "On the one side Spenser's pride
    and reserve, also his irritability, and on the other Philip's
    interest in alien matters which commanded his attention, made
    any real intimacy between the two an impossibility." Discusses
    Spenser's relations with his contemporaries and concludes that
    while he remains a great poet, "there is really little to admire
    in Spenser as a man." Spenser's attack on Irish ultimately was
    his undoing. Reprinted: 1910.1; Port Washington, N.Y.:
    Kennikat Press, 1970.

2   AUSTIN, ALFRED. "The Essentials of Great Poetry." QR 210:
    408-28.
        Notes that Spenser is frequently lyrical when he is not
    offering lyrical poetry. Discusses Epithalamion in development
    of lyric poetry.

3   BOAS, FREDERICK S., ed. Introduction to Giles and Phineas
    Fletcher Poetical Works. Vol. 2. Cambridge: Cambridge
    University Press, pp. xiii-xxiii.
        Presents considerable evidence to show that Phineas
    Fletcher is author of Brittain's Ida.

*4 BOEHM, KURT. "Spenser's Verbalflexion." Ph.D. diss.,
    Friedrich-Wilhelms-Universität, Berlin.
        For published edition, see 1909.5.

5   _____. Spensers Verbalflexion. Berlin: Mayer & Muller,
    59 pp.
        Analyzes Spenser's inflection of verbs under three major
    headings: verb endings, formation of tenses, list of available
    verbs. Published version of 1909.4.

6   CLARK, J. SCOTT. "Spenser, 1552(?)-1599." In A Study of
    English and American Poets: A Laboratory Method. New York:
    Charles Scribner's Sons, pp. 38-88.
        Reprint of 1900.3.

7   COLE, GEORGE W. Catalogue of Books . . . of the Library of
    Elihu D. Church. New York: Dodd, Mead, Co.; Cambridge:
    Cambridge University Press.
        Reprint of 1907.6.

8   COOPER, LANE. "The 'Forest Hermit' in Coleridge and
    Wordsworth." MLN 24:33-36.
        Notes that hermit described by Coleridge in Parts VI and
    VII of The Rime of the Ancient Mariner is similar to Spenser's
    description of Archimago and his hermitage in The Faerie Queene,
    I.i.34.

9   De SELINCOURT, HUGH. "The Successors of Spenser." In The
    Cambridge History of English Literature. Edited by A.W. Ward
    and A.R. Waller. Vol. 4. Cambridge: Cambridge University
    Press, pp. 149-67.
        Traces Spenser's influence. Reprinted: 1932.33.

10 DEVEREUX, W. "Spencer's Pedigree." JCHAS 15:101-2.
        Notes mention of Spencers (descendants of Edmund Spenser)
    in will of Daniel Adams, dated 24 April 1702. For other studies
    of Spenser's pedigree, see 1905.1; 1906.8.

11 FALKINER, CAESAR LITTON. "Spenser in Ireland." In Essays
    Relating to Ireland, Biographical, Historical, and Topograph-
    ical. London and New York: Longmans, Green & Co., pp. 3-32.
        Spenser closely connected to Ireland and Irish affairs.
    Points our Irish elements in Spenser's works with emphasis on
    The Faerie Queene.

12 FLETCHER, C.R.L. Historical Portraits, Richard II to Henry
    Wriothesley 1400-1600. Oxford: Clarendon Press, pp. 165-66.
        Reproduces Pembroke Hall portrait.

13 GABRIELSON, ARVID. Rime as a Criterion of the Pronunciation
    of Spenser, Pope, Byron, and Swinburne: A Contribution to the
    History of the Present English Stressed Vowels. Uppsala:
    Almqvist and Wiksells Boktryckeri, 211 pp., passim.
        A collection of rimes in two sections. "Rime-Lists" in-
    cludes rimes to obsolete words, rimes correct in present English,
    and rimes incorrect in present English. Second category con-
    siders relations of rimes to pronunciation of the rime-vowels.

14 GREENLAW, EDWIN. "The Influence of Machiavelli on Spenser."
    MP 7:187-202.
        Sees Machiavellian lion in A Veue of the Present State of
    Ireland and fox in Mother Hubberds Tale. Finds some influence
    of distorted Machiavellian doctrine (from Gentillet) on Mother
    Hubberds Tale, while identifying fuller influence of Il Principe
    on general scheme and statecraft of A Veue of the Present State
    of Ireland, which rightly interprets Machiavellianism. Considers
    A Veue of the Present State of Ireland a practical plan to re-
    lieve suffering in Ireland, not merely a defense of Grey's
    atrocities.

15   HALES, J.W., and SIDNEY LEE. "Edmund Spenser." In <u>Dictionary</u>
      <u>of National Biography</u>. Edited by Sidney Lee. Vol. 18.
      London: Smith, Elder; New York: Macmillan Co., pp. 792-806.
          Discusses all works from critical perspective and in rela-
      tion to Spenser's biography.

16   HINCKLEY, HENRY BARRETT. "Theories of Vision in English
      Poetry." <u>MLN</u> 24:125.
          Platonic and Pythagorean theory of sight "by emission"
      underlies passage from <u>The Faerie Queene</u>, II.xi.26.1-2.

*17   HOFFMAN, FRITZ. "Das Partizipium bei Spenser mit Berück-
      sichtigung Chaucers und Shakespeares." Ph.D. diss., Friedrich-
      Wilhelms-Universität, Berlin.
          For published edition, see 1909.18.

18   _____ . <u>Das Partizipium bei Spenser mit Berücksichtigung</u>
      <u>Chaucers und Shakespeares</u>. Berlin: Mayer & Müller, 48 pp.
          Chapter headings include: construction, meaning, syntax,
      art of composition, origin of participial stems, favorite parti-
      ciples, and evolution of Spenser's use of the participle. Pub-
      lished version of 1909.17.

19   HUME, MARTIN. "Spanish Influence in Elizabethan Literature."
      <u>Transactions of the Royal Society of Literature</u> 29:1-35.
          Notes influence of Montemayor's <u>Diana</u> on <u>The Shepheardes</u>
      <u>Calender</u>.

20   INGLEBY, C.M.; L. TOULMIN SMITH; and F.J. FURNIVALL, et al.
      <u>The Shakespeare Allusion Book: A Collection of Allusions to</u>
      <u>Shakespeare From 1591 to 1700</u>. 2 vols. London: Humphrey
      Milford, Oxford University Press, 1:1; 2:461-62, 474.
          Identifies Aëtion (<u>Colin Clouts Come Home Againe</u>) as
      Shakespeare and argues Spenser finished draft of poem in 1591
      and later revised it. Points out that allusions in <u>The Faerie</u>
      <u>Queene</u>, I.3.30 and IV.1.46 are wrongly attributed to Shakespeare,
      and that Willy (<u>Teares of the Muses</u>) is Tarlton, not Shakespeare.
      Reprinted: 1932.33

*21   JUSSERAND, JEAN A.A. JULES. <u>A Literary History of the English</u>
      <u>People, From the Origins to the Renaissance</u>. New York:
      Putnam.
          Reprint of London: T.F. Unwin, 1895. Translated version
      of 1904.21. Revised with new title: 1926.25.

22   KALUZA, MAX. <u>Englische Metrik in historischer Entwicklung</u>.
      Berlin: Emil Ferber, pp. 358-66, 380.
          Considers briefly Spenserian stanza, its influence and
      variations, and stanza of <u>Epithalamion</u>.

*23   LEVLOH, P. <u>Tennyson und Spenser</u>. Marburg: [publisher not
      known].
           Cited in 1923.6.

24   M., N., and A. "Spenser's 'Faerie Queene.'" <u>NQ</u> 119:190.
           Queries existence and publication of "three supplemental
      cantos to 'The Faerie Queene,' not by Spenser, but by another
      and inferior hand."

25   MACKAIL, J[OHN] W[ILLIAM]. "Spenser." In <u>The Springs of
      Helicon: A Study in the Progress of English Poetry from
      Chaucer to Milton</u>. New York, London, Bombay, and Calcutta:
      Longmans, Green & Co., pp. 73-133.
           In his own lifetime Spenser was leading representative of
      new English Poetry and has been a quarry and playground for gen-
      erations of poets following. Flexible and profuse, his poetry
      is characterized by a longing for the golden age of the past and
      insistence on the degeneracy of modern times. Briefly considers
      Spenser's Platonism, his relationship to Ariosto, and the shorter
      works. <u>The Faerie Queene</u> is pageant and allegory of life.
      Spenser thought in images, and <u>The Faerie Queene</u> drifts through
      sea of dreams, fluctuating between moral allegory and unmoralized
      romance. Finds Spenser lacking any narrative or dramatic gift.
      Concludes with discussion of strengths and weakness of Spenserian
      stanza. Reprinted: Lincoln: University of Nebraska Press, 1962.

26   MAYNADIER, HOWARD. "The Areopagus of Sidney and Spenser."
      <u>MLR</u> 4:289-301.
           Argues that although Sidney, Spenser, and their friends
      probably met occasionally, there exists little evidence to sup-
      port a formally organized Areopagus.

27   MEYNELL, ALICE. "Where <u>The Faerie Queene</u> Was Written."
      <u>Atlantic Monthly</u> 103:250-54.
           Recounts visit to Kilcolman and discusses Irish people's
      unpleasant memories of Spenser's tenure there.

28   MUSTARD, WILFRED P. "Later Echoes of the Greek Bucolic
      Poets." <u>American Journal of Philology</u> 30:245-83.
           Traces influence of Theocritus, Moschus, and Bion on con-
      tinental and English poetry, including <u>The Shepheardes Calender</u>.
      For supplement, see 1918.17.

29   NADAL, THOMAS WILLIAM. "Chaucer's Influence on Spenser."
      Ph.D. diss., Harvard University, 214 pp.
           Concludes that "while Spenser imitated Chaucer in meter,
      in style, and in language; while he has borrowed from him freely
      for incidents, situations, and descriptions; while he has copied
      phrases and passages entire, and has taken over whole poems for
      his models; yet it is an interesting fact that the allegory of
      Spenser gives evidence of very little Chaucerian influence."

Allegories of The Shepheardes Calender, Mother Hubberds Tale, and
Daphnaida are only ones remotely related to Chaucer. Main influences are in language and meter, as in archaic shepherd's language
of The Shepheardes Calender, and in use of humor, as in Mother
Hubberds Tale. Concludes that Muiopotmos is not allegorical, is
mock-heroic, and was influenced by Sir Thopas and Nun's Priest's
Tale. Influence on The Faerie Queene differs from that on other
works: The Faerie Queene "shows far less imitation of Chaucer's
diction, a comparatively small borrowing for character and incident, with a large indebtedness to Chaucer for description."
Notes that Colin Clouts Come Home Againe, Amoretti, and Fowre
Hymnes show little Chaucerian influence. Provides appendix on
Spenser's archaisms. For related studies, see 1908.30; 1910.18.

*30   PHILLIMORE, W.P.W., and THOMAS GURNEY. Middlesex Parish
      Registers, Marriages. London: Phillimore & Co., p. 145.
         Cited in 1923.6, which notes "'Edm. Spenser and Jone
      Bre[ttri]dge 21 July 1586' under 'Marriages at West Drayton.'"

31   R., G.S. "Spenser on the Finance Bill." SatR 108:81-82.
         Interprets incident in The Faerie Queene, V: Artegall's
      meeting with giant wielding scales.

32   REYHER, PAUL. Les masques anglais: étude sur les ballets et
      la vie de cour en Angleterre (1512-1640). Paris: Hachette &
      Co., pp. 142-46.
         The Faerie Queene reflects splendor of Elizabethan court
      and stimulated artists and poets of reigns of James I and Charles
      I. Spenser a principal inspiration and source for writers of
      masques. Concludes, after a discussion of artistry of several
      episodes in The Faerie Queene, that Spenser is a grand master of
      all arts: a painter, sculptor, decorator, musician. Reprinted:
      New York: Benjamin Blom, 1964.

33   ROYSTER, JAMES FINCH. "A Note on Spenser's Archaism and
      Cicero." MLN 24:30-31.
         Censures E.K.'s classical defense in Cicero of Spenser's
      use of archaisms in The Shepheardes Calender, showing Cicero to
      be no advocate of archaizing and E.K. to have taken passage of
      De Oratore out of context.

34   SHEAVYN, PHOEBE. The Literary Profession in the Elizabethan
      Age. Manchester: Manchester University Press, 258 pp.,
      passim.
         Notes Spenser's dissatisfaction with his position with Grey
      in Ireland as expressed in the allegory, presumably on Grey, in
      Virgil's Gnat. Comments on how Spenser supported himself and
      acquired patrons, on the risks of his political allegories, on
      his relationship with Ponsonby, on his relations with his con-
      temporaries, and on his popularity with readers in his time.
      Revised: ed. J.W. Saunders (Manchester: Manchester University
      Press; New York: Barnes & Noble, 1967).

35 SMITH, REED. "Allegory and Its Use by Spenser in His Minor
    Poems." Ph.D. diss., Harvard University, 435 pp.
        Analyzes allegory "in the abstract" in Part 1 so as to
    apply the "divisions and canons" to Spenser's minor works in
    Part 2. Treats all poems, except The Faerie Queene, noting
    that The Faerie Queene is Spenser's supreme example of allegory.
    Considers Spenser's extensive use of allegory due to his world
    view: "He was primarily interested in ideas, not men and women.
    He did not view the world directly, with all seeing eye, but
    mediately as reflected in an allegorical glass."

36 STRONACH, GEORGE. "Signatures of Spenser." Academy 77:519-20.
        Examines two extant samples of Spenser's handwriting.

37 TOYNBEE, PAGET. Dante in English Literature from Chaucer to
    to Cary. 2 vols. London: Methuen & Co., 1:xx-xxi, 80-82,
    309-15, 598-600, passim; 2:passim.
        Cites passages in Spenser that parallel Dante and concludes
    that "it is difficult to trace an undoubted connection between
    the two poets." Parallel passages may be more coincidence than
    deliberate imitation. Quotes nineteenth-century critics' views
    on matter.

                              1910

1   ADDLESHAW, PERCY. Sir Philip Sidney. London: Methuen;
    New York: Putnam's, pp. 259-71, passim.
        Reprint of 1909.1.

2   BASKERVILLE, C.R. "Two Parallels to 'Lycidas.'" Nation
    91:546-47.
        "May," lines 38ff., of The Shepheardes Calender noted as
    influence on St. Peter's speech in Lycidas; Spenser and subse-
    quently Milton influenced by Skelton's Colin Clout.

3   BRIGHT, JAMES WILSON, and RAYMOND DURBIN MILLER. The Elements
    of English Versification. Boston and London: Ginn & Co.,
    166 pp., passim.
        Cites examples of various types of lines, stanzas, and
    forms in Spenser. Reprinted: 1913.5.

4   CORY, HERBERT E[LLSWORTH]. "The Golden Age of the Spenserian
    Pastoral." PMLA 25:241-67.
        Traces influence of Spenserian pastoral, especially The
    Shepheardes Calender, upon English poetry from 1597 to 1700.
    Spenser's innovations peaked with Drayton and his followers,
    declined with Phineas Fletcher and Quarles.

5   CORY, HERBERT ELLSWORTH. "The Influence of Spenser on Eng-
    lish Poetry from 1579 to the Death of Keats." Ph.D. diss.,
    Harvard University, 491 pp.

                              43

    Presents detailed chronology of Spenser's influence from
his immediate admirers and imitators through the nineteenth century romantics. Shows sustained interest in and respect for
Spenser. For related studies, see 1911.8-9.

6   FEUILLERAT, ALBERT. John Lyly. Contribution à L'histoire de
    la Renaissance en Angleterre. Cambridge: Cambridge University
    Press, 661 pp., passim.
        Notes parallels and relationships between works of Spenser
and Lyly. Rejects identification of Willy (Teares of the Muses)
as Lyly or Sidney. Reprinted: New York: Russell & Russell,
1968.

7   GREENLAW, EDWIN A. "Spenser and the Earl of Leicester."
    PMLA 25:535-61.
        Interprets Mother Hubberds Tale as an allegorical warning
to the Queen of the dangers of the Alençon situation. Identifies Simier as the Ape, Burghley as the Fox, and Elizabeth as the
Lion. Poem shows definite influence of Chaucer and the Renard
cycle. Discussion of Virgils Gnat supports this interpretation.
On basis of tone and context of "Three Proper and wittie familiar
letters," suggests Spenser's connection with Leicester caused his
exile to Ireland and prompted him to write at least part of Mother
Hubberds Tale. Attack on Burghley not personal grievance, but
defense of his patron and aid to Puritans. Fixes dates of Mother
Hubberds Tale and Virgils Gnat at 1579-80 and prior to September
1585. Reprinted: 1932.24.

8   HANFORD, J. HOLLY. "The Pastoral Elegy and Milton's 'Lycidas.'"
    PMLA 25:403-47.
        Discusses Spenser (especially The Shepheardes Calender) as
part of the tradition stemming from Theocritus and Virgil and as
an influence on Milton.

9   HARPER, CARRIE ANNA. The Sources of the British Chronicle
    History in Spenser's "Faerie Queene." Byrn Mawr College
    Monographs. Monograph Series, vol. 7. Philadelphia: John C.
    Winston Co., 190 pp.
        Studies the nearly complete rhymed chronicle of kings of
Britain in The Faerie Queene, II.x and III.iii "to determine, as
exactly as may be, which of the possible sources Spenser used in
the preparation of his version of the chronicle, to note whether
he followed one authority or drew from several of his predecessors, and . . . to consider his method of selecting and arranging
his material." Reviews previous commentary on sources; establishes Spenser's method of working with a brief study of marriage
of the Thames and Medway in The Faerie Queene and brief study of
A Veue of the Present State of Ireland; lists probable sources of
Spenser's chronicle history; demonstrates that Geoffrey of Monmouth's Historia Regum Britannia is basis of Spenser's chronicle,
with Holinshed's Chronicle the next most probable other source;

quotes relevant parts of Spenser's chronicle, comparing stanzas
first to Geoffrey's <u>Historia</u>, secondly to Holinshed, thereafter
tracing what remains unaccounted for to other sources. Concludes
that "much of Spenser's chronicle agrees in detail as well as in
general outline with the <u>Historia</u>," with variations from other
sources. Appendix: "The theory that the British chronicle history was first planned as a separate work is not . . . suscepti-
ble of proof." Published version of 1908.19. Reprinted:
1910.10; New York: Haskell House, 1964.

10   _____. The Sources of The British Chronicle History in
      Spenser's "Faerie Queene." Philadelphia: John C. Winston Co.,
      190 pp.
            Reprint of 1910.9.

11   HOLME, JAMES W. "Italian Courtesy Books of the Sixteenth
      Century." <u>MLR</u> 5:145-66.
            First two <u>giornate</u> of Guazzo's <u>Civil Conversation</u> are
      rhetorical paraphrases of Platonic theories of beauty and love,
      and have many points in common with Spenser's <u>Fowre Hymnes</u>.

12   HYDE, DOUGLAS. A Literary History of Ireland. From Earliest
      Times to the Present Day. London: T. Fisher Unwin,
      pp. 493-96.
            Reprint of 1901.15.

13   KERLIN, ROBERT T. Theocritus in English Literature.
      Lynchburg, Va.: J.P. Bell Co., 203 pp., passim.
            Notes that Spenser "cannot be certainly affirmed to have
      known Theocritus--at least directly;" shows that Spenser fol-
      lowed Marot in The Shepheardes Calender. Points out Theocritan
      elements and parallels in Spenser's poetry and that "the dramatic
      character of Spenser's pastorals in general corresponds closely
      with that of the <u>Idylls</u>."

*14   KOEPPEL, EMIL. "John Day's Peregrinatio Scholastica in ihrem
      Verhältnis zu Spenser, Chaucer und den 'Gesta Romanorum.'"
      Die Neuren Sprachen, Festshrift Wilhelm Viëtor (Marburg),
      pp. 1-13.
            Cited in 1923.6.

15   LEE, SIDNEY. The French Renaissance in England. An Account
      of the Literary Relations of England and France in the Six-
      teenth Century. New York: Charles Scribner's Sons, Clarendon
      Press, pp. 261-63, passim.
            Shows strong ties between literatures of both countries
      and specific influence of various French writers on Spenser
      (i.e., Marot, Du Bartas, Ronsard, Desportes, Baïf).

16   LONG, PERCY W. "Spenser's Sir Calidore." ES 42:53-60.
          Concludes from appearance, reputation, date, social status
     of persons, and discourse of Sir Calidore with the author (The
     Faerie Queene, VI.x) that Calidore stands for Essex.

17   McKERROW, R.B., ed. A Dictionary of Printers and Booksellers
          in England, Scotland and Ireland, and of Foreign Printers
          of English Books 1557-1640. London: Blades, East and Blades,
          pp. 179-80, 217-18.
          Notes publication of Spenser's works in entries for
     Humphrey Lownes and William Ponsonby. Reprinted: Oxford:
     TRUEXpress for The Bibliographical Society, 1968.

18   NADAL, THOMAS WILLIAM. "Spenser's Muiopotmos in Relation to
          Chaucer's Sir Thopas and The Nun's Priest's Tale." PMLA 25:
          640-56.
          Suggests that Muiopotmos is "a purely mock-heroic poem"
     written "under the influence of two mock-heroic poems of Chaucer."
     Poem is not allegorical: "the whole spirit of Muiopotmos is
     foreign to that of Spenser's other allegorical poems." For
     related studies, see 1908.30; 1909.29.

*19 POWELL, FREDERCK YORK. "Some Words on Allegory in England."
          Privately Printed Opuscula issued to members of the Sette of
          Odd Volumes (London) 28:30-34.
          Cited in 1930.23. Reissue of "Some Words on Allegory in
     England," read to the Odd Volumes at their meeting 5 July 1895,
     by their brother Ignoramus. Private printing: Chiswick:
     Platrier Brothers, 1895.

20   PREVITÉ-ORTON, C[HARLES] W. Political Satire in English
          Poetry. Cambridge: Cambridge University Press, pp. 48-54.
          General commentary on satire in The Shepheardes Calender,
     Mother Hubberds Tale, and The Faerie Queene in context of his-
     torical development of political satire. Reprinted: New York:
     Russell & Russell, 1968.

21   ROSENTHAL, BRUNO. "Spensers Verhältnis zu Chaucer." Ph.D.
          diss., University of Kiel.
          For published edition, see 1911.34

22   SAINTSBURY, GEORGE. Historical Manual of English Prosody.
          London: Macmillen & Co., 347 pp., passim.
          Uses Spenser as example of various metrical forms, cites
     value of his experimentation, and discusses his influence on
     successive generations of poets. Reprinted with an introduction
     by Harvey Gross: New York: Schocken Books, 1966.

23   SANDISON, HELEN E. "Spenser's 'Lost Works' and their Probable
          Relation to His Faerie Queene." PMLA 25:134-51.

Takes Philo M. Buck (1908.9) to task for faulty method and occasional inaccuracy but emphasizes the probability of Buck's main contention that the greater number of Spenser's so-called lost works are to be found in Spenser's extant writings. Considers untenable and tenable identifications in Buck's list and concludes that, "aside from the identifications conveniently amassed by Mr. Buck," Spenser must have used The Faerie Queene "as a vast repository of his earlier productions, whether short finished poems, or fragments of abandoned projects."

24 SCHELLING, FELIX EMMANUEL. English Literature during the
   Lifetime of Shakespeare. New York: Henry Holt, 486 pp.,
   passim.
         General introduction to the poet and his works. Spenser
   was an innovator: "the paradox of Spenser's genius lies in his
   combination in harmonious union of a passionate love of the sen-
   suously beautiful with the purest and sternest spirit of his
   time." Reprinted: 1927.28.

25 SCHULZ, KONRAD. Die Satiren Halls. Ihre Abhängigkeit von
   den altrömischen Satirikern und inhre Realbeziehungen auf
   die Shakespeare-Zeit. Ph.D. diss., University of Berlin;
   Berlin: Palaestra; Mazer & Muller, passim.
         Discusses possible influence of Spenser on Hall's verse
   satires, specifically influence of themes of profanation of
   poetic art and disregard for knowledge from Teares of the Muses,
   view of the poet from The Shepheardes Calender, language from
   The Faerie Queene, and heroic couplet from Mother Hubberds Tale.

26 SILLS, KENNETH C.M. "Virgil in the Age of Elizabeth."
   Classical Journal 6:123-31.
         Notes Spenser's large debt to Virgil, especially in The
   Shepheardes Calender (Eclogues), Virgils Gnat (Culex), and The
   Faerie Queene (Aeneid).

27 SMITH, J.C. "The Problem of Spenser's Sonnets." MLR 5:273-81.
         Maintains that Amoretti and Epithalamion address Elizabeth
   Boyle; parts of Amoretti originally honored Lady Carey, but
   after she and Spenser quarrelled, he used sonnets in tribute
   of his new love.

*28 STEBBING, WILLIAM. The Poets: Geoffrey Chaucer to Alfred
   Tennyson. London and New York: Henry Froude; Oxford:
   Oxford University Press.
         Cited in 1923.6. Revised edition of 1907.31.

29 STOPES, Mrs. CHARLOTTE CARMICHAEL. William Hunnis and The
   Revels of The Chapel Royal. A Study of His Period and the
   Influences Which Affected Shakespeare. Materialien zur Kunde
   des älteren Englischen Dramas, 29. Louvain: A. Uystpruyst,
   p. 270.

Suggests that Spenser may have had William Hunnis in mind
for allusion in Teares of the Muses, lines 217-22: "because his
silence fits the date [1591, Hunnis had ceased writing], the
allusion to hunnie, and idle cell fit none of his [Spenser's]
greater known contemporaries."

30   TRENT, WILLIAM P. "Spenser." In Longfellow and Other Essays.
      New York: Thomas Y. Crowell & Co., pp. 53-71.
          Praises Spenser's art; compares him to Chaucer, Shakespeare,
      Milton, and others; defends him against modern detractors. Re-
      print of 1903.31.

31   VENN, JOHN. Grace Book Δ. Cambridge: Cambridge University
      Press, pp. 260, 290, 542.
          Lists Spenser's B.A. 1572-73 and M.A. 26 June 1576.

32   WESTROPP, THOMAS J. "Promontory Forts and Similar Structures
      in the County Kerry." JRSAI 40:179-213.
          Includes discussion of Smerwick and Spenser's defense of
      Lord Grey.

                              1911

1   BAYLEY, A.R. "Spenser and Dante." NQ 116:515.
          Suggests break with Rome may have caused Spenser's over-
      sight of Dante in letter to Raleigh. For related studies, see
      1911.2, 4; 1912.28.

2   BAYNE, THOMAS. "Spenser and Dante." NQ 124:115-16.
          Response to 1911.4. Spenser knew Dante well and adapted
      suggestions from him. Cites two examples of Spenser's use of
      Dante in The Faerie Queene at II.iii.40-41 and VI.x.10-16. For
      related studies, see 1911.1; 1912.28.

3   BÖHME, TRAUGOTT. Spensers Literarisches Nachleben bis zu
      Shelley. Palaestra, Untersuchung und Texte aus der deutschen
      und englischen Philologie, 93. Iterausgegeben von Alois
      Brandl, Gustav Roethe, und Erich Schmidt. Berlin: Mayer &
      Müller, 349 pp.
          Traces Spenser's influence on English poetry through
      seven stages: (1) from Spenser to Milton (1634), (2) Milton
      to Dryden (1634-67), (3) Restoration (1667-1700), (4) Age of
      Reason (1700-1730), (5) from 1730-1760, (6) Pre-Romantic era
      (1760-1793), (7) Romantic Period (1793-1825).

4   BRESLAR, M.L.R. "Spenser and Dante." NQ 116:447.
          Queries Spenser's failure to mention Dante in "Letter to
      Raleigh" as one of the allegorical works he consulted. For
      related studies, see 1911.1-2; 1912.28.

5   BRIGGS, WILLIAM DINSMORE.   "Spenser's Faerie Queene II.ii,
     and Boccaccio's Fiammeta."   In Matzke Memorial Volume Con-
     taining Two Unpublished Papers by John E. Matzke and Contribu-
     tions in His Memory by His Colleagues.   Leland Stanford Junior
     University Publications University Series.   Stanford: Stanford
     University, pp. 57-61.
         Demonstrates indebtedness of The Faerie Queene, III.ii to
     Boccaccio's Fiammetta.

6   BUCK, PHILO M., Jr.   "On the Political Allegory in The Faerie
     Queene."   Nebraska University Studies 11:159-92.
         Takes up Books I-III of The Faerie Queene individually,
     making numerous historical identifications, noting at the outset
     that "Spenser was a poet, not an historian, and the order he
     follows is seldom historical, nor are the characters ever more
     than occasionally consistent."

7   CORY, HERBERT E[LLSWORTH].   "Browne's Britannia's Pastorals
     and Spenser's Faerie Queene."   University of California
     Chronicle 2:189-200.
         For Britannia's Pastorals, Browne "imported scenes, charac-
     ters, and episodes from the Faerie Queene into Devonshire."
     Browne's model for story of loves and sorrows of Marina was
     story of Florimell in The Faerie Queene.   His story of Aletheia
     is "an elaborate redaction of several episodes of the first book
     of the Faerie Queene."   Published version of part of 1910.5.

8   _____.   The Critics of Edmund Spenser.   University of
     California Publications in Modern Philology, vol. 2.
     Berkeley: University of California Press, pp. 81-182.
         Recounts history of Spenser criticism and its significance
     in relationship to early twentieth-century opinions of Spenser.
     The chapter headings include: "The Age of Enthusiasm and Spenser-
     Worship," "The Age of Reason and the Rise of Literary Criticism,"
     "The Age of Literary Anarchy," "The Neo-Classical Despotism," and
     "The Triumph of Romanticism."   For related studies, see 1910.5;
     1911.9.   Reprinted: New York: Haskell House, 1964.   See McNeir-
     Provost no. 603.

9   _____.   "Spenser, Thomson, and Romanticism."   PMLA 26:51-91.
         Refutes two fallacious notions about neo-classical attitude
     toward Spenser: that he was an object of indifference and that
     the Augustans mocked him.   Augustans appreciated Spenser's moral
     earnestness and his allegory.   Cites numerous examples of Augustan
     imitations of Spenser.   Refutes argument that Spenser was a cause
     of romanticism.   Points out William Thomson's definite romantic
     tendencies early in eighteenth century and considers several gen-
     uine romanticists to demonstrate that they follow Spenser "subtly
     and deeply where the neo-classicists followed superficially and
     mechanically."   Studies Thomson's Castle of Indolence as a tran-
     sitional blend of Augustan and romantic elements.   For related
     studies, see 1910.5; 1911.8.   Published version of part of 1910.5.

10   CROTHERS, SAMUEL McCHORD. "The Romance of Ethics." In Among
      Friends. Boston and New York: Houghton Mifflin Co.,
      pp. 222-53.
           Uses Books I, II, V, and VI of The Faerie Queene as book of
      ethics from point of view of heroic youth, as an account of way
      in which virtues behave themselves in action.

11   CUNNINGHAM, GRANVILLE C. "Bacon and Edmund Spenser." In
      Bacon's Secret Disclosed in Contemporary Books. London:
      Gay & Hancock, pp. 77-127.
           Combines and expands 1908.11 and 1913.8, concluding that
      Bacon wrote The Shepheardes Calender, that Rosalind is Marguerite
      de Valois, that Bacon wrote Mother Hubberds Tale, and that in The
      Faerie Queene, I.ix Bacon announces his secret birth to Queen
      Elizabeth and her lawful husband, the Earl of Leicester.

12   DODGE, R.E. NEIL. "A Sermon on Source Hunting." MP 9:211-23.
           Challenges the soundness of arguments of "source hunt-
      ers, . . . who pad their lists of parallel passages and points
      of resemblance between authors with examples, which on examina-
      tion, are found to prove nothing at all." Specifically challenges
      Upham's claim (1908.38) that Spenser imitated DuBartas in his
      House of Alma, Nadal's claim (1910.18) that Spenser had Chaucer's
      Sir Thopas in mind when he wrote Muiopotmos, and Lee's (1904.26)
      and Kastner's (1908.23) claims that Spenser imitated Sonnets 68
      and 48 from Desportes's Amours de Diane.

13   FLETCHER, JEFFERSON B. "Benivieni's 'Ode of Love' and
      Spenser's 'Fowre Hymnes.'" MP 8:545-60.
           Finds Benivieni's Canzone della Amore celeste et divino
      (ca. 1488), rather than works of Bruno and Ficino, to be
      Spenser's most immediate source for the Platonism of the Fowre
      Hymnes. Compares parallel texts. For related study, see
      1911.14.

14   _____. "A Study in Renaissance Mysticism: Spenser's 'Fowre
      Hymnes.'" PMLA 26:452-75.
           Interprets Fowre Hymnes as unified exposition of Calvinism
      tempered by Neoplatonic mysticism; the two early hymns describe
      romantic love, which leads to religious love as expressed in the
      last two hymns. Shows influence of Italian Neoplatonists (espe-
      cially Benivieni) on Spenser's doctrine of love. Finds real
      significance of poems in their mystical theme ("the medieval
      renaissance 'religion' of beauty and love"): "Sapience is 'a
      divine person' (the Holy Ghost) and the true lover is not merely
      to learn wisdom . . . , he is eternally to live with Wisdom,
      which is the very God."

15   FULTON, EDWARD. "Spenser and Romanticism." Nation 92:445.
           Cory (1911.9) goes too far in minimizing Spenser's influ-
      ence on romanticism.

*16   GILLETTE, ALLETTA M. "Political Allegory in the Second Book
      of The Faerie Queene." Master's thesis, University of
      Washington.
          Cited in Stephens, 1950.

 17   GREENLAW, EDWIN A. "The Shepheardes Calender." PMLA 26:419-51.
          Rejects Kalendrier des Bergeres as Spenser's chief source,
      showing strong influence of sixteenth-century Chaucer canon and
      analogues in Googe's Eglogs for seasons motive, Colin-Rosalind
      romance, and ecclesiastical satire. Five "Moral" eclogues form
      core of poem and follow Chaucer in style and aim. Mother Hubberds
      Tale similar in theme and technique. Continues discussion in
      1913.14. For related studies, see 1912.23; 1913.2.

 18   GREENOUGH, JAMES BRADSTREET, and GEORGE LYMAN KITTREDGE.
      Words and Their Ways in English Speech. New York and London:
      Macmillan, pp. 118, 295, 354, 375.
          Reprint of 1901.11.

 19   HICKEY, EMILY. "Sir Calidore: A Paper for Girls." CW 93:
      632-45.
          Interprets moral allegory of Book VI of The Faerie Queene
      to conclude that Sir Calidore is model for contemporary behavior.

 20   HUNT, THEODORE W. "Spenser and Later Sonnet-Writers."
      Bibliotheca Sacra 68:264-84.
          Briefly comments on Spenser's innovations in the Visions
      and Amoretti.

*21   INGERSOLL, RUTH C. "The Influence of Spenser upon the Earlier
      Poems of Keats." Master's thesis, Wellesley College.
          Cited in Stephens, 1950.

 22   JOYCE, P.W. "Spenser's Irish Rivers." In The Wonders of
      Ireland and Other Papers on Irish Subjects. London, New York,
      Bombay, and Calcutta: Longmans, Green & Co.; Dublin: M.H.
      Gill & Son, pp. 72-114.
          Identifies the Irish rivers in The Faerie Queene, IV.xi,
      the Mutabilitie Cantos, and Colin Clouts Come Home Againe. Pro-
      vides list of identifications. Reprint of "Spenser's Irish
      Rivers," Fraser's Magazine, n.s. 17 (1878):315-33.

 23   LANGDON, IDA, ed. Introduction to Materials for a Study of
      Spenser's Theory of Fine Art. Ithaca, N.Y.: Cornell Univer-
      sity Press, pp. i-lxiii.
          Assembles "illustrative passages" from Spenser's work that
      reveal his theory of art. Discusses Spenser's concepts of nature
      and art, his attitudes toward the poet and imitative process, and
      the strong Platonic and Aristotelian influences evident in his
      works. Published version of 1911.24.

*24   LANGDON, IDA. "Materials for a Study of Spenser's Theory of
       Fine Art." Master's thesis, Cornell University.
          For published edition, see 1911.23.

25   LITTLEDALE, H. "A Note on Spenser's 'Amoretti.'" MLR 6:203.
          Sonnet 15 borrowed from Desportes (Diane, I, 32).

26   LONG, PERCY W. "Spenser's Sonnets 'As Published.'" MLR
       6:390-97.
          Maintains that Amoretti and Epithalamion praise different
   women and are not companion pieces.

27   MACINTIRE, ELIZABETH JELLIFFE. "French Influence on English
       Classicism." PMLA 26:496-527.
          Considers Areopagus an influential organized group, modeled
   on Pléiade; the group sought reform in English letters and experimented with various literary forms, with special emphasis on the
   classics. Comments on several works to show French influence on
   Spenser.

28   MERRILL, ELIZABETH. The Dialogue in English Literature.
       Yale Studies in English, vol. 42. New Haven: Yale University
       Press; New York: Henry Holt Co., pp. 36-37, 63-66, passim.
          Cites dialogues in "February" and "May" eclogues of The
   Shepheardes Calender as examples of "the more artificial courtly
   dialogues of the day." Spenser's dialogues are well-unified and
   superior to those in other pastoral writers' pastoral poems.
   Dialogue form of A Veue of the Present State of Ireland is "con-
   structed in so regular a way that it very closely illustrates the
   typical method of procedure of rather weighty expository dialogues, and invites comparison with the more substantial essay
   or treatise." Concludes that dialogue was used in Veue to make
   Spenser's passion for Ireland more appealing and less technical,
   but the dialogue lacks in giving speakers personality, in develop-
   ing a sense of historical place, and in creating drama in the
   conversation (it is routine question and answer). Reprinted:
   New York: Archon Books, 1969.

29   MUSTARD, WILFRED P., ed. Introduction to The Eclogues of
       Baptista Mantuanus. Baltimore: Johns Hopkins Press, pp. 50,
       134-35, 140, 142, 146.
          Notes Spenser's debt to Mantuan for parts of "July,"
   "September," and "October" eclogues of The Shepheardes Calender.

30   NORLIN, GEORGE. "The Conventions of Pastoral Elegy."
       American Journal of Philology 32:294-312.
          Discusses influence of classical pastoral elegy or dirge,
   especially those of Theocritus, Bion, Moschus, and Virgil, on
   modern poetry. Comments on "November" eclogue of The Shepheardes
   Calender and Astrophel, noting relevant continental influences.

31 PADELFORD, FREDERICK MORGAN. <u>The Political and Ecclesiastical
   Allegory of the First Book of "The Faerie Queene.</u>" University
   of Washington Publications in English, vol. 2. Boston, New
   York, Chicago, and London: Ginn & Co., 62 pp.
   Bases historical interpretation of <u>The Faerie Queene</u> on
   Spenser's identification of poem with Queen Elizabeth in "Letter
   to Raleigh" and on Spenser's appeal to Clio, the muse of history,
   in prologue to Book I. Establishes Spenser's ecclesiastical sym-
   pathies in golden mean between "self-righteous and barren Puritan
   and the sensuous Roman Catholic." Summarizes action of Book I
   and identifies historical personages figured forth in political
   and ecclesiastical allegory.

32 REUNING, KARL. "Das Altertumliche im Wortschatz der Spenser--
   Nachahmugen des 18. Jahrhunderts." Ph.D. diss., Ludwigs-
   Universität, Giessem.
   For published and revised editions, see 1912.35-36.

33 ROBIN, P. ANSELL. "Spenser's 'House of Alma.'" <u>MLR</u> 6:169-73.
   Modifies Sir Kenelm Digby's interpretation of <u>The Faerie
   Queene</u>, II.ix.22. The passage represents "the condition of the
   human body as determined by the mystical numbers seven and nine."
   Sees head as circle, body as triangle, legs as rectangle. Nine
   is assigned to the perfect form of the circle; seven is identified with the body after the Pythagorean belief that the embryo
   develops "according to the proportions of the harmony or octave,
   with its seven musical intervals."

34 ROSENTHAL, BRUNO. <u>Spensers Verhältnis zu Chaucer</u>. Berlin:
   A. Buschhardt, 61 pp.
   Considers allusions to Chaucer from Chaucer's time and
   Spenser's, including Spenser's allusions to Chaucer, and com-
   pares Chaucer's and Spenser's classical gods, allegories, char-
   acters, plots, and settings. Published version of 1910.21.

*35 SCHOLDERER, VICTOR. "English Editions and Translations of
   Greek and Latin Classics." <u>London Bibliographic Society
   Publications</u>, 1911.
   Cited in 1923.6, which notes comments on <u>Virgils Gnat</u>.

36 SPURGEON, CAROLINE F.E. <u>Chaucer devant La critique en
   Angleterre et en France depuis son temps jusqu'a nos jours</u>.
   Paris: Hachette & Co., 430 pp., passim.
   Presents thorough account and interpretation of Chaucerian
   criticism to 1910. Makes numerous references to Spenser, com-
   pares Chaucer's and Spenser's works, and concludes that Spenser
   is main figure in literary tradition extending from Chaucer.
   Refers to <u>The Faerie Queene</u>, <u>The Shepheardes Calender</u>, <u>Colin
   Clouts Come Againe</u>, <u>Daphnaida</u>, and <u>Mother Hubberds Tale</u>; notes
   Chaucer's influence on these. Includes extensive annotated bibliography and texts relating to Chaucer.

*37   TAYLOR, RUPERT. "The Political Prophecy in England." Ph.D.
       diss., Columbia University, pp. 131-32.
          Cited in Atkinson, 1937.

 38   THOMAS, HENRY. "The Romance of Amadis of Gaul." Transactions
       of the Bibliographical Society 11:251-84.
          Quotes Southey's remark that Spenser imitated "Amadis of
       Gaul" in the Masque of Cupid in The Faerie Queene.

 39   UPHAM, ALFRED HORATIO. The French Influence in English
       Literature. From the Accession of Elizabeth to the Restora-
       tion. New York: Columbia University Press, pp. 25-90, passim.
          Reprint of 1908.37.

 40   WARD, A.W. "Historical and Political Writings; II. Histories
       and Memoirs." In The Cambridge History of English Literature.
       Edited by A.W. Ward and A.R. Waller. Vol. 7. Cambridge:
       Cambridge University Press, pp. 202-31.
          Discusses A Veue of the Present State of Ireland.
       Reprinted: 1932.66.

 41   WHITE, JAMES GROVE. Historical and Topographical Notes, Etc.
       on Buttevant, Castletownroche, Doneraile, Mallow, and Places
       in Their Vicinity. Vol. 2. Cork: Gay & Co., pp. 69, 264.
          Notes Spenser's descendants and loss of portrait from
       Castle Saffron. For Volume 1, see 1905.26.

 42   WOODWARD, PARKER. "'Discourse of English Poetrie,' 1586."
       Baconiana, 3d ser. 9:256-61.
          Concludes that Bacon authored Discourse of English Poetrie:
       it promoted the writing of poetry, gave instruction in writing
       eclogues, "further imputed the authorship of the anonymously pub-
       lished 'Kalendar' to the absent Spenser," gave Bacon chance to
       reply to criticism, and "prepared the public for the printing of
       a quantity of other verses, the 'Faerie Queene' included, which
       Francis would appear to have had ready to issue under the Spenser
       ascription." Contends Bacon was "son to the Queen and Leicester"
       and that "Spenser had for a money payment sold to Francis the use
       of his name when required on title pages."

                                   1912

  1   BANNERMAN, W. BRUCE, ed. "Genealogical Notes to the Pedigree
       of the Smythies Family." Miscellanea Genealogia et Heraldica,
       4th ser. 4:354-63.
          Lists Sarah Spenser, poet's daughter, as wife of John
       Tavers of St. Barry's, Co. Cork.

  2   BAYLEY, A.R. "Author's Errors." NQ 117:358.
          Notes Spenser's confusion of brother of Edward IV with son
       of Edward III in A Veue of the Present State of Ireland. Response
       to 1912.37.

3   _____. "Author's Errors." NQ 125:358.
         Response to 1912.38.

4   _____. "Edmund Spenser, 1592." NQ 125:417.
         In response to 1912.20, places Spenser at Kilcolman in
     1592.

5   BRODRIBB, C.W. "An Epigram of Spenser." NQ 117:269.
         Questions error in first of four epigrams after sonnets in
     Globe edition.

6   BRUCE, J. DOUGLAS. "Spenser's Faerie Queene, Book III, Canto
     VI, St. 11 ff., and Moschus's Idyl, Love the Runaway." MLN
     27:183-85.
         Spenser influenced by Tasso's Prologue of the Aminta for
     the course of Venus's search for Cupid in Book III of The Faerie
     Queene, though he was partially influenced by Moschus.

7   CALDERHEAD, I.G. "In Defense of 'E.K.'" MLN 27:74-75.
         Answers Royster (1909.33) and defends E.K.'s comments on
     Spenser's use of archaisms in The Shepheardes Calender. E.K.
     does not cite Cicero with certitude; finds use of archaisms com-
     mon among classical and earlier English writers, and notes their
     artistic effect in Spenser's poem.

8   CORY, HERBERT E[LLSWORTH]. "Spenser, the School of the
     Fletchers, and Milton." University of California Publications
     in Modern Philology 2:311-73.
         Details Spenser's influence on Milton's works, including
     that which came to Milton through the early influence of group
     of Spenser imitators, The School of the Fletchers: Phineas and
     Giles Fletcher, Thomas Walkley, Thomas Robinson, Francis Quarles,
     Joseph Beaumont, and Samuel Woodford. Published version of part
     of 1910.5.

9   DeLATTRE, FLORIS. English Fairy Poetry: From the Origins to
     the Seventeenth Century. London: Henry Frowde; Paris:
     Henri Didier, pp. 80-91, passim.
         The Faerie Queene is both moral and political allegory
     intended to gain favor of Elizabeth. Fairy mythology unessential
     and artificial.

10   De MONTMORENCY, J.E.G. "The 'Other Poet' of Shakespeare's
     Sonnets." ContempR 101:885-89.
         Suggests that rival poet is Spenser; that Aëtion in Colin
     Clouts Come Home Againe refers to Shakespeare. Finds evidence of
     relationship between the two poets.

11   De SELINCOURT, E., ed. Introduction to The Poetical Works of
     Edmund Spenser. London, New York, and Toronto: Humphrey
     Milford, Oxford University Press, pp. vii-lxvii.

Biographical account and introduction to works, with sections on The Faerie Queene dealing with Spenser and Ariosto,
allegory, description, characterization, diction, versification,
and style. Reprinted: 1916.4; 1921.6; 1924.14; 1926.10; 1929.14;
1932.18; 1935.14; 1966.

12   DIXON, W. MACNEILE. "The Romantic Epic." In English Epic and
     Heroic Poetry. London: J.M. Dent & Sons; New York: E.P.
     Dutton & Co., pp. 146-69, passim.
         Sackville's Induction cited as the original of Spenser's
style. The Faerie Queene "a picture-book of the spiritual life."
Quotes Hurd as the most reasonable defense of the unity of The
Faerie Queene. Unity of The Faerie Queene consists in "the relation of its general adventures to one common original, the apoint-
ment of The Fairy Queen; and to one common end, the completion of
The Fairy Queen's injunctions. . . . it is a unity of design,
and not of action." Reprinted: New York: Haskell House, 1964.

13   DOUADY, JULES. "Spenser et la Reine des Fees." In La mer et
     les poètes Anglais. Paris: Hachette & Co., pp. 66-84.
         Descriptive plot of summary of Book II and other sections
of The Faerie Queene.

14   ECKERT, FLORENCE. "The Portrayal of Nature in Spenser."
     Master's diss., University of Chicago.
         Assesses originality of Spenser's similes. Finds borrow-
ings from Classical, Hebrew, and Italian sources for nature images
and much innovation in Spenser's depictions of nature. Suggests
that Spenser anticipates the Romanticists in some aspects of this
imagery.

15   EVANS, R.W. "Notes on River Bregog." JCHAS 18:201-3.
         Describes main channel of Bregog (near Kilcolman Castle)
to show accuracy of Spenser's references in Colin Clouts Come
Home Againe. For other studies of rivers, see 1904.20, 30;
1913.21; 1916.6.

16   FINSLER, GEORG. Homer in der Neuzeit von Dante bis Goethe.
     Italien. Frankreich. England. Deutschland. Leipsig and
     Berlin: B.G. Teubner, pp. 276-81.
         Briefly discusses Spenser's use of sources in The Faerie
Queene.

17   FRIEDLAND, LOUIS S[IGMUND]. "Milton Lycidas and Spenser's
     Ruines of Time." MLN 27:246-50.
         Suggests correlation between elegaic parts of Spenser's
poem and Lycidas, but does not identify Ruines of Time as Milton's
source.

18   _____. "Spenser's Early Poems: Studied in Connection with
     the Literature of the French Renaissance." Ph.D. diss., New
     York University, 132 pp.

Studies selected minor poems to show that Spenser's
"theoretic standards, his ideals, and the nature of his artistry"
parallel that of French Renaissance; specifically Spenser's works
reflect "a belated mediaevalism, an allegorical bend, a leaning
toward Platonic idealism." Argues that Spenser is author of A
Theatre For Worldlings. Concludes that "the refined melancholy
which Spenser derives largely from Du Bellay" serves as unifying
mood of Ruines of Rome, The Ruines of Time, The Visions of Bellay,
The Visions of Petrarch, and Visions of the Worlds Vanitie and
that these poems embody a theme of the major works: Spenser's
"dread of that mutability which renders all temporal things un-
stable, and leaves its trail of ruin everywhere." Concludes also
that poetic theories gleaned from minor poems parallel those of
Pléiade: including views on "the origin, nature and aim of poetry,
on the true poet and the proper poetic style, on the particulars
of diction, and on the methods of elevating a language to classic
rank." Points out, though, that Spenser made imaginative and
innovative use of the tenets, selected wisely from foreign sources,
experimented extensively with verse forms but always maintained
the "melodiousness" of his early poems.

19 GREENLAW, EDWIN A. "Spenser and British Imperialism." MP 9:
    347-70.
        "Spenser differed from all other literary men of his time
in that he persistently clung to that conception of a poet's
function that made him a vates, a 'seer,' a man who should warn
and advise, directly or through cloudy allegories, those who
ruled England." With the exception of Amoretti and Fowre Hymnes,
Spenser's writings are an interpretation of Elizabethan political
idealism. Rescues Spenser from reputation of being functionary
of Leicester or Essex and from his reputation as "morose and dis-
appointed applicant for the favors of the great." Demonstrates
through chronological study of Spenser's works that he was "a
farsighted student of government who saw clearly the great des-
tiny of his nation." A Veue of the Present State of Ireland
shows knowledge of Machiavelli's Il Principe. Reprinted:
1932.24.

20 H., A.C. "Edmund Spenser, 1592." NQ 125:310.
        Queries Spenser's location in 1592, identity of articles
in Spenser portraits, color of Spenser's hair, identity of
Spenser's grandfather.

21 HAZLITT, WILLIAM CAREW. Shakespear, Himself and His Works,
    A Study from New Points of View. London: B. Quaritch.
        Reprint of 1902.18.

22 HERFORD, C.H. "The Elizabethan Age in Recent Literary
    History." QR 216:353-73.
        Commentary on views of Spenser presented by Jusserand,
Lee, Walker, and Ward and Waller, respectively.

23   HIGGINSON, JAMES JACKSON. Spenser's Shepherd's Calender in
      Relation to Contemporary Affairs. New York: Columbia
      University Press, 364 pp.
          Part I discusses ecclesiastical and political satire in
      "February," "May," "July," and "September" eclogues. Considers
      Spenser "an ardent, thorough-going Puritan of the controversial
      type"; eclogues oppose Elizabeth and Burghley's policies. "Feb-
      ruary" focuses on execution of Norfolk. "May" satirizes abuses
      in Church of England, notably in Fox (High Church party) and Kid
      (Puritans) fable. "July" satirizes pretentiousness of Bishops
      (especially in Aylmer); identifies Roffy as Bishop Ely, not John
      Young, Bishop of Rochester [Higginson neglects Spenser's employ-
      ment by Young in 1578]. "September" attacks specific abuses in
      Church. Traces change in Spenser's Puritanism from "fierce search-
      ing radicalism" of The Shepheardes Calender to Low Church position
      of The Faerie Queene.
          Part II presents conjecture on biographical identifications.
      E.K. and Cuddie represent Edward Kirke. Identifies Palinode as
      Andrew Perne, Piers as Thomas Preston, Diggon Davie as Richard
      Greenham, Thomalin as Thomas Wilcox. Concludes that Rosalind
      represents a patron who probably resembled both Lady Carey and
      Mary Sidney, the Countess of Pembroke. Early patrons included
      Earl of Leicester and Sidney family; Spenser was probably ac-
      quainted with Philip Sidney, but sees little influence of Sidney
      of The Shepheardes Calender, which was largely written (begun in
      1573) before the organization of Areopagus. Notes differences in
      Spenser's and Sidney's poetic theories. Appendix refutes Green-
      law (1911.17). For Greenlaw's response, see 1913.14.

*24   JACKSON, BLANCHE G. "Study of Spenser's Teares of the Muses."
      Master's thesis, University of Washington.
          Cited in Stephens, 1950.

25   JAGGARD, WILLIAM. "Edmund Spenser, 1592." NQ 125:417.
          Response to queries in 1912.20 regarding Spenser's hair
      color in portraits.

26   KEBLE, JOHN. Keble's Lectures on Poetry. Translated by
      Edward Kershaw Francis. Vol. 1. Oxford: Clarendon Press,
      pp. 70, 82, 123-24, 156, 199, passim.
          Notes consistency of scene in Spenser's poetry. Discusses
      figure of Arthur as "the perfect type of a high-minded hero," but
      chides Spenser for employing him only in times of great need in
      The Faerie Queene. Comments on Spenser's similarities to Virgil,
      calling Spenser "the English Virgil."

27   KING, EMMA C. "Rhetorical Elements in the Poetry of Edmund
      Spenser." Master's diss., University of Chicago, 73 pp.
          Divides rhetorical figures of Spenser's poetry into two
      groups: "one dealing with elements of syntax and form, the
      other with figures into the structure of which the imagination
      should enter." Gives numerous examples from works.

28   LANGDON, IDA. "Spenser and Dante." NQ 117:33.
        Directs Breslar (1911.4) to Paget Toynbee's Dante in English
Literature which includes Spenser as one of many English authors
who was patently influenced by Dante. For related studies, see
1911.1-2.

29   LONG, PERCY W. "Review of Spenser's Minor Poems, Edited by
        Ernest de Sélincourt." Englische Studien 44:260-66.
        Considers Spenser's dating of Colin Clouts Come Home Againe
from Kilcolman not a ruse to conceal his identity, but "a bit of
literary playfulness to fall in with the Irish setting of the
pastoral, and to emphasize Spenser's debt to Raleigh for services
in rendering his title secure to the said house." Notes date of
publication of Daphnaida need not be date of dedication and supports view that "if written early enough, [it] might have formed
a very appropriate part of the Complaints."

30   OSGOOD, CHARLES G. "Spenser Concordance." NQ 125:48.
        Queries concordance announced in 1872; guesses that 1872
concordance was abandoned at half-way point and manuscript
destroyed.

31   OWEN, S.G. "Ovid and Romance." In English Literature and
        the Classics. Collected by G.S. Gordon. Oxford: Clarendon
        Press, pp. 167-95.
        Features common to Ovid and Spenser include "the faculty of
sustained narration and copious invention, the love of beauty,
of the beauty of physical form, and the brightness of external
nature." Lists legend of Ovid retold briefly by Spenser or woven
into The Faerie Queene, mostly from the Metamorphoses with a few
from Heroides and Fasti.

32   PACHEU, JULES. "Idéalistes & mystiques: Dante, Spenser,
        Bunyan, Shelley." In De Dante à Verlaine: Études D'idéalistes
        & mystiques. Paris: A. Tralin, pp. 67-134.
        Discusses influence of Dante's idealism, religious and
mystical spirit, and allegory on Spenser. Spenser's allegory
bears profound trace of medieval period, and The Faerie Queene
allegory is strange mix of the past, the present, the fantastic,
the political, and the mythological.

33   PADELFORD, FREDERICK MORGAN. "Talus the Law." SP 15:97-104.
        Illustrates Talus's significance as the law in the allegory
of The Faerie Queene, V, by citing each passage in which Talus
appears.

34   REED, EDWARD BLISS. English Lyrical Poetry. From Its Origins
        to the Present Time. New Haven: Yale University Press;
        London: Humphrey Milford, Oxford University Press, pp. 164-67,
        180-86, passim.
        Considers Amoretti second most important sonnet sequence
in English (after Shakespeare's) and Fowre Hymnes the best

expression of Neoplatonism in age. General introduction to all works. Reprinted: 1914.16.

35   REUNING, KARL. Das Altertümliche im Wortschatz der Spenser-Nachahmungen des 18. Jahrhunderts. Strassburg: Karl J. Trübner, 40 pp.
        Shows through examples of archaic language Spenser's influence on eighteenth-century imitations. Published version of 1911.32. For enlarged edition, see 1912.36.

36   _____. Das Altertümliche im Wortschatz der Spenser-Nachahmungen des 18. Jahrhunderts. Quellen und Forschungen zur Sprachund Culturgeschichte der germanischen Völker, herausgegeben von Alois Brandl, Erich Schmidt, Franz Schultz, [vol.] 116. Strassburg: Karl J. Trübner, 197 pp.
        Expands 1912.35. Includes a list of archaic words and where they are found in eighteenth-century poetry, a table of archaic words, an index of archaic words, and an appendix which includes three eighteenth-century imitations of Spenser.

37   S., H.K.St.J. "Author's Errors." NQ 117:248.
        Questions Spenser's confusion of Lionel, Duke of Clarence, with George, brother of Edward IV. For response, see 1912.2.

38   _____. "Author's Errors." NQ 125:248.
        Queries two authors' references to Spenser. For response, see 1912.3.

39   SCHOFIELD, WILLIAM HENRY. "Spenser." In Chivalry in English Literature: Chaucer, Malory, Spenser, and Shakespeare. Harvard Studies in Comparative Literature, 2. Cambridge, Mass.: Harvard University Press, pp. 127-79.
        After general biography, links Spenser to medieval chivalry through his interest in honor, fair play, temperance, and steadfastness. In The Faerie Queene Spenser united chivalric ideals with metaphysical conceptions of moral principles. Seeking favor, Spenser wrote The Faerie Queene to entertain and teach London court. As with Castiglione, chivalry was for Spenser principal profession of a courtly gentleman. Notes differences between Chaucer and Malory, and Spenser. Discusses ideal gentleman as Spenser sets him out in The Faerie Queene. Reprinted: Port Washington, N.Y.: Kennikat Press, 1964; New York: AMS Press, 1970.

40   THOMPSON, GUY ANDREW. Elizabethan Criticism of Poetry. Ph.D. diss., University of Chicago.
        For published edition, see 1914.19.

41   WESTROPP, THOMAS J. "Early Italian Maps of Ireland." Proceedings of the Royal Irish Academy 30, sec. C:361-428.
        Studies development of maps; relates somewhat to A Veue of the Present State of Ireland.

42   WINBOLD, S.E. Spenser and His Poetry. London: George G.
     Harrap & Co., 157 pp.
          Approaches Spenser's works through appreciation of his
     times, life, and relationships. Amid over eighty-five pages of
     quotations from Spenser's works, considers Spenser's education
     and classical and modern sources from which he drew his poetry,
     the relationship between his poetry and his political fortunes,
     and the relationship between his poetry and his romantic life.
     Consideration is given to his friendship with Raleigh, Harvey,
     Sidney and Kirke, his pastoralism, his part in molding sonnet
     sequence, and his enrichment of English language. Reprinted:
     Folcroft, Pa.: Folcroft Press, 1969; Poetry and Life Series,
     New York: AMS Press, 1971.

43   WOODBERRY, GEORGE E. "Spenser." In The Torch: Eight Lectures
     on Race Power in Literature. London and New York: McClure,
     Phillips & Co., pp. 113-36.
          Reprint of 1905.27.

44   WOODWARD, PARKER. Tudor Problems. London: Gay & Hancock,
     pp. 141-45, passim.
          Francis Bacon used "Spenser" as cover name: "There is
     strong indication that the Queen and the ladies and gentlemen
     of her Court knew that Francis was using the name Spenser as a
     cover for certain of his poetical writings." Suggests that
     "Immeritô" fits Bacon more than Spenser and that Bacon wrote
     the letters to Harvey.

45   YEATS, WILLIAM BUTLER. "Edmund Spenser." In The Cutting of
     an Agate. New York: Macmillan Co., pp. 213-55.
          Considers Spenser an impersonal poet of the State, "which
     had taken possession of his conscience." "Spenser had learned to
     look to the State not only as the rewarder of virtue but as the
     maker of right and wrong, and had begun to love and hate as it
     bid him." Spenser saw Ireland as an official would, rather than
     as a poet, and thus misunderstands Irish people and affairs and
     misrepresents situation in A Veue of the Present State of Ireland.
     Sees Spenser's poetic genius in pastoral poetry and visual imagery,
     not in allegory. Reprinted: 1919.18.

                              1913

1   ANON. "Poets Laureate." ContempR 104:129-33.
          Lists Spenser as appointed to laureateship in 1590; notes
     that he never was laureate, but only pensioned.

2   BASKERVILL, C.R. "The Early Fame of The Shepheardes Calender."
     PMLA 28:291-313.
          Refutes Greenlaw's conclusion (1911.17) that the publica-
     tion of The Faerie Queene accounts for popularity of The

Shepheardes Calender. Shows reputation of The Shepheardes
Calender and its influence on contemporary poetry to be sig-
nificant. Sees less satire in this poem and in Mother Hubberds
Tale than other commentators. For related study, see 1913.14.

3   BERLI, HANS. Gabriel Harvey der Dickterfreund und Kritiker.
    Zurich: Leeman, pp. 52-60, 88-93, 104-9.
        Comments on Sidney-Spenser relationship and notes that
    Spenser borrowed title for Teares of the Muses from Harvey's
    Musarum Lacrymae.

4   BORLAND, LOIS. "Montgomerie and the French Poets of the
    Early Sixteenth Century." MP 11:127-34.
        Notes Spenser's use of continuous linking quatrain form
    (Amoretti); Spenser and Montgomerie devised form independently.

5   BRIGHT, JAMES WILSON, and RAYMOND DURBIN MILLER. The Elements
    of English Versification. Boston and London: Ginn & Co.,
    166 pp., passim.
        Reprint of 1910.3.

*6 COOPER, LAURA T. "Spenser's Veue of the Present State of
    Ireland. An Introduction with Notes on the First 55 Pages
    in Grosart's Edition." Master's thesis, Cornell University,
    84 pp.
        Cited in Stephens, 1950.

7   CUNNINGHAM, GRANVILLE C. "The Dates of Spenser's Birth and
    Death." Baconiana 11:153-59.
        Challenges accepted dates of Spenser's birth and death.
    1679 folio contains picture of the monumental tablet erected to
    the poet in Westminster Abbey which records the dates of birth
    and death as 1510 and 1596. The dates were "restored" to 1553
    and 1598 by private subscription in 1778. In his seventeenth-
    century manuscript, "History from Marble," Thomas Dingley records
    epitaph on the tablet with the dates 1516 and 1596. Concludes
    that no testimony among Spenser's contemporaries supports the
    birth date of 1553.

8   _____. "'Ignoto.'" Baconiana, 3d ser. 11:224-36.
        Argues that "Ignoto" poems were written by Bacon, and that
    Bacon wrote The Shepheardes Calender; evidence includes comments
    on anonymous publications of The Shepheardes Calender from 1579
    to 1611 when Spenser's name first appears on it, unexplained;
    and comments on inclusion of "Ignoto" poems with The Faerie Queene.

9   D., B. "The Armor of Sir James Scudamore." BMMA 8:118-23.
        Recounts acquisition in 1911 of two incomplete sets of
    armor of Sir James Scudamore, well known at Elizabethan Court
    and of sufficient prominence to warrant reference in Spenser's
    The Faerie Queene.

10 DUNLOP, ROBERT. <u>Ireland Under the Commonwealth. Being a</u>
    <u>Selection of Documents Relating to the Government of Ireland</u>
    <u>from 1651 to 1659</u>. Vol. 1. Manchester: Manchester
    University Press, p. lix.
        Quotes <u>A Veue of the Present State of Ireland</u> to note
    Spenser's support of Lord Grey's "puritanical zeal."

11 FRIEDLAND, LOUIS SIGMUND. "Spenser's Earliest Translations."
    <u>JEGP</u> 12:449-70.
        Presents evidence to establish Spenser as author-translator
    of Van der Noot's <u>Theatre of Voluptuous Worldlings</u> (1569); tone,
    color, imagery, and phrasing parallel that in other Spenserian
    poems, most notably the <u>Visions of Bellay</u>.

12 FYNMORE, R. J. "St. Bridget's Bower, Kent." <u>NQ</u> 118:231.
        Not specific hill, but ridge above Baxley, Holingbourne.
    For related commentary, see 1913.32.

13 GRAHAM, WALTER. "Some Notes on Spenser and Bacon." <u>MLN</u> 28:
    212-14.
        Suggests source for Thomalin's emblem ("March," <u>The Shep-</u>
    <u>heardes Calender</u>) in Plautus' <u>Cistellaria</u>. Source for Willye's
    emblem ("August") in Publilius Syrus, although similar passage
    in Bacon influenced by Agesilaus.

14 GREENLAW, EDWIN [A]. "The Shepheardes Calender, II." <u>SP</u>
    11:3-25.
        Continues earlier article (1911.17). Maintains argument
    on popularity of <u>The Shepheardes Calender</u> in answer to Baskervill
    (1913.2) by citing additional evidence. Assesses Spenser's rela-
    tionship with Leicester and the reasons for Spenser's exile to
    Ireland (in reference to <u>Mother Hubberds Tale</u> and Higginson's
    comments, 1912.23). Refutes Higginson's commentary on "February"
    eclogue; considers Spenser's Puritanism more political than
    doctrinal.

15 GREENLAW, EDWIN A. "Sidney's <u>Arcadia</u> as an <u>Example</u> of
    Elizabethan Allegory." In <u>Anniversary Papers by Colleagues</u>
    <u>and Pupils of George Lyman Kittredge Presented on the Comple-</u>
    <u>tion of His Twenty-fifth Year of Teaching in Harvard University</u>
    <u>June MCMXIII</u>. Boston and London: Ginn & Co., pp. 327-37.
        Cites a passage of the letter to Raleigh as summary of
    Renaissance theory of allegory; notes example of Spenserian
    allegory in the <u>Arcadia</u>, and describes the <u>Arcadia</u> as a prose
    counterpart of <u>The Faerie Queene</u>.

16 HALL, EDGAR A. "Spenser and Two Old French Grail Romances."
    <u>PMLA</u> 28:539-54.
        <u>Perlesvaus</u> or an analogue agreeing with it is source of
    Briana-Crudor story in Book VI of <u>The Faerie Queene</u>. The <u>Conte</u>
    <u>du Graal</u> is main source of Percival element in Tristram story in
    the same book.

17   HARPER, CARRIE A.   "'Locrine' and the 'Faerie Queene.'"
      MLR 8:369-71.
            In response to Crawford (1901.6), suggests that the author
      of Locrine borrows material from The Faerie Queene and that bor-
      rowing is sufficient "to controvert any dating of the play earlier
      than 1590." For related studies, see 1905.16; 1906.6; 1916.14.

18   LONG, PERCY W.   "The Date of Spenser's Earlier Hymns."
      Englische Studien 47:197-208.
            Presents evidence to date hymns ca. 1590. Internal evidence
      parallels that in Amoretti and Teares of the Muses, which can be
      dated at about the same time.

19   _____.   "The Name 'Shepherds' Calendar.'" Archiv 131:429-30.
            Contends that modern spellings of poem's title should fol-
      low Spenser's intention of "applying an olde name to a newe
      worke": "applications rather than adaptation of the name re-
      quires that shepheardes be interpreted as plural."

20   _____.   "Spenser and the Plowman's Tale." MLN 28:262.
            Notes influence of pseudo-Chaucerian Plowman's Tale on
      ecclesiastical eclogues of The Shepheardes Calender, especially
      line 149 of "February." Supports echo with E.K.'s gloss.

21   MOORE, COURTENAY.   "The Bregog." JCHAS 19:40-42.
            Discusses meaning of Bregog (Breg) and Spenser's use of
      river and Irish name. For related studies of rivers, see 1904.20,
      30; 1912.15; 1916.6.

22   MORTON, EDWARD PAYSON.   "The Spenserian Stanza in the Eight-
      eenth Century." MP 10:356-91.
            Notes fifty-seven poems in regular Spenserian stanza by
      thirty-eight known poets and eight anonymous writers. Surveys
      eighteen in regular Spenserian stanza during first half of the
      eighteenth century and imitations written during the course of
      the century: thirty-four after the ten-line imitation of Prior,
      thirteen other ten-line imitations, twenty-two nine-line imita-
      tions, and thirty six-line imitations.

23   NICHOLLS, NORTON.   "Reminiscences of Gray." In The Letters of
      Thomas Gray. Edited by Duncan C. Tovey. London: G. Bell &
      Sons, pp. 275-92.
            Nicholls, friend of Gray, notes Gray's love for Spenser.

24   PADELFORD, F[REDERICK] M[ORGAN].   "Spenser and the Puritan
      Propaganda." MP 11:85-106.
            Discusses nature of sixteenth-century Puritanism and
      Spenser's attitude toward it (considers him a Low-Churchman).
      Shows that Fox and Ape of Mother Hubberds Tale (lines 342-574)
      satirize the Puritan protest and offers support for view from
      The Shepheardes Calender, which Spenser completed while secretary
      to Bishop Young (identification of Roffyn). Concludes that

Spenser was "a consistent advocate of the golden mean in matters ecclesiastical." For related studies, see 1914.14; 1916.21.

25 PADELFORD, FREDERICK MORGAN. "Spenser's Arraignment of the Anabaptists." JEGP 12:434-48.
    Interprets controversy between Artegall and the Gyant, The Faerie Queene, V.2, as a scathing denunciation of communism, as practiced by the Anabaptist sect, "a sect whose contentions were generally supposed to be those stated in the allegory, against whom the very arguments were used that are employed in the poem, whose followers were drawn from different nations, who were thought to arouse the ignorant and the designing, and to check whom the English government was forced to expell the leaders across seas without ceremony and to threaten the residue with force." Presents substantial evidence to support Spenser's arraignment of the Anabaptists in this canto and shows that this allegory is consistent with rest of Book V. Also shows that these views coincide with Spenser's ecclesiastical views and prevailing views of the day.

26 PETRIELLA, TEOFILO. La novella de Britomarte nella Regina Delle Fate de E. Spenser riportata alle sue fonti italiene. Salerno: Matteo Spudafore, 78 pp.
    Summarizes Britomart material in Books III, IV, and V of The Faerie Queene and concludes that Spenser's borrowings of details, paraphrases, and translations of Ariosto include: Guyon's defeat by Britomart; Britomart's magic lance; the episode at the House of Malecasta; Britomart in the Cave of Merlin; Britomart's encounter with Scudamore; Britomart and Amoret's adventures; the Britomart-Artegall tournament; and Britomart's impatience for Artegall's return and her jealousy of Radigund.

27 SCHELLING, FELIX E. The English Lyric. Boston: Houghton Mifflin Co.; Cambridge, Mass.: Riverside Press, 344 pp., passim.
    Spenser generally discussed in development of lyric.

28 SCHULTZ, VICTOR. "Das persönliche Geschlecht unpersönlicher Substantira (mit Einschluss der Tiernamen) bei Spenser." Ph.D. diss., Christian-Albrechts-Universität, Kiel.
    For published edition, see 1913.29.

29 _____. Das persönliche Geschlecht unpersönlicher Substantira (mit Einschluss der Tiernamen) bei Spenser. Heidelberg: Carl Winter, 114 pp.
    Studies the gender of impersonal nouns in Spenser's works, including nouns applied to the universe (i.e., planets, stars, Orion); the components of the earth; natural phenomena; manmade objects, including ships' names; parts and functions of the body; animal names; and abstractions. Published version of 1913.28.

30   SHAFER, ROBERT. "Spenser's Astrophel." MLN 28:224-26.
         Shows Spenser's indebtedness to Bion's Lament for Adonis
   (parallel passages); accounts for "uninspired tone" of Astrophel.

31   SMITH, GEORGE CHARLES MOORE, ed. Gabriel Harvey's Marginalia.
      Stratford-upon-Avon: Shakespeare Head Press, 343 pp., passim.
         Overview of correspondence and Spenser's relationship with
   Gabriel Harvey. Finds evidence in accounts of Giordano Bruno
   that Areopagus met regularly, but finds no support in letters
   "that Harvey was a regular visitor at Leicester House at the
   meetings of Sidney and Dyer's 'Areopagus.'" Finds "little evidence of meetings or correspondence between Harvey and Spenser"
   after 18 July 1586. For supplements, see 1933.61; 1934.59;
   1935.67.

32   SMITH, G[EORGE] C[HARLES] MOORE. "St. Bridget's Bower, Kent."
      NQ 118:150.
         Identity of hill mentioned in "July" eclogue of The Shep-
   heardes Calender. For related study, see 1913.12.

33   _____. "Spenser and Mulcaster." MLR 8:368.
         Identifies Wrenock ("December," The Shepheardes Calender)
   as Richard Mulcaster, headmaster of Merchant Taylors' School.

34   SMITH, REED. "The Metamorphoses in Muiopotmos." MLN 28:82-85.
         Finds poem mock-heroic, not allegorical, with pervasive in-
   fluence of Chaucer and significant influence, especially in structure, of Ovid's Metamorphoses.

35   SPURGEON, CAROLINE F.E. Mysticism in English Literature.
      Cambridge: Cambridge University Press, pp. 24-26.
         Fowre Hymnes embody a Platonism arrived at through the
   intellect but do not record a mystical experience.

*36   STEBBING, WILLIAM. The Poets: Geoffrey Chaucer to Alfred
      Tennyson. London and New York: Henry Froude; Oxford: Oxford
      University Press.
         Cited in 1923.6. Revised edition of 1910.28.

*37   STREATOR, G.I. "The Influence of Early Medieval Allegory upon
      Spenser's Faerie Queene." Master's thesis, University of
      Washington.
         Cited in Stephens, 1950.

38   THOMPSON, FRANCIS. "The Poet's Poet." In The Works of
      Francis Thompson. Vol. 1. Edited by Wilfrid Meynell.
      London: Burns & Oats; New York: Charles Scribner's Sons,
      pp. 140-46, passim.
         Abridged version of 1903.30. Reprinted: 1925.33;
   Westminster, Md.: Newman Press, 1949.

39   VENN, JOHN, and J.A. VENN. The Book of Matriculations and
     Degrees: A Catalogue of Those Who Have Been Matriculated or
     Been Admitted to Any Degree in the University of Cambridge.
     Cambridge: Cambridge University Press, p. 630.
         Lists Edmund Spenser: Pembroke, Sizor, Easter Term, 1569;
     A.B., 1572-73; A.M. 1576.

40   WINGFIELD-STRAFORD, ESME. The History of English Patriotism.
     Vol. 1. London and New York: John Lane; Toronto: Bell &
     Cockburn, pp. 220-25, passim.
         The Faerie Queene is "tinged with an ardent and whole-
     hearted love of England, such as not even Shakespeare surpassed."
     Spenser is wholly English in his choice of characters and sets
     forth his political opinions best in Book V, wherein he treats
     of Justice, "and Justice with him is the conception of ordered
     discipline, which had shaped the policy of the Tudors."

                              1914

1   BENEDETTI, ANNA. L'"Orlando Furioso" nella vita intellettuale
     del popolo inglese. Milan: R. Bemporad & Brothers, pp. 95-
     165, passim.
         Discusses in detail parallels between Ariosto and Spenser,
     concluding that Orlando Furioso was significant influence on The
     Faerie Queene. Presents parallel passages and references, canto
     by canto, and shows Spenser's influence on other poets.

2   BRIE, FRIEDRICH. "Shakespeare un die Impresa-Kunst seiner
     Zeit." SJW 50:9-30.
         Comments on The Shepheardes Calender and The Faerie Queene.

*3   BROWN, L.A. "The Moral Allegory of Book V of Spenser's
     Faerie Queene." Master's thesis, University of Washington.
         Cited in Stephens, 1950.

4   BRUNNER, K. "Die Dialektwörter in Spensers 'Shepherds
     Calender.'" Archiv 132:401-4.
         Presents brief analysis of northern dialect words used in
     The Shepheardes Calender.

5   FLETCHER, JEFFERSON B. "'Spenser's Earliest Translations.'"
     JEGP 13:305-8.
         Confirms Friedland's assertion of Spenser's authorship of
     the Theatre of Voluptuous Worldlings (see 1913.11). Comments on
     Ponsonby's part in preparation of Complaints volume: "Ponsonby's
     role reminds one strongly of that of 'E.K.' in the 'Calender,'
     to wit, one of very wise ignorance."

6   GREENOUGH, JAMES BRADSTREET, and GEORGE LYMAN KITTREDGE.
     Words and Their Ways in English Speech. New York and London:
     Macmillan, pp. 118, 295, 354, 375.
         Reprint of 1901.11.

7   HARMAN, EDWARD GEORGE. <u>Edmund Spenser and the Impersonations</u>
     <u>of Francis Bacon</u>. London: Constable & Co., 608 pp.
          "Spenser" the poet and Spenser the Irish settler were dif-
     ferent men. Challenges traditional Spenser biography, suggesting
     that Bacon wrote Spenser's works under concealment. Identifies
     historical personages in <u>The Faerie Queene</u>, implying that Spenser
     cannot be the author of that poem. Bacon was young enough to have
     written Spenser's early shorter works, Spenser being too old to
     have written so youthfully and aristocratically. Bacon also the
     author of Spenser's later short works and of the poems prefixed
     to <u>The Faerie Queene</u> generally attributed to Raleigh. In related
     chapters, identifies Bacon as the author of works by Shakespeare,
     Sidney, Gascoigne, Sir Humphrey Gilbert, and Raleigh. Reprinted:
     New York: AMS, 1975.

8   HERFORD, C.H., ed. Introduction to <u>Shepheards Calendar, Con-</u>
     <u>taining Twelve Eclogues Proportionable to the Twelve Months</u>.
     London and New York: Macmillan, pp. i-lxxviii.
          Reprint of 1907.15.

9   LONG, PERCY W. "Spenser and Sidney." <u>Anglia</u> 38:173-92.
          Contends that Areopagus was "a mere figure of speech," that
     Spenser knew Sidney slightly, and that Sidney's influence on
     Spenser was "momentary and aesthetically negligible." Concludes
     that evidence in letters and poetry allows only for conjecture.

10   _____. "Spenser's 'Muiopotmos.'" <u>MLR</u> 9:457-62.
          Interprets poem as conventional Renaissance love theme of
     lover (Clarion-Spenser) entangled in snare of the beloved
     (Aragnoll-Lady Carey). Spenser's dedication is key.

11   LOWES, JOHN LIVINGSTON. "Spenser and <u>The Miroir de l'Omme</u>."
     <u>PMLA</u> 29:388-452.
          The marriage of Pride and the World in Gower's <u>Miroir de</u>
     <u>d'Omme</u> is Spenser's major source for the progress of Seven Deadly
     Sins in <u>The Faerie Queene</u>, I.iv. The two accounts agree, with
     divergencies, "in the threefold conjunction of animals, symbolic
     objects, and maladies--a conjunction without other parallel--and
     with the adroit interweaving of Gower's description of the wedding
     feast with Spenser's narrative." Spenser also indebted to <u>Miroir</u>
     for the account of Sclaunder in IV.viii and for detailed descrip-
     tion of Envie and Detraction in V.xii.

*12 MORRILL, BESSIE H. "The Literary Letter in the Sixteenth
     Century." Master's thesis, Columbia University, 1914.
          Cited in Atkinson, 1937.

13   MUSTARD, WILFRED P. "Lodowick Bryskett and Bernardo Tasso."
     <u>American Journal of Philology</u> 35:192-99.
          Shows that Bryskett's "The Mourning Muse of Thestylis" is
     paraphrase of Tasso's "Selva nella morte del Signor Aluigi da
     Gonzaga."

14   PADELFORD, FREDERICK MORGAN. "Spenser and the Theology of
       Calvin." <u>MP</u> 12:1-18.
          Points out correspondences between Spenser's <u>Hymne of Heav-</u>
       <u>enly Love</u>, <u>Hymne of Heavenly Beautie</u>, <u>Mother Hubberds Tale</u>, <u>The</u>
       <u>Faerie Queene</u>, Book I and Calvin's <u>Institutes of the Christian</u>
       <u>Religion</u>. Spenser demonstrates his accord with Calvin in the doc-
       trines of the Trinity, the fall and atonement of man, man's de-
       pravity and redemption, God's revelation of himself through the
       external world, and predestination. The allegory of the religious
       life of man in <u>The Faerie Queene</u>, Book I is a poetic rendering of
       the third book of the <u>Institutes</u>. For related studies, see
       1913.24; 1916.21.

15   _____. "Spenser's Fowre Hymnes." <u>JEGP</u> 13:418-33.
          Modifies Fletcher's view of the <u>Fowre Hymnes</u> (1911.14) by
       showing that "while the earlier hymns are in complete accord with
       [a] Neo-Platonic theory of love, the later hymns are based upon
       Calvinistic doctrines that are squarely opposed to it and that
       admit of no compromise." Contrasts Castiglione's six stages of
       Platonic love with that in latter two hymns to point up the adap-
       tation of Neoplatonism to Calvinistic doctrine. Discusses con-
       ceptions of love in <u>The Faerie Queene</u>: "it does not support the
       neo-Platonic theory that love leads the lover away from and be-
       yond the beloved." <u>The Faerie Queene</u> "shows the equal worth of
       men and women and their mutual dependence. . . . Through love
       they find themselves socially. The 'Faerie Queene' lays emphasis
       upon the life of action, and the life of contemplation is not
       made an end in itself, but rather contemplation serves to make
       life dynamic." Concludes that Spenser ultimately rejects theory
       of Neoplatonists in <u>Hymne of Heavenly Love</u> and <u>Hymne of Heavenly</u>
       <u>Beautie</u>.

16   REED, EDWARD BLISS. <u>English Lyrical Poetry. From Its Origins</u>
       <u>to the Present Time</u>. New Haven: Yale University Press;
       London: Humphrey Milford, Oxford University Press, pp. 164-
       67, 180-86, passim.
          Reprint of 1912.34.

17   SPURGEON, CAROLINE F.E. <u>Five Hundred Years of Chaucer Criti-</u>
       <u>cism and Allusion (1357-1900)</u>. Part 1, <u>Text 1357-1800</u>.
       Chaucer Society Publications, no. 48. London: Keagan Paul,
       Trench, Trubner & Co., pp. 118, 132-34, 161, passim.
          Chaucerian allusions in <u>The Shepheardes Calender</u>, <u>The</u>
       <u>Faerie Queene</u>, <u>Colin Clouts Come Home Againe</u>, <u>A Veue of the</u>
       <u>Present State of Ireland</u>. Comments on the influence of Chaucer
       on Spenser by other poets, critics, and editors. Notes Spenser's
       imitation of Chaucer's language. For index see 1921.17. For
       supplement, see 1923.15. For other volumes, see 1918.26;
       1921.17; 1922.24; 1924.35. Reprinted: 1925.31; New York:
       Russell & Russell, 1960.

*18   STRANGNATT, MABEL V. "Blood Relationships in Spenser's
       Faerie Queene." Master's thesis, Columbia University.
              Cited in Stephens, 1950.

 19   THOMPSON, GUY ANDREW. Elizabethan Criticism of Poetry.
       Menasha, Wis.: George Banta Publishing Co., Collegiate Press,
       216 pp., passim.
              Considers state and nature of Elizabethan poetry under
       three major headings: "The State of Poetry; Causes; Remedies,"
       "The Nature and Function of Poetry," and "Form." Spenser con-
       sidered with others in discussions of complaints against debasers
       of poetry, lack of contemporary taste, and lack of patronage.
       Spenser associated poetry with patriotism, learning, and aris-
       tocracy. For Spenser, poetry is the manifestation of divine
       passion and functions on both moral and esthetic levels. Final
       Section deals with poetic style, new style of diction, and verse
       experimentation. Published version of 1912.40.

 20   WINSTANLEY, LILIAN, ed. Introduction to The Faerie Queene.
       Book II. Cambridge: Cambridge University Press, pp. vii-lxxix.
              Presents general focus for The Faerie Queene, noting
       Spenser's use of sources, his Platonism and Puritanism, and his
       varied poetic techniques. Examines in detail medieval, classical
       and Italian sources for Book II and Spenser's use of Aristotle in
       conceiving Temperance. Concludes with commentary on historical
       allegory of Book II. Gives examples from Book II to illustrate
       Spenser's archaic diction and his debt to Chaucer, Malory,
       Geoffrey, Holinshed, Homer, Virgil, Ariosto, Tasso, and others.
       Reprinted: 1928.60.

                              1915

  1   CORNS, ALBERT R., and ARCHIBALD SPARKE, eds. A Bibliography
       of Unfinished Books in the English Language: With Annotations.
       London: Bernard Quaritch, p. 215.
              Notes an unfinished attempt in 1783 to put The Faerie
       Queene, Book I into blank verse.

  2   CRANE, RONALD S. "The Vogue of Guy of Warwick from the Close
       of the Middle Ages to the Romantic Revival." PMLA 30:125-94.
              Of all the literary men of his time, Spenser took deepest
       interest in medieval romances. He had read Le Morte Darthur and
       Huon of Bordeau among the prose versions and probably read Bevis
       of Hampton and The Squire of Low Degree among the metrical. From
       them he drew hints for details and general conception of The
       Faerie Queene.

  3   DeM[ONTMORENCY], J.E.G. "The Red Cross Knight." ContempR
       107:659-63.

Calls for contemporary wedding of chivalry and truth, recommending the study of the allegory of Book I of The Faerie Queene which sets forth "the eternal strife of Right against Might, of honour, love, and chivalry, against craft, materialism, and hatred of goodness."

4   ERSKINE, JOHN. "The Virtue of Friendship in The Faerie Queene."
    PMLA 30:831-50.
        Spenser defines friendship in Book IV of The Faerie Queene
    as "a communion of souls, an achievement, in part, at least of
    that harmony which is the nature of God, and which was once in
    the universe." Spenser supports a minority position among phi-
    losophers and ranks "friendship as equal in importance and iden-
    tical in kind with holiness, temperance, chastity, justice, and
    courtesy." Suggests that Spenser knew Giraldi's Tre dialoghi
    della vita civile in the original and drew heavily on the long
    passage on friendship in third dialogue. Book IV seems at first
    sight to treat only of jealousies and quarrels because of diffi-
    culty Spenser encountered in making an allegory of his kind of
    friendship. The mystical union of souls implies no action; thus,
    "he was forced to discuss chiefly illustrations of the lack of
    it." Allegory of Book IV is a variation on a few themes: ways
    the virtuous enter into the communion of friendship, the ease
    with which false friends fall out, the warfare that the devil
    wages against all harmony, the temporary estrangement which dis-
    cord sometimes achieves between good men and women, the relation
    of love to friendship, all ideas which Giraldi had stated as
    abstractions.

5   GLOVER, T.R. "Spenser." In Poets and Puritans. London:
    Methuen & Co., pp. 1-33.
        Defends The Faerie Queene against critics of its structure.
    Considers Spenser's life and his relationship to his times. Dis-
    cusses poet's sense of humor. Concludes with a general discussion
    of The Faerie Queene. Reprinted: 1916.9; 1923.14.

*6 JORDON, JOHN CLARK. "Robert Green." Ph.D. diss., Columbia
    University.
        For published edition, see 1915.7.

7   _____. Robert Greene. New York: Columbia University Press,
    pp. 175, 185.
        Greene's Alphonsus is a response to Spenser's complaint in
    Teares of the Muses about the decay of poetry and the want of
    heroic themes. Published version of 1915.6.

*8 KLIEM, HANS. "Sentimentale Freundschaft in der Shakespeare-
    Epoche." Ph.D. diss., University of Jena.
        Cited in Atkinson, 1937.

9   OSGOOD, CHARLES GROSVENOR, ed. A Concordance to the Poems of
     Edmund Spenser. Washington, D.C.: Carnegie Institution of
     Washington, 997 pp.
          An alphabetical listing of words in Spenser's works based
     on the Globe edition, including corrections from Cambridge edition
     and variants from Oxford edition. Inflected forms of all words
     are listed separately, variants in spelling are normalized, and
     all quotations are indexed under normal spelling. Attempts to
     represent every word in Spenser by at least one quotation, though
     very common words (listed on p. xi) are omitted.

10   PADELFORD, FREDERICK MORGAN. "The Political, Economic, and
     Social Views of Spenser." JEGP 14:393-420.
          Politically, Spenser is a patriot who demonstrates in his
     works: love of native land and faith in England's destiny, con-
     fidence in national institutions and customs, strong belief in
     international relations, awareness of England's divine destiny,
     belief in the divine right of kings, the ideal of the state as
     an ethical agency. Economically, Spenser is out of sympathy with
     the commercial spirit of his age, attacks greedy landlords and
     land grabbers, is against preachers of radical economic and social
     change, and defends private property and economic inequality.
     Spenser's Irish policies include subjugation of the realm, tith-
     ing, assigned trades, and prohibition of grain speculation. His
     stand leaves no provision for poverty. Comments on A Veue of the
     Present State of Ireland, The Faerie Queene, Mother Hubberds Tale,
     and Teares of the Muses. Aligns Spenser with "such stout hearts
     and pushing spirits as Gilbert, Raleigh, and Sidney, who had
     dreams of world empire for England, and who advocated British
     imperialism with as much warmth as the sensitive autocracy of
     the Queen would permit."

*11 PARKER, ROSCOE E. "Archaisms in Spenser." Master's thesis,
     University of North Carolina.
          Cited in Stephens, 1950.

12   RINAKER, CLARISSA. "Thomas Warton: A Biographical and
     Critical Study." Ph.D. diss., University of Illinois.
          For published editions, see 1915.13, 1916.25.

13   _____. "Thomas Warton and the Historical Method in Literary
     Criticism." PMLA 30:79-109.
          Warton's Observations on the 'Fairy Queen' of Spenser is
     the first important piece of modern historical criticism in Eng-
     lish literature. He had the intelligent independence to discard
     the pseudo-classical rules and broad knowledge to supply material
     for more just criteria. Warton is superior to all previous crit-
     ics of Spenser because he recognized the inadequacy of classical
     rules, because he introduced the modern historical method of
     criticism with his recognition that no work of art can be inde-
     pendently judged without reference to influences, because he had

a better understanding than his colleagues of the true relation
between classical and modern literature, and because he allowed
in criticism a place for the spontaneous delight and enthusiasm
of the reader. Warton is first critic to study Spenser's indebtedness to the romances, to Chaucer, and to medieval moralities
and allegories, considering as well the influence of the renaissance and the classical revival. "Warton's essay put a new seal
of critical approval upon the <u>Faery Queen</u> and Spenser's position
as the poet's poet was established with the new school." Reprinted in slightly revised form: 1916.25.

14   RUTHERFORD, MARK. "Spenser and Kilcolman." In <u>Last Pages</u>
    <u>from a Journal</u>. Edited by Dorothy V. White. London and New
    York: Humphrey Milford, Oxford University Press, pp. 1-18.
       For annotation, see 1915.17.

15   STEEL, JAMES H. "Style in Spenser." <u>Proceedings of the Royal</u>
    <u>Philosophical Society of Glasgow</u> 46:146-205.
       Studies metrical style of Spenser's poetical works, conclud-
ing that Spenser's style does not show continuous development,
that <u>The Shepheardes Calender</u> is Spenser's only conscious experimentation, and that his style was fully matured when he published
first three books of <u>The Faerie Queene</u> in 1590.

16   WALLACE, MALCOLM WILLIAM. <u>The Life of Sir Philip Sidney</u>.
    Cambridge: Cambridge University Press, pp. 228-30.
       Spenser's dedication of <u>The Shepheardes Calender</u> to Sidney,
his reference to him in the dedication to <u>Teares of the Muses</u>,
and the Spenser-Harvey correspondence are sole sources of information about relations of the two men. Reprinted: New York:
Octagon Books, 1967.

17   WHITE, WILLIAM HALE. "Spenser and Kilcolman." In <u>Last Pages</u>
    <u>from a Journal</u>. Edited by Dorothy V. White. London and New
    York: Humphrey Milford, Oxford University Press, pp. 1-18.
       Recounts condition of Ireland during Spenser's stay and his
conversation with Bryskett and comments on the romance of <u>The</u>
<u>Faerie Queene</u>.

18   WINSTANLEY, LILIAN, ed. Introduction to <u>The Faerie Queene,</u>
    <u>Book I</u>. Cambridge: Cambridge University Press, pp. vii-lxxx.
       Discusses historical and political allegory of Book I, and
Spenser's sources: medieval romance, classical writings, and
renaissance humanist works. Reprinted: 1920.28; 1924.42;
1928.59; 1932.69; 1949, 1952, 1958. 1961.

<u>1916</u>

1   BENSE, J.F. "'Meliboeus Old' in Milton's <u>Comus</u>."
    <u>Neophilologus</u> 1:62-64.
       Suggests that Meliboeus respectfully refers to Spenser.

2   BOLWELL, ROBERT. "Notes on Alliteration in Spenser." <u>JEGP</u>
     15:421-22.
        Refutes contention that Spenser "knew the power of allitera-
     tion upon <u>w</u> to give the sense of vastness and desolation." Pre-
     sents evidence of 225 cases of alliteration upon <u>w</u> in stressed
     syllables to show that eighty-seven percent of examples are ex-
     ceptions to generally held view.

*3   _____. "The Pastoral Elements in Spenser's Poetry."
     <u>Western Reserve Bulletin</u>. 19:17-27.
             Cited in 1923.6.

4   De SELINCOURT, E., ed. Introduction to <u>The Poetical Works of</u>
     <u>Edmund Spenser</u>. London, New York, and Toronto: Oxford Uni-
     versity Press, pp. vii-lxvii.
             Reprint of 1912.11.

5   ERSKINE, JOHN. <u>The Elizabethan Lyric</u>. New York: Columbia
     University Press, pp. 107-16, 153-58, 176-82, 189-96, 302.
             Reprint of 1903.8.

6   FLOOD, WILLIAM H. GRATTAN. "Identification of Spenserian
     'Aubrian' River." <u>JCHAS</u> 22:143-44.
             Identifies "Aubrian" as Urrin River. Answers query of
     1904.20.

7   FRATRES ROSEAE CRUCIS. <u>Secret Shakespeare Seals. Revelations</u>
     <u>of Rosicrucian Arcana</u>. Nottingham: H. Jenkins, pp. 20, 28,
     30, 81, plates 22, 23, 60, 61, 70.
             Finds numerical and name (Red Cross Knight) emblems in <u>The</u>
     <u>Faerie Queene</u> to link Spenser with the Impresa 287, <u>A Choice of</u>
     <u>Emblems</u> (1585).

8   FULTON, EDWARD. "Spenser, Sidney, and the Areopagus." <u>MLN</u>
     31: 372-74.
             Maintains that Spenser and Sidney were close friends, but
     Areopagus was not a formally organized group.

9   GLOVER, T.R. "Spenser." In <u>Poets and Puritans</u>. 2d ed.
     London: Methuen & Co., pp. 1-33.
             Reprint of 1915.5.

10   GREENLAW, EDWIN. <u>An Outline of the Literature of the English</u>
     <u>Renaissance</u>. Chicago and New York: Sanborn & Co., passim.
             Includes introduction to age, statement of literary
     problems, chronological outlines, and bibliography.

11   _____. "Shakespeare's Pastorals." <u>SP</u> 13:122-54.
             Concludes that Spenser is indebted to Sidney's <u>Arcadia</u> for
     the Calidore-Pastorella story in Book VI of <u>The Faerie Queene</u> and
     influenced by Sidney in Books IV-VI. The Pastorella-Calidore

story is also "closely parallel to some of Shakespeare's pastorals in plot and in its interpretation of pastoralism," and "there are indications that it had direct influence on Shakespeare." Also cites Spenser as influence on Shakespeare's Jaques in As You Like It.

12   GREENOUGH, JAMES BRADSTREET, and GEORGE LYMAN KITTREDGE. Words and Their Ways in English Speech. New York and London: Macmillan, pp. 118, 295, 354, 375.
        Reprint of 1901.11.

13   GREENWOOD, GRANVILLE G. Is There a Shakespeare Problem? London and New York: John Lane, pp. 333, 399, 541, passim.
        Comments in passing on Spenser's autograph, images, and on allusions to Spenser.

14   HUBBARD, FRANK G. "Locrine and Selimus." In Shakespeare Studies by Members of the Department of English of the University of Wisconsin. Madison: University of Wisconsin Press, pp. 17-35.
        Disagrees with Crawford (1901.6; 1906.6). Concludes that "all the borrowings from the Complaints found in Selimus come by way of Locrine." For related studies, see 1905.16; 1913.17.

15   LEEMING, EDITH MARY. "Spenser and His Relations with Elizabeth, Lady Carey." Master's thesis, Columbia University.
        Considers evidence concerning Spenser's relationship with kinswoman-patron, Lady Carey, to conclude that most discussions rely largely on conjecture since scant evidence exists to substantiate a strong friendship-patronage. Forwards argument that Amoretti and Epithalamion celebrate Spenser's courtship and marriage to Elizabeth Boyle.

16   LONG, PERCY W. "Spenser and the Bishop of Rochester." PMLA 31:713-35.
        Extensive influence of Young and Grindal on Spenser, especially evident in The Shepheardes Calender and Mother Hubberds Tale (notably the ecclesiastical satire). Finds source for Spenser's "moralizing against ambition" ("February" and "July") in Young's homily, A Sermon Preached before the Queenes Maiestie, the second of March. An. 1575. Discusses Spenser's relationship with Leicester (response to Greenlaw, 1911.17).

17   _____. "Spenseriana: The Lay of Clorinda." MLN 31:79-82.
        Considers Spenser author of poem, based on strong unity between it and Astrophel and on similarities with other Spenser poems.

18   _____. "Spenser's Birth-date." MLN 31:178-80.
        Suggests that Spenser was born in 1550 (rather than 1552), based on evidence from Amoretti and elsewhere.

19   LYONS, JESSIE M. "Spenser's Muiopotmos as an Allegory."
      PMLA 31:90-113.
           Interprets poem in light of first two stanzas to be an
      allegory of the quarrel between Raleigh and Essex (1588-89).
      Clarion represents Raleigh, "the gay gardens" are Elizabeth's
      court, and Aragnoll depicts Essex. Poem is not mock-heroic,
      but employs some mock-heroic elements.

20   MADDEN, D[ODGSON] H. Shakespeare and His Fellows. An Attempt
      to Decipher the Man and His Nature. London and New York:
      Smith, Elder & Co., pp. 12-53.
           Identifies Shakespeare as Aëtion of Colin Clouts Come Home
      Againe; surmises a significant relationship between Spenser and
      Shakespeare.

21   PADELFORD, FREDERICK MORGAN. "Spenser and the Spirit of
      Puritanism." MP 14:31-44.
           Establishes the essential spirit of Elizabethan Puritanism
      as "the attempt to realize fidelity to the things of the spirit
      through infidelity to all other human faculties." Spenser, though
      he professed Calvinistic theology, "advocates that full and rich
      enjoyment of the sense and of the life of the intellect that was
      the glory of the Renaissance." Concludes that Spenser was an ex-
      ponent of the Renaissance with a faith in intellect's integrity.
      He was an apostle of beauty and a lover of good things of life,
      however contradictory his theological professions may have been
      to the spirit of the Renaissance. References to The Faerie Queene,
      Teares of the Muses, The Ruines of Time, Mother Hubberds Tale, and
      Epithalamion. For related studies, see 1913.24; 1914.14.

22   PECK, H.W. "Spenser's Faerie Queene and the Student Today."
      SR 24:340-52.
           The fusion of allegory and romance in The Faerie Queene
      causes confusion: allegory is uneven and characters difficult
      to understand. Briefly surveys the poem. Challenges the common
      advice about teaching The Faerie Queene, i.e., to ignore the
      allegory and to emphasize pictorial and imaginative qualities,
      and the metrical beauty, because to do so is to ignore the
      author's point of view. Suggests that best preparation for
      study of The Faerie Queene is a course in medieval history which
      will make the customs, conventions, and outer trappings of the
      medieval world seem natural. Such a course will prepare the
      student for the deeper study of the narrative, sources, and
      allegory. Other conditions diminish the poem's appeal: lack
      of structural unity, defective poetry, lack of humor, and lack
      of knowledge of human nature. These faults of the poem in struc-
      ture and content will be greatly diminished if the student ap-
      proaches the poem from the point of view of the author and his
      age.

*23   PURVIS, SUE E. "A Comparative Study of the Position of Woman
      in: The Faerie Queene (the Radigund Episode), Love's Labour's

Lost, The Princess, Man and Superman." Master's thesis,
Columbia University.
    Cited in Stephens, 1950.

24   RAHILLY, T.A. "Identification of the Hitherto Unknown River
     'Aubrian' of Spenser Fame." JCHAS 22:49-56.
         Identifies Spenser's "stony Aubrian" as the Breanagh River.

25   RINAKER, CLARISSA. Thomas Warton: A Biographical and Crit-
     ical Study. University of Illinois Studies in Language and
     Literature, Vol. 2, no. 1. Urbana: University of Illinois
     Press, pp. 37-58, passim.
         Briefly considers Warton's early reading of Spenser, his
     own Spenserian imitations, and evolution of Warton's History of
     English Poetry. "Criticism: The Observations on the Faerie
     Queene of Spenser, 1754-1762" is reprint, with one minor modi-
     fication, of 1915.13. Published version of 1915.13.

26   RYE, WALTER. "The Possible East Anglian Descent of the Poet
     Spenser." Papers of Norfolk and Norwich Archaeological Society
     19, pt. 2:175-82.
         Suggests poet Spenser may be related to Spensers of
     Lancashire; finds other Edmund Spensers there 1550-1650.
     Notes that "the strongest thing for the Lancashire descent
     is that the poet called one of his sons Laurence, a Christian
     name which occurs in the Lancashire pedigree."

27   SCOTT, MARY AUGUSTA. Elizabethan Translations from the
     Italian. Boston and New York: Houghton Mifflin Co.,
     pp. 137-39.
         Notes continental sources for Complaints.

28   SMITH, D. NICHOL. "Authors and Patrons." In Shakespeare's
     England. Vol. 2. Edited by Sidney Lee, C.T. Onions, et al.
     Oxford: Clarendon Press, pp. 182-211.
         Spenser did not think of receiving money for his poems, but
     was more likely to have paid the printer, content to have copies
     for distribution among his friends. His early poems helped him
     win private secretaryship to Lord Grey, but The Faerie Queene
     did not result in the high post Spenser hoped for to remove him
     from exile in Ireland. Notes that seventeen sonnets added to
     The Faerie Queene provide list of chief patrons of the time.
     Reprinted: 1932.59; 1950.

                              1917

*1   AMISS, MARGARET. "The Pageant in Literature with Particular
     Relation to The Faerie Queene." Master's thesis, Columbia
     University.
         Cited in Stephens, 1950.

2   BRIE, FRIEDRICH. "Umfang und ursprung der poetischen
     beseelung in der Englischen Renaissance bis zu Philip
     Sidney." Englische Studien 50:383-425.
         Notes Spenser's debt to Sidney in use of personification.

3   BUTLER, WILLIAM F.T. Confiscations in Irish History.
     Dublin: Talbot Press; London: T. Fisher Unwin, pp. 138-39.
         Recounts return of Kilcolman to Spenser's grandson William.
     Reprinted: 1918.5; Port Washington, N.Y. and London: Kennikat
     Press, 1970.

4   CLARK, J. SCOTT. "Spenser, 1552(?)-1599." In A Study of
     English and American Poets: A Laboratory Method. New York:
     Charles Scribner's Sons, pp. 33-88.
         Reprint of 1900.3.

5   CORY, HERBERT ELLSWORTH. Edmund Spenser: A Critical Study.
     University of California Publications in Modern Philology,
     Vol. 5. Berkeley: University of California Press, 478 pp.
         Attempts "to come to certain conclusions about Spenser only
     on the basis of a vast number of experiences of other readers of
     Spenser in every decade from 1579 to 1917." Contains individual
     chapters on The Shepheardes Calender; The Faerie Queene, I-III;
     Complaints, Elegies, Colin Clouts Come Home Againe; Amoretti,
     Epithalamion; The Faerie Queene, IV-VI; and Fowre Hymnes,
     Prothalamion, and Mutabilitie Cantos. Concludes with a discus-
     sion of the attitudes of Spenser's contemporaries and of later
     ages toward Spenser and a sketching of the more important critics
     and poets who were influenced by him, especially by Augustan imi-
     tators. Concludes that while changing attitudes toward science
     and philosophy prevent modern readers from thinking as Spenser
     did, "our lives still find perennial inspiration in his life and
     poetry." Reprinted: New York: Russell & Russell, 1965; see
     McNeir-Provost no. 604.

6   CROSLAND, T[HOMAS] W[ILLIAM] H[ODGSON]. The English Sonnet.
     London: Martin Secker, pp. 176-89.
         Finds Amoretti too numerous to sustain slight subject mat-
     ter. Considers rhyme scheme of Spenserian sonnet "jarring and
     disappointing." Reprinted: 1918.8; 1969.

7   De SELINCOURT, E., ed. Introduction to The Poetical Works of
     Edmund Spenser. London, New York, and Toronto: Humphrey
     Milford, Oxford University Press, pp. vii-lxvii.
         Reprint of 1912.11.

8   EMERSON, OLIVER FARRAR. "A New Word in an Old Poet." MLN
     32:250-51.
         Notes that "underlay" (lines 97-100, Virgils Gnat) is used
     instead of "underlie" for sake of rhyme; means only "lie under."

9   _____. "Spenser, Lady Carey, and the Complaints Volume."
       PMLA 32:306-22.
       Contends that the Complaints volume comprises four separate
booklets, the last four poems making one segment. These poems
exalt Lady Carey with the dedication of Muiopotmos being the envoy
for the four poems. Rejects suggestion that Lady Carey is the
woman of the Amoretti.

10   FLETCHER, JEFFERSON B. "The Painter of the Poets." SP 14:
       153-66.
       Suggests a better realization of Spenser's visual imagery
through study of pictures of Boticelli, Dürer, and other primi-
tive colorists, and the line engravings of Mantegna, "rather than
by reading into his word-pictures the studied chiaroscuro and
atmospheric spaces of Rubens or Veronese or Turner." Accounts
for another type of Spenser's visual imagery in models presented
by Emblem books.

11   GOUGH, ALFRED B. "Who Was Spenser's Bon Font?" MLR 12:140-45.
       Identifies Bon Font in The Faerie Queene, V.ix.26 as
Ulpian Fulwell.

12   GREENLAW, EDWIN. "'A Better Teacher Than Aquinas.'" SP 14:
       196-217.
       Two fundamental parallels between Spenser and Milton are
beliefs that poetry is a philosophy of teaching by example and
that virtue is active not passive. Spenser's account of love
and beauty worked a powerful influence on Milton's treatment of
the relationship between Raphael and Adam, and Adam's sin. The
Legend of Guyon illustrates Milton's notion of Temperance and is
the Model for the philosophic content of Paradise Lost. "The two
great 'adventures' corresponding to Guyon's experience with Mammon
and the story of the Bower of Bliss are Satan's fall through pride
and lust for power, and Adam's fall through that irrational principle of the soul which operates through lust." The construction
of the story of Adam and Eve after the fall is primarily influenced by Book I of The Faerie Queene. For related studies, see
1920.10; 1932.24.

13   LONG, PERCY W. "Spenser's Visit to the North of England."
       MLN 32:58-59.
       Questions theory based on glosses to "January" and "June"
eclogues that Spenser need not have visited northern England to
use northern dialect in The Shepheardes Calender. Suggests that
these dialectal features may have been acquired from northern-
born ushers at Merchant Taylors' School.

*14   MOFFATT, JAMES S. "Tennyson, Spenser, and the Renaissance."
       Master's thesis, University of North Carolina.
       Cited in Stephens, 1950.

15   OSGOOD, CHARLES G. "Spenser's Sapience." SP 14:167-77.
          Reads Fowre Hymnes not as a "mere philosophical or theo-
      logical document," but as "the confession of a profoundly sensi-
      tive and serious man, revealing the course of his spiritual
      development." The upward progression moves from early disappoint-
      ment in love, "to ultimate intense consciousness of eternal things,
      indeed to an equivalent of the Beatific Vision itself." Reviews
      major interpretations of Sapience to conclude that Spenser's in-
      tended meaning is obscure.

16   PADELFORD, F[REDERICK] M[ORGAN]. "The Women in Spenser's
      Allegory of Love." JEGP 16:70-73.
          On the basis of differentiation suggested by epithets and
      descriptive terms applied to them, interprets Amoret as embodi-
      ment of charm in woman, Belphoebe of chastity, Florimell of
      beauty, Radigund of strength, and Britomart, Spenser's example
      of perfect womanhood, as the harmonious embodiment of all these
      qualitites.

17   POWELL, CHILTON LATHAM. English Domestic Relations, 1478-1653:
      A Study of Matrimony and Family Life in Theory and Practice As
      Revealed by the Literature, Law, and History of the Period.
      New York: Columbia University Press, pp. 174, 181, 187-89, 191.
          Spenser indebted to thought and literature of Italy, but
      his moral philosophy is English because he casts chastity as a
      woman, in keeping with the teaching of the domestic books which
      use the word only in reference to women and because for Spenser
      chastity characterized the wife and mother, not the virgin only,
      which is in keeping with the thought of the English and German
      Reformation. His doctrines come mostly from the classics but
      were influenced by Christian moral philosophy and by moral and
      religious ideas of sixteenth century.

18   ROBERTSON, J[OHN] M[ACKINNON]. Shakespeare and Chapman. A
      Thesis of Chapman's Authorship of "A Lover's Complaint," and
      His Origination of "Timon of Athens." With Indications of
      Further Problems. London: T. Fisher Unwin, pp. 118-19.
          Identifies Aëtion (Colin Clouts Come Home Againe) as
      Drayton.

19   ROLLINS, HYDER E. "Notes on the 'Shirburn Ballads.'" JAF
      30:370-77.
          References in the ballad of "Willie and Peggie" used to
      identify Willy (Teares of the Muses) with Tarlton.

*20   SHERER, GERTRUDE R. "Platonism in the Religious Lyric from
      Spenser to Milton." Master's thesis, Stanford University.
          Cited in Stephens, 1950.

21   WALKER, HUGH. "The Revelation of England Through Her Poetry."
      Warton Lecture on English Poetry, 8. PBA 8:181-97.

Mentions Spenser among others to reveal character of English people through poetry.

1918

1   B., E.K. "Locrine and the Faerie Queene." Nation 107:296.
     Argues that The Faerie Queene influenced Locrine.

2   BENSLEY, EDWARD. "Spenser and 'The Shepherd's Calendar.'"
     NQ 123:138.
     Finds source for Colin emblem ("December") in 8 B.C.
anonymous Consolatio ad Liviam. Response to 1918.10.

3   _____. "Spenser's Faerie Queene: Sans Loy, Sans Foy, Sans
     Joy." NQ 136:226.
     Responds to Fleming's thesis (1918.12): "Apart from any
question of pronunciation . . . imaginative literature has long
enjoyed a license in the coining of proper names that shall be
appropriate to the character."

*4   BRIE, FRIEDRICH. "The Design of the Poets." In Sidney's
     Arcadia: Eine Studie zur Englischen Renaissance, in Quellen
     und Forschungen zur Sprach- und Culturgeschichte der
     Germanischen Völker. Strassburg: Karl J. Trubner,
     pp. 23-65.
          Cited in 1923.6.

5   BUTLER, WILLIAM F.T. Confiscations in Irish History. 2d ed.
     Dublin: Talbot Press; London: T. Fisher Unwin, pp. 138-39.
          Reprint of 1917.3.

6   COOK, ALBERT STANBURROUGH. "Five Spenserian Trifles." JEGP
     17:289-90.
          Emendations for Amoretti 19, 43, 45, 49, and Commendatory
Sonnet 1.

7   CRANE, RONALD S. "Imitation of Spenser and Milton in the
     Early Eighteenth Century." SP 15:195-206.
          Discusses Henry Felton's A Dissertation on Reading the
Classics and Forming a Just Style (1709) as an example of a work
which "brought the whole attitude underlying the Spenser and
Milton revivals into close and explicit harmony with a thoroughly
traditional conception of poetical imitation."

8   CROSLAND, T[HOMAS] W[ILLIAM] H[ODGEON]. The English Sonnet.
     New York: Dodd, Mead & Co., pp. 176-89.
          Reprint of 1917.6. Reprinted: Folcroft, Pa.: Folcroft
Press, 1969.

9   DeMOSS, W.F. "Spenser's Twelve Moral Virtues 'according to
     Aristotle.'" MP 16:23-38, 245-70.
        Challenges Jusserand's three main arguments (1906.13) that
     Spenser's and Aristotle's lists of virtues are not the same in
     number, and they are unlike in nature, and that Spenser's ideas
     concerning a list of twelve virtues derive from Lodowick
     Bryskett. After close study of The Faerie Queene and Nichomachean
     Ethics, concludes that the number of Spenser's virtues agrees with
     Aristotle's thirteen good qualities, one of which, Magnificence,
     includes the rest; that Spenser follows the method of Aristotle's
     moral philosophy at least in essentials; and that Spenser's and
     Bryskett's virtues are unlike in nature. Reprinted: 1920.5-6.

10   EAGLE, R.L. "Spenser and 'The Shepherds' Calendar.'" NQ
     123:12-13.
        Are words of Colin emblem ("December," The Shepheardes
     Calender) from Peacham's Minerva Britannia? For response, see
     1918.2.

11   EMERSON, OLIVER FARRAR. "Spenser's Virgils Gnat." JEGP 17:
     94-118.
        Compares Spenser's adaption with "Virgilian or pseudo-
     Virgilian" Culex, showing Spenser's expanded text (from 414
     lines to 688) to be a "pleasing poem of his youth" and an
     acceptable translation for its time.

12   FLEMING, CHARLES F. "Spenser's Faerie Queene: Sans Loy, Sans
     Foy, and Sans Joy." NQ 136:71.
        Argues that "these three names should be pronounced in such
     a way as to make them appear true knights and not enemies of the
     soul" because evil comes to men in guise of good and because "the
     allegory represents the conflict of goodness, not against openly
     declared wrong, but against fraud and pretense." For response,
     see 1918.3.

13   GREENLAW, EDWIN. "Spenser's Fairy Mythology." SP 15:105-22.
        "The realm of Gloriana is two-fold: England, in the his-
     torical allegory; the Celtic Otherworld in the fairy aspect."
     Notes Celtic analogues in The Faerie Queene, especially vision
     of the fairy mistress, the device by which Spenser establishes
     the basis of The Faerie Queene: "Spenser conceives the Tudor
     rule as a return to the old British line; he conceives Elizabeth
     Tudor as the particular sovereign, coming out of Faerie, whose
     return fulfils the old prophecy." Had the greatness of the last
     two decades of the sixteenth century occurred under a Tudor King,
     Spenser would have figured that king under the name of Prince
     Arthur. Since Elizabeth is a woman, the prophecy is fulfilled
     "through personifying, in Arthur, the spirit of Great Britain,
     now united to the Faerie Queene herself." Gloriana is a fairy
     sovereign; Arthur is a Briton. For Spenser, Fairy means Welsh.
     Gloriana is Elizabeth Tudor. Thus, "the old British spirit,

the real England, represented in Arthur, finds in her 'glory,' in
the rich connotation given that term in the Renaissance, and also
the powerful government . . . that was making England a great European power and was the prophecy of the coming British imperialism."

14   HUGHES, MERRITT Y. "Spenser's 'Blatant Beast.'" MLR 13:267-75.
       Whether or not the Blatant Beast particularly shadows Puri-
     tan calumniation, as Jonson's remark to Drummond of Hawthronden
     would suggest, "it certainly shadows a host of various kinds of
     calumniation committed by men of all professions in a century
     when libel did its worst in European politics."

15   LEFRANC, ABEL. Sous le masque de William Shakespeare. William
     Stanley Vi Comte de Derby. Paris: Payot & Co., pp. 199-237,
     passim.
       Comments on identifications in Colin Clouts Come Home
     Againe: Aëtion is not Shakespeare, but rather William Stanley;
     Amyntos is Ferdinando, Earl of Derby. Significance seen in
     Stanley family arms, which bore an eagle.

*16 LESTER, ROBERT M. "The Treatment of Nature in Elizabethan
     Pastoral Poetry Before 1600." Master's thesis, Columbia
     University.
       Cited in Stephens, 1950.

17   MUSTARD, WILFRED P. "Later Echoes of the Greek Bucolic
     Poets." American Journal of Philology 39:193-98.
       Supplement to 1909.28.

18   PADELFORD, FREDERICK MORGAN. "Talus: The Law." SP 15:97-104.
       In Book V of The Faerie Queene Talus represents the law and
     those who enforce it.

19   PALMER, GEORGE HERBERT. "Edmund Spenser." In Formative
     Types in English Poetry. The Earl Lectures of 1917. Boston
     and New York: Houghton Mifflin Co.; Cambridge, Mass.:
     Riverside Press, pp. 65-97.
       Contrasts Chaucer and Spenser as realist and idealist,
     suggesting connection between Spenser's severe life and high
     romance of his verse. Reprinted: Freeport, N.Y.: Books for
     Libraries Press, 1968.

20   PATCH, HOWARD R. "Notes on Spenser and Chaucer." MLN 33:
     177-80.
       Notes general similarities between the pageant of rivers
     in The Faerie Queene, IV.xi, and a scene in Dekker's Londons
     Tempe. Spenser's approximation of pageant customs suggests that
     his other pictures derive from pageants which he saw.

21   PAUL, FRANCIS. "The Shepheards Calender." American Catholic
     Quarterly Review 43:167-69.

Attempts to show that Spenser was, "without doubt, hostile to Catholicism, and intolerant in his hostility," especially in The Shepheardes Calender.

*22   PELTON, NELLIE F. "The Minor Poems of Edmund Spenser."
      Master's thesis, Johns Hopkins University.
      Cited in Stephens, 1950.

 23   QUILLER-COUCH, ARTHUR THOMAS. Studies in Literature. New
      York: G.P. Putnam's Sons, pp. 78-79, 185, 266.
         Notes that the originality of The Faerie Queene, a "romantic"
      work, is due to Spenser, not to his sources and influences. Con-
      siders Epithalamion and Meredith's Love in a Valley to be great-
      est songs of human love in English Literature.

*24   RESCHKE, HEDWIG. "Die Spenserstanze bei den Spensernachahmen
      des 19. Jahrhunderts." Ph.D. diss., University of Heidelberg.
         For published and revised edition, see 1918.25.

 25   _____. Die Spenserstanze im neunzehnten Jahrhundert.
      Anglistische Forschungen, no. 54. Herausgegeben von
      Dr. Johannes Hoops. Heidelberg: Carl Winters, 198 pp.
         Considers Spenserian stanza in relation to twenty-three
      major and minor poets and Spenserian stanza in translation. Pub-
      lished version, with additions, of 1918.24.

 26   SPURGEON, CAROLINE F.E. Five Hundred Years of Chaucer Criti-
      cism and Allusion (1357-1900). Part 2. Chaucer Society,
      2d ser. 49 and 50. London: Kegan Paul, Trench, Trubner &
      Co.; London and New York: Oxford University Press, pp. 25,
      218.
         Chronological list of criticism and allusion from 1801-
      1850. Notes Chaucer material, Todd's edition of Spenser in 1805,
      and Walter Savage Landor's comment on Spenser's soporific quality.
      Part 2 of five parts. For other volumes, see 1914.17; 1921.17;
      1922.24; and 1924.35. Reprinted: 1925.31; New York: Russell &
      Russell, 1960.

 27   TOLMAN, ALBERT H. "The Relation of Spenser and Harvey to
      Puritanism." MP 15:549-64.
         Assesses nature of Spenser's Puritanism. Finds him to be,
      like Harvey, a broad-minded Low-Churchman, who defended the epis-
      copal system. Notes influence on most of Spenser's works.

 28   WHITMAN, CHARLES HUNTINGTON. A Subject-Index to the Poems of
      Edmund Spenser. New Haven: Yale University Press; London:
      Humphrey Milford, Oxford University Press, 272 pp.
         "An index in so far as it includes the names of persons,
      places, animals, and things, whatever, in fact, has a function
      and definite meaning--whatever, in the compiler's judgment, would
      be likely to prove of interest to the student of Spenser and his
      age. It partakes also of the nature of a dictionary, in that it

includes brief explanations, allegorical and otherwise, whenever
such explanations seem necessary." Based on the Cambridge edition. Reprinted: 1919.17; New York: Russell & Russell, 1966.

1919

1 DRAPER, JOHN W. "The Glosses to Spenser's 'Shepheardes
   Calender.'" JEGP 18:556-74.
       Discussion identifies sources of diction of The Shepheardes
   Calender: words from Middle English, from other contemporary
   writers, loan words, and words coined by Spenser. Finds significant number of northern dialect words in poem, but are not
   "characteristically Lancastrine." Considers E.K.'s glosses joint
   effort with Spenser for most part.

2 _____. "Spenserian Biography: A Note on the Vagaries of
   Scholarship." Colonnade 14:35-46.
       Comparative view of facts and theories concerning Spenser's
   biography.

3 _____. "Spenser's Linguistics in The Present State of
   Ireland." MP 17:471-86.
       Considers the treatise "one of the early monuments of
   Celtic scholarship in English," but finds Spenser's knowledge
   of linguistics in it "sadly narrow" and his understanding of
   Celtic political matters "unsympathetic, at times almost to the
   point of savagery." For related studies, see 1922.7; 1926.12.

4 FOWLER, EARLE BROADUS. "Spenser and the Courts of Love."
   Ph.D. diss., University of Chicago.
       For published edition, see 1921.8.

5 GILBERT, ALLAN H. "Spenser's Imitations from Ariosto:
   Supplementary." PMLA 34:225-32.
       Supplements Dodge (1897). Spenser imitates Ariosto in
   canto conclusions and canto transitions. Lists parallels between Spenser and Ariosto not noted by Dodge, and conclusions
   and transitions in the manner of Ariosto. See R.E. Neil Dodge,
   "Spenser's Imitations from Ariosto," PMLA 12:151-204. For supplement to Gilbert's study, see 1920.7.

6 HARRIS, RENDEL. The Origin of the Doctrine of the Trinity.
   Manchester: Manchester University Press; London: Longmans,
   Green, & Co., p. 41.
       Discusses Trinity from New Testament sources and finds
   similar ideas in Hymne of Heavenlie Beautie, lines 186-206.

7 HARRISON, JOHN S. Platonism in English Poetry of the Sixteenth and Seventeenth Centuries. New York: Macmillan Co.,
   235 pp.
       Reprint of 1903.15.

8   JONES, H.S.V. Spenser's Defense of Lord Grey. University of
     Illinois Studies in Language and Literature 5:151-219.
          Consists of four chapters: "Spenser, Lord Grey, and
     Ireland"; "Nationalism and Tolerance in England and France";
     "Spenser and Les Politiques"; and "Spenser and Machiavelli."
     Examines Book V of The Faerie Queene and A Veue of the Present
     State of Ireland to demonstrate how Spenser's defense of Lord
     Grey is the poet's attempt to meet Queen Elizabeth on common
     ground. Considers political writers in France and England with
     whom Spenser would have been familiar, especially Jean Bodin,
     concluding that Grey's severity is consistent with clementia as
     distinguished by misericordia and that the English deputy "was
     never guilty of that atrocity of the mind which Seneca marks as
     the true antithesis of clemency." Final chapter disputes Green-
     law's contention (1909.14) that "the Veue of the Present State of
     Ireland defends the Lord Deputy's administration of Irish affairs
     according to the principles and precepts of the Machiavellian
     politic."

*9   MOFFATT, JAMES S. "Colin Clouts Come Home Againe." Ph.D.
     diss., University of North Carolina.
          Cited in 1923.6. Relates poem to pastoral, court of love
     conventions, and Breton's Pilgrimage to Paradise.

10   MUSTARD, W[ILFRED] P. "E.K.'s Classical Allusions." MLN
     34:193-203.
          Lists E.K.'s allusions and gives classical sources.

*11 NITCHIE, ELIZABETH. "Vergil and the English Poets." Ph.D.
     diss., Columbia University.
          For published edition, see 1919.12.

12   _____. Vergil and the English Poets. New York: Columbia
     University Press, passim.
          Surveys Virgil's influence and popularity in England during
     the Renaissance. Spenser knew pastoral tradition and adopts song-
     contest of Theocritus and Virgil, religious and moral satire of
     Mantuan, and the elegy of Marot. Spenser "introduces into his
     pastorals not only religious satire after the pattern of his
     Italian models, but also personal allegory after the manner of
     Virgil and his followers." References to The Shepheardes Calender,
     Colin Clouts Come Home Againe, Daphnaida, Astrophel. Reprinted:
     New York: AMS Press, 1966.

13   OSMOND, PERCY H. The Mystical Poets of the English Church.
     London: Society for Promoting Christian Knowledge; New York:
     Macmillan Co., pp. 17-25.
          Spenser first English poet to expound Plato's views on Love
     and Beauty. His Platonic idealism closely akin to mysticism and
     clearly evident in the Hymne in Honour of Love, the Hymne in
     Honour of Beautie, and A Hymne of Heavenly Beautie.

14   POWELL, C.L. "The Castle of the Body." SP 16:197-205.
     Points out parallels of Spenser's House of Alma (The Faerie
Queene, II.ix) with Grosseteste's Le Chasteau d'Amour, Sawles
Warde, and Piers the Plowman.

15   RENWICK, W.L. "The December 'Embleme' of 'The Shepheardes'
     Calender.'" MLR 14:415-16.
     "December" emblem adapted from Marot. Suggests that its
omission from first Quarto is due to its being a repetition of
"November" emblem.

16   SQUIRE, JOHN COLLINGS. "The Mantle of Sir Edwin" in his Books
     in General. New York: Alfred A. Knopf, pp. 75-80.
     Rejects Harman's view (1914.7) that Bacon wrote Spenser's
works.

17   WHITMAN, CHARLES HUNTINGTON. A Subject-Index to the Poems of
     Edmund Spenser. New Haven: Yale University Press, 272 pp.
     Reprint of 1918.28.

18   YEATS, WILLIAM BUTLER. "Edmund Spenser." In The Cutting of
     An Agate. New York: Macmillan Co., pp. 213-55.
     Reprint of 1912.45.

                              1920

1   BASKERVILL, CHARLES READ. "The Genesis of Spenser's Queene
     of Faerie." MP 18:49-56.
     Plan of The Faerie Queene partly influenced by entertain-
ments at Kenilworth and Woodstock in 1575. Spenser's Arthur
figures forth Leicester.

2   BERDAN, JOHN M. Early Tudor Poetry: 1485-1547. Studies in
     Tudor Literature. New York: Macmillan Co., 564 pp., passim.
     Discusses Spenser in terms of Platonism, the medieval tra-
dition and Chaucer. Sees The Faerie Queene as culmination of
four modifications of Tudor poetry: personified abstractions,
chivalry, satire, and historical allusions. Reprinted: New
York: Shoe String Press, 1961.

3   COULTER, CORNELIUS C. "Two of E.K.'s Classical Allusions."
     MLN 35:55-56.
     Identifies sources for The Shepheardes Calender, "March,"
lines 16, and "April," lines 122-23.

4   COURTHOPE, WILLIAM JOHN. "Court Allegory: Edmund Spenser."
     In A History of English Poetry. Vol. 2. London: Macmillan
     & Co., pp. 234-87.
     General introduction to Spenser and his works. Emphasis
on allegory in works: "Allegory not only provides the form of

his compositions; it is the very essence of his thought."
Reprinted: 1926.8; New York: Russell & Russell, 1962.

5   DeMOSS, WILLIAM FENN. "The Influence of Aristotle's Politics
     and Ethics on Spenser." Ph.D. diss., University of Chicago,
     75 pp.
          Reprint of 1918.9. See 1920.6.

6   _____. The Influence of Aristotle's "Politics" and "Ethics"
     on Spenser. Private ed. Chicago: University of Chicago
     Press, 70 pp.
          Introduction casts Spenser as man of his age in following
     Aristotle and in tending toward allegorical interpretation of
     classics. "Aristotle's influence on the Faerie Queene" is a
     reprint of 1918.9, with minor change in opening paragraph.
     Three remaining chapters discuss Aristotle's influence on
     "Mutabilitie Cantos," perhaps written as "Part of one of the
     completed books of the Faerie Queene"; A Veue of the Present
     State of Ireland; and The Shepheardes Calender and the minor
     poems.

7   DODGE, R.E. NEIL. "Spenser's Imitations from Ariosto:
     Addenda." PMLA 35:91-92.
          Supplements Gilbert's supplement (1919.5).

8   GAYLEY, CHARLES MILLS, and BENJAMIN PUTNAM KURTZ. Methods
     and Materials of Literary Criticism: Lyric, Epic, and Allied
     Forms of Poetry. Boston and New York: Ginn & Co., 911 pp.,
     passim.
          Spenser variously discussed in sections on history of
     lyric, theory of epic, and history of epic. Each section in-
     cludes annotated bibliography of criticism.

9   GREENLAW, EDWIN. "Spenser and Lucretius." SP 17:439-64.
          Spenser indebted to Lucretius for Garden of Adonis (The
     Faerie Queene, III.vi) and Mutabilitie Cantos. For response,
     see 1928.31. For related studies, see 1930.14; 1931.11; 1932.24;
     1934.63.

10   _____. "Spenser's Influence on Paradise Lost." SP 17:320-59.
          Illustrates important place of origin and government of
     world of Nature in Spenser's poetry. Attempts to show that
     "Spenser's Hymnes are not only Platonic but mystical in the
     medieval sense in their revelation of the way in which the Soul
     may rise to the actual presence of God; to show that they are
     not distinct but cumulative and present a systematic philosophy
     of contemplation; to show that his philosophy is worked out by
     two-fold means: the contemplation of God's dealings with Man
     and the contemplation of God's works as revealed in a vast cos-
     mogony; and to show, finally, that in this union of the ideal of
     God in nature and of a justification of the ways of God to man

we have, in a sense not found in any source yet named, the very
structure itself of Paradise Lost." Milton also directly influenced by "Mutabilitie Cantos." Suggests that Spenser patterns
his mysticism on Neoplatonic ideas drawn ultimately from Socrates'
speech in Plato's Symposium and Castiglione's use of the same in
The Courtier, Book IV (Bembo's speech). Shows that the three
stages, "purification, illumination, and perfection, or the true
contemplation, are developed from a beginning in pure Platonism
to the adaptation of religious ecstasy leading to the sight of
God himself." For related studies, see 1917.12; 1932.24; 1934.63.

11 GREENOUGH, JAMES BRADSTREET, and GEORGE LYMAN KITTREDGE.
    Words and Their Ways in English Speech. New York and London:
    Macmillan, pp. 118, 295, 354, 375.
        Reprint of 1901.11.

12 HUGHES, MERRITT Y. "Spenser and Utopia." SP 17:132-46.
        Recounts sixteenth-century social uprisings and notes mass
    of floating conservative opinion about social order reflected in
    Elyot, Tyndall, North, Cheke, and Sidney. Concludes that Spenser
    was democratic in recognizing that "gentle virtues sometimes
    spring in vulgar soil" and in guarding essential human equality
    which transcends blood and rank. But for democracy and various
    forms of socialism, he took more pains than any other Elizabethan
    writer to spell out his lack of sympathy. Suggests that histor-
    ical allegory in story of the Giant whom Artegall overthrows in
    Book V of The Faerie Queene lies in Ket's Rebellion in Norwich in
    1549.

13 HYDE, DOUGLAS. A Literary History of Ireland. From Earliest
    Times to the Present Day. London: T. Fisher Unwin,
    pp. 493-96.
        Reprint of 1901.15.

14 JACK, ADOLPHUS ALFRED. A Commentary on the Poetry of Chaucer
    and Spenser. Glasgow: Maclehose, Jackson & Co.; London:
    Simpkin, Hamilton & Co.; New York: Macmillan Co., pp. 141-362.
        Separate sections devoted to Chaucer and Spenser. Biog-
    raphy of Spenser followed by commentary on shorter works and
    The Faerie Queene. Places The Faerie Queene in the "School of
    Beauty." Finds Book I the best because of introductory air and
    the conduct of the allegory. Book II: narrow and confining;
    Book III: frankly romantic adventures lacking central allegor-
    ical figure. The second part of the poem is not a part at all,
    "on the contrary, a mere fragment which might . . . have been
    continued indefinitely." Book IV: "a mere run of romantic
    adventure" concerned with many matters other than friendship;
    Book V: "a veiled record of actual happenings;" Book VI: a
    masterpiece fit to rank with the first three books. Two remain-
    ing chapters consider "Criticism and Imitations" and "The Faeries
    of Spenser." Reviews criticism of Hughes, Warton, and Hurd and

considers two different streams of imitation: burlesque and
serious. Considers three origins of European Faerie race:
(1) vestiges of pagan mythology dispossessed by Christianity;
(2) local divinities of Gaul; (3) agricultural belief in earth
powers. Appendices: "Spenser's Similes," "Spenser's Pictures
of Soft Peace," and "On the Uses of Archaic Language." Reprinted:
Folcroft, Pa.: Folcroft Press, 1969.

*15   KING, R.W. "Spenser and Archaisms." Athenaeum 1:252.
          Cited in Atkinson, 1937.

16   LOONEY, J. THOMAS. "Shakespeare" Identified in Edward de Vere
          The Seventeenth Earl of Oxford. New York: Frederick A. Stokes
          Co., pp. 284-94, passim.
          Finds evidence in Edward de Vere's lyric poetry and circum-
stances to identify him, not William Shakspeare, as Willie of The
Shepheardes Calender and Teares of the Muses. Considers The
Shepheardes Calender "a series of burlesques upon prominent men
of the day." Considers correlation between Aëtion (Colin Clouts
Come Home Againe) and William Shakspeare also conjectural.

17   M., G. "Sir Walter Raleigh, His Connection With Munster."
          JCHAS 26:54-59.
          Notes Raleigh's frequent visits to Spenser at Kilcolman.

18   MUSTARD, W[ILFRED] P. "Notes on The Shepheardes Calender."
          MLN 35:371-72.
          Identifies source for "December" emblem (i.e., "Colins
Embleme").

19   OSGOOD, CHARLES G[ROSVENOR]. "The 'Doleful Lay of Clorinda.'"
          MLN 35:90-96.
          Forwards view that poem is Spenser's. Supports with list
of parallels (ideas, word usages, phrases, mannerisms, etc.) to
known Spenser poems.

20   _____. "Spenser's English Rivers." Transactions of the
          Connecticut Academy 23:65-108.
          Follows "Bartholomew's half-inch-to-the-mile maps, based on
ordnance maps," to demonstrate Spenser's first-hand knowledge of
English rivers. Presents results in "quotation and running commentary." Concludes that in The Faerie Queene, IV.ix, half the
matter is drawn from Camden's Britannia (1586), that Spenser used
1587 edition of Holinshed, and that "Canto ix owes but a small
portion of its material to the Epithalamion Thamesis."

21   OSGOOD, CHARLES GROSVENOR. "Virgil and the English Mind."
          In The Tradition of Virgil: Three Papers on the History and
          Influence of the Poet. Princeton, N.J.: Princeton University
          Press; London: Oxford University Press, pp. 23-40.

Hero of first book of The Faerie Queene, Saint George, bred
incognito by farm folk. Spenser akin to Virgil in building his
British Empire out of Georges, i.e., earthworkers. Spenser "had
a strong smack for etymologies--and it is no unmeaning coincidence
that the poet of the Georgics should find a hearkening ear in the
nation that chose the peculiar protection of Saint George."

22   PHETZING, AMELIA CAROLINE. "The History of the Fair Unknown."
     Master's thesis, University of Chicago, pp. 37-48, 57-65.
        Considers Spenser's place in the history of the "Fair Un-
     known," or "Gareth and Lynette." Notes points of similarity
     between Book I of The Faerie Queene and Libaeus Disconus, spe-
     cific imitations of Ariosto and Tasso, copyings from Chaucer,
     and borrowings from Bevis of Southampton. Also notes points of
     contact between Tennyson and Spenser.

23   SCHROEDER, KURT. Platonismus in Der Englischen Renaissance
     vor und bei Thomas Eliot, Nebst Neudruck von Eliot's
     "Disputacion Platonike," 1533. Berlin: Mayer & Müller,
     115 pp., passim.
        Studies Platonism in general with emphasis on Colet,
     Erasmus, More, Starkey, Eliot, Ascham, Campion, Mulcaster, and
     The Courtier. Mentions Spenser's Fowre Hymnes and The Faerie
     Queene in relation to these. For related study, see 1907.28.

24   SECCOMBE, THOMAS, and JOHN W. ALLEN. The Age of Shakespeare.
     Vol. 1. London: G. Bell & Sons, pp. 22-24, 29-42.
        Suggests that Amoretti characterize Spenser's "religious
     temperament and his peculiar idealism," yet are monotonous be-
     cause of sonnet form. Considers The Shepheardes Calender an
     experiment in language, form and subject matter. Finds allegory
     of The Faerie Queene "unintelligible," the stories unrelated,
     and the knights unrepresentative of their virtues. Concludes
     that The Faerie Queene is beautiful poem, but as an allegory it
     "must be held to be a failure."

25   SNYDER, EDWARD D. "The Wild Irish: A Study of Some English
     Satires Against the Irish, Scots, and Welsh." MP 17:687-725.
        General study in which A Veue of the Present State of
     Ireland is mentioned as a work which "sets forth with telling
     realism all the national failings of the Irish as seen by a
     cultivated Englishmen [sic]." Also notes Irish reference in
     The Faerie Queene (VII.vi) and in Colin Clouts Come Home Againe
     (lines 308-19).

26   TAYLOR, HENRY OSBORN. Thought and Expression in the Sixteenth
     Century. Vol. 2. New York: Macmillan Co., pp. 230-37.
        Distinguishes between the actual and the real in Spenser,
     the former his "horrid surroundings in Ireland or his disappoint-
     ments at Court," the latter the world of symbol and allegory,
     "moving in the life and strength of ethical principles and the

underlying validities of human conduct." The Faerie Queene lacks narrative unity because its matter is too multiform. Reprinted: New York: Ungar, 1959; Collier, 1962.

27   WILSON, J. DOVER. "A Note on Elisions in The Faerie Queene." MLR 15:409-14.
        Spenser used apostrophe to indicate syllabic loss.

28   WINSTANLEY, LILIAN, ed. Introduction to The Faerie Queene, Book I. Cambridge: Cambridge University Press, pp. vii-lxxx.
        Reprint of 1915.18.

29   WOODBERRY, GEORGE EDWARD. "Spenser." In The Torch: And Other Lectures and Addresses. New York: Harcourt, Brace & Howe, pp. 83-101.
        Reprint of 1905.27.

1921

1   BAYFIELD, M.A. "Elizabethan Abbreviation. Spenser." TLS, 1 and 8 September, pp. 562, 578.
        In The Faerie Queene, "where we have apostrophe with elision or such spellings as scattred, glistring, the missing vowel was meant to be uttered." Finds similar use of apostrophe in Jonson.

2   BLANCHARD, HAROLD H. "Italian Influence on the 'Faerie Queene.'" Ph.D. diss., Harvard University, 376 pp.
        Discusses influence of Boiardo, Aroisto, Tasso, Dante on Spenser. Finds less influence of Dante than of others: Dante informed Spenser's consciousness, while Spenser drew more directly from Boiardo, Ariosto, and Tasso (illustrates with parallel passages). Seems most extensive influence is from Ariosto, as in: "(1) The spirit of satire and burlesque as seen in the character of Braggadochio. (2) The tendency to operate characters through grotesque actions for the amusement of their creator and the reader. (3) Self-indulgence in the color and action of the world of romance and in the melody of its music for their own sake. (4) Cynicism, irony, vulgarity toward life in general, resulting in a general leveling of ideals."

3   BRIGHT, JAMES W. "On Some Characteristics of Spenser." MLN 31:189-91.
        Comments on Spenser's use of archaisms and on his idealism in The Faerie Queene.

4   BROADUS, EDMUND KEMPER. The Laureateship. A Study of the Office of Poet Laureate in England with Some Account of the Poets. Oxford: Clarendon Press, pp. 33-39.
        Examines tradition that Spenser was laureate; concludes that while document in Lord Chamberlain's office lists Spenser

as an official poet laureate, "there is absolutely no reason to
believe that Spenser enjoyed any court favor" and that the pension granted him "was apparently not paid." Notes Spenser's
dedications and praise for Elizabeth, his comments in letter to
Raleigh, and highest praise and admiration of his contemporaries
at time the laureate tradition was taking form as chief reasons
for traditional assumption that he was official poet laureate to
Elizabeth. Reprinted: 1932.10; Freeport, N.Y.: Books for
Libraries Press, 1966, 1969. See McNeir-Provost, nos. 125-6,
which show that the pension apparently was paid.

5   COVINGTON, F[RANK] F., Jr. "Elizabethan Notions of Ireland."
    Texas Review 6:222-46.
        Discusses A Veue of the Present State of Ireland in context
of general overview of Elizabethan commentaries on Ireland. Concludes from Spenser's account and from other documents that Veue
is "a tolerably accurate notion of the English attitude toward
Ireland in Elizabeth's reign," but does not entirely represent
poet's personal feelings for Ireland. Spenser voices official
position. Notes that while Spenser's suggestions for dealing
with Ireland met with disapproval in 1596-98, Lord Mountjoy
eventually used some of the same methods to subjugate Ireland.

6   De SELINCOURT, E., ed. Introduction to The Poetical Works of
    Edmund Spenser. London, New York, and Toronto: Humphrey
    Milford, Oxford University Press, pp. vii-lxvii.
        Reprint of 1912.11.

7   EINSTEIN, LEWIS. Tudor Ideals. New York: Harcourt Brace,
    376 pp., passim.
        Notes Spenser's involvement in affairs of his day.
    Reprinted: New York: Russell & Russell, 1962.

8   FOWLER, EARLE BROADUS. Spenser and the Courts of Love.
    Menasha, Wis.: George Banta Publishing Co., 137 pp.
        Demonstrates the fundamental influence of the allegory of
the court of love on The Faerie Queene through analysis of representative medieval examples. Categorizes basic elements of in-
door and outdoor settings, classifies types of characters within
the settings, and studies two of Spenser's adaptations of the
court of love allegory in the quasi-judicial conception of the
court and in the masque. Published version of 1919.4.

9   GALIMBERTI, ALICE. "Il Rinascimento cortigiano Edmondo
    Spenser e Guglielmo Shakespeare (1500-1600)." In Dante nel
    Pensiero Inglese. Firenze: Felice Le Monnier, pp. 33-53.
        Finds Book I of The Faerie Queene trite and childish, but
concludes from individual verses that while Spenser's work lacks
the sublime element of Dante's, the English poet nonetheless knew
and used works of the Italian.

10   HUGHES, MERRITT Y. "Some Aspects of the Relation of Edmund
      Spenser's Poetry to Classical Literature." Ph.D. diss.,
      Harvard University, 285 pp.
          Through a series of separate essays shows that "in his
      appreciation and use of Greek motives Spenser was guided prin-
      cipally by contemporary fashions. Careful investigation has
      failed to reveal more than two or three cases of Greek elements
      in his poetry which might not be most naturally explained by
      their occurrence in an Italian or French writer whom there is
      good reason to suppose that he read. The forms which the clas-
      sical elements invariably take in his poetry, and the spirit in
      which they are used, are always colored strongly by contemporary
      usages." Shows in Part 1, "Spenser and the Greek Pastoral Triad"
      (and in Appendix 1, "On the Possible Connection between Spenser's
      Astrophel and Bion's Lament for Adonis"), that "every trait in
      common between Spenser's minor poems and the pastoral elegies of
      Theocritus, Bion, and Moschus will be found in the work of the
      Pléiade." In Part 2, "The Relation of Virgil's Eclogues to the
      Shepheardes Calendar," finds Spenser's use of Virgilian material
      to be knowledgeable and unique, but sparse, in The Shepheardes
      Calender. In "The Virgilian Influence in the Faerie Queene"
      shows that Spenser makes allusions to and borrows episodes from
      the Aeneid and makes extensive use of Virgil's descriptions,
      details, epithets, similes, and phrases. In Appendix 2 discusses
      the correspondences between the Culex and Virgils Gnat. In Part
      3, "Spenser and Aristotle," examines Spenser's use of Nicomachean
      Ethics in The Faerie Queene to conclude that Spenser's extensive
      borrowings are mainly from secondary sources.

11   LEGOUIS, ÉMILE. "L'Épithalame' D'Edmund Spenser traduit en
      verse français." RLC 1:398-415.
          Brief, general introduction to a French translation of the
      poem; notes influence of Pléiade on rhyme scheme.

*12   LINDSEY, EDWIN S. "The Relation of Spenser to Sir Philip
      Sidney." Master's thesis, University of North Carolina.
          Cited in Stephens, 1950.

*13   MATTHES, PAULA. "Das umschreibende 'do' in Spensers Faerie
      Queene." Ph.D. diss., University of Tübingen.
          Cited in Atkinson, 1937.

14   PADELFORD, FREDERICK MORGAN. "The Virtue of Temperance in
      The Faerie Queene." SP 18:334-46.
          Book II is an allegory of continence, and its episodes
      cover every phase of Aristotle's continence and incontinence:
      in eating and drinking, physical intercourse, ambitious pursuits
      of honor and victory, inordinate pursuit of wealth, and anger.

*15   PORTER, MARY LOUISE. "The Holy Wars in Medieval and Modern
      English Literature." Master's thesis, Cornell University,
      217 pp.
          Cited in 1923.6.

*16   SOHR, LUDWIG.   "Die Visuellen Sinneseindrücke und akustischen
       Phänomene in Spensers poetischen Werken." Ph.D. diss.,
       University of Munich.
            Cited in Atkinson, 1937.

17   SPURGEON, CAROLINE F.E. <u>Five Hundred Years of Chaucer Criti-
       cism and Allusion (1357-1900)</u>. Part 3. Chaucer Society,
       2d ser. 52. London: Kegan Paul, Trench, Trubner & Co.;
       London and New York: Oxford University Press, pp. 16, 68.
            Chronological list of criticism and allusion from 1851-1900.
       Notes M.P. Case's comment on Spenser's request to be buried next
       to Chaucer and Walter Savage Landor's preference of Chaucer over
       Spenser. Part 3 of five parts. For other volumes see 1914.17;
       1918.26; 1922.24; 1924.35. Reprinted: 1925.31; New York:
       Russell & Russell, 1960.

18   STOPES, CHARLOTTE CARMICHAEL. "Thomas Edwards, Author of
       'Cephalus and Procris, Narcissus.'" <u>MLR</u> 16:209-23.
            Discusses Edwards as devoted imitator of Spenser; maintains
       that references in <u>Colin Clouts Come Home Againe</u> usually attributed
       to Shakespeare (i.e., Aëtion) actually praise Edwards. Identifies
       Amyntas as Ferdinando Stanley.

19   TOYNBEE, PAGET. <u>Britain's Tribute to Dante in Literature and
       Art. A Chronological Record of 540 Years (c. 1380-1920)</u>.
       London: Humphrey Milford, Oxford University Press, p. 8.
            Shows that Spenser "imitates Dante in numerous passages of
       <u>The Faerie Queene</u>."

20   TUELL, ANNE KIMBALL. "Note on Spenser's Clarion." <u>MLN</u> 36:
       182-83.
            Identifies Spenser with Clarion in <u>Muiopotmos</u>, Burghley
       with Aragnoll; finds clue to poem in name "Clarion." Considers
       poem a mock-heroic.

21   TUELL, ANNE K[IMBALL]. "The Original End of <u>Faerie Queene</u>,
       Book III." <u>MLN</u> 36:309-11.
            Spenser altered closing stanzas of Book III in 1590 edition
       because when he turned to Book IV he had further use for the
       separation of Amoret and Scudamour, but he failed to introduce
       these rejected stanzas when he had need for them near the end
       of Book IV.

*22   WARNER, GEORGE W., and JULIUS P. GILSON. <u>Catalogue of Western
       Manuscripts in the Old Royal and King's Collections</u>. London:
       British Museum, Department of MSS, 13B I, f. 214.
            Cited in 1923.6; includes letter from Sir W. Pelham on
       behalf of James Spenser.

23   WHITNEY, LOIS. "The Literature of Travel in <u>The Faerie
       Queene</u>." <u>MP</u> 10:143-62.

Lists various possible sources in travel history for The
Faerie Queene but concentrates on the voyage to the Bower of
Bliss in Book II. Considers parallels in the medieval Legend
of St. Brendan and lists other possible sources for individual
stanzas in canto xii: the True History of Lucian, The Travels
of Sir John Mandeville, Ferdinand Columbus's History of the Life
and Actions of Admiral Christopher Colon, John Sparke's The Voyage Made by Master John Hawkins, Hakluyt's Divers Voyages,
Thevet's Singularitez, and the Celtic Imram Curaig Maelduin.

24   WILSON, JOHN. "Spenser and His Critics." In Critical Essays
     of the Early Nineteenth Century. Edited by Raymond MacDonald
     Alden. New York: Charles Scribner's Sons, pp. 368-77.
          Abbreviated reprint of paper originally in Blackwood's
     Magazine (September 1834).

                              1922

 1   ACHESON, ARTHUR. Shakespeare's Sonnet Story 1592-1598.
     London: Bernard Quaritch, pp. 12-15, passim.
          Consideration of Menalcas ("June," The Shepheardes Calender)
     identified as John Florio and relationship to Parolles in Love's
     Labour's Won. Reprinted: 1933.1.

 2   ANON. "Pierre de Ronsard," TLS, 2 March, pp. 129-30.
          Compares Spenser with Ronsard. Shows Spenser to excel in
     epic, ode, and moral purity; Ronsard in sonnet, chanson, odette,
     and rhymed epigram. Spenser displays "a chaste, almost Puritan,
     reticence," while "Ronsard can Platonize and Petrarchize with
     the best."

*3   BOTTA, ANNE C. LYNCH. Handbook of Universal Literature.
     Boston: Houghton Mifflin Co., pp. 481-82.
          Reprint of 1902.7. For revised edition, see 1923.4.

 4   BROOKE, TUCKER. "Stanza Connection in The Faerie Queene."
     MLN 37:223-27.
          Spenser uses four devices to connect stanzas: running over
     rhyme from one stanza to the next, employing recurrent lines,
     beginning stanzas with relatives and close-binding conjunctions,
     and carrying over important words from the alexandrine into the
     first line of the next stanza.

 5   CARPENTER, FREDERICK IVES. "Desiderata in the Study of
     Spenser." SP 19:238-43.
          Need for modern variorum and new life of Spenser, new edi-
     tion of A Veue of the Present State of Ireland based on "all
     manuscripts," and new studies of Spenser-Harvey correspondence,
     other Spensers or Spencers of the poet's time, Spenser's circle,
     Spenser's autograph, the itinerary of Spenser's travels in

Ireland, the "Spenser Tradition," Spenser's debt to Ovid, and
Spenser as the founder of modern English poetic diction.

6   _____. "Spenser in Ireland." MP 19:405-19.
        Sets out in the form of notes and queries records and date
concerning Spenser as an office-holder.

7   COVINGTON, F[RANK] F., Jr. "Another View of Spenser's
     Linguistics." SP 19:244-48.
        Defends Spenser's linguistic vagaries in A Veue of the
Present State of Ireland, but argues that Spenser's knowledge of
the Celtic language and culture was somewhat narrow. For related studies, see 1919.3; 1926.12.

8   DRAPER, JOHN W. "Dr. Grossart's Rosalind." JEGP 21:675-79.
        Refutes Grossart's identification of Rosalind in The
Shepheardes Calender as Rose Dinley by showing that the grammar,
diction, and rhymes of the poem are not particularly Lancastrian.

9   _____. "Spenserian Biography; A Note on the Vagaries of
     Scholarship." The Colonnade, Yearbook of the Andiron Club of
New York City 14:35-46.
        General discussion of biographical aspects of Muiopotmos,
The Shepheardes Calender, and Amoretti.

*10   FRANK, TENNEY. Vergil, A Biography. New York: Henry Holt &
      Co., chapter 3.
        Discusses the Culex and Virgils Gnat.

11   GALLAND, RENÉ. "Un poète errant de la Renaissance: Jean
     Van Der Noot et l'Angleterre." RLC 2:337-50.
        Rejects Spenser as author of sonnets (A Theatre for World-
lings) on basis of his youth and inexperience, but sees possible
influence of Noot's l'Olympiade on some of Spenser's poetry.

12   GRIERSON, H.J.C. "Spenser's 'Muiopotmos.'" MLR 17:409-11.
        Rejects view that poem concerns Lady Carey. Reads poem as
allegory of poet's (butterfly-Spenser) outcome when he "comes
bustling into the web of schemes" of the politician (spider-
Burghley); specifically, allegory of Leicester-Burghley conflict
(1579-80), in which Spenser aligned with Leicester.

13   HALES, JOHN W. "The Poet's Poet." In Modern English Essays.
     Vol. 2. Edited by Ernest Rhys. London and Toronto: J.M.
     Dent & Sons; New York: E.P. Dutton, pp. 241-46.
        Moved by a "genuine poetic impulse, . . . Spenser created
a new world, which, from its first appearance in the firmament
of literature, had a special charm and fascination for his brother
artists, who, generation after generation, delighted to wander in
it." Reprinted: 1923.18.

*14   HEFFNER, HUBERT C. "Mysticism in Spenser's Fowre Hymnes."
      Master's thesis, University of North Carolina.
         Cited in Stephens, 1950.

 15   JENKINSON, HILARY. "Elizabethan Handwritings: A Preliminary
      Sketch." Library, 4th ser. 3:1-34.
         Discusses Spenser's handwriting and signature, noting that
      he probably wrote both the Secretary and the Italic hand. Fac-
      simile illustrations.

*16   MASCH, WERNER. "Studien zum italienischen Einflüss in
      Spensers Faery Queene." Ph.D. diss., University of Hamburg.
         Cited in Atkinson, 1937.

*17   MELDRUM, H.S. "The Pastime of Pleasure by Stephen Hawes: a
      Probable Source of Spenser's Faerie Queene." Master's thesis,
      University of Washington.
         Cited in Stephens, 1950.

 18   O'RAHILLY, THOMAS F. "Irish Poets, Historians, and Judges in
      English Documents, 1583-1615." Proceedings of the Royal Irish
      Academy 36.C:86-102.
         Comments on Spenser and A Veue of the Present state of
      Ireland.

 19   RENWICK, W.L. "The Critical Origins of Spenser's Diction."
      MLR 17:1-16.
         Discusses influence of the Pléiade on Spenser's diction:
      "Spenser worked on precisely the same lines as were laid down by
      Du Bellay and Ronsard: the ancient native literature to be stud-
      ied with a linguistic purpose; dialects, and particularly such as
      retained some archaic character, to be brought into the main
      stream of literary speech; technical terms to be put to poetical
      use; new forms to be created from existing roots; and lastly,
      words to be borrowed from ancient and modern foreign languages:
      the language to be plastic, not rigid, and the poet to be the
      final judge of fitness."

 20   _____. "Mulcaster and Du Bellay." MLR 17:282-87.
         Finds correspondence between Mulcaster's views on language
      and those of Du Bellay. Mulcaster noted as possible influence on
      Spenser's diction.

 21   _____. "Spenser and the Pléiade." MLR 17:287-88.
         Acknowledges Fletcher's study of Spenser's diction
      ("Areopagus and Pléiade," American Journal of Philology 2:1898).
      The article Renwick cites is not in this source.

*22   SCHOFFLER, HERBERT. Protestantismus und Literatur. Neue
      Wege zur englischen des achtzehnten Jahrhunderts. Leipzig:
      B. Tauchnitz, pp. 71-86.
         Cited in Atkinson, 1937. Includes "Das Wiedererwachen
      Spensero und Miltons."

*23   SPRUILL, MARY J. "Masque Elements in Spenser's Faerie Queene."
       Master's thesis, University of North Carolina.
            Cited in Stephens, 1950.

24   SPURGEON, CAROLINE F.E. Five Hundred Years of Chaucer Criti-
       cism and Allusion (1357-1900). Parts 4 and 5. 2 vols.
       Chaucer Society, 2d ser. 53 and 54. London and New York:
       Oxford University Press; London: Kegan Paul, Trench, Trubner
       & Co., 4:47; 5:104.
            Appendixes: additional English references to Chaucer,
       French and German allusions. Quotes Spenser allusion to Wife
       of Bath in The Faerie Queene, VI.iii.1 and notes Legouis's 1896
       thesis on Spenser and Chaucer. Parts 4 and 5 of five parts.
       For other volumes, see 1914.17; 1918.26; 1921.17; 1924.35.
       Reprinted: 1925.31; New York: Russell & Russell, 1960.

*25   STARNES, DeWITT T. "Bibliographical History of the Funeral
       Elegy in England from 1500-1639." Ph.D. diss., University
       of Chicago.
            Cited in Atkinson, 1937. Comments on influence of Chaucer's
       Book of the Duchess on Daphnaida.

26   THOMPSON, ELBERT N.S. "Between the Shepheardes Calender and
       the Seasons." PQ 1:23-30.
            Discussion, in part, of Spenser's influence (especially of
       "December" eclogue) on Robert Farlie's Kalendarium Humanae Vitae;
       The Kalender of Mans Life (1638), which reflects the plan and
       themes of Spenser's poem.

27   WELPLY, W.H. "The Family and Descendants of Edmund Spenser."
       JCHAS 28:22-34.
            Presents data to confirm Elizabeth Boyle as Spenser's wife
       and notes evidence in Public Record Office on Spenser's purchase
       of lands in Cork.

28   WILLIAMSON, GEORGE C. Lady Anne Clifford Countess of Dorsett,
       Pembroke and Montgomery. 1590-1676. Her Life, Letters and
       Work. Kendal, England: Titus Wilson & Son, p. 63.
            First monument to Spenser erected at Westminster (1612) by
       Lady Anne.

                                   1923

*1   ANDERSON, HATTIE R. "Spenser's Ideal of Conduct as Exemplified
       in the Allegory of The Faerie Queene." Master's thesis, Uni-
       versity of Colorado.
            Cited in Stephens, 1950.

*2   BARRINGTON, SYBIL. "Edmund Spenser's Letter to Sir Walter
       Raleigh: a letter prefixed to The Faerie Queene, Edited with

Introduction and Notes." Master's thesis, University of
North Carolina.
    Cited in Stephens, 1950.

3   BEHLER, MALLY. "Die Beziehungen zwischen Sidney und Spenser."
     Archiv 146:53-59.
        Concludes that Sidney and Spenser exchanged ideas, but
     finds little evidence to substantiate the existence of Areopagus
     group. For related studies, see 1930.19; 1931.42.

4   BOTTA, ANNE C. LYNCH. Handbook of Universal Literature.
     Boston: Houghton Mifflin Co., pp. 481-82, passim.
        General comments on works and Spenser's place in literary
     tradition. Notes influence of Ariosto and Tasso on The Faerie
     Queene and that Arthur's appearances in poem unify the separate
     books. Revised edition of 1902.7; 1922.3.

5   BUTLER, W.F. "The Clan Carthy." JCHAS 29:51-59.
        Notes events on and near rivers known to Spenser in
     Buttevant and Doneraile.

6   CARPENTER, FREDERICK IVES. A Reference Guide to Edmund
     Spenser. Chicago: University of Chicago Press, 333 pp.
        Compilation attempts to be comprehensive bibliographical
     guide to Spenser's writings and writings about him. Annotates
     more important items; some scattered commentary. Headings:
     The Life; The Works; Criticism, Influence, Allusions; and Vari-
     ous Topics. Full index. Reprinted: New York: Peter Smith,
     1950; New York: Kraus Reprint Co., 1969.

7   _____. "Spenser Apocrypha." In The Manly Anniversary Studies
     in Language and Literature. Chicago: University of Chicago
     Press, pp. 64-69.
        Examines De Rebus Gestis Britanniae, a Latin chronicle by
     "E.S.," and concludes that the work is not by Spenser.

8   CHAMBERS, E.K. The Elizabethan Stage. Vol. 3. Oxford:
     Clarendon Press, pp. 207, 328.
        Alabaster's Eliseis mentioned in Colin Clouts Come Home
     Againe; identifies Alcon as Lodge. Reprinted: 1934.12.

9   DAVIS, BERNARD E.C. "Our Pleasant Willy." NQ 145:323-24.
        Argues that Willy (Teares of the Muses) is actor Richard
     Tarlton, not Shakespeare, and the "gentle spirit" is Lyly. Sug-
     gests that Spenser added "Willy" stanza as tribute to Tarlton and
     coincidentally placed it near that alluding to Lyly.

*10 De MARR, HARKO G. "A History of Modern English Romanticism."
     Ph.D. diss., University of Amsterdam.
        For published versions, see 1924.11-12.

11   FORREST, H.T.S. Five Authors of "Shake-speares Sonnets."
     London: Chapman & Dodd, pp. 203, 206, 215-16.
          Suggests Spenser as "rival poet."

12   GARNETT, RICHARD, and EDMUND GOSSE. English Literature An
     Illustrated Record. From the Age of Henry VIII to the Age
     of Milton. Vol. 2. New York: Macmillan Co., pp. 109-30.
          Reprint of 1904.12.

13   GARROD, H.W. "Spenser and Elizabeth Boyle." TLS, 10 May,
     p. 321; 24 May, p. 355.
          Suggests that Elizabeth Boyle married three times before
     she married Spenser and was widowed at time of her marriage with
     Spenser. Notes that Elizabeth's "immense readiness to marry
     other suitors" contrasts with hesitant lady of Amoretti. For
     response, see 1923.42.

14   GLOVER, T.R. "Spenser." In Poets and Puritans. 2d ed.
     London: Methuen & Co., pp. 1-33.
          Reprint of 1915.5.

15   GRAVES, THORNTON S. "Some Chaucer Allusions (1561-1700)."
     SP 20:469-78.
          Supplements Spurgeon (1914.17).

16   GREENLAW, EDWIN. "The Captivity Episode in Sidney's Arcadia."
     In The Manly Anniversary Studies in Language and Literature.
     Chicago: University of Chicago Press, pp. 54-63.
          Character of Braggadochio in Book II of The Faerie Queene
     influenced by the Pamela-Cecropia episode in Sidney's Arcadia.
     Reprinted: Freeport, N.Y.: Books for Libraries Press, 1968.

17   _____. "Some Old Religious Cults in Spenser." SP 20:216-43.
          Cites Alanus de Insulis as Spenser's source for Castle of
     Alma, judgment of Nature, Garden of Adonis, Adgistes, Cybele, and
     Temple of Isis. Concludes with five observations: (1) the con-
     siderable extent of passages brought into relationship with one
     another and the large part of Spenser's poetry which they repre-
     sent; (2) Spenser's mysticism is founded on Nature; (3) part of
     Spenser's seeming incoherence belongs to his time; (4) Spenser
     is a prelude to the new spirit of scientific research; (5) love
     is the unifying force in Spenser's universe.

18   HALES, JOHN W. "The Poet's Poet." In Modern English Essays.
     Vol. 2. Edited by Ernest Rhys. London and Toronto: J.M.
     Dent & Sons; New York: E.P. Dutton, pp. 241-46.
          Reprint of 1922.13.

19   HARMAN, EDWARD G. Gabriel Harvey and Thomas Nashe. London:
     J.M. Ouseley & Son, pp. 4-7, 20-23, 118-21, 164-67.
          Maintains that "Spenser" is a pen name for Francis Bacon.

20   HOUSTON, PERCY HAGEN. <u>Doctor Johnson. A Study in Eighteenth
      Century Humanism</u>. Cambridge, Mass.: Harvard University
      Press, pp. 129-36, passim.
          On Johnson's approval of Spenser as a moral teacher and
      Johnson's criticism of imitators of Spenserian pastoral.

21   HUGHES, MERRITT Y. "Spenser and the Greek Pastoral Triad."
      <u>SP</u> 20:184-215.
          Assesses Spenser's direct relationship to pastoral tradi-
      tion of Theocritus, Bion, Moschus, rejecting view that Spenser
      depended on Greek tradition for inspiration. Shows Spenser's
      relationship to classical tradition to be nominal, while real
      influence on <u>The Shepheardes Calender</u> and other poems comes from
      Italian and French pastoralists, especially Marot and poets of
      the Pléiade. Spenser's treatment of love is antithetical to
      that of Theocritus and other classical writers; use of archaisms
      and dialect in <u>The Shepheardes Calender</u> is closer to tradition of
      Ronsard and Du Bellay than to Theocritus.

22   JENKINSON, HILARY. "On Autographs." <u>History</u>, n.s. 8:98-110.
          Suggests that Spenser had two handwritings, which would
      account for the different signatures attributed to him.

*23   KELSO, RUTH. "The Institution of the Gentleman in English
      Literature of the Sixteenth Century. A Study in Renaissance
      Ideals." Ph.D. diss., University of Illinois.
          Published: 1926.26; Revised: 1929.28.

24   KINGSFORD, C.L. "Essex House, Formerly Leicester House and
      Exeter Inn." <u>Archaeologia</u> 73:1-50.
          Harvey introduced Spenser to Sidney, who probably obtained
      for the poet his uncle's patronage. Spenser living in Leicester
      House in 1579 when he wrote to Harvey that he and Sidney were in
      close association. Spenser stayed in Essex House in 1596 and
      wrote <u>Prothalamion</u> there.

*25   KÖHLER, KARL. <u>Das Epitheton ornans in der englischen Poesie
      von Chaucer bis Spenser</u>. Freiburg: [publisher unknown].
          Cited in 1923.6.

26   LEGOUIS, ÉMILE. <u>Edmund Spenser</u>. Les grands écrivains
      étrangers. Paris: Libraire Bloud & Gay, 359 pp.
          Written mainly as general introduction for French readers
      of Spenser. Devotes seven chapters to interrelationships of
      Spenser's life, shorter works, friendship with Leicester, resi-
      dences in Ireland, and court disappointments; four chapters to
      <u>The Faerie Queene</u>, which cover allegory, romance, pageantry, and
      music and scenery. Reprinted: 1926.31; 1930.25; ed. Pierre
      Legouis (Paris: Didier, 1956). Partly reprinted and edited:
      1926.30; 1933.41.

27   LILJEGREN, S.B. "Studies in Philology ed. by Greenlaw--Dey--
      Howe. Vol. xx.2, Published Quarterly by the University of
      North Carolina Press." Anglia Beiblatt 34:362-65.
          Summarizes 1923.21.

*28   McMURPHY, SUSANNAH JANE. "Spenser's Use of Ariosto for
      Allegory." Ph.D. diss., University of Washington.
          For published edition, see 1924.25.

29   MAXWELL, CONSTANTIA. Irish History From Contemporary Sources
      (1509-1610). London: George Allen & Unwin, pp. 60, 73-76,
      151, 171, 250-52, 339, passim.
          Cites A Veue of the Present State of Ireland among docu-
      ments necessary for study of Irish history; reproduces passages
      with some commentary. Finds that "Spenser alone of the writers
      of the period takes a scholarly view of the Irish customs."
      Notes Spenser's associations and service in Ireland. Finds
      Spenser's view of Irish law (that it be fashioned out of the
      customs and conditions of the people) appropriate and sound.

*30   MILLICAN, CHARLES B. "Antiquarianism in Edmund Spenser."
      Master's thesis, University of North Carolina.
          Cited in Stephens, 1950.

31   O'BRIEN, GEORGE, ed. Advertisements for Ireland. Being a
      description of the State of Ireland in the reign of James I,
      contained in a manuscript in the library of Trinity College
      Dublin. Dublin: Royal Society of Antiquaries of Ireland,
      71 pp.
          Cites Spenser's A Veue of the Present State of Ireland.

32   PADELFORD, FREDERICK MORGAN. "The Spiritual Allegory of The
      Faerie Queene, Book One." JEGP 22:1-17.
          Spiritual allegory of Book I of The Faerie Queene is "the
      growth in grace, through experience and instruction, of a Chris-
      tian gentleman." Formally, allegory is indebted to medieval and
      Italian Renaissance romances, morality plays and moral allegories
      of early Tudor period, and to Aristotle's Ethics. Spiritually,
      Spenser is indebted to the idealism of Protestant Christianity,
      especially as Calvin defines it in the Institutes, and to the
      idealism of Plato and his Italian followers.

33   PLOMER, HENRY R. "Edmund Spenser's Handwriting." MP 21:
      201-7.
          Presents evidence to show that Spenser used both Italian
      and Secretary forms of handwriting.

34   _____. "Spenser's Handwriting." TLS, 26 April, p. 287.
          Document in Irish State Papers "sets at rest the vexed
      question" of Spenser's handwriting.

*35   POPE, EMMA FIELD. "The Reflection of Renaissance Criticism
       in Edmund Spenser's Faerie Queene." Ph.D. diss., University
       of Chicago.
            Published version: 1926.44.

 36   RENWICK, W.L., ed. Introduction to Spenser. Selections with
       Essays by Hazlitt, Coleridge, and Leigh Hunt. Oxford:
       Clarendon Press, pp. v-xv.
            Discusses Spenser's poetic theory and style. Notes that
       by time Spenser published The Shepheardes Calender (at age 27)
       he was master of his art, so his "obscured" allusions and borrow-
       ings are deliberate, not due merely to "a century of 'romantic'
       criticism." Reprinted: 1929.36; 1946.

 37   RICKERT, EDITH. "Political Propaganda and Satire in A Mid-
       summer Night's Dream." MP 21:133-54.
            Notes a precedent for political allegory in Spenser and
       Lyly that may have influenced Shakespeare in writing A Midsummer
       Night's Dream. Spenser developed "trick" of using several char-
       acters in same piece to flatter the Queen.

*38   ROWE, KENNETH T. "Spenser and Ovid." Ph.D. diss., Rice
       Institute (Houston).
            Cited in 1930.23.

 39   SAINTSBURY, GEORGE. A History of English Prosody. From the
       Origins to Spenser. Vol. 2. London: Macmillan & Co.,
       pp. 350-69.
            Reprint of 1908.32.

 40   SEATON, ETHEL. "Phineas Fletcher--A New MS." TLS, 22 March,
       p. 199.
            Fletcher MS (in Sion College Library) includes Venus and
       Anchises, identical in substance to "Brittain's Ida," which
       previously was thought to be Spenser's. Lines added to Venus
       and Anachises prove Fletcher's authorship.

 41   SHEPPARD, S. "Third Pastoral Appended to His Epigrams."
       SP 20:274-76.
            Notes in dialogue of Linus and Coridon their comments on
       former shepherds Tityrus and Colin Clout who "was the Prince of
       Shepherds nam'd."

 42   WELPLY, W.H. "Spenser and Elizabeth Boyle." TLS, 24 May,
       pp. 355-56.
            Rejects Garrod's assumptions (1923.13) about Elizabeth
       Boyle's marriages by showing inconsistencies in his dates.

1924

1   BALDWIN, T.W.   "The Three Francis Beaumonts."   MLN 39:505-7.
         Praise for Spenser in Lady Newdigate-Newgate's Gossip from
Francis Beaumont, Master of the Charterhouse, not from Beaumont
the dramatist.

*2   BAUER, R.   "Die Iren und die irischen Verhältnisse der
         Elisabethanischen Zeit in der Dorstelling von Edm. Spenser
         und den 'Calenders of the Carew Papers' Ein Beitr. zu eng.-
         irischen Kulturgeschichte."   Ph.D. diss., University of
         Halle.
         Cited in Atkinson, 1937.

3   BERDAN, JOHN M.   "The Family of The Faerie Queene."   Johns
         Hopkins Alumni Magazine 12:267-87.
         Considers the Italian "ancestors" of The Faerie Queene:
Pulci, Boiardo, Ariosto, Tasso.

4   CARPENTER, FREDERICK IVES.   "G.W. Senior and G.W.I."   MP 22:
         67-68.
         Speculation on identity of authors of sonnets prefixed to
Amoretti.

5   _____.   "The Marriages of Edmund Spenser."   MP 22:97-98.
         Comments on two records of the marriages of Edmund Spenser.

6   COLE, GEORGE WATSON.   "Bibliographical Pitfalls -- Linked
         Books."   Papers of the Bibliographical Society of America
         18:12-30.
         Focuses on bibliographer's problems with books published as
one volume, but found in separate parts, e.g., Spenser's A Veue
of the Present State of Ireland published by James Ware with histories by Campion and Hanmer.

7   COVINGTON, F[RANK] F., Jr.   "Biographical Notes on Spenser."
         MP 22:63-66.
         Conjectures on Spenser's residence in Ireland: his land-
holding, friends, and activity in Dublin.

8   _____.   "Spenser in Ireland."   Ph.D. diss., Yale University,
         pt. 1, 143 pp., pt. 2, 258 pp.
         Focuses on "the facts of Spenser's Irish residence" and the
references and allusions to Ireland in Spenser's poetry and prose:
Part 1 is biography of Spenser with emphasis on years in Ireland;
Part 2 details Irish influences in Spenser's works. Concludes in
Part 1 that Spenser's life in Ireland was not a punishment or an
exile; that he was encouraged to go by Lodowick Bryskett and
Edward Waterhouse; that he enjoyed friends and confortable income
at Kilcolman; and thus his controversies with Lord Roche were due
in part to fact that Roche's lands surrounded Kilcolman. Concludes

in Part 2 that large number of Irish references and allusions in
The Faerie Queene and A Veue of the Present State of Ireland show
Spenser to be well informed on Irish geography, topography, land-
scape, classes of people, manners, and customs. Notes that
Spenser displays "typically English attitude, of superiority and
distrust, toward the Irish" in The Faerie Queene and A Veue of
the Present State of Ireland. Notes Spenser's sources for Irish
antiquities and history as Holinshed, Camden, and Buchanan, as
well as unprinted sources and Irish chronicles. Includes discussion of Colin Clouts Come Home Againe. Part 2, Chapter 7,
Published: 1924.9.

9   COVINGTON, FRANK F., Jr. "Spenser's Use of Irish History in
     The Veue of the Present State of Ireland." University of Texas
     Bulletin, Studies in English 4:5-38.
        Presents detailed evidence to conclude "that Spenser's
     knowledge of Irish history was fairly wide, although not pro-
     found or exact." Discusses Spenser's inexactness and careless-
     ness with details, yet "he possessed a knowledge of minutiae not
     to be gained from general reading"; Spenser's reliance on
     Holinshed's Chronicles and his use of other books, legends and
     traditions, frequently distilling facts from several sources into
     one passage; Spenser's critical attitude toward Irish sources,
     but his careless use of material (even legendary material) in
     English sources (this "he seems to have accepted as sober fact");
     Spenser's regard for all data from an English viewpoint--"while
     at times his adherence to his sources, particularly to Holinshed,
     is rather close, he seems generally to have depended upon his
     memory--which was not infallible--for his fact." Provides in-
     sights into Spenser's life in Ireland.

*10   DeBLACAM, HUGH. "Secret of Spenser." Literary Review 5:1-2.
         Cited in Atkinson, 1937.

11   De MARR, HARKO GERRIT. Elizabethan Romance in the Eighteenth
      Century. Zalt-Bommel: N.V. Van de Garde & Co., passim.
         Considers eighteenth-century editions of Spenser, Spenserian
      stanza and diction in seventeenth centuries. Traces influence of
      Spenser, with special emphasis on Milton. Reprinted with new
      title: 1924.12; New York: Haskell House, 1964.

12   _____. A History of Modern English Romanticism: Elizabethan
      and Modern Romanticism in the Eighteenth Century. Vol. 1.
      London: Humphrey Milford, Oxford University Press, pp. 1-109,
      221-32, passim.
         Treats in detail Spenser's influence in seventeenth and
      eighteenth centuries, distinguishing imitators as Elizabethan
      and Augustan Spenserians: "the Elizabethan Spenserians admired
      the romantic quality of Spenser, they imitated his sensuous glow;
      the Augustan Spenserians admired the epic quality of Spenser, they
      imitated him in a mood of burlesque, which soon changed into a
      serious spirit." These two types eventually "merged into the

modern Spenserians, who applied Spenser's stanza in their own way
and for their own purposes." Includes chapters and bibliography
on "English Editions of Spenser . . . in the Eighteenth Century";
"The Spenserian Stanza in the Seventeenth and Eighteenth Centuries"; "Spenserian Diction in the Seventeenth and Eighteenth
Centuries"; "Elizabethan Spenserians"; "The Life and Works of
Samual Croxall, D.D."; and "Augustan Spenserians." Concludes
that total influence of Spenser and Milton upon modern romanticism lies in three areas--form, diction, and, most important,
imaginative power; and that "the genuine Spenserianism of the
eighteenth century was . . . more a belated Elizabethan Romanticism than an early outburst of Modern Romanticism." Study also
includes thorough discussion of Spenser's influence on Milton.
Reprint of 1923.11; 1924.11. Reprinted: New York: Haskell
House, 1964.

13   De REUL, PAUL. "Le poète Spenser, à propos d'un livre récent."
      Revue de L'Université de Bruxelles 29, no. 3:268-80.
            Discusses Spenser's works in general mainly from perspec-
      tive of Legouis (1923.26). Concludes: "Le charme de Spenser,
      c'est la Renaissance en fleur, le printemps qui se change en été,
      le moment exquis où le moyen âge anglais, sous l'encourageant
      sourire d l'Italie, découvre les Grâces antiques."

14   De SELINCOURT, E., ed. Introduction to The Poetical Works of
      Edmund Spenser. London, New York, and Toronto: Humphrey
      Milford, Oxford University Press, pp. vii-lxvii.
            Reprint of 1912.11.

15   DRAPER, JOHN. "The Narrative-Technique of The Faerie Queene."
      PMLA 39:310-24.
            Concludes that form of The Faerie Queene was "dictated by
      the Italian criticism of the forty years preceding," but content
      came from various areas: Italian poets, Malory, English romances,
      classics.

16   DUNLOP, ROBERT. "An Unpublished Survey of the Plantation of
      Munster in 1622." JRSAI 54:128-46.
            Presents excerpts from British Museum Sloane MS 4756,
      fol. 80, dating after 1622, James I having appointed a commission
      for the survey. Notes condition of Spenser's property and de-
      scribes his new house.

17   FAIRCHILD, HOXIE NEALE. "The Classic Poets of English Litera-
      ture: II. Edmund Spenser." Literary Digest International
      Book Review 2:542-43.
            Introduction to Spenser through brief consideration of Book
      I of The Faerie Queene in terms of complex mingling of medieval,
      pagan, and Christian elements, the distinctive stanza form, the
      meandering narrative, and the moral and political allegory.

18   HAINES, C.R. "Timon: And Other Emendations." TLS, 6 March,
      p. 144.
           Supports view that Rosalind in The Shepheardes Calender is
      Rose Daniel; identifies Menalcas as Florio, whom Rose married.

19   HOLLOWELL, B.M. "The Elizabethan Hexametrists." PQ 3:51-57.
           General discussion of movement (1570-1590) in English
      prosody to introduce classical meters into English poetry;
      Spenser named among others.

20   KNOWLTON, E.C. "Genius as an Allegorical Figure." MLN 39:
      89-95.
           Spenser in general tradition against intemperance of the
      flesh which developed on the basis of Alan of Lille's precepts.
      For a related study, see 1928.28.

21   LANGDON, IDA. Milton's Theory of Poetry and Fine Art. An
      Essay with a Collection of Illustrative Passages from His
      Works. New Haven: Yale University Press; London: Humphrey
      Milford, Oxford University Press, pp. 13, 30-31, 39, 65, 76,
      134, 140, passim.
           Refers to Spenser as influence on Milton and for parallels
      to Milton. Comments on Platonic influences, relationships be-
      tween The Faerie Queene and Paradise Lost, and Spenser's and
      Milton's condemnation of poetasters. Reprinted: New York:
      Russell & Russell, 1965.

22   LAW, ROBERT ADGER. "Tripartite Gaul in the Story of King
      Leir." Texas Studies in English 4:39-48.
           In The Faerie Queene, II.x.29, "Celtica" is "the central
      division of Gaul." Cordelia "was sent to Aganip of Celtica."

23   LONGFIELD, ADA. "Anglo-Irish Trade in the Sixteenth Century
      as Illustrated by the English Customs Accounts and Port Books."
      Proceedings of the Royal Irish Academy 36.C:317-25.
           Comments on A Veue of the Present State of Ireland.

*24   McGILL, WINIFRED. "A Study of the Spirit of Edmund Spenser."
      Master's thesis, University of Washington.
           Cited in Stephens, 1950.

25   McMURPHY, SUSANNA JANE. Spenser's Use of Ariosto for Allegory.
      University of Washington Publications in Language and Litera-
      ture, vol. 2. Seattle: University of Washington Press, 1-54.
           A study in three parts. First considers nature, extent, and
      method of Spenser's borrowings from Ariosto's "genuine" allegory,
      i.e., allegory intended by Ariosto and not devised by commentators
      and translators. Considers secondly possible relationship between
      changing style of Books III and IV of The Faerie Queene and changes
      in nature of Spenser's borrowings from Ariosto. In these books
      Spenser converts romance elements in Ariosto, i.e., non-allegorical
      characters, actions, and places, to purposes of his own allegory.

Considers finally Ariosto as source for characters and their fortunes in Spenser's political allegory. Published version of 1923.28. Reprinted: Folcroft, Pa.: Folcroft Press, 1969.

26   MARSH, E. "An Emendation in Spenser's <u>Prothalamium</u>." <u>London Mercury</u> 9, no. 51 (January):300.
     "Brides" in line 176 should read "Birdes."

*27 MARTIN, CLIFF, ed. "Edition of <u>View of Ireland</u>." Ph.D. diss., Cornell University, 538 pp.
     Cited in Atkinson, 1937.

*28 MOCK, H.B. "Influence of Ovid on Spenser." Ph.D. diss., University of North Carolina.
     Cited in National Union Catalog.

29   NICOLSON, MARGARET ERSKINE. "Realistic Elements in Spenser's Style." <u>SP</u> 21:382-98.
     Demonstrates six kinds of realism in Spenser's poetry: (1) reference to rural nature in general or to specific places or things; (2) references to rural life; (3) personal or psychological descriptions relating to people; (4) touches of realism or local color introduced by means of a few words; (5) colloquialisms of rustic conversation; (6) realistic descriptions of court, clergy, and other walks of life. Studies "the realistic touches that give vividness to the pastoral scenes in the <u>Calender</u>, that give much of the sting to the satire in <u>Mother Hubberd's Tale</u> and that by contrast lend an added brilliance to the romance of the <u>Faerie Queene</u>."

30   PADELFORD, FREDERICK M. "The Allegory of Chastity in <u>The Faerie Queene</u>." <u>SP</u> 21:367-81.
     Book III of <u>The Faerie Queene</u> does not depart from Spenser's original design. The book expounds virtue of chastity, and is unified and organic. Cites two reasons for position of chastity in the poem: (1) if the three books were published to secure royal favor and financial assistance, they should include an embodiment of Queen Elizabeth; (2) chastity logically follows continence (temperance).

31   PIENAAR, W.J.B. "Spenser's 'Complaints.'" <u>TLS</u>, 4 Decmeber, p. 825.
     Presents line readings to show Spenser's careful use of sources (mainly Du Bellay's <u>Songe</u>) in <u>Visions of Bellay</u>, <u>Visions of Petrarch</u>, and <u>A Theatre for Worldlings</u>.

*32 PIERCE, G.A. <u>Red Cross Knight and the Legend of Britomart</u>. New York: John Martin's Bookhouse.
     Cited in 1930.23.

*33   SAURAT, DENIS. "Les idées philosophiques de Spenser."
       Yearbook of the New Society of Letters at Lund 1 (December).
       Lund: Gleerup; London: Oxford University Press.
            For translated edition, see 1930.42.

 34   SHIPLEY, JOSEPH T. "Spenserian Prosody: The Couplet Forms."
       SP 21:594-615.
            Studies prosody of Mother Hubberds Tale, Colin Clouts Come
       Home Againe, and "February," "May," and "September" eclogues of
       The Shepheardes Calender to show close correspondence between
       use of octosyllabic and heroic couplet forms in Spenser and
       Chaucer. Argues Spenser's knowledgeable use of Chaucerian final
       "e."

 35   SPURGEON, CAROLINE F.E. Five Hundred Years of Chaucer Criti-
       cism and Allusion (1357-1900): Introduction. London: Oxford
       University Press; London and New York: Kegan Paul, Trench,
       Trubner & Co., pp. xxiii-xxv.
            Mentions Spenser's admiration for Chaucer and his allusions
       to him in his works. For other volumes, see 1914.17; 1918.26;
       1921.17; 1922.24. Reprinted: 1925.31; New York: Russell &
       Russell, 1960.

 36   TAYLOR, A.E. "Spenser's Knowledge of Plato." MLR 19:208-10.
            Concludes from errors in two passages in The Faerie Queene
       that "Spenser's knowledge about Socrates does not go beyond a
       confused recollection of certain works of Cicero."

 37   WEIBEL, K. "Phineas Fletcher's Purple Island in Ihrer
       Abhangigkeit von Spenser's Faerie Queene." Englische Studien
       58:321-67.
            Discusses parallels between Spenser and Fletcher and lines
       of influence.

*38   WELLS, HENRY W. "Poetic Imagery Illustrated from Elizabethan
       Literature." Ph.D. diss., Columbia University.
            For published edition, see 1924.39.

 39   _____. Poetic Imagery Illustrated from Elizabethan Literature.
       New York: Columbia University Press, pp. 58-68, 138-68,
       passim.
            Discusses eight types of imagery: Decorative, Sunken,
       Violent, Radical, Intensive, Expansive, Exuberant, Humorous.
       Spenser represents the Intensive, an image "of high imaginative
       value in which clarity and concentration associate the minor term
       with pictorial art." Shows Spenser to be "the first master in
       Elizabethan poetry" of Intensive imagery with numerous examples
       from The Faerie Queene. Commentary on Decorative imagery of The
       Shepheardes Calender, Prothalamion, and Epithalamion, and ele-
       ments of other types of imagery in Spenser's poetry. Published
       version of 1924.38.

40   WELPLY, W.H. "Edmund Spenser: Some New Discoveries." NQ
     146:445-47.
         Presents biographical data on Elizabeth Boyle and Spenser's
     children, Sylvanus, Peregrine, and Catherine. For correction,
     see 1924.41.

41   _____. "Edmund Spenser: Some New Discoveries." NQ 147:35.
         Corrects earlier assertion (1924.40) on name of Spenser's
     daughter.

42   WINSTANLEY, LILIAN, ed. Introduction to The Faerie Queene,
     Book I. Cambridge: Cambridge University Press, pp. vii-lxxx.
     Reprint of 1915.18.

                              1925

*1   ARIAIL, J.M. "Some Immediate English Influences, Faerie
     Queene, Books I-III." Ph.D. diss., University of North
     Carolina.
         Cited in National Union Catalog.

*2   BEATTY, ELSIE. "The Criticism of Spenser During the Eighteenth
     Century." Master's thesis, University of Illinois.
         Cited in Stephens, 1950.

 3   BLANCHARD, HAROLD H. "Imitations from Tasso in The Faerie
     Queene." SP 22:189-221.
         A continuation of Koeppel's study of parallel passages in
     The Faerie Queene and Tasso's poems. Lists twenty-one parallels,
     in the order they appear in The Faerie Queene, with the Rinaldo
     and the Gerusalemme Liberata.

 4   _____. "Spenser and Boiardo." PMLA 40:828-51.
         Demonstrates that "Spenser had read the Orlando Innamorato,
     that it lay in his memory along with his reading of other romances
     of chivalry, and that parts of it asserted themselves when occa-
     sion was offered in the creation of his own poem." Cites fifteen
     parallel passages.

 5   COVINGTON, F[RANK] F., Jr. "A Note on Faerie Queene IV.iii.27."
     MLN 40:253.
         Cites Spenser's comparison of the fluctuating fortunes of
     the battle between Cambell and Triamond to the powerful tide in
     the river Shannon (IV.iii.27) as one of Spenser's earliest speci-
     fic references in The Faerie Queene to his Irish environment.

 6   COVINGTON, FRANK F., Jr. "Spenser and Alexander Neckham."
     SP 22:222-25.
         Finds possible source for Spenser's pageant of the rivers
     in The Faerie Queene, IV.xi in the De Laudibus Divinae Sapientiae

                              111

of Alexander Neckham (1157-1217) or in excerpts from it included
in 1590 edition of Camden's Britannia.

7   DAVIS, BERNARD E.C. "The Text of Spenser's 'Complaints.'"
     MLR 20:18-24.
          Compares Folio edition (1611) of Complaints with Quarto
     (1591) to show that Spenser helped prepare volume for publica-
     tion. Speculates on reasons for textual revision in satire of
     The Ruines of Time and omission of Mother Hubberds Tale from
     first Folio edition.

8   DUCKETT, ELEANOR SHIPLEY. Catullus in English Poetry. Smith
     College Classical Studies, no. 6. Edited by Julia Harwood
     Caverno and Florence Alden Cragg. Menacha, Wis.: George
     Banta Publishing Co., pp. 108-13, 130-31, 146-47.
          Prints excerpts from Epithalamion and The Faerie Queene
     beside Catullus's Carmen 61, Carmen 62, and Carmen 64 as part
     of demonstration of Latin's poet's influence on English poetry
     from Herrick to twentieth century.

*9   GREENLAW, EDWIN A. "The New Science and English Literature in
     the Seventeenth Century." Tudor and Stuart Club Lecture, 1925.
     Johns Hopkins Alumni Magazine 13:331-59.
          Cited in Atkinson, 1937. Comments on scientific learning
     in Mother Hubberds Tale and The Faerie Queene.

*10 ____. "An Outline of English Thought in the Sixteenth Cen-
     tury." Proceedings of Dr. Greenlaw's Seminary "C," 1925-26,
     no. 1. Manuscript. Baltimore: Johns Hopkins University
     Library.
          Cited in Atkinson, 1937.

11   HARMAN, EDWARD GEORGE. The "Impersonality" of Shakespeare.
     London: Cecil Palmer, pp. 274-91, 310-26, passim.
          Identifies Timias as Essex and Scudamour as Raleigh in
     The Faerie Queene.

*12 HEFFNER, RAY. "Spenser and the British Sea-Power." Master's
     thesis, University of North Carolina.
          Cited in Stephens, 1950.

13   HUGHES, MERRITT Y. "Spenser's Debt to the Greek Romances."
     MP 23:67-76.
          Discusses Heliodorus, Longus, and Achilles Tatius as
     direct influences on The Faerie Queene. Concludes that Spenser
     ultimately derived from Longus or Heliodorus four motifs in the
     Pastorella story: escape from sacrifice, exposure, being car-
     ried to a cave, and riddling prophecy. None is developed in a
     way to commit them to a definite Greek source, and all had ana-
     logues in Renaissance Literature.

14   LEA, KATHLEEN M. "Conceits." <u>MLR</u> 20:389-406.
      Spenser brought to his conceits the colored world of
Ariosto, the mysticism of Ficino, memory of pageants he wit-
nessed in the streets or masques given in the halls of nobility.

15   LEE, SIDNEY. <u>Great Englishmen of the Sixteenth Century</u>.
      London: G.G. Harrap.
         Reprint of 1904.27.

*16   LEIBLE, ARTHUR B. "<u>Mother Hubberds Tale</u>, Edited with Intro-
      duction, Notes, and Glossary." Master's thesis, Indiana
      University.
         Cited in Stephens, 1950.

17   McELDERRY, BRUCE ROBERT, Jr. "Spenser's Poetic Diction."
      Ph.D. diss., University of Iowa, 239 pp.
         Reviews criticism of Spenserian diction to twentieth cen-
tury, and sixteenth century theory and practice in diction; analyzes E.K.'s glosses in <u>The Shepheardes Calender</u> of familiar
words, variations of meaning, and archaisms; discusses further
use of dialect and archaism and further innovations in later
works; also discusses Spenser's traditional diction. Appendix:
"complete alphabetical lists of the words which . . . were part
of Spenser's 'individual' diction, that is words used by Spenser
which were not a part of the accepted literary language when he
began to write." Words categorized as archaisms, dialect words,
importations, coinages, variations, and adoptions.

*18   MAXWELL, WILLIAM C. "Word-Compounding in Spenser." Ph.D.
      diss., University of Washington.
         Cited in Atkinson, 1937.

19   MILLS, LAURENS J. "The Renascence Development in England of
      the Classical Ideas about Friendship." Ph.D. diss., Univer-
      sity of Chicago, pp. 260-73.
         Spenser's ideas of friendship in Book IV of <u>The Faerie
Queene</u> represent pure return to Aristotelianism, though he was
possibly influenced by frequent treatment of the theme in current literature.

*20   MITCHELL, ANNA F. "<u>Colin Clouts Come Home Againe</u>, Edited with
      Introduction, Notes, and Glossary." Master's thesis, Indiana
      University.
         Cited in Stephens, 1950.

*21   NEWBOLT, HENRY. "Some Poets and Their Scenery." In <u>Essays by
      Divers Hands, Being the Transactions of the Royal Society of
      Literature of the United Kingdom</u>. Edited by John Drinkwater.
      N.s. 5. Oxford: Oxford University Press, pp. 130-32.
         Cited in Atkinson, 1937. Notes influences on <u>The Shepheardes
Calender</u>.

*22   NIX, MARTHA J.   "A Study of the Influence of the Morality
      Plays on Spenser's Faerie Queene, Master's thesis, University
      of Washington.
         Cited in Stephens, 1950.

23   NOTCUTT, H. CLEMENT.   "Spenser's Wonderful Line."   Spectator
     135:305.
         Responds to query (1925.32), citing "Spenser's wonderful
     line" in The Faerie Queene, I.xi.45.

24   OSGOOD, CHARLES G[ROSVENOR].   "Lycidas 130, 131."   RES 1:339-41.
         If Milton's "two-handed engine at the door" is the iron
     flail of Talus, Milton may have recalled Talus's battering of
     the castle of Munera and Pollente or Munera's attempt to divert
     him from his vengeance in The Faerie Queene, V.ii.   This would
     assume the enemies of the Church to be within the fold and that
     vengeance awaits them just outside.   If the enemies threaten from
     without, Milton may have thought of Britomart's sleepless night
     in Dolon's castle under Talus's careful watch, or of Talus watch-
     ing all night before Britomart's pavilion, against attack from
     Radigund, or of his exposure of Braggadochio and Trompart, or of
     his redressing ills and establishing justice in Irena's realm.
     Thus, Talus "wields everywhere his weapon . . . to drive our
     corruption, usurpation, injustice, and all other political ills
     with which Milton particularly charged Episcopacy."   Concludes
     that these lines "are but another instance of the allusive
     Alexandrian splendour in which he [Milton] excelled all rivals."

25   PARKER, ROSCOE E.   "Spenser's Language and the Pastoral
     Tradition."   Language 1:80-87.
         Contends that "Spenser's pastoral poetry is purposely more
     archaic than his non-pastoral. . . .   The pastoral Colin Clout
     is more archaic in diction than the earlier chivalric Faerie
     Queene," which shows that Spenser, "following the well-established
     pastoral tradition, consciously used a specialized diction for
     pastoral poetry."

26   PEARSON, A.F. SCOTT.   Thomas Cartwright and Elizabethan Puri-
     tanism 1535-1603.   Cambridge: Cambridge University Press,
     pp. 188-89.
         Identifies Thomalin ("March," The Shepheardes Calender) as
     Thomas Cartwright, whose works reflect Thomalin's Puritan argu-
     ments; suggests that choice of Hugh Singleton as printer of The
     Shepheardes Calender strengthens Spenser's Puritan sympathies.

27   POCK, WALTER EDWIN.   "The Poet's Poet."   TLS, 1 January, p. 9.
         Phrase used first in reference to Shelley.   Lamb first to
     apply it to Spenser.

28   RENWICK, W.L.   Edmund Spenser: An Essay on Renaissance Poetry.
     London: Edward Arnold & Co., 198 pp.

In first four chapters discusses humanistic and poetic backgrounds. As a young student, Spenser "learned the theory of the new poetry: to cultivate the mother tongue by the imitation of the best learning and . . . of the best models to be found." Spenser taught in school and by Latin, Italian, and French poets and critics to apply humanist system to vernacular poetry. In "The Kinds of Poetry" discusses genres in which Spenser wrote the new poetry, their precedence in ancient and modern poetry, and his guidance by modern theory and commentary. The Faerie Queene is Spenser's attempt to reconcile old native virtues and new literary demands. Discusses shorter works and Complaints. Third chapter, "Style and Language," discusses growth of Spenser's style out of his treatment of language. Deals with relationship between foreign and native tongues, and outgrowth of style from form, with the added criteria of decorum, inventiveness, and individuality. Spenser adapted techniques of French predecessors to his own improvement of the English language. Fourth chapter extends consideration of style to "Verse and Metre." "Imitation; Matter, Allegory," the fifth chapter, discusses variety and scope of Spenser's imitations, the variety of matter, his debts to Latin, Italian, and French writers, and various modes of allegory. Spenser's "Philosophy" variously borrowed from Lucretius, Cicero, Italian Neoplatonists, Aristotle, Calvin, and the Bible, and incorporated into his work. Spenser, a constructive idealist. Final chapter, "'The Prince of Poets in his Tyme,'" is a comprehensive discussion of Spenser's vocation as poet and his vision of poetry: "That he might be a great poet, that England might be seen among the nations in poetry as in war and traffic and exploration, that he might construct a comprehensive ideal of life and make it attractive to men, Spenser studied how poetry should be written, and first of all how it had been written." He laid foundations for all succeeding generations of poets. Reprinted: London: Methuen, 1965.

29   SCHIRMER, WALTER F. "Das Sonett in der englischen Literatur." Anglia, 49, 1-31.
       Notes Spenser's sonnet form.

*30   SHERRICK, HAZEL L. "A Study of Edmund Spenser's Mutability." Master's thesis, University of Washington.
       Cited in Stephens, 1950.

31   SPURGEON, CAROLINE F.E. Five Hundred Years of Chaucer Criticism and Allusion, 1357-1900. 3 vols. Cambridge: Cambridge University Press, passim.
       Reprint in three volumes of 1914.17; 1918.26; 1921.17; 1922.24; 1924.35. Reprinted: New York: Haskell House, 1960.

32   STEELE, AGNES M.A. "A Query." Spectator 135:16.
       Queries location of "Spencer's [sic] wonderful line." For response, see 1925.23.

33   THOMPSON, FRANCIS. "The Poet's Poet." In The Works of Francis
     Thompson. Vol. 1. Edited by Wilfrid Maynell. London: Burns
     & Oats; New York: Charles Scribner's Sons, pp. 140-46, passim.
          Abridged version of 1903.30. Reprint of 1913.38.

34   VEN-TEN BENSEL, ELISE FRANCISCA WILHELMINA MARIA van der.
     The Character of King Arthur in English Literature.
     Amsterdam: H.J. Paris, pp. 159-67.
          Contrasts Arthur of The Faerie Queene with Arthur of
     Malory's Morte Darthur in terms of Spenser's hero's threefold
     personality, twofold allegorical nature, and his actual role as
     fairy-prince. Reprinted: New York: Haskell House, 1966.

*35 WEBB, WILLIAM S. "Studies in the Renaissance Fable with
     Special Reference to Spenser." Master's thesis, University
     of North Carolina.
          Cited in Stephens, 1950.

                                1926

1   ALBRIGHT, EVELYN MAY. "The Faerie Queene in Masque at the
     Gray's Inn Revels." PMLA 41:497-516.
          Shows that "the Proteus masque contains a fairly explicit
     announcement, to the court of Elizabeth, of the impending publi
     cation of Part II of The Faerie Queene, in connection with the
     acknowledgement of it as source; and that parts of Book IV and
     V (as yet unpublished) gave suggestions for two little masques,
     of Amity and of Proteus, in the Christmas Revels at Gray's Inn
     and at court in the winter of 1594-5."

*2   BINKLEY, HAROLD C. "Letter-Writing in English Literature."
     Ph.D. diss., Harvard University.
          Cited in Atkinson, 1937. Includes Spenser-Harvey
     correspondence.

3   BOAS, F.S. Preface to Venus and Anichises. Edited by Ethel
     Seaton. Oxford: Oxford University Press, pp. v-viii, xlix-li.
          Disproves Spenser's authorship.

4   BOAS, GUY. Chaucer and Spenser. London and Edinburgh:
     Thomas Nelson & Sons, 262 pp.
          General introduction to poets with selections from major
     works. Interprets Mother Hubberds Tale as satire on Anjou affair
     with lion representing Elizabeth, Anjou as the ape, Burghley as
     fox, and Leicester as Mercury. This satire led to Spenser's exile.
     Interprets The Faerie Queene as political and moral allegory in
     praise of Elizabeth who appears as Gloriana, Belphoebe, Britomart,
     Mercilla, and Una.

5   BUYSSENS, E. "Calvinism in the Faerie Queene of Spenser."
    Revue belge de philologie et d'histoire 5:37-69, 381-400.
         Compares Calvin and Spenser, concluding that Book I of
    The Faerie Queene is, under allegorical form, a detailed state-
    ment of Calvin's doctrine of salvation as set out in the
    Institution Cretienne. For related study, see 1934.11.

6   CALDWELL, JAMES RALSTON. "Dating a Spenser-Harvey Letter."
    PMLA 41:568-74.
         Argues that the 5 October letter, which reveals something
    of Spenser's relationship with Leicester and mentions the
    Areopagus, divides neatly into two parts; the Latin poem and
    final paragraph were written on 5 October and the rest on 15
    and 16 October.

7   CAWLEY, ROBERT R. "A Chaucerian Echo in Spenser." MLN 41:
    313-14.
         Finds verbal echo of Chaucer's House of Fame (lines 2141-51)
    in The Faerie Queene, I.iv.16.7-8.

8   COURTHOPE, WILLIAM JOHN. "Court Allegory: Edmund Spenser."
    In A History of English Poetry. Vol. 2. London: Macmillan &
    Co., pp. 234-87.
         Reprint of 1920.4.

9   COVINGTON, F.F., Jr. "An Early Seventeenth-Century Criticism
    of Spenser." MLN 41:386-87.
         Notes Thomas Heywood's quote, apparently from memory, from
    The Shepheardes Calender in The Hierarchie of the Blessed Angells
    (1635).

10 De SELINCOURT, E., ed. Introduction to The Poetical Works of
    Edmund Spenser. London, New York, and Toronto: Humphrey
    Milford, Oxford University Press, pp. vii-lxvii.
         Reprint of 1912.11.

11 DOWNS, BRIAN W. Cambridge Past and Present. London: Methuen
    & Co.; New York: George H. Doran Co., pp. 121-22.
         Spenser, Pembroke's "greatest nurseling," enjoyed the com-
    pany of Edmund Kirke and Gabriel Harvey. Recounts Harvey's
    attempts to persuade Spenser to write quantitative verse.

12 DRAPER, JOHN W. "More Light on Spenser's Linguistics." MLN
    41:127-28.
         Considers two etymologies ("tanistry" and "Scot") which
    Spenser perhaps derived from Camden and Holinshed. For related
    studies, see 1919.3; 1922.7.

*13 DURKEE, CORA L. "Britannia's Pastorals as a Spenserian Imita-
    tion." Master's thesis, Yale University Press.
         Cited in Stephens, 1950.

14   FINNEY, CLAUDE L. "Keats's Philosophy of Beauty: An Inter-
      pretation of the Allegory of Endymion in light of the Neo-
      Platonism of Spenser." PQ 5:1-19.
          Spenser's conceptions of nature, art, friendship, and love,
      especially in The Faerie Queene and Fowre Hymnes, provide basis
      for Keats's Neoplatonic philosophy of beauty in Endymion.

*15   FORD, MILDRED. "Spenser's Characterization in The Faerie
      Queene." Master's thesis, University of Colorado.
          Cited in Stephens, 1950.

*16   FRIEDRICH, W.G. "Christian Mysticism in Spenser's Fowre
      Hymnes," "Elfin," "Notes on the Faerie Queene," "Spenser's
      Cup of Gold with Wine and Water," and "Spenser's Tree of
      Life and the Legend of the True History of the Cross." Pro-
      ceedings of Dr. Greenlaw's Seminary "C," 1926-27, nos. 28, 31,
      38, 40, 60, 65. Manuscript. Baltimore: Johns Hopkins Uni-
      versity Library.
          Cited in Atkinson, 1937.

17   GARNETT, RICHARD, and EDMUND GOSSE. English Literature An
      Illustrated Record. From the Age of Henry VIII to the Age of
      Milton. Vol. 2. New York: Macmillan Co., pp. 109-30.
          Reprint of 1904.12.

18   GREENLAW, EDWIN. "Two Notes on Spenser's Classical Sources."
      MLN 41:323-26.
          Finds source for lines 233-43 of Colin Clouts Come Home
      Againe in Apollonius Rhodius's Argonautica and for The Faerie
      Queene, II.iii.41 in Hesiod's Works and Days.

19   GREENOUGH, JAMES BRADSTREET, and GEORGE LYMAN KITTREDGE.
      Words and Their Ways in English Speech. New York and London:
      Macmillan, pp. 118, 295, 354, 375.
          Reprint of 1901.11.

*20   HARD, FREDERICK. "Spenser's Use of Chiaroscuro." Proceedings
      of Dr. Greenlaw's Seminary "C," 1926-27, no. 16. Manuscript.
      Baltimore: Johns Hopkins University Library.
          Cited in Atkinson, 1937.

*21   HENDRICKS, IRA K. "The Use of the Spenserian Stanza before
      1798." Master's thesis, Stanford University.
          Cited in Stephens, 1950.

22   HUGHES, MERRITT Y. "Burton on Spenser." PMLA 41:545-67.
          Demonstrates that in Anatomy of Melancholy Robert Burton
      unconsciously left a valuable set of notes on Spenser's works.

23   HULL, ELEANOR. A History of Ireland and Her People. Vol. 1.
      From Earlier Times to the Tudor Period. Dublin: Phoenix
      Publishing Co., pp. 365, 386, 432-34, 471.

Notes A Veue of the Present State of Ireland as source for
deplorable conditions in Ireland. Comments on Spenser's loyalty
to Lord Grey, the model for Artegall in The Faerie Queene, V.
Cites use of Irish places and names in Spenser's descriptions.

24   JONES, H.S.V. "The Faerie Queene and the Medieval Aristotelian
      Tradition." JEGP 25:283-98.
      Points out that Renaissance writers freely mix Aristotelian,
Platonic, and Christian elements, which is typical of medieval
Catholic thought; Spenser's ethical system in The Faerie Queene
follows this pattern. Links Spenser to Hooker, who adopted
Thomistic system of laws, but concludes that Spenser's thought
parallels more closely that of Philip Melanchthon, specifically
his Enarrationes upon the Ethics of Aristotle: Melanchthon ac-
comodates Christian and classic codes of conduct in his
Enarrationes by "crossing Aristotle with the Ten Commandments";
the result is "a list of virtues corresponding closely with those
which Spenser has celebrated in the Faerie Queene." Notes that
Spenser probably read Melanchthon as a student. Finds
Melanchthon's influence in Spenser's conception and emphasis on
Holiness (Book I); the joining of Continence and Chastity (Books
II, III) with the seventh commandment; joining Friendship (Book
IV) with the sixth commandment; joining Justice (Book V) with the
fifth and eighth commandments; joining Courtesy (Book VI) with
the ninth commandment. Thus, "in spite of his political Protes-
tantism and his sympathy with reform, the culture of Edmund
Spenser, like that of the Anglican Church, however abundantly
it might have used the resources of Renaissance art, is funda-
mentally conservative, medieval, and Catholic."

25   JUSSERAND, JEAN A.A. JULES. A Literary History of the English
      People. Time of Renaissance. Age of Elizabeth. New York:
      G.P. Putnam's Sons, pp. 438-509.
      Includes detailed biography and survey of Spenser's achieve-
ments, with general commentary on each work. Gives particular
emphasis to The Shepheardes Calender and The Faerie Queene.
Revised version of 1904.21.

*26   KELSO, RUTH. The Institution of the Gentleman in English
      Literature of the Sixteenth Century. A Study in Renaissance
      Ideals. Urbana: University of Illinois Press.
      Cited in Atkinson, 1937. Published version of 1923.23.
For revised edition, see 1929.28.

27   LANDRUM, GRACE WARREN. "Spenser's Use of the Bible and His
      Alleged Puritanism." PMLA 41:517-44.
      Considers Spenser's borrowings from forty-nine books of
Bible, concluding that his preference is Cranmer's Bible, or the
Great Bible. Suggests that Spenser might be a Precisionist, a
churchman who declined to ally himself with any distinct group
of dissenters and remained in favor of modified Anglicanism.
Hymne of Heavenly Love and Hymne of Heavenly Beautie are

predominantly Christian in both phrasing and conception. Identifies Sapience with Second Person of Trinity as the Logos. Appendix "purports to be a complete list of the biblical texts to
which Spenser refers or alludes in his poetry and prose." For
correction, see 1929.9.

*28   LEE, RENSELAER W. "Platonism in Spenser." Ph.D. diss.,
      Princeton University.
           Cited in National Union Catalog.

29   LEGOUIS, ÉMILE. A History of English Literature. The Middle
      Ages and the Renaissance. Translated by Helen Douglas Irvine.
      Vol. 1. New York: Macmillan Co., pp. 173-85, passim.
           General introduction to Spenser and his poetry. Notes in-
      fluences on Spenser and Spenser's influence on others. Reprinted:
      1930.25; 1933.40; 1947; 1951; 1954.

30   _____. Spenser. London and Toronto: J.M. Dent & Sons,
      New York: E.P. Dutton & Co., 147 pp.
           Translates and edits for English readers parts of 1923.26;
      1926.31. Calls attention to "the great and lasting glories of
      Spenser's poetry" and examines "certain claims made for him with
      less justification." Includes chapters on Spenser's character,
      his moral and religious ideas, his literary tenets, a chapter on
      his personal history (Amoretti and Epithalamion) and two chapters
      on The Faerie Queene. Sees tension in Spenser's poetry and life:
      "He was born to be inspired by an enthusiasm for earthly and
      physical beauty, yet the more ascetic spirit of Christianity was
      constantly calling upon him to renounce such vanities." Illus-
      trates with analyses of The Shepheardes Calender, Complaints, and
      Fowre Hymnes. Concludes that "Platonism is the only philosophy
      that deserves notice in Spenser's works. And in so far as it is
      moral, it is also the only moral doctrine that Spenser sings with
      a note of fervour in his voice. The rest of his moralizing is
      mere contention--it is trite, tame, shallow, nerveless." Notes
      literary traditions and conventions Spenser borrowed. Finds
      Amoretti and Epithalamion unified and most personal of Spenser's
      poetry. Presents detailed analysis of pictorial elements of The
      Faerie Queene, showing influence of tapestries, pictures, pageants,
      and dumb-shows/pantomime on Spenser. Notes his particular abil-
      ity to make the abstract concrete. Concludes that "the Fairy
      Queen is nothing but a succession of similar visions without much
      moral or intellectual value, but all of them bearing the same
      vivid impress. The entire romance, from the first page to the
      last, might easily be cut up to form an immense gallery of sepa-
      rate pictures, and we should lose but little of its substance,
      still less of its poetic beauties." Considers mask tradition a
      chief influence on The Faerie Queene: Spenser found allegory,
      mythology, romance, and pastoral combined in the mask. Shows
      that in The Faerie Queene "Spenser was to keep the mask's gor-
      geous scenery, the scenic movement and changes, the actors'

gestures and mimicry . . . to reproduce the alternatives of mask
and antimask, that is, of beautiful and grotesque . . . [and
give] an equivalent for the stage-music in his harmonious stanzas." Spenser's greatness lies in his artistic abilities, rather
than in his moral allegories. Reprinted: 1933.41.

31   _____. Edmund Spenser. Les grands ecrivains étrangers.
      Paris: Libraire Bloud et Gay, 359 pp.
         Reprint of 1923.26.

32   LEMMI, C.W. "Monster-Spawning Nile-Mud in Spenser." MLN
     41:234-38.
         Quotes Spenser's uses of "slime" in The Faerie Queene,
     I.i, III.vi, II.x, and III.iv, noting that for Spenser "slime
     becomes synonymous . . . with bodily substance," and "the chief
     source of these ideas, especially as regards the specific allu-
     sions to the mud of the Nile, is to be found in the Historical
     Library of Diodorus Siculus." Concludes that Greek and Roman
     philosophers are Spenser's source for the general doctrine that
     creatures are produced from mud under the influence of the sun's
     heat. Note also "Three Monsters in the Faerie Queene," and
     "Notes on the Faerie Queene." Proceedings of Dr. Greenlaw's
     Seminary "C," 1926-27, nos. 2, 7, 8, 19, 33, 35, 38, 57, 61, 64.
     Manuscript. Baltimore: Johns Hopkins University Library.
     Cited in Atkinson, 1937. For response, see 1930.27.

*33   MALTBY, JEANNETTE E. "Spenser's Use of the Bible in The
      Faerie Queene, Books I and II." Master's thesis, University
      of Washington.
         Cited in Stephens, 1950.

34   MEZGER, FRITZ. "Kannte Spenser irische Gedichte?" Archiv
     150:232-33.
         Comments on Spenser's use of Irish allusions.

35   _____. "Spensers Quellenangaben." Archiv 150:233-34.
         Notes Spenser's use of classical sources.

36   MOWAT, R.B. "Oxford, Cambridge, and Literature." QR 247:
     347-63.
         In a discussion of relationship between English writers and
     universities, notes Spenser's mention of Cambridge and Oxford in
     pageant of the rivers in Book IV of The Faerie Queene.

37   NOTCUTT, H. CLEMENT. "The Faerie Queene and Its Critics."
     E & S 12:63-85.
         A defense of the structure of The Faerie Queene. Threefold
     method attempts (1) "to glance briefly at three misconceptions
     which seem to underlie many of the accusations that are brought
     against the poem"; (2) "to make a brief examination of one of
     the later books with a view to ascertaining whether any kind of

scheme or plan can be recognized in it"; and (3) "to follow one
of the stories running through a considerable part of the poem
in order to see what light it may throw on Spenser's way of
handling his materials." First misconception (theory that each
book must center on a single knight) is dismissed because it
goes beyond anything that Spenser promised, would involve a
monotonous uniformity, ignores fundamental differences between
themes of various books, and overlooks the possibility of a different scheme. Second misconception (the charge of loose ends)
is dismissed because Books I and II hang together, Books III to
V represent a separate group, and Book VI represents the beginning of a new group. Third misconception (interpretation of
historical allegory) is dismissed because Spenser's major concern
is moral allegory, topical allusions being used only for illustration. Answers objections that poem lacks form by pointing out
(a) at the beginning of each book, Spenser provides a link to
the one preceding; (b) soon after the opening of each book Spenser
introduces an illustration of the qualities opposed to the virtue
of the book; and (c) in all but the third book, Arthur comes to
the aid of the endangered knight. Sets out the form of Book IV
in terms of the contrast between Ate and Concord, demonstrating
that the knights of Books III and V are brought to friendly relations in middle of Book IV. Vindicates Spenser of charge of
"losing his grip on his subject," concluding that the story of
Florimell in Books III-V, a very intricate story which runs
through "the very parts of the poem that have been judged to be
most carelessly put together, is in reality handled in such a
way that in each book it is directly related to the idea with
which, according to Spenser's plan, that book was intended to
deal."

*38   O'CONNOR, J.M. "Spenser's Use of the St. George Legend, The
      Fair Unknown, and Other Medieval Romance Themes in Book I of
      The Faerie Queene." Master's thesis, University of Washington.
           Cited in Stephens, 1950.

39   PADELFORD, FREDERICK M., and WILLIAM C. MAXWELL. "The Compound
      Words in Spenser's Poetry." PMLA 25:498-516.
           Considers the compound words which Spenser coined or used
      for conscious poetic effect. Lists compound words in Spenser's
      works, words excluded from list "because commonly used," and, in
      table form, number of times each type of compound occurs in a
      particular poem, the total number of compounds in a poem, and
      the frequency of occurrence. Concludes that Book V was written
      before the first ten cantos of Book IV of The Faerie Queene.
      Notes influence of Pléiade on English writers in their innova-
      tive use of compound words.

40   PADELFORD, F.M., and MATTHEW O'CONNOR. "Spenser's Use of the
      St. George Legend." SP 23:142-56.

Considers influence of St. George tradition on Book I of
The Faerie Queene, noting possible sources in Caxton's collection
of saints' lives, A Festival, compiled by John Mirk; Mantuan, or
Barclay's translation of Mantuan in The Lyfe of the Glorious Mar-
tyr Saint George; and a tapestry poem by John Lydgate. For
related study, see 1927.15.

41   PIENAAR, W.J.B. "Edmund Spenser and Jonker Jon van der Noot."
     ES 8:33-44, 67-76.
          Contends that Theodore Roest translated the poems (A Theatre
     for Worldlings) and Spenser assisted by putting the poems into
     verse. French version was basis for the translations, but Italian
     and Dutch versions were also consulted. Notes influence of A
     Theatre for Worldlings on Spenser's works, especially The Faerie
     Queene.

42   POPE, E[MMA] F[IELD]. "The Critical Background of the
     Spenserian Stanza." MP 24:31-53.
          Spenser turned to Italian sources for his metric scheme, to
     Dante's terza rima, "a medium dignified by its use in a great
     epic," which Spenser "transformed in all the music of its tone
     quality and syllabic form into the nearest equivalent of his
     native language." Nine-line madrigal was direct model for
     stanzaic form.

*23 POPE, EMMA FIELD. The Reflections of Renaissance Criticism in
     Edmund Spenser's "Faerie Queene." Chicago: University of
     Chicago Press, 400 pp.
          Cited in 1930.23. Discusses Spenser's use of sources.
     Published version of 1923.35.

44   _____. "Renaissance Criticism and the Diction of The Faerie
     Queene." PMLA 41:575-619.
          Traces influence of contemporary criticism on diction of
     The Faerie Queene in two parts: "the first traces the Renaissance
     theory of diction from its inception in the classics through its
     development in Italy, France, and England; the second analyzes
     the characteristics of Spenser's diction and seeks to establish
     the relationship existing between the theory of his age and his
     practice." Concludes that "Spenser followed the tenets of criti-
     cism: he restored ancient words, he drew from dialects, he bor-
     rowed from foreign tongues, he lengthened, contracted, combined,
     compounded, and created words. In all these processes he has
     observed the moderation enjoined by critics from Aristotle to
     Ronsard. He was under the influence not of Greece, of Rome,
     Italy, France, or England alone, but of that composite body,
     Renaissance criticism, which embraced the combined teachings of
     all these nations, and was universally known to poets and schol-
     ars." For response, see 1927.6.

45   SAURAT, DENIS. "La 'Sapience' de Spenser et La 'Shekhina' de
     la Cabale." RLC 6:5-15.

> Finds influence of Cabalists in Sapience of the <u>Hymne of Heavenlie Beautie</u>: "Spenser célèbre la <u>Matrona</u> des cabalistes." Concludes: "Plus encore que dans les détails du personnage de Sapience, c'est dans cette identité de rôle entre <u>Sapience</u> et la <u>Schekhina</u>, alors que régulièrement l'amour divin relève du rôle de Jésus-Christ, que l'on peut voir une influence cabaliste sur les conceptions et memê les sentiments de Spenser."

*46   SAVAGE, D.J. "Spenser's Relation to Puritanism." Proceedings of Dr. Greenlaw's Seminary "C," 1926-27, no. 51. Manuscript. Baltimore: Johns Hopkins University Library.
> Cited in Atkinson, 1937.

*47   SESSUMS, A.C. "Notes on the Faerie Queene" and "Spenser's Use of Proverbs." Proceedings of Dr. Greenlaw's Seminary "C," 1926-27, nos. 16, 49, 55. Manuscript. Baltimore: Johns Hopkins University Library.
> Cited in Atkinson, 1937.

48   SHANNON, GEORGE P. "The Heroic Couplet in the Sixteenth and Seventeenth Centuries, With Special Reference to the Influence of Ovid and the Latin Elegaic Distich." Ph.D. diss., Stanford University, pp. 58-65.
> Discusses Chaucerian influence on metrics of <u>The Shepheardes Calender</u> and <u>Mother Hubberds Tale</u>. In Spenser "we have seen the Chaucerian couplet in the most modern form it was to attain."

*49   SMITH, CHARLES G. "Notes on the Faerie Queene" and "The Place of Love in Spenser's World-Order." Proceedings of Dr. Greenlaw's Seminary "C," 1926-27, nos. 25, 29, 35, 44, 47. Manuscript. Baltimore: Johns Hopkins University Library.
> Cited in Atkinson, 1937.

*50   TAYLOR, HILDA. "Topographical Poetry in England During the Renaissance." Ph.D. diss., University of Chicago, 216 pp.
> Cited in Atkinson, 1937.

51   TRENEER, ANNE. <u>The Sea in English Literature from Beowulf to Donne</u>. London: University Press of Liverpool, Hodder & Stoughton, pp. 107-209, passim.
> Examines Spenser's sea imagery and use of sea legends in three passages: Guyon's trip to the Bower of Bliss, Book II, <u>The Faerie Queene</u>; the fantasia of Florimell and Marinell, Books III, V; and description of the sea in <u>Colin Clouts Come Home Againe</u>. "In the Guyon story the sea is the sea of life; in the story of Florimell it is a sea of pictures and fancies; in 'Colin Clouts Come Home Again' we are nearer the actual sea as Spenser experienced it." Notes sea images in <u>Muiopotmos</u> and <u>Ruines of Time</u>.

52   TWISS, HENRY F. "Mallow and Some Mallow Men." <u>JCHAS</u> 31: 61-71.

Notes Spenser's visits to Mallow and residence of poet's descendant (Edmund Spenser, died 23 October 1789) in Mallow.

53   Van WINKLE, COURTLANDT, ed. Introduction and notes to
      Epithalamion. New York: F.S. Crofts, pp. 3-39.
          Discusses Spenser's text and epithalamic tradition to show
      that Catullan form is chief model for Spenser's poem and that
      poem is influenced significantly by Neoplatonism. Analyzes
      Spenser themes, personal allusions, and metrics. Extensive
      notes.

*54   WEBB, W.S. "Mulcaster and Spenser." Proceedings of Dr.
      Greenlaw's Seminary "C," 1926-27, no. 36. Manuscript.
      Baltimore: Johns Hopkins University Library.
          Cited in Atkinson, 1937.

*55   _____. "Spenser's Acquaintance with Hebrew" and "Spenser and
      Virgil." Proceedings of Dr. Greenlaw's Seminary "C," 1926-27,
      nos. 32, 67. Manuscript. Baltimore: Johns Hopkins University
      Library.
          Cited in Atkinson, 1937.

56   WELLS, WHITNEY. "Spenser's Dragon." MLN 41:143-57.
          Spenser follows the romances in only one or two minor de-
      tails for his dragon description in The Faerie Queene, I.xi.
      Suggests source for the description in The Vision of Tundale.

57   WILSON, F.P. "Spenser and Ireland." RES 2:456-57.
          Bill of imprest in the accounts of the Treasurer of the
      Wars in Ireland, Sir Henry Wallop, (MS. Rawl. A. 317--Bodleian
      Library) suggests that Spenser was in Ireland on 30 May 1590.

                              1927

1   ADAMS, R. BINGHAM. "Ferdinando Freckleton." NQ 153-88.
          Christening of an Edmund Spenser at St. Mary Magdalene,
      Bermondsey, Surrey, 18 April 1553. Is is the poet?

2   ALBRIGHT, EVELYN MAY. Dramatic Publication in England 1580-
      1640: A Study of Conditions Affecting Content and Form of
      Drama. Monograph Series of the Modern Language Association
      of America. New York: D.C. Heath; London: Oxford University
      Press, pp. 150-51.
          Notes that King James of Scotland brought claim against
      Edmund Spenser in November 1596 for satire on himself and his
      deceased mother in Books IV-VI of The Faerie Queene.

3   ANON. "The Poet's Poet." Bookman (London) 72:261-62.
          Spenser portrait.

                              125

*4   BALLIÈRE, PAUL. <u>Poetès allemands et poètes anglais</u>. Paris:
     [publisher not known], pp. 187-91.
         Cited in Atkinson, 1937, who notes discussion of <u>Amoretti</u>.

*5   BAMBER, JURETTA V. "The Renaissance Paradox in Spenser."
     Master's thesis, University of Louisville.
         Cited in Stephens, 1950.

6   BULLOCK, WALTER L. "A Comment on Criticism in the Cinque-
     cento." <u>PMLA</u> 42:1057-60.
         Considers Pope's study (1926.44) of Italian theorists
     "somewhat misleading through its failure to mention the most
     important authorities, and through its inexactitude in certain
     minor details." Regards Bembo and Speroni essential to discus-
     sion of <u>cinquecento</u> theories. Sees parallel between Spenser's
     method and those of Bembo's <u>Prose della Volgar Lingua</u> and
     Speroni's <u>Dialogo delle Lingue</u>. Notes also importance of Cicero
     "among the classic authorities influential on the Renaissance."
     For supplement, see 1931.8. For response, see 1931.40.

7   BUSH, DOUGLAS. "Some Allusions to Spenser." <u>MLN</u> 42:341-16.
         Lists several allusions not included in Carpenter (1923.6).

8   BUSHNELL, NELSON SHERWIN. "The Style of Keats's Spenserian
     Stanzas, Sonnets, and Odes." Ph.D. diss., Harvard University,
     343 pp.
         Concludes that Keats followed Spenserian pattern closely,
     while experimenting freely with sonnet and ode.

9   CONWAY, EUSTACE. "Anthony Munday." In <u>Anthony Munday and
     Other Essays</u>. New York: privately printed, pp. 9-62.
         Links Spenser with Munday by noting similarities between
     Spenser's descriptions in <u>The Shepheardes Calender</u> and Munday's
     poetry. Identifies Palinode in <u>The Shepheardes Calender</u> and Palin
     in <u>Colin Clouts Come Home Againe</u> as Munday.

*10 DUNBAR, H. FLANDERS. "Symbolism in Medieval Thought and Its
     Consummation in <u>The Divine Comedy</u>." Thesis, Columbia
     University, p. 500.
         For published edition, see 1929.15.

*11 EDMUNDS, JAMES M. "A Study of the Amoret Story in the Third
     and Fourth Books of <u>The Faerie Queene</u>." Master's thesis,
     Johns Hopkins University.
         Cited in Stephens, 1950. Theses develops "The Amoret Story."
     Proceedings of Dr. Greenlaw's Seminary "C," 1926-27, no. 56.
     Manuscript. Baltimore: Johns Hopkins University Library.

12   ERSKINE, JOHN. "Life: The Great Adventure: The Story of
     <u>The Faerie Queene</u>." <u>Delineator</u> 110:29, 66, 69.

Brief summary of The Faerie Queene with emphasis on letter
to Raleigh and Spenser's language. Reprinted in expanded version:
1928.12; 1935.17; Cleveland and New York: World Publishing Co.,
1941.

*13   FRENCH, P.W.   A Commentary and Questionnaire on "The Faerie
       Queene." London: Pitman, 32 pp.
              Cited in National Union Catalogue.

14   GARROD, H.W. "Abberation in Rhyme." TLS, 14 April, p. 265.
              Notes nine passages in The Faerie Queene for which Spenser
       or the printer substituted unrhyming synonyms for rhyming words
       and notes seven other instances of the same phenomenon in Eliza-
       bethan sonnets.

15   GREENLAW, EDWIN. "Una and Her Lamb." MLN 42:515-16.
              Response to Padelford and O'Connor's suggestion (1926.40)
       that "the original of Una and her lamb may be found in old ver-
       sions of the legend of St. George in which the king's daughter is
       represented as led to the sacrifice in company with a sheep."
       Suggests no one literary source for Spenser's version of St.
       George legend, concluding that "it was part and parcel of folk
       belief and courtly entertainment in his time and long before."
       For supplement, see 1931.47. For response, see 1926.40.

16   HEWLETT, JAMES H. "Interpreting a Spenser-Harvey Letter."
       PMLA 42:1060-65.
              Disagrees with Caldwell (1926.6). Sees difference in mood
       between October and April letters. Presents Harvey's "travel
       letter" of 23 October 1579 as an indication of Spenser's serious-
       ness in writing and hopes for achievement.

17   LAWRENCE, C.E. "The Personality of Spenser." QR 249:154-67.
              Sketches personal view of Spenser from the works, notes
       strong influence of Chaucer.

18   _____. "The Poet's Poet." Bookman 72:261-62.
              Spenser's influence on Keats, Shelley, Wordsworth, Milton,
       and Shakespeare.

19   MAGNUS, LAURIE. English Literature in Its Foreign Relations
       1300 to 1800. London: Kegan Paul, Trench, Trubner & Co.;
       New York: E.P. Dutton & Co., pp. 24-26.
              Presents general introduction to Spenser in context of
       historical development of the age and literary traditions. Notes
       chief classical, Italian, and French influences on Spenser, con-
       siders him a reformer of language, and cites The Faerie Queene
       as Spenser's supreme achievement.

20   MAGOUN, F.P., Jr. "The Chaucer of Spenser and Milton." MP
       25:129-36.

Suggests Chaucerian source for Spenser's Blandamour in
The Faerie Queene.

*21 MARSHALL, M.L. Representative Spenserian Sonnets. Landover,
     Md.: Dreamland Press.
          Cited in Atkinson, 1937.

 22 PARTRIDGE, A.F. "Spenser's Mistress, Rosalind." NQ 153:
     389-90.
          Identifies Rosalind as kinswoman of Francis Wilkes. For
     related study, see 1927.35.

*23 PIERCE, MARJORIE BRAND. "The Allusions to Spenser up to
     1650." Master's thesis, University of Chicago, 173 pp.
          Cited in Stephens, 1950.

 24 PLOMER, HENRY R., and TOM PEETE CROSS. The Life and Corres-
     pondence of Lodowick Bryskett. Chicago: University of
     Chicago Press, pp. 41-46, passim.
          Documents close friendship between Spenser and Bryskett.
     Both served and respected Lord Grey, and felt Grey's departure
     from Ireland to be a misfortune. Finds evidence to believe
     Spenser became deputy clerk of Council of Munster in 1584.
     Overall background for Spenser's involvement in Irish affairs.

 25 RICHTER, MARGARET ROSE. "Spenser's Use of Arthurian Romance."
     Ph.D. diss., Stanford University, 356 pp.
          Identifies ninety-five motifs in The Faerie Queene and
     provides analogues in primarily Old French Arthurian romances,
     "taking into account the direct borrowing of material, the imi-
     tation of romance conventions in language and structure, and, to
     some extent, the indirect borrowing through use of Italian writ-
     ers who had drawn upon the romances." Concludes that The Faerie
     Queene is "made up of fundamentally Arthurian material, fused
     with similar motifs, gleaned elsewhere, of like origin in myth
     and folk-lore and therefore capable of being fused into a har-
     monious whole. It represents not one people or period, but the
     accumulated racial heritage of the European peoples."

 27 ROSENBACH, A.S.W. Books and Bidders: The Adventures of a
     Bibliophile. Boston: Little, Brown, & Co., pp. 148-151.
          Recounts acquisition of presentation copy of The Faerie
     Queene (1590), Spenser's own copy, inscribed to himself, dated
     1590, and also inscribed to Elizabeth Boyle with the complete
     first sonnet of the Amoretti. Notes also the acquisition of an
     English travel book which Spenser presented to Gabriel Harvey and
     which Harvey annotated with happy comments about his friendship
     with Spenser.

 27 SANDISON, HELEN E. "Spenser's Mansilia." TLS, 8 September,
     p. 608.

Identifies Mansilia in <u>Colin Clouts Come Home Againe</u> with
Helena, Marchioness of Northhampton on evidence from her epitaph
on Salisbury cathedral monument and from British Museum,
Lansdowne Roll 9. "Mansilia" may be a derivation of adjective
<u>mansueta</u> or <u>mansues</u>, which "fits her well."

28 SCHELLING, FELIX EMMANUEL. <u>English Literature during the</u>
    <u>Lifetime of Shakespeare</u>. New York: Henry Holt, 486 pp.,
    passim.
        Reprint of 1910.24.

29 SCOTT, JANET G. "The Sources of Spenser's 'Amoretti.'" <u>MLR</u>
    22:189-95.
        Finds Tasso to be an important source for <u>Amoretti</u>, notably
    71 (<u>Rime</u> 14), 72 (<u>Rime</u> 47), and 78 (<u>Rime</u> 167).

30 STOVALL, FLOYD. "Feminine Rimes in <u>The Faerie Queene</u>." <u>JEGP</u>
    26:91-95.
        One example of regular feminine rhyme in Books I-II; 163
    examples in Books IV-VII. One example of irregular feminine
    rhyme in I-III; 125 in IV-VII. Concludes that Spenser first
    thought (Books I-III) feminine rhyme impaired dignity of his seri-
    ous poem but changed his mind and deliberately used feminine rhyme
    in early cantos of Book IV. Conscious purpose became less acute;
    thus gradual decrease in feminine rhymes in Books V and VI.

*31 THOMPSON, NATHALEE Q. "Spenser's Treatment of Love and
    Friendship Compared with Castiglione's." Ph.D. diss.,
    University of Chicago.
        Cited in Atkinson, 1937.

32 TILLEY, M.P. "The Comedy <u>Lingua</u> and <u>The Faerie Queene</u>." <u>MLN</u>
    42:150-57.
        Immediate source of T. Tomkis's <u>Lingua</u> is story of Alma in
    <u>The Faerie Queene</u>, II.ix.

33 VENN, JOHN, and J.A. VENN, comps. <u>Alumni Cantabrigiensis:</u>
    <u>A Biographical List of All Known Students, Graduates and</u>
    <u>Holders of Office at the University of Cambridge from the</u>
    <u>Earliest Times to 1900</u>. Pt. 1, vol. 4. Cambridge: Cambridge
    University Press; New York: Macmillan Co., p. 321.
        Brief biographical listing.

34 WANN, LOUIS. "The Role of the Confidant(e) in the Renaissance
    Epic." <u>Anglia</u> 51:63-74.
        Glauce, Nurse to Britomart, and the Palmer of Guyon are two
    genuine instances of confidants in <u>The Faerie Queene</u>. They are
    alike because each is completely faithful to welfare of his or
    her superior, different because Palmer is something of a sage
    because of his superior knowledge, whereas Glauce appears to be
    only a devoted Nurse.

35   WELPLY, W.H. "Spenser's Mistress, Rosalind." NQ 153:389.
          Data to identify Rosalind: Aubry MS, Lady Dryden's pedi-
      gree, Sir Erasmus Dryden's knowledge of Chancery lawsuit. For
      related study, see 1927.22.

*36   WOLLERMAN, IRA D. "The Court in the Poetry of Edmund Spenser."
      Master's thesis, Indiana University.
          Cited in Stephens, 1950.

                                  1928

1   ALBRIGHT, EVELYN MAY. "Spenser's Reason for Rejecting the
      Cantos of Mutability." SP 25:93-127.
          Demonstrates that "the Mutability cantos were certainly
      intended as part of a book in The Faerie Queene; that the theme
      of the book was probably to have been English affairs in Ireland;
      that this early version of part of a book on Ireland was rejected
      by Spenser because he sent it to Harvey for criticism and a cir-
      cle of Cambridge friends to whom he read it criticised it severely;
      that Spenser conserved a good part of the matter of Mutability in
      his published works, using a bit of it for the preface to a new
      book on Irish affairs (Book V) and other bits elsewhere in the
      early poems with a changed emphasis and tone which may be trace-
      able to Harvey's criticism." Places date of composition of the
      Mutabilitie cantos at 1579-1580. For related studies, see
      1929.3; 1930.4, 36; 1931.4; 1932.1; 1935.56.

2   B., R.S. "Edmund Spenser, His Connection With Co. Northants."
      NQ 154:69.
          Little evidence to link poet with Burnley Spensers. For
      related studies, see 1928.9, 13, 23.

3   BELL, EDNA F. "Imitations of Spenser from 1706 to 1774."
      Master's thesis, University of Oklahoma, 170 pp.
          Limits discussion to serious imitations of The Faerie Queene,
      Fowre Hymnes, Epithalamion, Prothalamion, and The Shepheardes
      Calender, Spenser's works most popular in eighteenth century.
      Treats plan, structure, and story of Spenser's poem; "then the
      various major imitations of [the] particular poem [are] dis-
      cussed according to their general structure, style, imagery,
      and philosophy." Shows "how the imitators became numerous, how
      they until the time of Beattie's 'The Minstrel' very consciously
      adhered to his diction; how they varied his form of the stanza;
      how they patterned after his style and manner, even to the use
      of his simplicity of style for purposes of burlesque; how they
      liked his allegory, Platonic philosophy and satire; how they were
      fond of referring to certain characters which he had made famous;
      and, lastly, how they had paid tribute to his artistry."

4   BELLAMY, CHARLES H.   "The Poets-Laureate." <u>Manchester</u>
     <u>Quarterly</u> 54:249-72.
          Notes that Spenser never claimed title of laureate, nor did
     any of his contemporaries grant it to him; no recognized court
     office of Poet Laureate existed in Elizabeth's time.

5   BRADNER, LEICESTER. "Forerunners of the Spenserian Stanza."
     <u>RES</u> 4:207-8.
          No experimentation with nine-line stanza in <u>The Shepheardes</u>
     <u>Calender</u>. Concludes that medial and final couplets peculiar to
     Spenser's stanza "may have come from native sources, aided by
     [Spenser's] own ingenuity." Spenser linking of final couplet
     with rest of stanza comes from Italian madrigal.

*6   BRIE, FRIEDRICH. <u>Imperialistiche stromungen in der englischen</u>
     <u>literatur</u>. Halle: M. Niemeyer, passim.
          Cited in Atkinson, 1937.

*7   BRUCE, J.D. "Edmund Spenser [with selections]." In <u>Columbia</u>
     <u>University Course in Literature Based on the World's Best Lit-</u>
     <u>erature</u>. vol. 11. Edited by John W. Cunliffe et al. New
     York: Columbia University Press.
          Cited in Atkinson, 1937.

*8   CAMPBELL, JEANNETTE H. "The Influence of <u>The Shepheardes</u>
     <u>Calender</u> upon the Formal Pastoral of the Period 1579-1602."
     Master's thesis, University of Chicago.
          Cited in Atkinson, 1937.

9   CLIFTON, A.S.W. "Edmund Spenser, His Connection with
     Northants." <u>NQ</u> 154:195.
          Notes Round's <u>Peerage and Family History</u> as link between
     poet and Althorp Spencers. For related studies, see 1928.2, 13,
     23.

10   CRANE, CLARA W. "A Source for Spenser's Story of Timias
     and Belphebe [<u>sic</u>]." <u>PMLA</u> 43:635-44.
          Suggests an incident in the Old French romance of <u>Violette</u>
     as a possible source for the reconciliation of Timias and
     Belphoebe in Book IV of <u>The Faerie Queene</u>.

11   DeHAAS, CORNELIUS E. <u>Nature and the Country in English Poetry</u>
     <u>of the First Half of the Eighteenth Century</u>. Amsterdam:
     H.J. Paris, 301 pp., passim.
          Notes influence of <u>The Shepheardes Calender</u> on eighteenth-
     century rural poetry. Reprinted: Folcroft, Pa.: Folcroft
     Press, 1970.

12   ERSKINE, JOHN. "<u>The Faerie Queene</u>." In <u>The Delight of Great</u>
     <u>Books</u>. Indianapolis: Bobbs-Merrill Co., pp. 75-96.
          Expanded version of 1927.12. Reprinted: London: Eveleigh
     Nash and Grayson, 1935.12.

13   EVANS, F. "Edmund Spenser, His Connection with Co. Northants."
      NQ 154:29.
           Poet related to Northampton Spensers, rather than to Burnley
      Spensers. For related studies, see 1928.2, 9, 23.

14   FAIRCHILD, HOXIE NEALE. The Noble Savage: A Study in
      Romantic Naturalism. New York: Columbia University Press,
      pp. 194, 251, 258, 300, 357, 442.
           Southey and Campbell wrote in Spenserian stanzas; Spenser
      exemplifies romantic fusion of infinite and finite; Spenser's
      medievalism an influence on early romanticists. Reprinted:
      New York: Russell & Russell, 1961.

15   FLASDIECK, HERMANN M. Der Gedanke einer englischen Sprach-
      akademie in Vergangenheit und Gegenwart. Jena: Verlag der
      Frommaunschen Buchhandlung, pp. 6-7.
           Comments in chapter "Renaissance und Revolution" on Spenser-
      Harvey correspondence and Areopagus.

*16   GWIN, H.H. "The Influence on Keats of Spenser, Milton, and
      Shakespeare." Master's thesis, University of Virginia.
           Cited in Stephens, 1950.

17   HAGGETT, DOROTHY GENE. "Spenser's Original Contributions to
      the English Language, Adapted from Words of Romanic and Clas-
      sical Origin." Master's thesis, University of Washington,
      41 pp.
           Illustrates with tables that "Spenser introduced into Eng-
      lish vocabulary from the Romanic and Classical languages some
      eighty words of his own origination, gave a particular meaning
      to approximately fifty words already in use, and was quick to
      endorse around eighty more words not used before 1500. Of these,
      by far the majority came from the Romanic languages, particularly
      the French, and some sixty have Latin roots."

18   HARD, FREDERICK. "Studies in Aesthetic Influences on Edmund
      Spenser." Ph.D. diss., Johns Hopkins University, 188 pp.
           Studies Spenser's works, environment, and background to
      determine his attitude toward fine arts of his time and extent
      to which his aesthetic interests affected his poetry. Considers
      literary and actual sources of Spenser's sensitivity to architec-
      ture, music, tapestries, and painting and illustration.

19   HEFFNER, RAY L. "The Earl of Essex in Elizabethan Literature."
      Ph.D. diss., Johns Hopkins University, pp. 6-30.
           In Artegall, Spenser presents "Essex the leader of the for-
      ward school, and the hope of England for a great and imperial
      policy." Partially reprinted: 1934.29.

*20   HEINEMANN, ELFRIEDE. "Das Bild der Dame in der Erzählenden
      Dichtung Englands von Malory bis Spenser." Ph.D. diss.,
      Wilhelms University, 113 pp.
           For published edition, see 1928.21.

21   _____. "Das Bild der Dame in Spensers Faerie Queene." In
      Das Bild der Dame in der Erzählenden Dictung Englands von
      Malory bis Spenser. Quakenbruck: Robert Kleinert, pp. 62-97.
           Considers Spenser's women under categories: noble birth,
      beauty, view of love, inner merits, chastity, temperance, charm,
      steadfastness, bravery, and piety. Published version of 1928.20.

22   HENLEY, PAULINE. Spenser in Ireland. Cork: Cork University
      Press, 231 pp.
           Focuses not on Spenser of allegory and romance, but on
      Spenser "the ruthless apostle of coercive government, the grimly
      precise exponent of the statecraft of Elizabethan England." Con-
      siders A Veue of the Present State of Ireland an "exposition of
      the gospel of savage repression" that did much to kindle the bit-
      terness of the Irish but did little to influence Elizabeth's
      policies. Details Spenser's political involvement (ultimately
      insignificant and would have gone unnoticed had he not been
      prominent poet) with chapters "With Grey in Ireland," "Spenser
      as an 'Undertaker,'" "The Poet at Kilcolman," and discusses
      Irish influences in Spenser works with chapters, "Further Irish
      Influences and Allusions," "The Ruin of the Plantation," "Spenser
      and Political Thought," and a biographical chapter, "The Poet's
      Descendants." Identifies Irish allusions in Colin Clouts Come
      Home Againe and The Faerie Queene, many related to area and his
      life around Kilcolman. Sees conflict in Spenser between poetic
      nature and political opportunist. Poet Spenser delved into Irish
      lore and legend, was influenced by Irish literature (points out
      relationship between ancient lore and parts of The Faerie Queene
      and A Veue of the Present State of Ireland and notes possible
      influence of Irish metrical form on Spenser's innovations in
      verse, using Colin Clouts Come Home Againe as chief example).
      Concludes on Spenser's Irish political views: "Narrowminded and
      intolerant, all too anxious to accept the official point of view,
      he made no use of the opportunity that he had of forming an inde-
      pendent opinion on the claims of the Irish people. He diligently
      noted the political views of his own countrymen who were serving
      in Ireland, and the plan that he eventually puts forward for the
      subjugation of the country is the outcome, not of his own expe-
      rience or thought, but of the discussion he had heard from time
      to time among English officials." Thus, Spenser's Irish views
      are often inconsistent, slanderous, and ignorant in blind defense
      of Elizabethan policy. Reprinted: New York: Russell & Russell,
      1969.

23   HIERONYMUS. "Edmund Spenser, His Connection with Co.
      Northants." NQ 154:123.
           Evidence to relate poet to Northampton Spensers. For
      related studies, see 1928.2, 9, 13.

24   HULBERT, VIOLA BLACKBURN. "A New Interpretation of Spenser's
      Muiopotmos." SP 25:128-48.

Finds substantial evidence to read poem as allegory of
Sidney-Oxford quarrel (1579); identifies Sidney with fly and
Burghley with spider.

*25   HULBERT, VIOLA B[LACKBURN]. "Spenser's Twelve Moral Virtues
      According to Aristotle and the Rest." Ph.D. diss., University
      of Chicago.
         Cited in 1931.58.

*26   HUNTER, MADELYN C. "The Relations Between Edmund Spenser and
      William Cecil, Lord Burghley." Master's thesis, University of
      Iowa.
         Cited in Stephens, 1950.

27   IRVING, WILLIAM HENRY. "An Imitation of the Faerie Queene."
      MLN 43:80.
         Notes existence of A Canto of the Fairy Queen, written by
      Spenser, never before published (1739) which tells of Red Cross
      Knight's visits with Archimago to foreign lands.

28   KNOWLTON, E.C. "The Genii of Spenser." SP 25:439-56.
         Supplements 1924.20. "Familiar with encyclopaedic exposi-
      tions of genius and with mediaeval adaptations of the figure to
      ethical doctrine, he [Spenser] conceived two Genii for his alle-
      gorical pattern. The false Genius he associated with sloth and
      ill-directed passion, deadly sins, infidelity to chivalry, de-
      basement of the creative functions in art and life. The true
      Genius he associated with eternally active creation, healthful
      pleasure, sound education in loving and living." The former is
      the Genius of the Bower of Bliss, the latter that of the Garden
      of Adonis. For previous study, see 1924.20.

29   LEE, RENSSELAER W. "Castiglione's Influence on Spenser's
      Early Hymns." PQ 7:65-77.
         Maintains that for the Neoplatonism of first two hymns
      Spenser owes larger debt to The Courtier, Book 4, "line for line,
      than to either Ficino, Bruno, or Benivieni." Contends that "the
      hymns to Love and Beauty are a concentrated expression of the
      philosophy which, more than any other, informs the whole of the
      Fairy Queen."

30   LEMMI, C.W. "The Influence of Trissino on The Faerie Queene."
      PQ 7:220-23.
         Shows Trissino's influence on Spenser through parallels
      between The Faerie Queene, Books I and II, and L'Italia Liberata
      dai Goti.

31   LEVINSON, RONALD B. "Spenser and Bruno." PMLA 43:675-81.
         Challenges Greenlaw's thesis (1920.9) "that certain portions
      of the Faerie Queene are animated by a spirit of Lucretian scepti-
      cism at odds with that Christianized Neoplatonism which has

commonly been recognized as Spenser's sole philosophy." Suggests
that "a possible escape from this dilemma can be effected through
the assumption of a borrowing of certain elements from the philosophy of Giordano Bruno, in whose system an attempt is made to
reconcile precisely that contradiction between spiritualism and
materialism in which Spenser seems to be involved. It was Bruno's
continual attempt to combine the Lucretian account of a change-
less material substance with the Platonic doctrine of the change-
lessness of spiritual substance." Bruno's doctrine reaches focal
clarity in the Spaccio. Also demonstrates two parallels between
Bruno's Spaccio and the cantos of Mutability. For related studies,
see 1930.14; 1932.24; 1934.63.

32   NAYLOR, E.W. "Spenser (1552-99); Skelton (1460?-1529); and
     Chaucer (1340-1400)." In The Poets and Music. London and
     Tornoto: J.M. Dent, pp. 133-59.
          Suggests possible sources in Egyptian lore and in Cicero
     for notions in Spenser's description of Castle of Alma in The
     Faerie Queene, II.ix.22. Reprinted: 1928.

*33 NUTTING, HAZEL D. "Spenserian Criticism in the Past Decade."
     Master's thesis, University of Colorado.
          Cited in Stephens, 1950.

34   PARROTT, ALICE. "A Critical Bibliography of Spenser from
     1923-1928." SP 25:468-90.
          An attempt to complete F.I. Carpenter's Reference Guide
     (1923.6) for the years 1923-1928. Includes additional entries
     for earlier years made in Carpenter's own copy of the Guide.

35   PIENAAR, W.J.B. "Arthur's Shield in The Faerie Queene."
     MP 26:63-68.
          Arthur's shield is shield of faith.

36   PRAZ, MARIO. "Machiavelli and the Elizabethans." PBA 14:
     49-97.
          Notes Spenser's adoption of Machiavellian maxims "almost
     word by word" in A Veue of the Present State of Ireland, concepts
     antithetical to those in The Faerie Queene.

37   PURDY, MARY M. "Elizabethan Literary Treatment of the Proposed
     Marriages of Queen Elizabeth." Ph.D. diss., University of
     Pittsburgh, pp. 497-522.
          Considers relationship between Elizabeth and Leicester a
     main concern in Spenser's poetry: veiled allusions in "April"
     and "October" eclogues of The Shepheardes Calender; allusions in
     Mother Hubberds Tale; Lobbin represents Leicester in Colin Clouts
     Come Home Againe; tributes to Leicester in Prothalamion and
     Ruines of Time; and chief tribute to Leicester, as Arthur, in
     The Faerie Queene. Interprets all books of The Faerie Queene to
     be, at least in part, allegory of Leicester-Elizabeth
     relationship.

38   RENWICK, W.L., ed. Introductions to <u>The Complete Works of</u>
      <u>Edmund Spenser</u>. 4 vols. London: Scholartis Press.
           For individual volumes, see 1928.39; 1929.35; 1930.39;
      1934.55.

39   _____. Introduction and notes to <u>Complaints</u>. London:
      Scholartis Press, 273 pp.
           Considers <u>Mother Hubberds Tale</u> only noteworthy poem in
      volume. Notes that critics seek too much allegory in <u>Complaints</u>,
      especially in attacks on Burghley in <u>Teares of the Muses</u>. Spenser
      emphasizes in <u>Complaints</u> the "World Vanity--the fleetingness of
      strength and power and beauty." Links poems to other works on
      similar theme: eclogues of Mantuan, <u>Zodiacus Vitae</u> of Palingenius,
      and works by duBartas, Greville, and Davies. Poems also reveal
      Spenser's antiquarian interests and his expertise at imitation
      and innovation.

40   REUNING, KARL. "<u>The Shepherd's Tale of the Powder Plot</u>, Eine
      Spenser-Nachahmung." In <u>Beiträge zur Erforschung der Sprache</u>
      <u>und Kultur Englands und Nordamerikas</u>. Vol. 4, pt. 2,
      pp. 8-154.
           Discusses William Bedell's obscure imitation of Spenser's
      The Shepheardes Calender.

*41   RICHTER, MARGARET R. "Spenser's Use of Arthurian Romance."
      Ph.D. diss., Stanford University.
           Cited in 1931.58.

42   ROYSTER, JAMES F. "E.K.'s <u>Elf<Guelph, Goblin<Ghibelline</u>."
      <u>MLN</u> 43:249-52.
           Discussion of E.K.'s gloss on "June," line 25, <u>The Shep-</u>
      <u>heardes Calender</u>, on etymology of "elf" and "goblin." Shows
      E.K.'s use repeated in works as late as Skinner's <u>Etymologicon</u>
      <u>Linguae Anglicanae</u> (1671).

*43   RUSSELL, I. WILLIS. "Allegory of <u>Mother Hubberds Tale</u>."
      Proceedings of Dr. Greenlaw's Seminary "C," 1928-29, no. 30.
      Manuscript. Baltimore: Johns Hopkins University Library.
           Cited in Atkinson, 1937.

*44   _____. "Some Notes on <u>Mother Hubberds Tale</u>." Proceedings of
      Dr. Greenlaw's Seminary "C," 1928-29. no. 11. Manuscript.
      Baltimore: Johns Hopkins University Library.
           Cited in Atkinson, 1937.

*45   _____. "Spenser's <u>Virgils Gnat</u> and the Earl of Leicester."
      Proceedings of Dr. Greenlaw's Seminary "C," 1928-29, no. 17.
      Manuscript. Baltimore: Johns Hopkins University Library.
           Cited in Atkinson, 1937.

*46   _____. "Three Notes on Spenser's <u>Mother Hubberds Tale</u>."
        Proceedings of Dr. Greenlaw's Seminary "C," 1928-29, no. 19.
        Manuscript. Baltimore: Johns Hopkins University Library.
            Cited in Atkinson, 1937.

 47   SANDISON, HELEN ESTABROOK. "Arthur Gorges, Spenser's Alycon
        and Ralegh's Friend." <u>PMLA</u> 43:645-74.
            Biographical study that has relevance to <u>Daphnaida</u>; estab-
        lishes "the fact that Spenser's dedication of the <u>Daphnaida</u>, as
        of January 1, 1591, is to be taken to mean 1591 new style, not
        1592."

*48   SCHULZE, IVAN L. "The Relationship between Spenser and
        Elizabethan Pageantry and Chivalry." Proceedings of Dr.
        Greenlaw's Seminary "C," 1928-29, no. 34. Manuscript.
        Baltimore: Johns Hopkins University Library.
            Cited in Atkinson, 1937.

*49   SCOTT, MYRA E. "Problems Arising in the Interpretation of
        Spenser's <u>Shepheardes Calender</u> in Relation to Contemporary
        Affairs." Master's thesis, Stanford University.
            Cited in Stephens, 1950.

*50   STRATHMANN, ERNEST A. "Criticism of Spenser's <u>Muiopotmos</u>."
        Proceedings of Dr. Greenlaw's Seminary "C," 1928-29, no. 8.
        Manuscript. Baltimore: Johns Hopkins University Library.
            Cited in Atkinson, 1937.

*51   _____. "Note on Separate Publication of the <u>Complaints</u>."
        Proceedings of Dr. Greenlaw's Seminary "C," 1928-29, no. 32.
        Manuscript. Baltimore: Johns Hopkins University Library.
            Cited in Atkinson, 1937.

*52   _____. "Spenser and Lady Carey." Proceedings of Dr. Green-
        law's Seminary "C," 1928-29, no. 21. Manuscript. Baltimore:
        Johns Hopkins University Library.
            Cited in Atkinson, 1937.

*53   STREET, HELEN K. "A Study of Spenser's <u>Mother Hubberds Tale</u>."
        Master's thesis, Tulane University.
            Cited in Stephens, 1950.

 54   TUVE, ROSEMOND. "Red Crosse Knight and Mediaeval Demon
        Stories." <u>PMLA</u> 44:706-14.
            Spenser's foundling, Red Cross Knight, is reminiscent of
        "often-recurring romantic infancies [--the shreds and patches
        gathered by an eclectic imagination and fused, as was Spenser's
        habit, into a new whole, coherent, convincing, true, yet none-
        theless suggestive of those tales of other foundlings--] from
        Romulus and Remus, Valentin and Orson, down to Libeaus Desconus
        and the Young Perceval--which were Spenser's unrealized literary
        inheritance."

55   VAUGHAN, MARY F. "Pageants and Processions in Spenser's
      Poetry." Master's thesis, Oklahoma University, 43 pp.
         Compares pageants, masques, and processions in The Faerie
      Queene, Fowre Hymnes, Epithalamion, and Prothalamion with those
      of the middle ages. Cites numerous examples of Spenser's
      borrowings.

56   "VERITAS." "The Hidden Hand." Baconiana 3d ser. 19:205-8.
         Notes Bacon's knowledge of Hebrew and Chaldean and his use
      of sacred symbols in the woodcuts of "his 1611 Spenser."

57   WARD, B.M. The Seventeenth Earl of Oxford, 1550-1604.
      London: John Murray, pp. 359-69.
         Suggests that "Pleasant Willy" of Teares of the Muses and
      "Willy" in March and August eclogues of The Shepheardes Calender
      is Philip Sidney, not Lyly or Tarleton; that "Gentle Spirit" of
      Teares of the Muses is Oxford.

*58   WEBB, WILLIAM S. "Spenser and Vergil." Ph.D. diss., Johns
      Hopkins University.
         Partially reprinted: "Vergil in Spenser's Epic Theory."
      ELH 4 (1937):62-84; See McNeir-Provost no. 1732.

59   WINSTANLEY, LILIAN, ed. Introduction to The Faerie Queene,
      Book I. Cambridge: Cambridge University Press, pp. vii-lxxx.
         Reprint of 1915.18.

60   ____. Introduction to The Faerie Queene, Book II. Cambridge:
      Cambridge University Press, pp. vii-lxxix.
         Reprint of 1914.20.

61   ZEITLER, W.I. "The Date of Spenser's Death." MLN 43:322-24.
         Presents evidence to support 13 January 1599, rather than
      16 January.

                              1929

*1   ADAM, ROBERT B. The Robert B. Adam Library Relating to Dr.
      Samuel Johnson and His Era. Vol. 3. London and New York:
      Oxford University Press, p. 225.
         Cited in National Union Catalog. Mentions Spenser.

 2   AINSWORTH, EDWARD GAY. "The Orlando Furioso in English Liter-
      ature Before 1640." Ph.D. diss., Cornell University, pp. 95-
      161, passim.
         Presents an extensive discussion of Ariosto's influence on
      The Faerie Queene with an effort "to contrast the spirit and tem-
      perament of Ariosto and Spenser, showing what modifications
      Spenser made in his borrowings from Ariosto, contrasting the
      effectiveness with which the two poets used many of the same

devices, and suggesting that Spenser gradually learned the technique of narrative by experimenting with the methods of Ariosto."
Cites numerous parallels in themes, plots, incidents, similes and
metaphors, characters, but sees real differences in purpose--
Spenser's is more serious while Ariosto excels as story-teller.
Finds more influence on Books IV-VI due probably to Harington's
1591 translation of Orlando Furioso.

3   ALBRIGHT, EVELYN MAY. "On the Dating of Spenser's 'Mutability'
      Cantos." SP 26:482-98.
         Challenges Belden's thesis (1929.6) that Fletcher is in-
debted to the Mutabilitie cantos for Christs Victorie and defends
her dating of Mutabilitie at 1579-1580 against Belden's suggestion that Spenser could not have written Mutabilitie before 1586.
For related studies, see 1928.1; 1930.4, 36; 1932.1; 1935.56.

4   _____. "Spenser's Cosmic Philosophy and His Religion." PMLA
      44:715-59.
         In view of Greenlaw (1920.9; 1920.10) and Saurat's (1929.41)
denial of Spenser's religious faith, re-examines "Spenser's views
on the universe, the creation of the world, and of vegetable and
animal life, the immortality of the soul, the existence of God,
and the relations of God to the universe." Interprets Mutabilitie,
the Garden of Adonis, and Colin Clouts Come Home Againe (lines
799-883) as "youthful attempts at a world philosophy, largely
under the influence of Empedocles as to cosmic theory, with a
curious admixture of notions from Genesis and a few ideas from
Aristotle." Hymne of Heavenlie Beautie and Hymne of Heavenlie
Love reveal not only ideas of Benivieni, Ficino, Castiglione,
but also ideas from Platonic, Neoplatonic, Aristotelian, and
Christian philosophies. Discounts Lucretius as significant
source. Responds point for point to Greenlaw, suggests seven
major concepts of the philosophy of Empedocles with which Spenser
agrees, and concludes to ten facts which demonstrate that Lucretius is not the source of Spenser's theory of the origin of things.
Concludes Spenser's views to be rational and conservative, with
no scientific interests except astronomy. For related studies,
see 1929.3; 1930.14; 1931.11; 1932.1; 1934.63.

*5 BEER, N.A. A History of British Socialism. London:
      G. Bell, pp. 46-47.
         Cited in Atkinson, 1937, which notes Beer's comments on
Spenser as anticommunist and antidemocratic.

6   BELDEN, H.M. "Alanus de Insulis, Giles Fletcher, and the
      Mutabilitie Cantos." SP 26:131-44.
         Possibly having seen Mutabilitie cantos prior to their
publication in 1609, Fletcher was prompted to seek out De Planctu
Naturae of Alanus de Insulis as a source for his Christs Victorie
in Heaven. Challenges Albright's dating (1928.3) of Mutabilitie
at 1579-1580, suggesting a date no earlier than 1586. For related studies, see 1928.1; 1930.4, 36; 1932.1; 1935.56.

7 _____ . "Two Spenser Notes." MLN 44:526-31.
         Spenser influenced by the Helen of Euripides for roles of
   Proteus and Florimell in The Faerie Queene and by pseudo-
   Virgilian Ciris for part of a speech by Britomart's nurse, Glauce.

8 BHATTACHERJE, MOHINIMOHAN. Studies in Spenser. Calcutta:
   University of Calcutta Press, 93 pp.
         Book V of The Faerie Queene based on Plato's conception of
   justice, although Spenser follows Aristotle in giving instances
   of injustice; Spenser indebted to Pico della Mirandola for Neoplatonism in Fowre Hymnes; Spenser indebted to Plato for poetic
   theory; Bruno's influence on Spenser; Spenser indebted to
   Castiglione for Sir Calidore in The Faerie Queene, Book VI and
   for Mother Hubberds Tale.

9 BOATWRIGHT, EVELYN. "A Note on Spenser's Use of Biblical
   Material." MLN 44:159.
         Corrects Landrum's (1926.27) incorrect chapter reference to
   Ephesians in letter to Raleigh. The "v." which she reads as a
   roman numeral is an abbreviation for the latin vide intended to
   refer the reader to all of St. Paul's letter to the Ephesians.

*10 BRINKLEY, ROBERT. "Sir Richard Blackmore's Arthurian Epics."
   Proceedings of Dr. Greenlaw's Seminary "C," 1929-30, [no
   number]. Manuscript. Baltimore: Johns Hopkins University
   Library.
         Cited in Atkinson, 1937.

11 BUSH, DOUGLAS. "Some Allusions to Spenser." MLN 42:314-16.
         Finds allusions to Spenser, not mentioned by Carpenter, in
   seven works published between 1592 and 1801.

12 COE, ADA HUME. "Spenser and Ovid." CW 22:91-92.
         Suggests that Spenser borrowed description of Wood of
   Error in The Faerie Queene, I.i.8-9 from Ovid's Metamorphoses
   10.86-105. For related studies, see 1929.13, 26, 43.

13 COOPER, LANE. "Spenser and Ovid." CW 22:166.
         In response to Coe (1929.12), points out that Skeat made
   clear in 1894 the relationship between passages on the Wood of
   Error in The Faerie Queene, I.i.8-9 and Chaucer's Parelement of
   Foules, lines 176-182. For related studies, see 1929.12, 26, 43.

14 De SELINCOURT, E., ed. Introduction to The Poetical Works of
   Edmund Spenser. London, New York, and Toronto: Humphrey
   Milford, Oxford University Press, pp. vii-lxvii.
         Reprint of 1912.11.

15 DUNBAR, H. FLANDERS. Symbolism in Medieval Thought and Its
   Consummation in "The Divine Comedy." New Haven: Yale
   University Press; London: Oxford University Press, p. 500.

Distinguishes between symbolic allegory and personification allegory, noting that the two appear side by side in The Faerie Queene. Published version of 1927.10. Reprinted: New York: Russell & Russell, 1961.

16   FAVERTY, FREDERIC E. "A Note on the Areopagus." PQ 5:278-80.
     Doubts existence of Areopagus as formally organized group. Suggests that Spenser and Harvey used the word as a "pedantic pleasantry," since "the word Areopagus was applied in the latter half of the sixteenth century to any group of persons which arrogated to itself the province of a judiciary body."

*17 FRITTS, KATHERINE T. "Spenser and Platonism." Master's thesis, Columbia University.
     Cited in Stephens, 1950.

18   GREENLAW, EDWIN. "Britomart at the House of Busirane." SP 26:117-30.
     Considers analogues of elements in The Faerie Queene and in the English Wagner Book and Amadis of Gaul, part of a group of tales about castles of wonder, all of which echo the Vulgate Lancelot. Considers also Arthur of Little Britain, "the greatest single influence to be traced in Spenser's Poem," especially Arthur's adventure at Port Noire at the castle built on Mount Perilous. Concludes that "the center of the story of Britomart at Busirane's castle is some version of the Grail mysteries." In terms of the allegory, to the scornful exposition of court love at Castle Joyeous and "to his poetical representation of the mysteries of reproduction and the origin of life" in the Garden of Adonis, Spenser adds a third representation of love in the House of Busirane, "an imaginative treatment of the religion of love degenerated into a cult, . . . a love that is no true religion."

19   GREENOUGH, JAMES BRADSTREET, and GEORGE LYMAN KITTREDGE. Words and Their Ways in English Speech. New York and London: Macmillan, pp. 118, 295, 354, 375.
     Reprint of 1901.11.

20   GRIERSON, HERBERT JOHN CLIFFORD. Cross Currents in English Literature of the Seventeenth Century. The Messenger Lectures, Cornell University, 126-27. London: Chatto and Windus, pp. 25-28, 29-65, passim.
     Contrasts Spenser's and Milton's purposes in writing epics. Spenser fails to bridge gap between secular and sacred poetry in The Faerie Queene and is closer to Petrarch than to Dante in his conception of love. Considers the "spirit" and "form" of The Faerie Queene "most harmonious . . . when, retaining moral allegory as a shield," Spenser "reverts in spirit to the allegory from which his own ultimately derives, the Romance of the Rose," especially in Books III-VI. Concludes: Spenser could not "effect

a real compromise between the courtly sensuous chivalrous poetry
of the Renaissance, the dream of love and chivalry, revived with
less of conviction, but a more elaborate embellishment of presen-
tation, and the intenser spirit of Protestant, Puritan, or Catholic Christianity intent on otherworldly values. The values of
The Faerie Queene, and there are such, are not Christian as
Bunyan and Foster understood Christian, but Humanist." Notes
that in Fowre Hymnes "Spenser's vein is more Petrarchan than
Platonic." Reprinted 1948; New York: Harper & Brothers, 1958.

21   HALL, WILLIAM C. "The Sonnet." Manchester Quarterly 55:
     262-83.
         Notes that quatrains of Spenserian sonnet are linked to and
     based upon stanza of The Faerie Queene.

22   HANKINS, JOHN E. "The Harpalus of Spenser's Colin Clout."
     MLN 44:164-67.
         Identifies Harpalus as George Turberville, who refers to
     himself as Harpalus in his Epitaphes, Epigrams, Songs, and Son-
     nets (1567); supports Emil Koeppel identification (1891).

23   HUGHES, MERRITT Y. Virgil and Spenser. University of
     California Publications in English, vol. 2, no. 3. Berkeley:
     University of California Press, pp. 263-418.
         Part 1: "The Pastorals," with an interchapter on Virgils
     Gnat; Part 2: "The Epic and the Romance." On the basis of
     Spenser's use of four "virgilian" motifs of Ronsard, Bäif, and
     Du Bellay in "August" eclogue of The Shepheardes Calender, the
     contrast between Spenser's shadowing himself in Colin Clout and
     Virgil's shadowing himself in various personae, their differing
     conceptions of "nature," and the scant testimony from Spenser's
     contemporaries of Spenser's relation to Virgil, concludes that
     "Virgil's influence upon the Calender seems to have been slight,
     indirect, and distorted." Spenser was attracted by both of
     Virgil's minor epics, translating the Culex, reproducing part
     of the Ciris in The Faerie Queene. Notes that the freedom of
     epic style in these poems "may have helped him to achieve in
     the Gnat a syntax and a cadence which begins to resemble that
     of the Faerie Queene." Doubts the influence of Virgil on nar-
     rative structure of The Faerie Queene, but posits multiple in-
     fluences from ancients, Italy, France. Notes Spenser's greatest
     debt to Virgil is story of Glauce and Britomart (Book III, The
     Faerie Queene), taken from the Ciris. Sees resemblance between
     Spenser's Belphoebe and Virgil's Venus. Cites parallels between
     Spenser and Virgil but adds that "Spenser in planning The Faerie
     Queene, included both the plans which Virgil rejected. He ad-
     mitted British chronicle history and its encrusting legends to-
     gether with all the mythological lore of the classical epics and
     of medieval romance." Concludes that while "Spenser misunder-
     stood Virgil," he admired him; thus, Virgil was an important
     factor in the creation of The Faerie Queene.

24   ____. "Virgilian Allegory and The Faerie Queene." PMLA 44:
        696-705.
            Suggests that the Belphoebe of The Faerie Queene derives
        not only from the Venus of the Aeneid but also from allegorical
        interpretations of the Virgilian Venus which Spenser inherited
        from Landino, Speroni, Scaliger, and Tasso.

25   JEFFREY, VIOLET M. John Lyly and the Italian Renaissance.
        Paris: Librairie Ancienne Honoré Champion, p. 92.
            Notes Spenser's influence on Lyly.

26   JOHNSTON, MARY. "Once More Spenser and Ovid." CW 22:208.
            To the tree list of Coe (1929.12) and Cooper (1929.13),
        adds "the earlier, if shorter, list of trees given by Catullus
        64.288-291 as the wedding-gift brought by the river-god Peneos
        from forest-girt Tempe."

27   KANE, ROBERT J. "Tobacco in English Literature to 1700 with
        Special Reference to the Authorship of the First English Work
        Thereon." Ph.D. diss., Harvard University, pp. 21-22.
            Credits Spenser with phrase "divine tobacco" and cites
        possible allusion to tobacco in "soveraine weed" reference made
        by Belphoebe to wounded Timias.

28   KELSO, RUTH. The Doctrine of the English Gentleman in the
        Sixteenth Century, with a Bibliographical List of Treatises
        on the Gentleman and Related Subjects Published in Europe to
        1625. University of Illinois Studies in Language and Litera-
        ture, vol. 14. Urbana: University of Illinois Press, 287 pp.,
        passim.
            Notes Spenser's intent to portray a gentleman by his moral
        qualities and cites The Faerie Queene to exemplify gentlemanly
        traits of courtesy, temperance, and good horsemanship. Published
        version of 1923.23; revised version of 1926.26. Reprinted:
        Gloucester: Peter Smith, 1964.

29   LEMMI, C.W. "The Symbolism of the Classical Episodes in The
        Faerie Queene." PQ 8:270-87.
            Acknowledges Spenser's indebtedness to Boccaccio, Alanus,
        and Lucretius, but suggests that Spenser "was indebted to the
        Mythologiae of Natalis Comes for the symbolism of most of the
        episodes of classical origin to be found in The Faerie Queene."
        For response, see 1930.5.

30   LEWIS, CHARLTON MINER. The Principles of English Verse.
        Edited by Chauncey Brewster Tinker. 2d ed. New Haven:
        Yale University Press, pp. 77-79.
            Spenser material exactly as in 1906 edition. Pagination
        differs because original plates were melted down during World War
        I and type had to be reset. Revised edition of 1906.16.

*31   MEZGER, FRITZ. <u>Der Ire in der englischen Literatur bis zum
       Anfang des 19 Jahrhunderts</u>. Leipzig: Palestra, pp. 37-43.
             Cited in Atkinson, 1937. Comments on <u>A Veue of the Present
       State of Ireland</u>.

*32   MILLER, JOSEPH R., Jr. "Spenser's Influence on Milton's Prose
       and Poetry." Manuscript study. Charlottesville: University
       of Virginia Library.
             Cited in 1931.58.

*33   PEARSON, LU EMILY. "Elizabethan Love Conventions." Ph.D.
       diss., Stanford University.
             For published edition, see 1933.52.

 34   PIENAAR, W.J.B. <u>English Influences in Dutch Literature and
       Justus Van Effen as Intermediary: An Aspect of Eighteenth
       Century Achievement</u>. Cambridge: Cambridge University Press,
       pp. 10-11, 225.
             Jonker Jon van der Noot fired Spenser with the enthusiasm
       of the Pléiade; Van Effen called <u>The Faerie Queene</u> "a torso of a
       projected epic."

 35   RENWICK, W.L., ed. Introduction and notes to <u>Daphnaida and
       Other Poems</u>. London: Scholartis Press, 244 pp.
             Considers all poems in the volume, with partial exception
       of <u>Fowre Hymnes</u>, "occasional" poems of worth: "Many lessons in
       the craft of writing await the careful reader of these poems
       written by a master of the old--and neglected--craft called
       Rhetoric." Sees significant influence of Chaucer's <u>Book of the
       Duchess Blanche</u> on <u>Daphnaida</u> and of Chaucer's pastoral technique
       on <u>Colin Clouts Come Home Againe</u>. Finds <u>Amoretti</u> conventional
       and <u>Epithalamion</u> innovative and fresh. Considers Neoplatonism
       basis for <u>Fowre Hymnes</u>, but Spenser's use of sources is inconsis-
       tent: Spenser's "Platonism, as expounded here, is imperfect and
       alloyed, and its influence has been much exaggerated, but one
       doctrine remains constant in his thought, the belief in the
       divine nature of beauty. He did not ascend the 'Platonic ladder'
       from earthly to heavenly beauty; the earth that its Creator found
       good sufficed for him; but he saw that the Creator had made it
       beautiful, that its beauty came from Him, and was the mark of its
       divine origin."

 36   _____. Introduction to <u>Spenser, Selections with Essays by
       Hazlitt, Coleridge and Leigh Hunt</u>. Oxford: Clarendon Press,
       pp. v-xv.
             Reprint of 1923.36.

 37   RENWICK, W.L. "Spenser's Galathea and Naæra." <u>TLS</u>,
       14 March, pp. 206-7.
             Presents circumstantial evidence to identify in <u>Colin
       Clouts Come Home Againe</u> Galathea with Lady Wallop and Naæra with
       the Countess of Ormonde. For related study, see 1933.33.

38   RUSSELL, I. WILLIS. "Biblical Echoes in <u>Mother Hubberds</u>
<u>Tale</u>." <u>MLN</u> 44:162-64.
        Notes three biblical references in lines 433ff that differ
from ones previously cited.

*39   _____. "The Sources of Spenser's <u>Mother Hubberds Tale</u>."
Master's thesis, Johns Hopkins University.
        Cited in Stephens, 1950.

40   SANDISON, HELEN E. "Three Spenser Allusions." <u>MLN</u> 44:159-62.
        Notes three poems by Joseph Hall, Hugh Holland, and T. May,
contemporaries or nearly so of Spenser, which bring praises of
Spenser into connection with those given to other poets.

41   SAURAT, DENIS. <u>La littérature et l'occultisme: Études sur</u>
<u>la poésie philosophique moderne</u>. Paris: Les Éditions Rieder,
184 pp.
        Contains first four chapters of text translated by Bolton
(1930.42) but does not include the chapter on Spenser. For
related study, see 1929.4.

42   SCOTT, JANET. "Les sources et l'apport personnel." In <u>Les</u>
<u>sonnets élisabéthains</u>. Bibliothèque de la revue de
littérature comparée, 60. Paris: Librairie Ancienne Honoré
Champion, pp. 159-77, passim.
        Comments on Spenser's debt to Tasso and Desportes.

43   SEDGWICK, W.B. "Spencer [sic] and Ovid Again." <u>CW</u> 22:184.
        In response to Coe (1929.12), points out Spenser's imita-
tion of Chaucer's <u>Parlement of Foules</u> in description of Wood of
Error in <u>The Faerie Queene</u>, I.i.8-9. For related studies, see
1929.13, 26.

44   SMIT, J[OHAN]. <u>Bilderdijk et La France</u>. Amsterdam: H.J.
Paris, p. 199.
        Notes Spenser's influence on <u>Bilderdijk</u>: "Il n'y a que
Spenser et Milton qui soient loués sans réserve."

45   THEOBALD, BERTRAM G. "The Monuments to Bacon, Shakespeare
and Spenser." <u>Baconiana</u> 20:14-28.
        Using "marginal acrostics" and three of Bacon's "codes of
numerical cipher," concludes that Spenser's name shows up on
Bacon's and Shakespeare's tombstones and that Bacon's name shows
up on Spenser's.

46   _____. <u>Shake-speare's Sonnets Unmasked</u>. London: Cecil
Palmer, 117 pp., passim.
        Attempts to prove that Bacon wrote Shakespeare's sonnets
and dramatic literature, while Spenser wrote the other non-
dramatic works.

*47   WATSON, SARA R. "Spenser and Sixteenth Century Chivalry."
      Master's thesis, Western Reserve University.
          Cited in Stephens, 1950.

 48   WOOD, HERBERT. "Spenser's Great-Grandson." TLS, 14 February,
      p. 118.
          Letter from John Wainwright, Baron of the Irish Court of
      Exchequer, dated 3 August 1736, reports sale of Kilcolman Castle
      to pay grandson's debts.

                                  1930

 1   ATKINSON, DOROTHY FRANCIS. "A Study of the Punctuation of
      Spenser's Faerie Queene." Ph.D. diss., University of
      Washington, 237 pp.
          Concludes: literary men of late Elizabethan period had a
      system of punctuation similar to the modern; they regarded this
      system as having affinities with that of such classical authors
      as Cicero and Quintillian; Spenser's system in accord with con-
      temporary theorists and is remarkably systematic, despite a few
      inconsistencies; punctuation is Spenser's own rather than his
      printer's.

 2   BAROWAY, ISRAEL. "Imagery: 2. In the Influence of the Song
      of Songs Upon Edmund Spenser." In "Studies in the Bible as
      Poetry in the English Renaissance." Ph.D. diss., Johns
      Hopkins University, pp. 67-97.
          Studies images in Amoretti, Epithalamion, Colin Clouts Come
      Home Againe, and The Faerie Queene which parallel images in Song
      of Songs. For additional study and published edition, see
      1933.5; 1935.4.

 3   BENSLY, EDWARD. "Literary Queries: Tennyson, Spenser."
      NQ 158:319.
          Notes source of quote on delight in reading The Faerie
      Queene in conversation between Pope and "an old lady." Response
      to 1930.41.

 4   BUSH, DOUGLAS. "The Date of Spenser's Cantos of Mutability."
      PMLA 45:954-57.
          Challenges Albright's dating of the Mutabilitie cantos
      (1928.1; 1929.3) and her substitution of Empedocles for Lucretius
      as a dominent influence on Spenser (1929.4). For related studies,
      see 1930.36; 1932.1; 1935.56.

 5   BUYSSENS, E. "The Symbolism in Faerie Queene Book I." PQ
      9:403-6.
          Challenges Lemmi's thesis (1929.29) that Spenser was in-
      debted to Natalis Comes for the symbolism of most of the episodes
      of classical origin in The Faerie Queene. Acknowledges influence

                                  146

of Comes, but concludes that "the symbolic significance of his allegory in Book I is pure Calvinism."

6   CLARK, EVA TURNER. Shakespeare's Plays in the Order of Their Writing. A Study based on the Records of the Court Revels and Historic Allusions. London: Cecil Palmer, pp. 649-53, passim.
        Notes parallel allusions in Shakespeare and Spenser, notably The Shepheardes Calender and Teares of the Muses. Discussion of Muiópotmos in section on allusions to poems inspired by the Earl of Oxford; identifies Clarion as Oxford.

7   CUMMING, W.P. "Ovid as a Source for Spenser's Monster-spawning Mud Passages." MLN 45:166-68.
        Challenges Lemmi's assignment of the origin of Spenser's Monster-spawning Nile-mud passages in The Faerie Queene to the Historical Library of Diodorus Siculus (1926.32), noting that whatever other sources Spenser used, he used Ovid for his notions of abiogenesis.

8   DUSTOOR, P.E. "Legends of Lucifer in Early English and in Milton." Anglia 54:213-68.
        Mentions Spenser's use of archangels in Fowre Hymnes.

*9 EMERSON, FRANCIS W. "The Squire's Tale of Chaucer, Spenser, and Lane." Master's thesis, Vanderbilt University.
        Cited in Stephens, 1950.

10 FITZGERALD, JOHN J. "Documents Found at Castlewhite, Co. Cork." JRSAI 60:79-83.
        Notes that Castlewhite was sold in 1637, "to Sir Robert Travers and Zachary Travers, sons of John Travers, who was married to a sister of the poet Spenser."

11 GIBBON, JOHN MURRAY. Melody and the Lyric: From Chaucer to the Cavaliers. London and Toronto: J.M. Dent & Sons; New York: E.P. Dutton, pp. 87-88.
        Notes that Richard Carlton wrote four madrigals from stanzas in The Faerie Queene and that one Stanza in The Faerie Queene (II.xii.33) reflects the contemporary vogue of madrigals.

12 GOLDER, HAROLD. "Bunyan and Spenser." PMLA 45:216-37.
        Advises extreme caution against accepting the hypothesis that Bunyan borrowed from Book I of The Faerie Queene for his Pilgrim's Progress on bases that there is not evidence, except for parallels, that Bunyan owned, borrowed, or read The Faerie Queene; that the excellences of The Faerie Queene conflict with Bunyan's Puritanism; that The Faerie Queene would be beyond the ordinary reading of Bunyan's class; that Bunyan's and Spenser's accounts agree in no essential detail.

13   GRAY, M.M. "The Influence of Spenser's Irish Experiences on
     The Faerie Queene." RES 6:413-28.
          Traces influences of Spenser's Irish experiences "not only
     in the background and incident, but in the emotional and imagina-
     tive life of the poet as these are reflected in the poem." Ex-
     amines Irish influences in the first, second, fifth, and sixth
     books of The Faerie Queene. For response, see 1931.31.

14   GREENLAW, EDWIN. "Spenser's Mutabilitie." PMLA 45:684-703.
          Answers responses to three of his earlier essays (1920.9-10;
     1923.17) on the subject of the Garden of Adonis and Mutabilitie.
     Dismisses Levinson's concern over the incongruity of Lucretian
     elements in a poet who is predominently a Platonist with the com-
     mon knowledge of Spenser's "practice of combining in a single
     passage matters drawn from widely different sources." Also chal-
     lenges validity of Levinson's argument that Bruno influenced
     Spenser in Garden of Adonis passage and in Mutabilitie. Denies
     Albright charge (1929.4) that Greenlaw presents Spenser as an
     atheist who has broken his Platonic faith. Challenges Albright's
     dating of Mutabilitie at 1579-80 (1928.1; 1929.3), upholding
     Belden's later dating (1929.6). For related studies, see
     1928.31; 1929.4; 1932.24; 1933.7; 1934.63.

15   HAMER, ENID. The Metres of English Poetry. London: Methuen
     & Co., 349 pp., passim.
          Close study of Spenser's metrics, notably Spenserian stanza
     and metres of The Shepheardes Calender, Mother Hubberds Tale,
     Amoretti, and Epithalamion. Reprinted: 1951, 1966.

16   HARD, FREDERICK. "Spenser's 'Clothes of Arras and Toure.'"
     SP 27:162-85.
          Though he follows medieval tradition, Spenser's description
     of tapestries in The Faerie Queene, III.i.34-39 and III.xi.28-46
     direct reader's attention to tapestries Spenser might have actu-
     ally seen. Brief history of tapestry in England, concluding that
     tapestry lore is congenial to Spenser's mind and spirit. Con-
     cludes with comparative study of Spenser's tapestries and actual
     tapestries of Spenser's lifetime.

17   HARRIS, ROBERT BRICE. "The Beast in English Satire from
     Spenser to John Gay." Ph.D. diss., Harvard University,
     pp. 46-88, passim.
          Traces development of beast satire from Mother Hubberds
     Tale through first quarter of eighteenth century. Spenser estab-
     lished models that integrated old and new conventions: in fables
     of The Shepheardes Calender ("May," "Fox and Kid"; "July," "Eagle
     and Shellfish"; "September," "Roffy and Lowder") and in Mother
     Hubberds Tale. Notes Spenser's ability to comment on political
     situations under guise of allegory and satire, and his use of
     heroic couplet and other new metrical forms. Discusses similari-
     ties between Virgils Gnat and Muiopotmos, and discusses extensive
     list of works influenced by Mother Hubberds Tale.

18   HARRISON, T.P., Jr. "The Faerie Queene and the Diana." PQ
     9:51-56.
        Suggests that Spenser may have employed the Diana of
     Montemayor, particularly the continuation of Alonzo Perez, in
     episodes of Pastorella and Calidore (VI.ix) and Placidas and
     Amyas (IV.vii).

19   _____. "The Relations of Spenser and Sidney." PMLA 45:712-31.
        Chronology and character of poets' work suggest exchange of
     ideas, even though little evidence exists to substantiate exist-
     ence of Areopagus group. Finds correspondences especially in
     poetic theories and experimentation with classical metres. For
     related studies, see 1923.3; 1931.42.

20   HEFFNER, RAY. "Spenser's Allegory in Book I of the Faerie
     Queene." SP 27:142-61.
        Concludes from a study of relationship between The Faerie
     Queene and reports of pageants presented to Elizabeth on her
     progress to her coronation in 1558-59: that Spenser got from
     pageants a suggestion for Una and his allegorical method in Book
     I; that Spenser chose religion as subject for Book I because it
     was first problem to confront Elizabeth and first of her virtues;
     and that Spenser's contemporaries saw Book I as allegory of Queen
     Elizabeth and her relation to the establishment of Pure Religion.

21   JENKINS, CLAUDE. "The Church and Religion in the Age of
     Shakespeare." History, n.s. 15:199-211.
        Refers to Church's comments on Spenser's regard for Ireland
     (A Veue of the Present State of Ireland).

22   JONES, H.S.V. A Spenser Handbook. New York: Appleton-
     Century-Crofts, 419 pp.
        Chapters on Spenser's Age and Life are followed by individ-
     ual chapters on each of his works, including eight on The Faerie
     Queene. Final chapter considers language and versification.
     Each chapter ends with a bibliography of references.

23   JONES, MABEL LAVERNE. "Recent Interest in Edmund Spenser
     (1910-1930)." Master's thesis, University of Oklahoma, 213 pp.
        Bibliographic study (mainly an annotated bibliography)
     divided according to "Books and Articles Involving Direct Refer-
     ence to Spenser's Work" and "Books and Articles Emphasizing Phases
     of Special Interest Other than the Works."

24   LATHAM, MINOR WHITE. The Elizabethan Fairies: The Fairies of
     Folklore and the Fairies of Shakespeare. Ph.D. diss., Columbia
     University; New York: Columbia University Press, 313 pp.,
     passim.
        Considers The Faerie Queene, The Shepheardes Calender, and
     the Epithalamion in various contexts: origins of fairies,
     changelings, traditional and literary fairies, belief that

fairies are visible and actual spirits, the need for a new race
of fairies to overcome traditional wickedness associated with
fairies, Diana's sovereignty over fairies, and the connection
of fairies to the Church of Rome. Reprinted: Folcroft, Pa.:
Folcroft Press, 1970; New York: Octagon Books, 1972.

25   LEGOUIS, ÉMILE. Edmund Spenser. Les grands écrivains
      étrangers. Paris: Libraire Bloud et Gay, 359 pp.
           Reprint of 1923.26.

26   LEIBLE, ARTHUR B. "Conventions of Animal Symbolism and
      Satire in Spenser's Mother Hubberds Tale." Ph.D. diss.,
      University of Chicago.
           Notes parallels between satire of Mother Hubberds Tale and
      The Shepheardes Calender, pointing out popular satire patterns
      Spenser followed. Identifies three tracts by William Turner
      that relate to Mother Hubberds Tale.

27   LEMMI, C.W. "The Allegorical Meaning of Spenser's
      Muiopotmos." PMLA 45:732-48.
           Interprets Muiopotmos as "an allegory of the life and death
      of Sir Philip Sidney much like Astrophel." Poems tell same tale;
      the butterfly image suits Sidney; the Astery episode alludes to
      Stella; the allegory fits Sidney's life. Identifies Sidney in
      Clarion, Anjou in Aragnoll, Elizabeth in Venus, Penelope Devereux
      in Astery, Lettice Knolles in Psyche, and Anjou's envoys, La Mole
      and Simier, in Sport and Play. For responses, see 1931.13, 52.

28   MILLICAN, CHARLES BOWIE. "Spenser and the Arthurian Legend."
      RES 6:167-74.
           Suggests influence of Prince Arthur's London Roundtable, of
      which Richard Mulcaster was a member, on Spenser's choice of
      Arthurian legend for The Faerie Queene. Reprinted: 1930.29.

29   _____. Spenser and the Arthurian Legend. London: Sidgwick &
      Jackson, 8 pp.
           Offprint of 1930.28. For additional studies, see 1930.30;
      1932.47.

*30   _____. "Studies in Spenser and the Arthurian Legend."
      Ph.D. diss., Harvard University.
           For related study, see 1930.29. For published and revised
      edition, see 1932.47.

31   MURRY, JOHN MIDDLETON. "The Poet's Poet." TLS, 27 February,
      pp. 149-50.
           Discusses appreciation of Spenser in nineteenth and early
      twentieth centuries, and Spenser as teacher of poets. Notes
      Spenser's sense of beauty as greatest influence, especially on
      Keats: "Much is sometimes made of Spenser's moral intention in
      composing The Faerie Queene; and, indeed, Spenser rather paraded

it himself. But in reality this moral intention amounts to
little. . . . When it came to a struggle between his morality
and his sense of beauty, the sense of beauty, very properly,
triumphed. The sense of beauty did with Spenser precisely what
it did with his pupil Keats, 'it obliterated all consideration.'
Spenser as a philosopher was hopelessly inconsistent, as a moral-
ist hopelessly divided." Considers Spenser's "music" insurpass-
able and Epithalamion "one perfect poem," the culmination of all
Spenser's poetry. Book VI of The Faerie Queene contains same
spirit and life as Epithalamion: "the five books which precede
it are romance, the sixth is simply romantic, in the sense in
which As You Like It and A Winter's Tale are romantic." Reprinted:
1931.35; Freeport, N.Y.: Books for Libraries, 1968; in John Clare
and Other Studies (London and New York: Peter Nevill, 1950),
pp. 73-84; in J. Middleton Murry Selected Criticism 1916-1957
(London: Oxford University Press, 1960), pp. 76-85.

32   MUSTARD, W[ILFRED] P. "E.K.'s Note on the Graces." MLN 45:
     168-69.
        Traces allusions in classical works for E.K.'s gloss on
"April," line 109, The Shepheardes Calender.

33   NELSON, LOUISE A. "Muiopotmos." Calcutta Review 3d ser.
     37:339-41.
        Relates Muiopotmos to Chaucer's Sir Thopas and Nun's
Priest's Tale and interprets poem in terms of Raleigh-Essex
quarrel.

34   OSGOOD, CHARLES G[ROSVENOR]. "Spenser and the Enchanted
     Glass." Johns Hopkins Alumni Magazine 19:8-31.
        Defends moral values of The Faerie Queene, especially
Spenser's iconoclastic idealism drawn from many philosophers.
Draws sharp distinction between ideal world as Spenser conceived
it and all that is finite. Considers two moral issues of great
import to the poem and to Spenser himself: continence (to include anger, love of honor, and love of gain as well as carnal
desires) and chronic despondency. Concludes that The Faerie
Queene presents "truer intimations of moral values" than does
the real world. Tensions between real and ideal and true and
false in poem reflect Spenser's life.

35   OSGOOD, CHARLES GROSVENOR; JUNIUS S. MORGAN; and KENNETH
     McKENZIE. "Virgil and the English Mind." In The Tradition
     of Virgil. Princeton: Princeton University Press, pp. 26-40.
        General discussion of Virgil's appeal during Renaissance;
Spenser cited in this context.

36   PADELFORD, FREDERICK M. "The Cantos of Mutabilitie: Further
     Considerations Bearing on the Date." PMLA 45:704-11.
        Suggests late date of composition for Mutabilitie based on
comparative statistical study of frequency of compound words,

run-on lines, feminine endings, explanatory phrases, appositions, apostrophes, and rhetorical questions. For related studies, see 1928.1; 1929.3, 6; 1930.4; 1932.1; 1935.56.

37   _____. "The Muse of the Faerie Queene." SP 27:111-24.
        On basis of external evidence and classical and Italian tradition, suggests Calliope as the muse of The Faerie Queene. For response, see 1932.5.

*38   PEARSON, LU EMILY. "The Love Conventions of the English Sonnet, A Study of the Elizabethan Protest against Petrarchism." Ph.D. diss., Stanford University, 1930.
        For published and revised edition, see 1933.52.

39   RENWICK, W.L., ed. Introduction and notes to The Shepherd's Calendar. London: Scholartis Press, 240 pp.
        Thoroughly discusses text, allusions, allegory, and significance of The Shepheardes Calender.

40   ROWE, KENNETH THORPE. "Sir Calidore: Essex or Sidney?" SP 27:125-41.
        Disputes Long's identification of Sir Calidore as Essex (1910.16; 1914.9) and re-establishes Sidney as the inspiration of Sir Calidore. For response, see 1934.29.

41   S. "Literary Queries: Tennyson, Spenser." NQ 158:279.
        For response, see 1930.3.

42   SAURAT, DENIS. "Spenser's Philosophical Ideas." In Literature and Occult Tradition: Studies in Philosophical Poetry. Translated by Dorothy Bolton. London: L. MacVeagh; New York: Dial Press, pp. 163-238.
        Considers Spenser's philosophical ideas vague, but finds much philosophical "feeling" in his poetry. Distinguishes two types of feeling, which together, present Spenser's philosophy: (1) those associated with natural order--"the feeling that nature is alive; the feeling that nature is fruitful; the association of sensuality with the feeling for nature; the lively sense of the vicissitudes of nature"; (2) those associated with "a very keen sense of the vicissitudes of human destiny and of course the world in general." Finds Spenser essentially pagan and somewhat skeptical, but notes frequent elements of Christian theology in his works, notably in The Faerie Queene and the Fowre Hymnes. Arrives at six aspects of Garden of Adonis often at variance: reincarnation of some souls; fruitfulness of nature in her species; chaos-substance and transitoriness of forms; time the great destroyer; beauty of the lovemaking season; immortality of being throughout its changes. Finds old Christian notion of two orders in Mutabilitie Cantos: earthly order subject to change and perfect heavenly order. Notes cabalistic influence on Spenser in his conception of Sapience, which corresponds to

the Schekhina in the Zohar (See 1926.45). Translated version of
1924.33; 1929.41. For related study, see 1934.63. Reprinted:
Port Washington, N.Y.: Kennikat Press, 1966.

43 SCHULZE, IVAN L. "Elizabethan Chivalry, Pageantry, and
    Masque in Spenser." Ph.D. diss., Johns Hopkins University,
    195 pp.
        The tournament, pageant, and masque supplied "raw materials
    for every purpose that Spenser had before him" in writing The
    Faerie Queene. They have "left their mark upon the structure of
    the work as a whole, as well as upon single episodes. In addi-
    tion they supplied dynamic sources for Spenser's treatment of
    Elizabeth, her courtiers, his own patrons, religious and secular
    affairs, in the cloudy allegories of his poem."

44 SHEPARD, ODELL. The Lore of the Unicorn. London: George
    Allen & Unwin, p. 87.
        Quotes Spenser's unicorn simile in The Faerie Queene,
    II.v.10.

45 SISSON, CHARLES J. "Grafton and the London Gray Friars."
    Library, 4th ser. 11:121-49.
        Notes that physician John Vandernodt is not poet-author of
    A Theatre for Worldlings.

46 SMITH, CHARLES G. "Spenser's Theory of Friendship." Ph.D.
    diss., Johns Hopkins University, 157 pp.
        For published edition, see 1935.65.

47 STOLL, ELMER EDGAR. Poets and Playwrights: Shakespeare,
    Jonson, Spenser, Milton. Minneapolis: University of
    Minnesota Press, pp. 167-202, passim.
        Variously discusses Spenser's patriotism, interest in new
    world, naivete, and differences in temperament from Milton. Con-
    centrates in "Spenser" on Spenser's role as high priest of roman-
    ticism. Defines romanticism and renaissance; discusses basis of
    Spenser's romanticism in love of beauty awakened by classical and
    Italian influences; contrasts characters of Una and Britomart;
    compares Spenser to Milton, noting Spenser's influence; concludes
    that Spenser is descriptive, picturesque, and sentimental poet.
    Reprinted: New York: Russell & Russell, 1965.

*48 STRATHMANN, ERNEST A. "A Critical Edition of Spenser's
    Muiopotmos." Ph.D. diss., Johns Hopkins University.
        Partially reprinted: 1935.71.

49 THEOBALD, BERTRAM G. Francis Bacon Concealed and Revealed.
    London: Cecil Palmer, 389 pp., passim.
        Identifies "Immerito" as Bacon, not Spenser, since there
    exist little biographical data on Spenser after he left Cambridge.
    "It is evident that scholars have been far too hasty in assuming

that 'Immerito' was the pen-name of Spenser, merely because the
anonymous <u>Shepheardes Calender</u> was included in a posthumous collection of works ascribed to him during his lifetime." Contends
that all Spenser's works were written by Bacon.

, 50   TILLYARD, E.M.W. <u>Milton</u>. London: Chatto & Windus, 396 pp.,
passim.
       Considers Spenser's influence on Milton "undoubted":
"Milton must have had Spenser almost by heart." Notes that
poets share ideas on nature of poetry and that "Sepnser in his
own stanza, in parts of <u>Colin Clout</u>, in <u>Epithalamion</u>, may have
been Milton's model for sustaining his verse, for constructing
the long verse paragraph." Finds most significant Spenserian influence in <u>Paradise Regained</u>, from Book II of <u>The Faerie Queene</u>:
"The temptations in each are pretty similar and it is quite
likely that Archimago suggested Satan's first disguise. More
important still, the allegorical twilight in Milton might be
compared with the dimness of Mammon's Cave, and the banquet in
the wilderness to the Bower of Bliss." Reprinted: 1949. Revised: New York: Barnes & Noble, 1966, 1967.

51   TRNKA, B. <u>On the Syntax of the English Verb from Caxton to
Dryden</u>. Travaux du cercle linguistique de Prague, 3. Prague:
Jednota Ceskoslovenskych Matematiku a Fysiku, 95 pp., passim.
     Examples of and comments on Spenser's archaic language.

52   UPCOTT, L.E. "The Poet's Poet." <u>TLS</u>, 6 March, p. 19.
       Points out that the atmosphere, the descriptions, and much
of the language of Spenser's Bower of Bliss (<u>The Faerie Queene</u>,
II.xii) derive from Tasso's Garden of Armida (<u>La Gerusalemme
Liberata</u>, c., xvi).

*53   VANEK, OLGA M. "Spenser's Interest in Medieval Romance as
Illustrated in the First Book of <u>The Faerie Queene</u>." Master's
thesis, University of Illinois.
       Cited in Stephens, 1950.

*54   WALLACE, CALVIN R. "A Comparative Study of Church's Glosses
and Annotations of Spenser's <u>Faerie Queene</u>." Master's thesis,
University of Tennessee.
       Cited in Stephens, 1950.

55   WYLD, HENRY CECIL. "Spenser's Diction and Style in Relation
to Those of Later English Poetry." In <u>A Grammatical Miscellany
Offered to Otto Jespersen on His Seventieth Birthday</u>. Edited
by N. Bøgholm, Aage Brusendorff, and C.A. Bodelsen. Copenhagen:
Levin & Munksgaard; London: George Allen & Unwin, pp. 147-65.
       Examines <u>The Faerie Queene</u> with regard to diction proper:
special words, metaphorical expressions, and the choice and ap-
plication of epithets; and style: balance, antithesis, contrast;
repetition of similar ideas; and amplification. Concludes that

"the main features of eighteenth century poetic diction, in the
special sense, and certain characteristics of style, usually
associated with Pope and his School, are all to be found in the
Faerie Queene," coming either directly from Spenser or via
Milton. Considers Spenser a storehouse of poetical words and
phrases and a master of versification and verbal expression:
"He attains at once to perfection, and embodies all the grace
and dignity of which English was capable." Includes careful
examination of language of Spenser and Pope.

1931

1   ALDEN, RAYMOND M. English Verse. Specimens Illustrating Its
    Principles and History. New York: Henry Holt & Co.,
    pp. 106-9, passim.
        Reprint of 1903.1.

2   ARBER, AGNES. "Edmund Spenser and Lyte's 'Nievve Herball.'"
    NQ 160:345-47.
        Presents evidence to link stanza in "April" eclogue, The
    Shepheardes Calender, with Henry Lyte's A Nievve Herball as
    source for Spenser's flower and plant names.

3   BALL, LEWIS F. "The Morality Theme in Book II of The Faerie
    Queene." MLN 46:371-79.
        Cites examples of influence on Book II of The Faerie Queene
    of conventional features of later morality plays in which "themes
    of an ethical or social nature were introduced and indeed often
    occupied the foremost place."

4   BENNETT, JOSEPHINE WATERS. "Spenser and Gabriel Harvey's
    Letter-Book." MP 29:163-86.
        Refutes Albright's theory (1928.1) that the fourth book of
    the so-called letters to Spenser in Harvey's Letter-Book is a
    reply to the Cantos of Mutabilitie. Points out that the first
    letter is fiction, meant perhaps for John Wood, nephew of his
    patron; that the second is literary fiction; that the third is
    literary in character and meant to be addressed to John Wood;
    that there is no evidence that the fourth was sent to Spenser.
    For response, see 1932.1.

5   _____. "Spenser's Hesiod." American Journal of Philology
    52:176-81.
        For his account of the Nereids in The Faerie Queene,IV.xi.
    48-51, Spenser depended upon Bobinus Mombritius's Latin verse
    translation of Hesiod's Theogony.

6   _____. "The Theme of Spenser's Fowre Hymnes." SP 28:18-57.
        Dates composition of Hymnes between Spring 1595 and Septem-
    ber 1596, thus showing "the essential unity of theme, symmetry of

plan, and climactic progression of the whole work." Discusses
chief influences (Benivieni, Castiglione, Ficino, Pico) on Fowre
Hymnes and notes how Spenser adapted the structural pattern of
Dante's Paradiso: "In the first hymn Spenser described the ray-
ing downward of the divine influence of love. In the second hymn
it was the descent of beauty. . . . In the third hymn we have
the answering, upward aspiration of the human soul toward divine
love, and in the fourth hymn Spenser is dealing with the ascent
of the human soul to the presence of divine Beauty." For response,
see 1932.52.

7   BRINKLEY, R. FLORENCE. "Blackmore's Portrayal of Spenser."
     MLN 46:313-16.
          Notes reference to The Faerie Queene in Blackmore's epic,
     Eliza (1705).

8   BULLOCK, WALTER L. "Reply to E.F. Pope." PMLA 46:287-88.
          Maintains original view of cinquecento criticism (1927.6)
     with few corrections listed here. For related studies, see
     1926.44; 1927.6; 1931.40.

9   BULLOUGH, GEOFFREY, ed. Introduction to The Philosophical
     Poems of Henry More. Manchester: Manchester University Press,
     pp. xlii-xliv, lxiii-lxviii.
          Notes heavy influence of allegory, imagery, and phraseology
     of The Faerie Queene on Psychozoia, and more than incidental
     echoes of Fowre Hymnes in the same poem.

10   CLARK, EVA TURNER. Hidden Allusions in Shakespeare's Plays.
     A Study of the Oxford Theory Based on the Records of Early
     Court Revels and Personalities of the Times. New York:
     William Farquhar Payson, pp. 643-47.
          Identifies Clarion in Muiopotmos as Oxford, "the writer of
     the plays we know as Shakespeare's"; images in poem correspond to
     imagination operative in plays. Willy in Teares of the Muses
     identified as Oxford.

11   CUMMING, WILLIAM P. "The Influence of Ovid's Metamorphoses
     on Spenser's 'Mutabilitie' Cantos." SP 28:241-56.
          Demonstrates Spenser's primary debt to two passages in the
     Metamorphoses for the pictorial style, pageantry, and illustra-
     tions given by Mutabilitie in her defense in the "Mutabilitie"
     cantos. Refutes Greenlaw's overemphasis of Spenser's debt to
     Lucretius (1920.9) and Albright's (1929.4) ascription of Spenser's
     cosmic philosophy to Empedocles. For related study, see 1934.63.

12   DENKINGER, EMMA MARSHALL. Immortal Sidney. New York:
     Brentano's, passim.
          Mentions possible relationship between Sidney and Spenser.

13 _____. "Spenser's Muiopotmos Again." PMLA 46:272-76.
    Refutes Lemmi (1930.27), finding his argument and identifi-
cations inconsistent. Suggests that Francis Walsingham be identified with the Stella references here and in Astrophel. For
related study, see 1931.52.

14 ECCLES, MARK. "Spenser's First Marriage." TLS, 31 December,
    p. 1053.
    Verifies Spenser's marriage to Machabyas Chylde; cites
St. Margaret's Church Parish Record 1539-60, entry of 27 October
1579. For related studies, see 1932.31, 37.

15 ERSKINE, JOHN. The Elizabethan Lyric. New York: Columbia
    University Press, pp. 107-16, 153-58, 176-96, 302.
    Reprint of 1903.8.

*16 FEVER, MARTIN. "Similes in The Faerie Queene of Edmund
    Spenser." Master's thesis, Rutgers University.
    Cited in Stephens, 1950.

17 FRISBEE, GEORGE. Edward De Vere: A Great Elizabethan.
    London: Cecil Palmer, pp. 64-75.
    Attempts to show, on basis of "ciphers" in various passages
of Spenser's works, that Edward De Vere, Earl of Oxford, wrote
Spenser's works.

18 GARNETT, RICHARD, and EDMUND GOSSE. English Literature An
    Illustrated Record. From the Age of Henry VIII to the Age of
    Milton. Vol. 2. New York: Macmillan Co., pp. 109-30.
    Reprint of 1904.12.

19 GOLDER, HAROLD. "Bunyan's Giant Despair." JEGP 30:361-78.
    Spenser and seventeenth-century Spenserians were among many
writers who pursued theme of despair.

20 GORDON, GEORGE. "Virgil in English Poetry." PBA 17:39-53.
    Mentions Spenser as Virgil's most precocious English pupil
and notes that Spenser was less prepared than Virgil for poetry
and that his debts to Virgil are innumerable. Notes Spenser's
influence on Milton. Reprinted: The Discipline of Letters
(Oxford: Clarendon Press, 1946), pp. 19-34; London: Haskell
House, 1964.

21 GREENOUGH, JAMES BRADSTREET, and GEORGE LYMAN KITTREDGE.
    Words and their Ways in English Speech. New York and London:
    Macmillan, pp. 118, 295, 354, 375.
    Reprint of 1901.11.

22 HAMER, DOUGLAS. "Spenser's Marriage." RES 7:271-90.
    With references to Amoretti and Epithalamion concludes that
Spenser married twice: in 1580 to the mother of three children,
and to Elizabeth Boyle, the mother of Peregrine.

23   HARD, FREDERICK. "Lamb on Spenser." SP 28:656-70.
         Comments and allusions in Lamb's works reveal admiration
for Elizabethans and suggest Lamb may have envisioned a fuller
study of Spenser. Reprinted: Royster Memorial Studies, ed.
Louis B. Wright et al. (Chapel Hill: University of North
Carolina Press, 1931), pp. 124-38.

24   ___. "Spenser and Burghley." SP 28:219-34.
         Reinforces, with much topical data, satire on Burghley in
Fox of Mother Hubberds Tale (lines 1171-82); Burghley built personal mansions while neglecting royal palaces and certain nobility.

25   HEFFNER, RAY. "Spenser's Acquisition of Kilcolman." MLN
     46:493-98.
         Correction of Carpenter's and Henley's dating of Spenser's
acquisition (27 June 1586). Evidence better supports acquisition
date of 22 May 1589, and occupancy between 3 September 1588, and
24 March 1558/59. Notes Spenser's quarrel with Lord Roche over
title to estate.

26   HERBERT, A.S. "Chevisaunce." TLS, 19 March, p. 234.
         Identification of chevisaunce ("April," The Shepheardes
Calender) as honeysuckle.

27   HOWARD, LEON. "Melville and Spenser--A Note on Criticism."
     MLN 46.291-92.
         Identifies Spenserian sources in quotations that accompany
the ten sketches in The Encantadas, or Enchanted Isles. For
related study, see 1932.62.

28   HULBERT, VIOLA BLACKBURN. "A Possible Christian Source for
     Spenser's Temperance." SP 28:184-210.
         Christianity and writing of church fathers, not Nichomachean
Ethics, are source of Spenser's concept of temperance in Book II
of The Faerie Queene.

29   LANZ, HENRY. The Physical Basis of Rhyme: An Essay on the
     Aesthetics of Sound. Stanford: Stanford University Press;
     London: Oxford University Press, p. 259.
         Cites Spenserian stanza as example of harmonic form which
is possible only on the basis of nine lines.

30   Le BEL, EUGENE C. "Christian and Medieval Theology in
     Spenser's 'Hymne of Heavenly Love' and 'Hymne of Heavenly
     Beautie.'" Master's thesis, University of Chicago, 82 pp.
         Concludes that first two hymns have atmosphere of pagan
antiquity, while last two are religious and Christian: "the
dominant influence on the first two hymns is platonism and its
myths, the predominant influence on the last two is christian
and medieval theology, colored by the platonic idea of love for
beauty."

31   LEWIS, C.S. "Spenser's Irish Experiences and The Faerie
     Queene." RES 7:83-85.
          Disagrees with Gray (1930.13) that Malory and his predeces-
     sors are sources for Spenser's episodes in The Faerie Queene.
     Suggests influence of Ariosto and Boiardo.

32   LOTSPEICH, HENRY GIBBONS. "Classical Mythology in the Poetry
     of Edmund Spenser." Ph.D. diss., Princeton University.
          For published edition, see 1932.43.

33   LOWENBERG, J. "Philosophy and Literature." University of
     California Chronicle 33:267-92.
          Notes Spenser's keen interest in "a possible region of un-
     exampled and ideal perfection."

*34 MITCHELL, PEARL B. "An Analysis of the Aesthetic Qualities
     of Spenser's Poetry." Master's thesis, Stanford University.
          Cited in Stephens, 1950.

35   MURRY, JOHN MIDDLETON. "The Poet's Poet." In Countries of
     the Mind. 2d ser. London: Oxford University Press,
     pp. 63-77.
          Reprint of 1930.31.

36   NETHERCOT, ARTHUR H. Abraham Cowley. The Muses Hannibal.
     London: Humphrey Milford; Oxford: Oxford University Press,
     passim.
          Brief mentions of Spenser's influence on Cowley.

37   OSGOOD, CHARLES G[ROSVENOR]. "Comments on the Moral Allegory
     of the Faerie Queene." MLN 46:502-7.
          Though he calls it the "Book of Temperance," Spenser actu-
     ally discusses continence in Book II of The Faerie Queene, perhaps
     taking his hint from Book IV of The Courtier; Cymochles represents
     the invariably incontinent man; Spenser's discussion of theme of
     erotic love not limited to Books III and IV, and in over one hun-
     dred instances in The Faerie Queene "he exhibits the widest grada-
     tions of the grand passion, from the highest conception to the
     lowest;" Maleger is physical disease; Braggadochio and Satyrane
     demonstrate Spenser's ability to portray character.

*38 PACKARD, FAITH E. "Spenser's Influence on the Pictorial
     Landscape of Certain Eighteenth Century Poets." Master's
     thesis, Wellesley College.
          Cited in Stephens, 1950.

39   PADELFORD, FREDERICK MORGAN. "Spenser and The Pilgrimage of
     the Life of Man." SP 28:211-18.
          Points out parallels between The Faerie Queene and
     De Guileville's The Pilgrimage of the Life of Man, concluding
     that The Pilgrimage "may well have formed a part of Spenser's

wide background reading." Notes De Guileville's possible influence on "May" and "September" eclogues of The Shepheardes Calender in the condemnation of false shepherds and of the buying and selling of holy offices.

40   POPE, EMMA FIELD. "'A Comment on Criticism in the Cinquecento': A Reply." PMLA 46:276-87.
      Refutes Bullock (1927.6) on same basis as earlier study (1926.42) and on ground that Bembo, Speroni, Tolomei, Gelli, Varchi, and Cicero are irrelevant: "These Italian works, and others in the series dealing primarily with the vulgar, were excluded as but little pertinent to the subject at hand. Based fundamentally on points which have their inception in Dante's De Vulgari Eloquentia, these 'ragionamenti' are sharply localized discussions of Italian problems" and, thus, focus "chiefly in quibbling technicalities of nomenclature: Is the language of Dante, of Petrarch, of Boccaccio to be designated as Florentine, Tuscan, Italian, or the Vulgar?" Contends that none of these treatises reach definite conclusions. Defends her method of paraphrasing. For related study, see 1931.8.

41   PURCELL, J.M. [Note on Muiopotmos.] PMLA 46:945-46.
      Comments on Denkinger's assessment of Sidney-Lady Rich affair: "The Philip Sidney-Penelope Rich affair has no basis in any contemporary record." Also notes that date of Penelope Devereux's marriage to Lord Rich is speculation (probably some time after 10 March 1581).

42   _____. "The Relations of Spenser and Sidney." PMLA 46:940.
      Notes parallel between studies by Harrison (1930.19) and Behler (1923.3).

*43   ROBERTS, J. RUSSELL. "Spenser's Use of Classical Mythology." Master's thesis, State College of Washington.
      Cited in Stephens, 1950.

44   ROBERTSON, JOHN M. Marlowe, A Conspectus. London: George Routledge & Sons, 192 pp., passim.
      Notes insertions of Spenser's lines in Marlowe's plays and parallels between Tamburlaine, II, and The Faerie Queene. For related studies, see McNeir-Provost nos. 1247, 1730.

45   RYLANDS, GEORGE. "English Poets and The Abstract Word." In Essays and Studies by Members of the English Association. Vol. 16. Edited by H.J.C. Grierson. Oxford: Clarendon Press, pp. 53-84.
      Notes how effectively Spenser controls concrete and abstract language in Epithalamion and The Faerie Queene. Also points out numerous imitators of Spenser.

46   St. CLAIR, FOSTER YORK. "The Myth of the Golden Age from
     Spenser to Milton." Ph.D. diss., Harvard University,
     pp. 1-7, 33-48.
          Discusses Ovid and Du Bartas as chief sources for myth of
     golden age which became vehicle for social and political commen-
     tary in late sixteenth century. Notes golden age allusions in
     Mother Hubberds Tale as clue to Spenser's satire on communism
     and allusions in The Faerie Queene, Books III, IV, V, and
     Mutabilitie Cantos, as integral aspects of Spenser's themes.

47   SCHULZE, IVAN L. "The Maiden and Her Lamb, Faerie Queene,
     Book I." MLN 46:379-81.
          Supplements Greenlaw's argument (1927.15) that is it un-
     necessary to cite one literary source for Spenser's use of
     St. George legend. Cites "additional instances of the occurrence
     of the legend to illustrate its wide dissemination and to show
     that the maiden and the lamb frequently appeared together." Note
     also "Mary Stuart as Duessa" and "The Witch and Her Beast." Pro-
     ceedings of Dr. Greenlaw's Seminary "C," 1926-27, no. 39, 1928-
     29, no. 6. Manuscript. Baltimore: Johns Hopkins University
     Library. Cited in Atkinson, 1937.

48   _____. "Spenser's Belge Episode and the Pageants for Leicester
     in the Low Countries, 1585-86." SP 28:235-40.
          Shows that "the pageants presented in honor of Leicester in
     Holland, in 1585-86, profoundly influenced Spenser's allegory in
     one of the most important episodes in Faerie Queene."

49   SHEPHARD, OSCAR H. "Sir Philip Sidney." Manchester Quarterly
     57:1-25.
          Briefly discusses Spenser in relation to Sidney's life and
     works.

50   STIRLING, BRENTS. "Spenser and Thomas Watson, Bishop of
     Lincoln." PQ 10:321-28.
          Suggests that the Oak ("February," The Shepheardes Calender)
     represents Watson, which helps explain Spenser's comments on
     Catholicism in a tale apparently about old age. Ascham, Harvey,
     and possibly Spenser respected Watson's scholarship.

51   _____. "Terpsichore's Lament and 'Pleasant Willy.'" JEGP
     30:556-62.
          Draws relationship between Terpsichores's lament (Teares
     of the Muses) and Elizabethan jig to show that "Pleasant Willy"
     is not Tarlton, thus dating the poem much earlier than 1588 and
     giving more basis to the protests against abuses cited in the
     poem.

52   STRATHMANN, ERNEST A. "The Allegorical Meaning of Spenser's
     Muiopotmos." PMLA 46:940-45.

Rejects Lemmi's interpretation (1930.27), showing that the attempt to establish a connection between Astrophel and Muiopotmos fails on two counts: "only two out of five fairly extended parallels are between poems certainly written by Spenser; and the parallels are not convincing when examined in their content." Poem is less allegorical than Lemmi makes it. For related study, see 1931.13.

53   _____. "Spenser's Legends and Court of Cupid." MLN 46:
     498-501.
         Finds evidence in Douce MS 280 in Bodleian Library to show
     that these works were available as late as 1597-1603.

*54 TYLER, ROLAND W. "The Pictorial Elements in Spenser's Faerie
     Queene." Master's thesis, Boston University.
         Cited in Stephens, 1950.

*55 WALLACE, ALLIE B. "A Study of Some of the Proper Names in
     Spenser's Faerie Queene." Master's thesis, Oklahoma A and M
     University.
         Cited in Stephens, 1950.

56   WILSON, MONA. Sir Philip Sidney. London: Duckworth,
     pp. 123-26.
         Comments on Areopagus (may or may not have existed as for-
     mally organized group) and Spenser's metrical innovations. Re-
     printed: 1932.68; London: R. Hart-Davis, 1950.

57   WINSLOW, ANNE. "Rhythmic Variations in Spenser's Faerie
     Queene." Vassar Journal of Undergraduate Studies 5:179-93.
         Considers varied rhythms effected by Spenser's long and
     short phrases, rhyme, upward and downward accents, alternating
     accents, alliteration and assonance, spondaic feet, polysyllables
     and monosyllables, different consonants, long and short vowels.

58   WYLLIE, J.W., and R.W. CHURCH. "A Spenser Bibliography for
     1928-1930." Mimeographed. Charlottesville: University of
     Virginia Library.
         Revised: 1932.72.

1932

1   ALBRIGHT, EVELYN MAY. "Spenser's Connections with the Letters
     in Gabriel Harvey's 'Letter-Book.'" MP 29:411-36.
         Refutes Bennett's claim (1931.4) that Harvey changed the
     person he wrote four letters to from Spenser to John Wood, whom
     Harvey chose as the sponsor of at least two projected publica-
     tions. Also refutes Bennett's claim that Cantos of Mutabilitie
     were written much later than 1580, and Padelford's argument
     (1930.36) for late date for Mutabilitie on the basis of increased

use of feminine rhymes and run-on lines. For related studies,
see 1928.1; 1929.3-4, 6; 1935.56.

2   ANON. "The Language of Edmund Spenser." Word Study 7, no. 3
    (January):1.
         Briefly notes Spenser's innovations, influence on later
    poets, and some attitudes toward use of archaisms.

*3 ARMISTEAD, ROBERT. "Spenser's Theory of Loyalty." Master's
    thesis, Baylor University.
         Cited in Stephens, 1950.

4   BENNETT, JOSEPHINE WATERS. "Spenser's Garden of Adonis."
    PMLA 47:46-80.
         Attempts to present "an interpretation of the whole passage
    which treats it as a single, continuous, and serious allegory,
    based entirely upon a body of well-known Platonic and Neo-Platonic
    conceptions about the organization of the universe, and containing
    no elements of the Lucretian theory of origins." Concludes that
    "the garden of Adonis is an otherworld paradise where Venus, the
    mother, or source of all forms, protects and enjoys Adonis, the
    father and generator of forms in process of acquiring the vital
    force necessary for 'shaping their house of clay.' Here the
    forms of all living things, and of souls as well, grow 'as they
    created were' by the Word of God. Out of the garden the souls
    go down into generation, and the forms of other things go out
    also, to give 'forme and feature' to the substance supplied by
    chaos, and so 'invade the state of life.'" For related study,
    see 1934.63. Reprinted with revision: 1936.3.

5   _____. "Spenser's Muse." JEGP 31:200-219.
         Challenges Padelford's suggestion (1930.37) that Calliope
    is muse of The Faerie Queene and concludes that Clio presides
    over the poem.

*6 BERRY, ALBERT M. "Edition of Spenser's Colin Clout's Come
    Home Again." Master's thesis, Columbia University.
         Cited in Stephens, 1950.

7   BLAIR, LAWRENCE. "The Plot of the Faerie Queene." PMLA 47:
    81-88.
         Concludes that "the plot of the Faerie Queene defies an
    analysis that would seek to make it, as a whole, like any other
    plot that we know. In parts it is formal; in parts, it is seem-
    ingly formless. We must then, in looking for the unifying element
    in the Faerie Queene, look elsewhere for it than in its construc-
    tion." For related studies, see 1933.9, 53-54.

*8 BODDY, MARGARET P. "Some Aspects of the Ovidian Elements in
    Spenser's Poetry." Master's thesis, University of Minnesota.
         Cited in Stephens, 1950.

9   BOUGHNER, DANIEL C. "The Psychology of Memory in Spenser's
     Faerie Queene." PMLA 47:89-96.
          Sets forth Spenser's psychology of memory in order "to make
     clear the relationship of his system to the current Elizabethan
     doctrines, and to establish the purpose of certain departures
     from those doctrines."

10   BROADUS, EDMUND KEMPER. The Laureateship. A Study of the
     Office of Poet Laureate in England With Some Account of the
     Poets. Oxford: Clarendon Press, pp. 33-39.
          Reprint of 1921.4.

*11 BRYAN, CHARLEYNE. "A High-School Edition of Canto VIII of
     Book III of Spenser's Faerie Queene." Master's thesis,
     University of Minnesota.
          Cited in Stephens, 1950.

12   BUCKLEY, GEORGE T. Atheism in the English Renaissance.
     Chicago: University of Chicago Press, passim.
          Mentions Spenser in relation to Harvey, DuBartas, and
     Raleigh. Reprinted: New York: Russell & Russell, 1965.

13   BUSH, DOUGLAS. "Spenser." In Mythology and the Renaissance
     Tradition in English Poetry. Minneapolis: University of
     Minnesota Press, pp. 86-123, passim.
          Spenser mingles ancient, medieval, and modern elements in
     "one current of poetic expression." His "ornamentation ranges
     from allusions, similes, paraphrases, to narratives or pictures
     occupying a number of stanzas." Whether he borrows from Homer
     or not, he alters the spirit of what he borrows to suit his
     Renaissance orthodoxy. His debt to Virgil is post-classical
     and medieval, and he expands on Ovid. "However important the
     classical sources, The Faerie Queene owes most of its material
     and more than a little of its narrative technique to medieval
     romance, and of course to Ariosto's version of romance as well."
     Concludes that "Spenser's treatment of myth . . . is largely
     colored by the medievalism apparent in his fable, in his narra-
     tive and descriptive technique, in his own thought and feeling,
     and by the theory and practice of continental literature of the
     sixteenth century." Reprinted: New York: Pageant Book Co.,
     1957; rev. ed.: New York: W.W. Norton & Co., 1963.

14   CASSIER, ERNST. Die platonische Renaissance in England und
     die Schule von Cambridge. Leipzig and Berlin: B.G. Teubner.
     Translated by James P. Pettegrove as The Platonic Renaissance
     in England. London: Thomas Nelson & Sons, pp. 112-16.
          Considers Platonism in The Faerie Queene, Hymne of Heavenly
     Love, and Hymne of Heavenly Beautie to be "most complete expres-
     sion" of Platonism of the Elizabethan Age. Stresses homogeniety
     of Spenser's thought, i.e., adventures of knights in The Faerie
     Queene are similar to spiritual process that pervades the Hymnes.

*15   CONNELL, JACK J. "Arms and Armour in Edmund Spenser."
       Master's thesis, Rutgers University.
         Cited in Stephens, 1950.

16   COURTHOPE, WILLIAM J. "The Poetry of Spenser." In The Cam-
       bridge History of English Literature. Edited by A.W. Ward
       and A.R. Waller. Vol. 3. Cambridge: Cambridge University
       Press, pp. 211-46.
         Reprint of 1908.10.

*17   De LACY, HUGH. "Astrology in the Poetry of Edmund Spenser."
       Master's thesis, University of Washington.
         For published version, see 1934.14.

18   De SELINCOURT, E., ed. Introduction to The Poetical Works of
       Edmund Spenser. London, New York, and Toronto: Humphrey
       Milford, Oxford University Press, pp. vii-lxvii.
         Reprint of 1912.11.

19   De SELINCOURT, HUGH. "The Successors of Spenser." In The
       Cambridge History of English Literature. Edited by A.W. Ward
       and A.R. Waller. Vol. 4. Cambridge: Cambridge University
       Press, 149-67.
         Reprint of 1909.9.

20   DRAPER, JOHN W. "Classical Coinage in the Faerie Queene."
       PMLA 47:97-108.
         Divides Spenser's coinages of classical proper names into
three groups: "historical or mythological persons to whom Spenser
alludes; classical names transferred to the Faerie Queene with no
apparent allusion either to those who bore them in Greek or Roman
times or to the etymological meaning of the word itself; and
. . . those that Spenser took from classical words the meanings
of which were appropraite to the characters or actions of the
persons concerned."

21   ELIOT, T[HOMAS] S[TEARNS]. "Christopher Marlowe." In Essays
       on Elizabethan Drama. London: Faber & Faber, pp. 24-27.
         Notes Marlowe's borrowings from Spenser (The Faerie Queene,
I.vii.32 for Tamburlaine, II, Act IV, sc. iv) and influence of
Spenser on Marlowe's blank verse. Reprinted: 1934.17; New York:
Harcourt, Brace & Co., 1956. For related studies, see McNeir-
Provost nos. 1247, 1730.

*22   FRIEDERICH, WERNER P. Spiritualismus und Sensualismus in der
       englischen Barockly-rik. Vienna and Leipzig: W. Braumüller,
       p. 197.
         Cited in Atkinson, 1937. Notes contrasts between Spenser
and Donne.

23   FRISBEE, GEORGE. "Edmund Spenser." <u>SLR</u> 8:795.
        Suggests that "Edmund Spenser" is pen name of Edward De
Vere, Earl of Oxford.

24   GREENLAW, EDWIN. <u>Studies in Spenser's Historical Allegory</u>.
        Johns Hopkins Monographs in Literary History, 2. Baltimore:
        Johns Hopkins Press; London: Oxford University Press, 220 pp.
        A collection of four essays, the latter two being reprints
(1910.7; 1912.19). "The Battle of the Books" recounts the controversy surrounding Polydore Vergil's rejection of Geoffrey of
Monmouth's account of Arthur and of the deeds of the Britons, the
battle of books which ensued, and the importance of this controversy to a full understanding of Spenser's theme in <u>The Faerie
Queene</u>. "Elizabethan Fact and Modern Fancy" challenges Winstanley
(1915.18) and others' elaborate identification of character and
incident in <u>The Faerie Queene</u>, traces theory and practice of
historical allegory in England in masques, court entertainments,
and drama and cites Hall's Chronicle (1548) as "the clue to the
interpretation of both Shakespeare's chronicle plays and of
Spenser's <u>Faerie Queene</u>," as well as the masques and pageants
of their time. Concludes that historical allegory is simple and
general and that historical allusions and topical elements are
"ornaments and graces, not the underlying structure, of the <u>Faerie
Queene</u>." Includes "Commentary and Bibliographical Notes" on four
essays. Reprinted: New York: Octagon Books, 1967; See McNeir-
Provost no. 729.

25   GREENLAW, EDWIN; CHARLES GROSVENOR OSGOOD; and FREDERICK
        MORGAN PADELFORD, eds. <u>The Works of Edmund Spenser. A
        Variorum Edition</u>. 11 Vols. Baltimore: Johns Hopkins Press.
        Volumes published separately 1932-1949; See McNeir-Provost
nos. 409-16.

26   GREG, W.W., ed. <u>English Literary Autographs 1550-1650</u>.
        Selected and edited with J.P. Gilson, R.B. McKerrow, Hilary
        Jenkinson, and A.W. Pollard. Oxford: Oxford University
        Press, plates 39, 40.
        Brief biographical account, discussion of Spenser's English
hand and Italian script, and reproductions of official public
record office documents in Spenser's hand. Reprinted: Nendeln,
Liechtenstein: Kraus Reprint, 1968.

27   HAMER, DOUGLAS. "Edmund Spenser: Descendants." <u>NQ</u> 162:370.
        Queries date of death of Rev. Edmund Spenser Tiddemann and
his relationship to Rev. Philip Goldworthy Tiddeman who is included in genealogy of Edmund Spenser. For related studies, see
1932.28, 67; 1933.68-69.

28   _____. "Edmund Spenser: Some Further Notes." <u>NQ</u> 162:380-84.
        Addenda and questions on Welply's biographical data. For
related studies, see 1932.27, 67; 1933.68-69.

29   _____. "Sir Robert Tynte's Sons." NQ 163:62-63.
      Evidence to show that William Tynte, of Cahirmony, is only
son of Robert Tynte and Elizabeth Boyle.

30   _____. "Spenser; Travers." NQ 162:352.
      In tracing his own ancestry in 1852, F.C. Spenser formu-
lated theory that Spenser was born in Lancashire. Refers to
letter from John Travers which states that an Elizabethan an-
cestor of Travers family married Sarah Spenser (Edmund's sister)
and that John Travers possessed legal documents with signature
of Spenser's oldest son and various Spenser-family vouchers,
including one from Lancashire.

31   _____. "Spenser's First Marriage." TLS, 14 January, p. 28.
      Cautiously accepts view (Eccles, 1931.14, and others) that
Spenser had married Machabyas Chylde as cited in St. Margaret's
Parish Record.

32   HARRISON, CHARLES T. "The Ancient Atomists and English Human-
ists of the Seventeenth Century." Ph.D. diss., Harvard
University, pp. 5-6.
      Mentions Spenser's use of Lucretius.

33   INGLEBY, C.M.; L. TOULMIN SMITH; F.J. FURNWALL; et al. The
Shakespeare Allusion Book: A Collection of Allusions to
Shakespeare from 1591 to 1700. 2 vols. London: Humphrey
Milford, Oxford University Press. 1:1; 2:461-62, 474.
      Reprint of 1909.20.

*34   INGRAM, GLADYS A. "The Music of Spenser's Faerie Queene."
Master's thesis, Oklahoma A and M University.
      Cited in Stephens, 1950.

*35   JACKSON, RUTH. "The Influence of Castiglione's Courtier upon
Spenser's Fowre Hymnes." Master's thesis, University of
Oregon.
      Cited in Stephens, 1950.

36   JENKINS, RAYMOND. "Spenser and the Clerkship in Munster."
PMLA 47:109-21.
      Presents evidence to show that after 1584 Spenser served as
Bryskett's deputy as clerk in the Council of Munster. Studies
Spenser's relations with Bryskett, the Sidney family, and Lord
Grey. Concludes that Spenser "emerges as an authority on all
parts of Ireland, possessed of a much larger experience with
Irish problems than we have heretofore imagined," making A Veue
of the Present State of Ireland a more significant document.

37   _____. "Spenser's Hand." TLS, 7 January, p. 12.
      Cites lines from Daphnaida to support Eccles' view
(1931.14) that St. Margaret Parish Record cites marriage of

Spenser and Machabyas Chylde. Identifies State Papers at Public
Record Office in Spenser's hand.

38   JONES, H.S.V. "Magnanimity in Spenser's Legend of Holiness."
      SP 29:200-206.
           Addresses question of how Arthur, the Chief of the Christian
      knights can represent Magnanimity, the most Hellenic of virtues.
      Scholastic philosophers developed long before Spenser a Christian
      version of magnanimity, derived from animus, which means voluntas
      as well as fortitudo. "If Arthur represents voluntas as well as
      fortitudo, the first book of the Faerie Queene may be sugges-
      tively compared with such educational moralities as The Marriage
      of Wit and Science, The Marriage of Wit and Wisdom, and Mind,
      Will, and Understanding." Concludes that Spenser's "mediaeval
      understanding of highmindedness [magnanimity] . . . makes clear
      the great importance which he attached to the will in the conduct
      of moral life."

39   JUDSON, A.C. "Spenser's Theory of Courtesy." PMLA 47:122-36.
           Proposes "to enumerate and comments on the chief 'articles
      in that familiar creed of courtesy' to whose adherence by Spenser
      Professor Jones (1930.22) calls our attention; next, to notice
      certain other articles of the creed which are dealt with by
      Spenser," viz. proper distinctions in treatment of different
      ranks and classes, hospitality to strangers, discourtesy, and
      slander; and "to discuss . . . the most significant aspect of
      Spenser's treatment of courtesy," i.e., "that true courtesy is
      fundamentally a matter of the heart rather than of manners."
      Concludes that Spenser fuses two conceptions of courtesy in
      Book VI of The Faerie Queene: he "concurs in many of the ideas
      about courtesy that constitute the Renaissance doctrine of the
      gentleman," and "he presents the knightly Christian ideal."

*40   KEENAN, ANNA M. "James Thomson as a Follower of Spenser."
      Master's thesis, University of Minnesota.
           Cited in Stephens, 1950.

*41   KOLLER, KATHERINE. Studies in Colin Clout's Come Home Againe.
      Ph.D. diss., Johns Hopkins University, 60 pp.
           See 1934.35 for reprint of Chapter 1, "Spenser and Raleigh."

42   LEE, SIDNEY. "The Elizabethan Sonnet." In The Cambridge
      History of English Literature. Edited by A.W. Ward and
      A.R. Waller. Vol. 3. Cambridge: Cambridge University Press,
      pp. 247-72.
           Reprint of 1908.25.

43   LOTSPEICH, HENRY GIBBONS. Classical Mythology in the Poetry
      of Edmund Spenser. Princeton Studies in English, no. 9.
      Princeton: Princeton University Press, 126 pp.

An alphabetical list of Spenser's myths and their sources
in classical mythology, preceded by an introduction which considers Spenser's indebtedness to Boccaccio and Natalis Comes who
use same traditional modes of interpreting myths as Spenser: the
physical, the euhemeristic, and the moral.   Concludes that Spenser
equates myth and poetry because of his instinct as a poet and because of received tradition.   Classic myth came to Spenser "rich
in meaning and association given it by generations of poets and
commentators;" he used it in many ways to serve his intentions:
"as poetic ornament for the high style; as a way of pointing out,
through analogies and formal similes, the links of kinship between the people and actions of his created world and those of
the world of classical antiquity."   From classical mythology he
drew "abundant material for moral allegory," which became "central to the most important avowed purpose of his work."   Published version of 1931.32.   Reprinted: New York: Octagon
Books; Gordian Press, 1965.

44   McELDERRY, BRUCE ROBERT, Jr.   "Archaism and Innovation in
     Spenser's Poetic Diction." PMLA 47:144-70.
        Contends that Spenser's use of archaisms ("traceable in not
more than 320 words") has been "greatly exaggerated"; that there
is slight reliance on dialect, even in The Shepheardes Calender,
and almost none in later poetry; and that his innovations in
language ("they number nearly six hundred words, forms, and
meanings,") are "only very incidentally reckless or ignorant."

45   McPEEK, JAMES A.   "The Influence of Catullus on English Litera-
     ture to 1700." Ph.D. diss., Harvard University, pp. 59-65,
     136-80, passim.
        Concludes that there is slight influence of Catullus'
Carmen on Amoretti and that chief influence on Epithalamion is
Marc-Claude de Buttet's Epithalame, with only incidental borrow-
ings from Catullus' Manlius and Junia and du Bellay's Epithalame.

46   MARTIN, WILLIAM CLIFF.   "The Date and Purpose of Spenser's
     Veue." PMLA 47:137-43.
        Dates A Veue of the Present State of Ireland midsummer,
1596; associates first part with Essex, rather than with Drake
who died in 1596.   Suggests that the work is Spenser's reconcilia-
tion with Essex in hopes of gaining court favor through him.

47   MILLICAN, CHARLES BOWIE.   Spenser and the Table Round: A
     Study in the Contemporaneous Background for Spenser's Use
     of the Arthurian Legend.   Harvard Studies in Comparative
     Literature, vol. 8.   Cambridge, Mass.:   Harvard University
     Press, 237 pp.
        Spenser's use of Arthurian material is "a feature of the
antiquarian movement which derived its impetus from the vigorous
policy of Henry VII" and subsequent Welsh enthusiasm and linking
of House of Tudor to the return of Arthur's reign.   Movement

aided by Leland, Kelton, and Bale's defense against Polydore
Vergil of Arthur's authenticity as portrayed by Geoffrey of
Monmouth. During Elizabeth's reign, "the tide of Arthurian
enthusiasm in England reached its flood," with numerous genealogies tracing Elizabeth's line to Arthur. Tudor right of Arthurian succession a tradition by Spenser's time. Spenser influenced
by Mulcaster and the latter's membership in a fellowship of
Arthur's knights. Robinson's account of the London Round Table,
commended by Elizabeth, a gauge of Arthurian popularity.
Humphrey Lhuyd, William Lambard, Richard Harvey, and others
defend Geoffrey's Arthur and condemn Polydore Vergil through
Elizabeth's reign. In combining these Arthurian influences and
his classical training, Spenser is in line with Renaissance theories of poetry. Notes that Arthurian connection continued
through early Stuart years and concludes that combined influences inevitably led Spenser to use of Arthurian material in
The Faerie Queene. Published and revised version of 1930.29-30.
Reprinted: New York: Octagon Books, 1967.

48   MOORE, G.S. "The Influence of Dante on Spenser." The Moraga
      Quarterly 3:60-68.
         Dante and Spenser wrote under similar literary and polit-
ical influences. Concludes from brief comparative study that
Spenser was influenced by Dante because of similarity of idea
and phraseology.

*49   MUNCIE, NINA B. "The Importance of Myth in The Faerie Queene
      as Exemplified by Spenser's Use of it in the Story of Florimell
      the Fayre, with Special Attention to Myth-Classification."
      Master's thesis, Oklahoma A and M University.
         Cited in Stephens, 1950.

*50   NEVIN, ALICE M. "Seasonal Allusions in Spenser and Milton."
      Master's thesis, Western Reserve University.
         Cited in Stephens, 1950.

51   OSBORN, ALBERT W. Sir Philip Sidney en France. Paris:
      Libraire Ancienne Honoré Champion, pp. 43, 45, 157, 159.
         Notes influence of Pléiade on Sidney and Spenser.

52   PADELFORD, FREDERICK MORGAN. "Spenser's Fowre Hymnes: A
      Resurvey." SP 29:207-32.
         Reasserts view that the Hymnes, mainly the latter two,
correspond to Calvin's theology, which has basis in St.
Augustine's theology and that of the Christian Mystics. Considers Platonic elements of the poem incidental to the Christian
elements. Sees parallel in treatment of Platonism in Benivieni's
Admonitione. Answer to Bennett, 1931.6. For response, see
1935.5.

170

53   POTTS, ABBIE FINDLAY. "The Spenserian and Miltonic Influence
     in Wordsworth's Ode and Rainbow." SP 29:607-16.
          Finds significant influence of Prothalamion, Epithalamion,
     and Fowre Hymnes on Wordsworth's poetry, especially evident in
     form, spirit, and imagery of "Intimations of Immortality" ode.

54   ROBIN, PERCY ANSELL. Animal Lore in English Literature.
     London: John Murray, pp. 15, 54-57, 73, 119-24, passim.
          Examines use of and sources for Spenser's animal refer-
     ences, such as dragon and sea monsters in The Faerie Queene, I,
     II; and beasts in Mother Hubberds Tale. Divides study according
     to species.

55   ROLLINS, HYDER E., ed. Francis Davison. A Poetical Rhapsody
     1602-1621. Vol. 2. Cambridge, Mass.: Harvard University
     Press, pp. 109-10.
          Notes that Willy in A Poetical Rhapsody refers to Sidney,
     but identifies Willy in Teares of the Muses as Richard Willey or
     Willes.

*56 SENDON, MARY K. "Spenser's Use of Proverbs." Master's thesis,
     Baylor University.
          Cited in Stephens, 1950.

57   SHARP, ROBERT L. "The Revolt Against Metaphysical Poetry:
     A Study in the Development of Neo-Classicism in England."
     Ph.D. diss., Harvard University, pp. 24-27, 43-50, passim.
          Refers to Spenser-Harvey correspondence and E.K.'s glosses
     on The Shepheardes Calender "to show that the free art and fine
     invention group was not inarticulate in criticism" and "to show
     the impossibility of exact boundaries in the criticism of this
     period." Discusses Spenser, Jonson, and Donne as summation of
     Elizabethan poetic traditions and as inspiration for seventeenth-
     century traditions, especially their attitudes "towards clarity,
     smoothness, and extravagance of thought and diction."

*58 SHULL, VIRGINIA M. "The Descriptive Background of The Faerie
     Queene." Master's thesis, Yale University.
          Cited in Stephens, 1950.

·59 SMITH, D. NICHOL. "Authors and Patrons." In Shakespeare's
     England, An Account of the Life and Manners of his Age. Vol.
     2. Oxford: Clarendon Press, pp. 182-211.
          Reprint of 1916.28.

*60 STARR, KATHRYN. "Dress in Edmund Spenser's Faerie Queene."
     Master's thesis, Rutgers University.
          Cited in Stephens, 1950.

*61 STEIN, HAROLD. "Studies in Spenser's Complaints." Ph.D.
     diss., Yale University.
          For published edition, see 1934.61.

62   THOMAS, RUSSELL. "Melville's Use of Some Sources in The
      Encantadas." AL, no. 1 (January):432-56.
         Twenty (out of twenty-four) quotations in preface to
      "Sketches" are Spenser's. Examines Melville's adaptations of
      quotes. For related study, see 1931.27.

63   van KRANENDONK. A.G. "Spenserian Echoes in A Midsummer Night's
      Dream." ES 14:209-17.
         On basis of parallels concludes that there is a connection
      between the Pyramus and Thisbe scene in A Midsummer Night's Dream
      and the first three books of The Faerie Queene.

64   W., G.H. "Edmund Spenser: Cateline." NQ 162:175-76.
         On relationship between Sir Robert Cateline and poet.

65   _____. "Newcomb, Penn, Spenser, and Tesdale." NQ 162:191.
         On Spenser's descendant, Thomas Newcomb, translator of
      Hervey's Contemplations on the Night.

66   WARD, A.W. "Historical and Political Writings; II. Histories
      and Memoirs." In The Cambridge History of English Literature.
      Edited by A.W. Ward and A.R. Waller. Vol. 7. Cambridge:
      Cambridge University Press, pp. 202-31.
         Reprint of 1911.40.

67   WELPLY, W.H. "Edmund Spenser: Being an Account of Some
      Recent Researches into His Life and Lineage, With Some Notice
      of His Family and Descendants." NQ 162:110-14, 128-32, 146-50,
      165-69, 182-87, 202-6, 220-24, 239-42, 256-60.
         Presents extensive biographical data with emphasis on
      poet's lineage. For related studies, see 1932.27-28; 1933.68-69.

68   WILSON, MONA. Sir Philip Sidney. New York: Oxford Univer-
      sity Press, pp. 123-26.
         Reprint of 1931.56.

69   WINSTANLEY, LILIAN, ed. Introduction to The Faerie Queene,
      Book I. Cambridge: Cambridge University Press, pp. vii-lxxx.
         Reprint of 1915.18.

*70   WORMELL, HELEN E. "Some Aspects of the Early Biographies of
      Spenser and Milton." Master's thesis, University of North
      Carolina.
         Cited in Stephens, 1950.

71   WURTSBAUGH, JEWEL. "Two Centuries of Spenserian Scholarship
      (1609-1805)." Ph.D. diss., Johns Hopkins University.
         From the folio edition of The Faerie Queene to the first
      variorum of Spenser's works, studies in considerable detail edi-
      tions, commentaries, and biographical accounts, relative chiefly
      to accuracy of text, scope and interest of the annotations,
      critical theories, anecdotes and facts of the poet's life, but

with some view to showing that the Spenserian problems were only
one phase of the larger questions of scholarship growing out of
the critical standards and opinions in the seventeenth and
eighteenth centuries. For published edition, see 1936.53.

72   WYLLIE, J.W., and R.W. CHURCH. "A Spenser Bibliography for
     1928-1930." Mimeographed. Charlottesville: University of
     Virginia Library.
         Revised version of 1931.58.

1933

1   ACHESON, ARTHUR. Shakespeare's Sonnet Story 1592-1598.
     London: Bernard Quaritch, pp. 12-15, passim.
         Reprint of 1922.1.

2   ALLEN, DON CAMERON. Francis Meres's Treatise "Poetrie," A
     Critical Edition. University of Illinois Studies in Language
     and Literature, vol. 16, nos. 3-4. Urbana: University of
     Illinois Press, 158 pp., passim.
         Considers Meres's comments on Spenser significant; mentions
     Spenser with others in relation to Meres.

3   ANON. "Ariosto." TLS, 8 June, pp. 385-86.
         Like Ariosto, Spenser is "fascinated by the fair and also
     by the foul" and portrays both vividly, but differs from Ariosto
     because the general aim of his poem has "an intrinsic nobility,"
     while Ariosto's scheme "gave but smallest occasion for matters
     of spiritual concern."

4   ANON. "The New Poet." TLS, 28 September, pp. 637-38.
         Finds Spenser's allegory strained and mechanical, his
     language innovative. Overall, his poetry is "protracted, con-
     tinuous and unfailing . . . without the help either of the grand
     style or of dramatic variety."

5   BAROWAY, ISRAEL. "The Bible as Poetry in the English Renais-
     sance: An Introduction." JEGP 32:447-80.
         Develops 1930.2.

6   BAYLEY, M.F. "The English Renaissance." Baconiana 21:139-42.
         Bacon wrote nearly all the literature of the Elizabethan
     age, including the works of Spenser.

7   BENNETT, JOSEPHINE WATERS. "Spenser's Venus and the Goddess
     Nature of the Cantos of Mutabilitie." SP 30:160-92.
         Examines "Spenser's description of Nature and the philo-
     sophical context of the Cantos in their relations to the revived
     and Christianized Neo-Platonism of the Renaissance." Challenges
     Greenlaw's interpretation of the Cantos in terms of Lucretian

materialism (1930.14). Spenser's cosmos has three "worlds," the
invisible, the celestial, and the sublunary each of which represents a stage of creation from highest to lowest. The first is
pure thought; the second, the world soul, which has two phases:
as it turns in the direction of pure thought and contemplates the
Ideas in the Mind of God it is the world soul and as it turns
toward the world it acts as the animus mundi and is called Nature;
the third is the visible world. Venus also has three phases:
super-celestial Venus identical with Sapience; celestial Venus
identical with Nature; worldly Venus. Thus, Venus is a single
emanation represented in three worlds. The second emanation is
masculine "as it constitutes the world soul and feminine as it
acts as efficient cause of creation, or Nature." Challenges
Greenlaw's Lucretian interpretation with the premise that
"Spenser's Nature is a Neo-Platonic Goddess who emanates from
ultimate divinity, a manifestation of the Venus-power which, at
its highest, is Sapience, and at its lowest is earthly Venus.
Jove is not the Supreme deity, but only the ruler of the 'heavens' or celestial world which embraces the eight spheres of the
visible universe." Reprinted and revised: 1936.3.

8   BEUTNER, Sister MARY LOUISE. "Spenser and the Emblem Writers."
    Master's thesis, St. Louis University, 107 pp.
        Discusses Emblem Books and their influence on Spenser,
especially evident in The Shepheardes Calender and some of the
Complaints. For Beutner's diss. on same topic, see McNeir-
Provost no. 1272.

9   BLAIR, LAWRENCE. [Reply to Mr. Perkinson.] PMLA 48:297-99.
        Attempts "to show that such errors as Mr. Perkinson points
out do not materially impair the fundamental conceptions of my
paper." For related studies, see 1932.7; 1933.53-54.

10 BROOKE, C.F. TUCKER. "Gentle Master Spenser." SLR 9:625-26.
        Considers reasons for reading Spenser "today," focusing on
The Faerie Queene as "the ideal novel, the picture of life as it
is" and the poet's "uncanny skill in narrative" to which "he adds
a power of description unsurpassed in English poetry."

11 BRYCE, J.C. "Spenser's 'XII. Morall Vertues.'" TLS,
    10 August, p. 537.
        Suggests Spenser's familiarity with Aegidius Columna
Romanus's categorical list of Aristotle's twelve virtues in
De Regimine Principum (1473).

12 BURT, M.K. "Verse Ancient and Modern." Revue de l'enseigne-
    ment des langues vivantes 50:420-22.
        Notes briefly the resemblance of Spenser's poetry to
Chaucer's adding that Spenser gives "a more studied grace,
richer ornament, tones more luxuriously sweet, the poetry becomes more self conscious, more definitely a thing of art."

13   BUYSSENS, E. "Spenser's 'Prosopopoia,' Lines 241-2." NQ
     164:190.
          Notes imperfect rhyme here to be similar to that in parts
     of The Faerie Queene. For related study, see 1933.42.

14   BYRON, H.J. "Edmund Spenser's First Printer, Hugh Singleton."
     Library, 4th ser. 14:121-56.
          Finds Spenser's choice of Singleton not accidental. Sug-
     gests Singleton was part of group, which included Spenser and
     John Stubbe (The Discoverie of a Gaping Gulf, 1579), that re-
     sisted Elizabeth and Burghley's policies and opposed the Anjou
     marriage. The Shepheardes Calender and Mother Hubberds Tale
     needed sympathetic printer.

15   CHAMBERS, E.K. Sir Thomas Wyatt and Some Collected Studies.
     London: Sedgwick and Jackson, pp. 146-51, 157, 159, 167,
     182-83, 193-96, 202-3.
          Notes that Spenser and Donne represent two types of pastor-
     alists, that The Shepheardes Calender revived interest in pastoral
     poetry in England, and cites general classical, continental, and
     native influences on Spenser. The Shepheardes Calender "inspired
     the old forms with a Chaucerian freshness and a new melody."
     Considers Spenser's variety of rhythms and his figuring forth
     of contemporaries under pastoral names in Colin Clouts Come Home
     Againe. Calls The Faerie Queene a mirror of the characteristic
     Elizabethan outlook. Comments on Spenser's court disappointment,
     his friendship with Raleigh, his transitory influence on early
     seventeenth-century poetry. Reprinted: New York: Russell &
     Russell, 1965.

16   CHANCELLOR, E. BERESFORD. The Literary Ghosts of London:
     Homes and Footprints of Famous Men and Women. London:
     Richards, p. 48.
          Notes Spenser's birthplace, his service to Essex, and
     circumstances of his death.

17   COLLINS, JOSEPH BURNS. "Christian Mysticism in the Eliza-
     bethan Age." Ph.D. diss., The Johns Hopkins University,
     pp. 276-344.
          Places Spenser in tradition of Christian mystical writers
     and interprets The Faerie Queene, I as "pilgrimage of life"
     allegory. Canto 10 (House of Holiness) depicts man's conversion
     and training toward perfection, while other Book I episodes repre-
     sent man's struggle (and eventual victory) against sins of world,
     flesh, and devil. Sees unity of the Fowre Hymnes in their adher-
     ence to mystical philosophy, rather than in Neoplatonism or
     Calvinism. First two hymns present idealized human love, while
     the second two celebrate a heavenly counterpart and embody
     Christocentric and Theocentric types of contemplation,
     respectively.

18   CRAIG, HARDIN; A.C. JUDSON; and RAY HEFFNER. "Spenser
     Allusions." PMLA 48:623-28.
          Lists items published before 1940 relevant to Spenser Allu-
     sion Book omitted from Carpenter's bibliography (1923.6).

19   CRAIGIE, WILLIAM. The Northern Element in English Literature.
     Toronto: University of Toronto Press, p. 25.
          Notes that "the dialect in Spenser's Shepherd's Calendar
     of 1579 is midland and southern in the main, but contains a few
     northern words and forms which are explained by the commentator,
     sometimes with an indication of their origin."

20   DAVIS, B.E.C. Edmund Spenser: A Critical Study. Cambridge:
     Cambridge University Press, 267 pp.
          Two introductory biographical chapters followed by three
     on humanism, romance, and allegory, which establish Spenser as
     an eclectic poet who combines classical and medieval, romance
     and epic, concrete and abstract, Platonic and Aristotelian.
     Three chapters on diction, imagery, and verse consider the vari-
     eties and influences of Spenser's experiment with language, the
     range of his imagery, the variety and harmony of his versifica-
     tion, and the popularity of his stanza. Final chapter surveys
     influence on Spenser's philosophy of such widely divergent author-
     ities as Plato and Aristotle, the Bible and the Kabbala, Lucretius
     and Ovid, Latin stoics and medieval schoolmen, Italian Platonists
     and Protestant divines, concluding that Spenser blends these
     sources into romantic world of The Faerie Queene. Reprinted:
     New York: Russell & Russell, 1962. See McNeir-Provost no. 622.

*21   de REUL, PAUL. Edmund Spenser. Introduction, traduction et
     notes. Paris: La Renaissance du Livre, 237 pp.
          Cited in National Union Catalog.

22   DRAPER, JOHN W. "Spenser's Use of the Perfective Prefix."
     MLN 48:226-28.
          Spenser's 120 correct uses of perfective prefix suggest
     that Spenser's reading of Middle English was wide and detailed.

*23   ELLIS, ESTHER. "Spenser's Fairy Land." Master's thesis,
     University of Tennessee.
          Cited in Stephens, 1950.

24   FRENCH, J. MILTON. "Lamb and Spenser." SP 30:205-7.
          Shows Spenser's influence on Lamb over thirty year period.
     See 1933.29.

25   FRISBEE, GEORGE. "Gentle Master de Vere." SLR 9:667.
          Response to Brooke (1933.10). "Edmund Spenser" is pen name
     of de Vere. Amoretti, 1 not written to Elizabeth Boyle, but to
     Mary Sidney by de Vere. Uses acrostics to support conjecture.

26   GILBERT, ALLAN H.   "Spenser's Cymochles."   MLN 48:230.
        Cymochles' "relation to his closely associated brother is
more evident, if his name is derived from καûμα, meaning burning,
glow, especially the burning heat of the sun" than if derived
from κûμα, meaning the dashing of waves.

27   GREENOUGH, JAMES BRADSTREET, and GEORGE LYMAN KITTREDGE.
        Words and Their Ways in English Speech. New York and London:
        Macmillan, pp. 118, 295, 354, 375.
        Reprint of 1901.11.

28   HARASZTI, ZOLTÁN.   "The Poet of Pure Fancy."   More Books
        8:213-22.
        Mentions that Ariosto's Orlando Furioso exerted its great-
est influence on English letters not through translation but
through The Faerie Queene, which was published a year before
Harington's translation of Orlando.

29   HARD, FREDERICK.   "Lamb and Spenser Again."   SP 30:533-34.
        Disagrees with French's assessment (1933.24) of Spenser's
influence on Lamb.

30   HARRISON, T.P., Jr.   "Spenser and the Earlier Pastoral Elegy."
        University of Texas Bulletin, Studies in English 13:36-53.
        Studies Spenser's pastoral elegies: "November," The
Shepheardes Calender, Astrophel, Lay of Clorinda, The Ruines of
Time (lines 281-343), and parts of Daphnaida. Shows that
Spenser's innovative achievements in these poems equal those
of The Faerie Queene. Details pastoral elements of Spenser's
works and examines sources (classical, Italian, and French) to
show Spenser's great debt to continental pastoral elegists.
Illustrates "unity in Spenser's conceptions of elegiac matter"
by considering these works in relation to one another."

31   _____.   "Spenser and Shelley's 'Adonais.'"   University of
        Texas Bulletin, Studies in English 13:54-63.
        Concludes that cumulative effect of comparing Shelley with
Spenser shows "Shelley was deeply impressed by the elegiac poems
of Spenser," more so by Astrophel than by The Shepheardes
Calender.

32   HEFFNER, RAY.   "Did Spenser Die in Poverty?"   MLN 48:221-26.
        Presents evidence to support usual notion that Spenser did
die in poverty. For related studies, see McNeir-Provost
nos. 125-6.

33   HENLEY, PAULINE.   "Galathea and Neaera."   TLS, 6 July,
        p. 464.
        Accepts Renwick's identification in Colin Clouts Come Home
Againe with Elizabeth Sheffield, Lady Ormonde (1929.37), but
finds evidence to identify Galathea with Frances Howard, widowed
Countess of Kildare and daughter of the Lord High Admiral.

34   HOLLAND, H[UBERT] H. Shakespeare, Oxford and Elizabethan
      Times. London: Denis Archer, p. 86, passim.
           Suggests connection between Spenser's poem to Thalia in
      Teares of the Muses and Shakespeare's Venus and Adonis: "Either
      Shakespeare's Adonis is intended for some person who is also
      Spenser's Willy, or Spenser intends Willy to be Shakespeare, and
      paraphrases his Venus and Adonis to show that fact."

35   JENKINS, RAYMOND. "Spenser at Smerwick." TLS, 11 May, p. 331.
           Letter written at Limerick, 28 November 1580 (in BM Addi-
      tional MSS 33, 924, fol. 6) "proves" Spenser was at battle of
      Smerwick and surrender of Fort del Ore. Concludes that Irenaeus
      in A Veue of the Present State of Ireland "is not merely Spenser's
      mouthpiece but that he is Spenser," making the Veue "a biograph-
      ical document which details many experiences in the poet's Irish
      career and which illuminates many an incident in the 'Faerie
      Queene,' particularly in the 'Legend of Justice.'" Both Veue
      and "Legend of Justice" justify Grey's methods in Ireland.

36   JOHNSON, FRANCIS R. A Critical Bibliography of the Works of
      Edmund Spenser Printed before 1700. Baltimore: Johns Hopkins
      Press, 75 pp.
           Critical catalogue of Spenser editions in collection of the
      Tudor and Stuart Literary Club at The Johns Hopkins University
      with the collation of other copies known to exist in other public
      and private libraries. Three objectives: "first, to give a de-
      tailed and accurate bibliographical description of the copy used;
      second, to note important variants exhibited by other copies of
      the same edition, and, where possible, to give a logical explana-
      tion of why these variants exist; third, to note any bibliograph-
      ical peculiarities which would indicate the possibility of textual
      corrections having been made in some copies, but not in others."
      Reprinted: London: Dawsons of Pall Mall, 1966; 1967; Folcroft,
      Pa.: Folcroft Press, 1969. See McNeir-Provost no. 61.

37   JOHNSTON, MARY. "Parasites in Plautus and Spenser." CW
      26:104.
           Spenser's Braggadocchio (The Faerie Queene, II.iii.9.2-9
      and 17.7) parallels Terence and Plautus's parasite and braggart
      soldier.

38   JUDSON, ALEXANDER CORBIN. Spenser in Southern Ireland.
      Bloomington: Principia Press, 59 pp.
           Recounts 1929 visit to area around Kilcolman, identifies
      geographical features found in Spenser's works, and includes
      eighteen photographs with appropriate captions from Spenser's
      works. For related study, see 1935.68.

39   LAMB, CHARLES. "Version of Popular Fallacies (corrigé de la
      version erreurs répandues)." Revue de l'enseignement des
      langues vivantes 50:232-33.
           Notes Spenser's "platonizing" in A Hymne in Honour of Beautie.

40   LEGOUIS, ÉMILE. Edmund Spenser. Les grandes écrivains
     étrangers. Paris: Libraire Bloud et Gay, 359 pp.
          Reprint of 1923.26.

41   _____. Spenser. London and Toronto: J.M. Dent & Sons;
     New York: E.P. Dutton & Co., 147 pp.
          Reprint of 1926.30.

42   MABBOTT, THOMAS OLLIVE. "Spenser's 'Prosopopoia,' Lines
     214-2." NQ 164:62-63, 266-67.
          Notes Spenser's use of m and n sounds and suggests im-
     perfect rhyme of lines be noted as possible error from dropping
     type. For related study, see 1933.13.

*43 McCABE, Sister MARY ALPHONSE, O.S.U. "Spenser's Use of Repe-
     tition in The Faerie Queene." Master's thesis, St. Louis
     University.
          Cited in Stephens, 1950.

*44 MERTEN, MARIA. "Michael Draytons 'Poly-Olbion' im Rahmen Der
     Englischen Renaissance." Ph.D. diss., Westfälischen Wilhelms-
     Universität zu Münster.
          For published edition, see 1934.44.

45   MOHL, RUTH. The Three Estates in Medieval and Renaissance
     Literature. New York: Columbia University Press, pp. 227-29,
     305-6, passim.
          Finds adaptations of états du monde literary form in
     Mother Hubberds Tale with Ape's and Fox's climb upward in soci-
     ety; sees close correspondence with Des estats du siècle.

46   O'RÍORDÁIN, SEÁN P. "The Place Names and Antiquities of
     Kinalmeaky Barony, Co. Cork." JCHAS 38:16-19.
          Notes burial of Catherine Spenser in Kilbrogan Churchyard.

47   P., E.J.S. "Notes and News." Bodleian Quarterly Record 7:
     291-95.
          The Faerie Queene mentioned as "one of the more famous
     books" in "the wonderful growth of literature" during the reign
     of Elizabeth.

*48 PADEN, JOHN E. "The Influence of Ovid's Metamorphoses on
     Spenser's Faerie Queene." Master's thesis, Oklahoma A and M
     University.
          Cited in Stephens, 1950.

49   PARKS, GEORGE B. "Gloriana's Annual Feast." TLS, 29 June,
     p. 447.
          Challenges Sprague's (1933.62) "ingenious suggestion that
     Gloriana's knights set out 'a year apart' on their respective
     quests," concluding that there is "no way of establishing an
     'annual' chronology."

50　　PARMENTER, MARY. "Colin Clout and Hobbinol:　A Reconsidera-
tion of the Relationship of Edmund Spenser and Gabriel Harvey."
Ph.D. diss., The Johns Hopkins University.
　　　　On basis of correspondence, shows relationship to be one of
"respect" more than one of "familiarity."　Considers correspondence to be "synthetic satirical devices" all written by Harvey,
even though letters include facts.　Letters extend pastoral char-
acterizations of The Shepheardes Calender (i.e., Colin-Immerito,
Hobbinol-Harvey).　Notes also that the personal elements of The
Shepheardes Calender are overemphasized "to deprecate or minimize
the satire of Church and State" in poem.　Concludes that Areopagus
is Harvey's adaptation of traditional "senate of poets," used in
correspondence as witty literary device that enables him to comment on quantitative English versifying, and that notion of
Areopagus as formal group is due mainly to nineteenth-century
Spenser biographers.　Finds Spenser-Harvey influence mutual,
with Spenser possibly influencing Harvey more than Harvey Spenser.

51　　PATTISON, BRUCE. "The Roundelay in the August Eclogue of
The Shepheardes Calender." RES 9:54-55.
　　　　Accounts for apparent roughness in rhythm of roundelay by
suggesting that Spenser wrote it with a contemporary song tune in
mind rather than a conventional meter; notes tradition for this.

52　　PEARSON, LU EMILY. Elizabethan Love Conventions.　Berkeley:
University of California Press, pp. 158-75, passim.
　　　　Discusses Spenser's fusion of Petrarchan and Platonic conventions in Amoretti to present a love that is both passionate
and spiritual:　in this Spenser comes "very close to his ideal
of harmonizing heavenly and earthly love."　Published version of
1930.38.　Reprinted:　New York:　Barnes & Noble, 1976.

53　　PERKINSON, RICHARD H. "The Plot of The Faerie Queene."
PMLA 48:295-97.
　　　　Points out "factual errors and fundamental misconceptions"
in Blair's (1932.7) consideration of plot of The Faerie Queene.
For related studies, see 1933.9, 54.

54　　　　　　. [Rejoinder to Mr. Blair.] PMLA 48:299-301.
　　　　Response to 1933.9.　Insists that two of Mr. Blair's errors
"are fundamental misconceptions, and as such destroy his contention."　For related studies, see 1932.7; 1933.53.

55　　PILLSBURY, STANLEY R. "The Four Hundredth Anniversary of the
Birth of Queen Elizabeth (September 7th, 1533)." New York
Public Library Bulletin 37:857-59.
　　　　Mentions display of a first edition of The Faerie Queene,
opened to the dedication to Queen Elizabeth.

56　　PONS, M. "Apprecier l'art de Spenser d'après le second livre
de la Reine des Fees." Revue de l'enseignement des langues
vivantes 50:150-55.

Discusses allegory of Book II and links it to rest of The
Faerie Queene.

*57   PRIEST, HAROLD MARTIN. "Tasso in English Literature, 1575-
       1675." Ph.D. diss., Northwestern University.
       Cited in Atkinson, 1937.

 58   READ, CONGERS. Bibliography of British History, Tudor Period,
       1485-1603. Oxford: Clarendon Press, nos. 2579, 3950a, 3959,
       3972.
       Useful mainly for historical aspects of age.

 59   ROPE, H.E.G. "Catholicism in Elizabethan Literature."
       Month, 162:250-54.
       Notes nostalgia for Roman faith in literature from Spenser
    to Shirley.

 60   SCHULZE, IVAN L. "Notes on Elizabethan Chivalry and The
       Faerie Queene." SP 30:148-59.
       Shows "that Elizabethan chivalry was not only worthy of
    Spenser's attention but also that it must be considered as source
    material along with the romances."

 61   SMITH, G.C. MOORE. "Printed Books with Gabriel Harvey's
       Autograph or MS. Notes." MLR 28:78-81.
       Supplements Gabriel Harvey's Marginalia (1913.31). For
    additional studies, see 1934.59; 1935.67.

 62   SPRAGUE, ARTHUR COLBY. "Gloriana's Annual Feast." TLS,
       27 April, p. 295.
       Suggests that the "xxi. severall dayes" of Gloriana's
    feast are not consecutive but that Gloriana held the annual feast
    twelve times, the knights setting out a year apart. For response,
    see 1933.49.

 63   STEWART, RANDALL. "Hawthorne and The Faerie Queene." PQ
       12:196-206.
       Concludes on basis of external evidence, allusions, plots,
    contrivance of situation, and characterization that "Hawthorne's
    creative conceptions were colored by his recollections of The
    Faerie Queene."

 64   STIRLING, BRENTS. "The Concluding Stanzas of Mutabilitie."
       SP 30:193-204.
       Notes variation between Mutabilitie, vii.58 and viii.1-2:
    "in the first the mutable order, of itself, reigns over change
    through dilation of things and their return to themselves and
    perfection by motion of fate, while in the second, permanence
    and rest lie in ultimate amalgamation with the Sabbaoth God."
    Suggests that Spenser unifies the two passages through a well-
    diffused Neoplatonic doctrine as found in Boethius's De
    Consolatione Philosophiae. For related study, see 1935.70.

65   STRATHMANN, ERNEST A. "A Manuscript Copy of Spenser's Hymnes."
     MLN 48:217-21.
         Suggests that copies of Hymne in Honour of Beautie and
     Hymne of Heavenly Beautie in Harleian MS 6910 are abbreviated
     versions.

66   SUGDEN, HERBERT W. "The Grammar of Spenser's Faerie Queene."
     Ph.D. diss., Duke University.
         For published edition, see 1936.45.

67   TUVE, ROSEMOND. "A Mediaeval Commonplace in Spenser's
     Cosmology." SP 30:133-47.
         Contends that Spenser's conception of Love (e.g., Colin
     Clouts Come Home Againe, lines 839 ff., Hymne in Honour of Love,
     lines 57 ff.) was commonplace in late medieval and renaissance
     thought, especially the Empedoclean ideas of "Love's separation
     and ordering of the parts of the world, the discord of the ele-
     ments and their reconciliation by Love, and continuing of life
     and of forms through Love's power." Illustrates point with ex-
     amples from Batman vppon Bartholome, Cornelius Agrippa, the
     Roman de la Rose, Chaucer's Boethius, and Googe's Zodiacus Vitae.
     Reprinted: Essays: Spenser, Herbert, Milton (Princeton:
     Princeton University Press, 1970), pp. 49-63.

68   WELPLY, W.H. "More Notes on Edmund Spenser." NQ 165:92-94,
     111-16.
         Additional details on Spenser's lineage. Supplements
     1932.27, 67. For related studies, see 1932.28; 1933.69.

69   _____. "Spenser in Ireland." TLS, 18 May, p. 348.
         Questions whether or not James Spenser, constable of Castle
     Limerick, is poet's father. For related studies, see 1932.27-28;
     67-68.

*70 WILHOUT, MARGARET J. "The Allegorical Representation of
     Puritanism in Spenser's 'The House of Alma,' Fletcher's 'The
     Purple Island,' and Bunyan's 'The Holy War.'" Master's thesis,
     University of Illinois.
         Cited in Stephens, 1950.

71   WILLIAMS, CHARLES. "The Evasion of Identity: (i) Spenser."
     In Reason and Beauty in the Poetic Mind. Oxford: Clarendon
     Press, pp. 51-62.
         Spenser's allegorical characters are "suggestively similar"
     to virtues and vices which they represent but not identical to
     them.

72   WINKLER, GERDA. "Das Relativum bei Caxton und seine Ent-
     wicklung von Chaucer bis Spenser." Ph.D. diss., University
     of Berlin, pp. 58-59, 77-82.

Concludes that Spenser did not always follow the natural speech of his time: he loves innovations of a purely individual type, which extend to his use of the relative. Compares and contrasts Caxton's and Spenser's uses of the relative.

73 WURTSBAUGH, JEWEL. "The 1758 Editions of The Faerie Queene." MLN 48:228-29.

Notes three editions of The Faerie Queene dated 1758: an octavo based on Hughes's version of the poem (1715), Upton's quarto in two volumes, and Church's octavo in four volumes, the latter two published by Tonson. Church's and Upton's editions were published within nine days of each other, "a sufficient reason for neither Upton nor Church referring to the work of the other."

1934

1 ALLEN, PERCY. Anne Cecil, Elizabeth, and Oxford. London: D. Archer, pp. 158-238.

Devotes three chapters to interpretation of political allegory in Mother Hubberds Tale, Muiopotmos, and The Faerie Queene and relationship of these works to the real "Shakespeare," Lord Oxford.

2 ANDREWS, CHARLES M. "An Early Edition of Spenser's Poems." Yale University Library Gazette 9:20-22.

Notes acquisition of 1611 edition of poems that excludes Mother Hubberds Tale. Suggests poem was omitted because it "reflected on Lord Burghley, whose son, Robert Cecil, was living in 1611." Poem was included in editions published after Cecil's death in 1612.

3 ANON. "Prof. Fletcher Lectures on Dante and Spenser." Vassar Miscellany News, 11 April, p. 3.

Summarizes Jefferson B. Fletcher's views: both The Faerie Queene and The Divine Comedy serve political purposes, glorification of England and Italy respectively; ideal man of Dante and Spenser has duty to maintain perfect state; virtue is basis for nobility. Considers Dante a Christian Aristotelian, Spenser "something of a Christian Platonist." Notes likely influence of Dante on Spenser. Lecture noted also by The Poughkeepsie Eagle, 7 April 1934.

4 BALL, LEWIS F. "The Background of the Minor English Renaissance Epics." ELH 1:63-89.

Defines two types of Renaissance epic: one patterned after Homer and Virgil that relies on Neo-Aristotelian theories (e.g., Trissino, Tasso, Ronsard, Blackmore); the other, a particularly English type that focuses on theme rather than on a hero and uses British history rather than allegory for ethical instruction.

Comments on Spenser in relation to these and links The Faerie
Queene to epics of other writers, such as Drayton's Poly-Olbion.

5   BAROWAY, ISRAEL. "The Imagery of Spenser and the Song of
Songs. JEGP 33:23-45.
Contends that "unquestionably Spenser translated the Song
of Songs into English verse," for "various of his poems bear the
unmistakable impress of the spirit, if not the letter, of the
imagery of Canticum Canticarum;" seen most notably in Amoretti,
Epithalamion, Colin Clouts Come Home Againe, and The Faerie
Queene. Reprinted: 1934.6.

*6   _____. The Imagery of Spenser and the Song of Songs. Urbana:
University of Illinois Press.
Cited in Atkinson, 1937. Reprint of 1934.5.

7   BATESON, F.W. English Poetry and the English Language. An
Experiment in Literary History. Oxford: Clarendon Press,
pp. 30-33.
Illustrates diffuseness and repetition in Elizabethan style
with sonnet 59 of Amoretti. Reprinted: New York: Russell &
Russell, 1961; Oxford: Clarendon Press, 1973 (each revised and
include new introductions). See McNeir-Provost no. 502.

8   BESTOR, ARTHUR EUGENE, Jr. "Emerson's Adaptation of a Line
from Spenser." MLN 49:265-67.
Notes influence of Muiopotmos on Emerson.

9   BRADNER, LEICESTER. "An Allusion to Bromley in the Shepherds'
Calendar." MLN 49:443-45.
Strengthens Spenser's connection with Bishop Young of
Rochester with identification of "S. Bridgets bowre" ("July,"
lines 41-44) as the well of St. Blaze, a shrine on the premises
of the Bishop's Bromley residence.

10   BURKE, CHARLES BELL. "Humour in Spenser." NQ 166:113-15.
General statement of the fact of humor in Spenser's works.

11   BUYSSENS, E. "Spenser's Allegories." TLS, 11 January, p. 28.
Book I of The Faerie Queene is faithful allegory of Calvin's
doctrine of Salvation by faith as set out in Institution
Chrétienne. For earlier study, see 1926.5.

12   CHAMBERS, E.K. The Elizabethan Stage. Vol. 3. Oxford:
Clarendon Press, pp. 207, 328.
Reprint of 1923.8.

13   DANNENBERG, FRIEDRICH. "Shakespeare Sonette: Herkunst,
Wesen, Deutung." SJW 70:37-43.
Places Amoretti in historical development of sonnet.

14   De LACY, HUGH. "Astrology in the Poetry of Edmund Spenser."
      JEGP 33:520-43.
         Established widespread belief in art of astrology with four
      types of evidence: number of books concerning it entered in
      Stationer's Register, 1557-1600; practicing astrologers of the
      day; belief among intellectuals Spenser knew or might have known;
      astrological passages in the works of Spenser's contemporaries.
      Examines three kinds of astrological passages in Spenser's poetry:
      "those used primarily for literary embellishment, those decora-
      tive and causal but commonplace, those which are causal and more
      or less technical." Concludes that Spenser's astrological pas-
      sages "reveal unmistakable and abiding interest in the art."
      Published version of 1932.17.

15   De SELINCOURT, E. "Spenser." In Oxford Lectures on Poetry.
      Oxford: Clarendon Press, pp. 106-30.
         Spenser found elastic form in his chivalrous fairy land,
      "where every event had some moral significance, and where many
      an incident glanced at current public affairs," satisfying his
      interest in the real world and his yearning after ideal physical,
      moral, and spiritual beauty. Spenser's innate pictorial imagina-
      tion "was doubtless fostered and developed by his close and ardent
      study of works of plastic and decorative art," and of the pageants
      of his youth, which might well be described as "living pictures."
      Considers examples of Spenser's pictorial composition, but con-
      cludes that "poetry is not painting . . . if it evoke an image it
      is by means of sound that the image is evoked. Spenser brought
      to perfection that mysterious pre-established harmony which ex-
      ists between the rhythm and colour of words and the varied human
      emotions." Spenser's music unifies the strange, diverse world
      of The Faerie Queene. Individual charm of Spenser's poetic nar-
      rative depends on the fusion of his pictorial and musical genius.
      Points out examples of Spenser's "constant penetration into the
      things of life" which are often represented as "a mere succession
      of lovely pictures." As poem develops, pure allegory yields to
      intimate psychology.

16   DOGGETT, FRANK A. "Donne's Platonism." SR 42:274-92.
         Spenser mentioned as Neoplatonist.

17   ELIOT, T.S. "Christopher Marlowe." In Essays on Elizabethan
      Drama. London: Faber & Faber, pp. 24-27.
         Reprint of 1932.21.

18   FAUST, GEORGE P. "A Spenser Parallel." MLN 49:393.
         Points out verbal parallel of The Faerie Queene, I.vii.17
      in sixteenth-century version of Sir Degare.

19   FLETCHER, JAMES M.J. "Edmund Spenser and the Dorset Stour."
      Notes and Queries for Somerset and Dorset 21:180-82.

Comments on river Stour (<u>The Faerie Queene</u>, IV.xi.32): Spenser's allusion suggests "that a six-headed river-god would be a monstrous thing to see,--<u>deformis</u>,--and that he [Spenser] may have had in mind the Cyclopes or Cerberus . . . mentioned in closing canto of his previous chapter." Concludes that the whole passage reveals Spenser's knowledge of Stour River and its environs.

20   FLETCHER, JEFFERSON BUTLER. <u>Literature of the Italian Renaissance</u>. New York: Macmillan Co., 347 pp., passim.
      Discusses significant Italian influence on Spenser. Treats writers separately and mentions Spenser in appropriate contexts. Reprinted: Port Washington, N.Y.: Kennikat Press, 1964.

21   FLETCHER, JEFFERSON B[UTLER]. "Some Observations on the Changing Style of the <u>Faerie Queene</u>." SP 31:152-59.
      Working from recognized opinion that "the successive books of <u>The Faerie Queene</u> reflect changes both in spirit and in narrative technique, in values and in artistry, and that these changes, gradual in the earlier books, become quickened in Book Four," demonstrates Spenser's "waning use of color and light . . . by tabulating the words that denote or connote color, those that denote or connote light, shade, or darkness, and by considering other changes significantly related to these basic considerations."

22   FOWLER, EARLE B. <u>Spenser and the System of Courtly Love</u>. Louisville: Standard Printing Co., 91 pp.
      Follows a brief history of courtly love with demonstration of courtly commonplaces in <u>The Faerie Queene</u>, including positive and negative mental and temperamental symptoms and effects. Considers the courtly canons which regulate conduct of knights and ladies in <u>The Faerie Queene</u> and which "largely determine their philosophy of love." Suggests that dramatic and realistic qualities in the Paridell-Hellenore episode in the third book of <u>The Faerie Queene</u> are partly due to "Spenser's use of the traditional Ovidian code in the details of Paridell's wooing and winning of Hellenore." However, Spenser "utterly rejects the ethical and moral implications of the traditional code and upholds an ideal love philosophy compounded of Puritan and Platonic elements" in <u>The Faerie Queene</u>, the <u>Fowre Hymnes</u>, <u>Colin Clouts Come Home Againe</u>, and <u>Amoretti</u>. Reprinted: 1935.21; New York: Phaeton Press, 1968; Folcroft, Pa.: Folcroft Press, 1969. See McNeir-Provost no. 683.

23   FRIEDRICH, WALTER GEORGE. "The Astrophel Elegies, A Collection of Poems on the Death of Sir Philip Sidney (1595)." Ph.D. diss., The Johns Hopkins University.
      Supports Spenser's authorship of <u>Astrophel</u> and editorship of collection of elegies with which it appeared; finds authorship of <u>The Doleful Lay of Clorinda</u> open question. Dates composition of <u>Astrophel</u> between fall of 1589 and end of 1591. Notes

traditional classical sources for poems. Assesses Spenser-Sidney
relationship in light of Spenser-Harvey correspondence, Spenser's
works, and contemporary literature to conclude that both cooper-
ated in significant literary movement, were close friends, and
that Sidney was Spenser's first patron. Includes bibliographical
description of 1595 Quarto of <u>Colin Clouts Come Home Againe</u> and
extensive line notes on poems.

24 GAMGUE, B.B. "Elizabeth and Literary Patronage." <u>PMLA</u>
 49:1041-49.
  Notes Elizabeth's patronage and pension to Spenser for <u>The
 Faerie Queene</u>.

25 GRISMER, FRANK A. "Spenser's Epithalamion." <u>TLS</u>, 26 April,
 p. 303.
  Interprets first stanza to suggest that "Spenser had a
 bride for whom he began the poem, but she apparently died. A
 revision of the poem appears to have been begun, but never completed. For response, see 1934.56.

26 HARD, FREDERICK. "Princelie Pallaces: Spenser and Elizabethan Architecture." <u>SR</u> 42:293-310.
  Suggests that Spenser's use of architectural imagery indicates "a conviction of the importance . . . of the art." Divides
 Spenser's use of architecture into two classes: "buildings whose
 function it is to convey to the reader the appropriate emotional
 significance of a given situation" and buildings used chiefly
 "as a pictorial device, for the purpose of giving either a
 romantic setting . . . or for specific realism of background."
 Concludes that Spenser's structures are suggested by buildings
 which he had actually seen and admired. References mainly to
 <u>The Faerie Queene</u> and <u>Mother Hubberds Tale</u>.

27 HARRISON, T.P., Jr. "Spenser and Boccaccio's <u>Olympia</u>."
 <u>The University of Texas Bulletin</u>, no. 3426; <u>Studies in
 English</u>, no. 14, pp. 5-30.
  Concludes from comparative study that "<u>Olympia</u> illustrates
 literary and theological traditions which find direct or ultimate
 expression not only in Spenser's pastoral <u>Calender</u> but in the
 <u>Daphnaida</u>, the <u>Fowre Hymnes</u>, and the <u>Faerie Queene</u>, I.x."

28 _____. "Spenser, Ronsard, and Bion." <u>MLN</u> 49:139-45.
  Counters popular view that "March" eclogue of <u>The Shepheardes Calender</u> and <u>Astrophel</u> were influenced directly by Bion's
 Fourth and First Idylls respectively. Shows Spenser's poems to
 be closer to Ronsard's paraphrases, <u>l'Amour oyseau</u> (1560) and
 <u>Adonis</u> (1563). Minimizes Spenser's direct knowledge of classical
 sources.

29 HEFFNER, RAY. "Essex, the Ideal Courtier." <u>ELH</u> 1:7-36.
  Challenges Rowe's identification of Sidney and Sir Calidore
 (1930.40) and demonstrates that Earl of Essex was celebrated as

model courtier in his own day and that "all the characteristics
of Calidore may be applied to Essex." Concludes that Spenser
includes Essex in character of Sir Calidore, though his fundamental conception of ideal courtier was not based on Essex to the
exclusion of others. Reprint of 1928.19.

*30 HUDSON, CHARLES M. "Edmund Spenser: Background and Perform-
     ance." Master's thesis, Vanderbilt University.
        Cited in Stephens, 1950.

 31 HUDSON, HOYT H. "John Hepwith's Spenserian Satire upon
     Buckingham: With Some Jacobean Analogues." Huntington
     Library Bulletin, no. 6 (November):39-71.
        Shows influence of Spenser's satiric Mother Hubberds Tale
     on Hepwith's satire against Buckingham, The Caledonian Forrest
     (printed 1641); also influence of Spenser on Niccols's The Cuckow
     (1607) and The Beggers Ape (1627), somewhat of a sequel to Mother
     Hubberds Tale.

 32 HUGHES, MERRITT Y. "Zeitgeist and Style, An Apology for
     Heinrich Wolfflin Against Martin Schultze." SR 42:482-91.
        Shows Wolfflin's critical theory to be of value in explain-
     ing Spenser's praise of a baroque painting as "the 'life-resembling
     pencill' of Zeuxis."

 33 JUDSON, ALEXANDER CORBIN. A Biographical Sketch of John
     Young, Bishop of Rochester, With Emphasis on His Relations
     With Edmund Spenser. Indiana University Studies, no. 103.
     Bloomington: Indiana University Press, 41 pp.
        Considers Spenser's contact with Young and Grindal (no
     earlier than 1578) to be significant in shaping ecclesiastical
     ideas of "May," "June," and "September" eclogues of The Shep-
     heardes Calender. Does not align Spenser with particular reli-
     gious faction, but regards him as advocate of reform in the
     Church in "the true spirit of Christianity."

*34 KAHIN, HELEN ANDREWS. "Controversial Literature about Women:
     A Survey of Literature of This Type with Special Reference
     to the Writings of the English Renaissance." Ph.D. diss.,
     University of Washington.
        Cited in National Union Catalog.

 35 KOLLER, KATHERINE. "Spenser and Ralegh." ELH 1:37-60.
        Spenser's poetry colored by friendship with Raleigh;
     identifies Timias in The Faerie Queene as Raleigh, Artegall as
     Lord Grey; suggests that Spenser delayed publication of Colin
     Clouts Come Home Againe from 1591 to 1595 as part of his "loyal
     support of his friend Ralegh, who in 1595 was striving for a
     complete restoration to royal favor." Reprint of 1932.41.

36   LAW, ROBERT A. "Holinshed as Source of <u>Henry V</u> and <u>King</u>
     <u>Lear</u>." <u>University of Texas Studies in English</u> 14:38-44.
         Notes that Spenser was among many who told Lear story
     before Shakespeare.

37   LEE, SIDNEY. "The Elizabethan Age of English Literature."
     In <u>Cambridge Modern History</u>. Edited by A.W. Ward, G.W.
     Prothero, and Stanley Leathers. Vol. 3. Cambridge:
     Cambridge University Press; New York: Macmillan, pp. 364-421.
         Reprint of 1905.18.

38   LEMMI, CHARLES W. "Britomart: The Embodiment of True Love."
     <u>SP</u> 31:133-39.
         Britomart embodies true love; Belphoebe embodies chastity;
     Amoret is "a type of maiden long regarded as ideal."

39   _____. "The Episode of Mordant and Amavia in <u>F. Q.</u>, I, 1."
     <u>PQ</u> 13:292-95.
         Interprets Acrasia allegorically as "the climax of intem-
     perate pleasure," lust, or "the reproductive energies of nature."
     The wine which she gives Mordant is the "sensual, polluted soul
     Mordant bears away with him." She warns him that he will die
     when his soul comes in contact with "the living water of purity
     . . . for spiritual death is precisely inability to receive
     purity."

40   LOWELL, D.O.S., and CHARLES KNAPP. "Vergilianism." <u>CW</u> 28,
     no. 6 (12 November):41-48.
         Mentions Spenser in discussion of <u>Culex</u>.

*41 McCRACKEN, MILDRED L. "The Plan and Conduct of <u>The Faerie</u>
     <u>Queene</u>." Master's thesis, University of Oklahoma.
         Cited in Stephens, 1950.

42   McMANAWAY, JAMES G. "'Occasion,' <u>Faerie Queene</u> II.iv.4-5."
     <u>MLN</u> 49:391-93.
         Suggests contemporary emblem books as immediate source for
     Occasion.

43   MAYNARD, THEODORE. <u>The Connection Between the Ballade,</u>
     <u>Chaucer's Modification of It, Rime Royal, and The Spenserian</u>
     <u>Stanza</u>. Ph.D. diss., Catholic University of America; Mensha,
     Wis.: George Banta Publishing Co., 107-31, passim.
         Carefully details the development of the Spenserian stanza:
     "Not until the Romantic Movement was the symmetrical beauty of
     the Spenserian stanza fully acknowledged. That symmetry and
     unity make me reject the suggestions that the Spenserian stanza
     is either <u>ottava rima</u> (with an added internal line) or is based
     upon <u>terza rima</u>, or is a modification of the madrigal (which has
     a different line), or is even the Chaucerian octave with an
     alexandrine tacked on. The evidence offered in this study is

that the Spenserian stanza grew naturally, and inevitably, from
a native stock, which, though ultimately derived from the French
ballade, was employed in England: rime royal." Spenserian stanza
has roots in Chaucer's rime royal. Notes that Spenser's use of
this stanza is very successful and cause for failure of his sonnet form: while the form fit most of his poetic material well,
it did not work with Amoretti. Amoretti are written with rhyme
ababbcbccdcdee "because the pattern of his stanza had become
part of the texture of his mind. Add a foot to the ninth line
of his sonnets, and discard the remaining five, and the result
is a Spenserian stanza."

44   MERTEN, MARIA. Michael Draytons "Poly-Olbion" im Rahmen Der
      Englischen Renaissance. Oranienburg: Druck Immaculatahaus,
      pp. 13-26.
         Discusses Spenser's influence on Drayton, concluding that
      he borrows from Spenser for his images, but he does not follow
      Spenser "mindlessly and slavishly." In final analysis, Drayton's
      images bear only superficial resemblance to Spenser's for "cer-
      tainly, Drayton possessed with all his veneration for Spenser,
      enough poetic gift and originality not to go so far in the imita-
      tion of his master to follow him completely as regarding content."
      Published version of 1933.44.

*45   MILLER, VIDA. "Terminology of Supernatural Beings in Chapman,
      Daniel, Drayton, Marlowe, and Spenser." Master's thesis,
      University of North Carolina.
         Cited in Stephens, 1950.

46   NEFF, MERLIN L. "Spenser's Allegory of the Toll Bridge."
      PQ 13:159-67.
         Traces history of monopolies on public utilities for per-
      sonal gain in England, noting that private tolls on bridges,
      roads, and ferries were among abuses in Spenser's day and that
      these abuses were an issue in Ireland during Spenser's residence
      there. Concludes that Artegall's episode with Pollente and
      Munera in The Faerie Queene, V.ii allegorically sets forth "the
      danger of private monopolies of public utilities as exemplified
      in toll bridges."

47   NEILL, KERBY. "Spenser's Shamefastnesse, Faerie Queene, II,
      ix, 40-44." MLN 49:387-91.
         Spenser's Shamefastnesse is not Aristotelian mean, but
      represents an extreme. Concludes that Spenser had no source
      for this idea, but that "it was part of his literary and ethical
      inheritance." Note also "The Source of Spenser's Temperance."
      Proceedings of Dr. Greenlaw's Seminary "C," 1931, [no number].
      Manuscript: Baltimore: Johns Hopkins University Library.
      Cited in Atkinson, 1937.

48   OSGOOD, CHARLES G[ROSVENOR]. "Verse in Spenser's Prose."
     ELH 1:1-6.
          Observes strong iambic character of the prose in A Veue of
     the Present State of Ireland and the Axiochus.

49   PADELFORD, FREDERICK MORGAN, ed. Introduction to The Axiochus
     of Plato Translated by Edmund Spenser. Baltimore: Johns
     Hopkins Press, 89 pp.
          Reproduces facsimile 1592 edition. Argues that Spenser
     translated the Axiochus, that this work influenced his later
     ideas, that phrasing in the translation parallels that in The
     Faerie Queene and in other known Spenser works, and that chief
     source is Welsdalius publi. 1568.

50   PANTLING, CONSTANCE. "Poetic Wit, The Renaissance and Seven-
     teenth Century" (From a lecture by T.S. Eliot at the British
     Institute). Revue de l'enseignement des langues vivantes
     51:86-182, passim.
          Comments on pastoral and Petrarchan qualities of The Shep-
     heardes Calender and notes Spenser's "tendency toward a purely
     English idiom and a natural simplicity."

51   PRICE, MARY BELL, and LAWRENCE MARSDEN PRICE. The Publication
     of English Literature in Germany in the Eighteenth Century.
     University of California Publications in Modern Philology,
     vol. 17. Berkeley: University of California Press; London:
     Cambridge University Press, p. 224.
          Notes a partial translation of The Faerie Queene into
     German in 1788. Reprinted: 1955.

*52 PROCTOR, LETA G. "Some Parallel Motives in Spenser's Faerie
     Queene and Homer's Iliad." Master's thesis, Oklahoma A and M
     University.
          Cited in Stephens, 1950.

53   PURCELL, JAMES M. Sidney's Stella. New York and London:
     Oxford University Press, pp. 58-66, passim.
          Discusses identity of Stella and dedication of Spenser's
     Astrophel: "Since the elegy is dedicated to Sidney's widow, to
     infer that Penelope Devereux was the Stella of a real passion is
     to accuse both Spenser and Frances Walsingham Sidney of a cal-
     lousness of which they could not be guilty." Links Stella of
     Spenser's Astrophel with Anne Cecil: "With Anne the heroine,
     Spenser's dedication to Sidney's widow is less offensive, and
     Burghley's antagonistic attitude toward Spenser is more intel-
     ligible." Concludes that "in 1594 the name of Sir Philip Sidney
     had not yet become associated with that of Penelope Rich either
     as an admirer or as paramour."

54   RATHBORNE, ISABEL E. "Another Interpretation of Muiopotmos."
     PMLA 49:1050-68.

Considers <u>Muiopotmos</u> an unfinished segment of a long mock-epic poem modeled after the pseudo-Homeric <u>Batrachomyomachia</u> and Heywood's <u>The Spider and the Flie</u>. Finds allegorical connotations in poem: it is "in some sense a parody of <u>The Faerie Queene</u>" in the same way the <u>Batrachomyomachia</u> parodies the <u>Iliad</u>.

55   RENWICK, W.L., ed. Introduction and notes to <u>A View of the Present State of Ireland</u>, edited principally from MS Rawlinson B 478 in the Bodleian Library and MS 188.221 in Caius College Cambridge. London: Scholartis Press, 330 pp.
    Dates <u>A Veue of the Present State of Ireland</u> 1596; presents extensive background on Ireland in Spenser's time; and concludes that Spenser's real purpose is to criticize "the whole regime, Irish, English-Irish and English alike." Notes that because of the numerous constraints on Spenser in his writing the <u>Veue</u>, it must be read in light of the more human ideal expressed in <u>The Faerie Queene</u>.

56   _____. "Spenser's <u>Epithalamion</u>." <u>TLS</u>, 3 May, p. 322.
    Rejects Grismer's reading of the poem (1934.25). <u>Epithalamion</u> is complete unified, joyous poem. "Short time" indicates contrast between short time of earth and eternity.

57   SMITH, CHARLES G. "The Ethical Allegory of the Two Florimels." <u>SP</u> 31:140-51.
    Attempts to show about the two Florimells in <u>The Faerie Queene</u>, II, III, and IV: "first, that the true Florimel, representing true beauty--beauty which has its source in a beautiful soul--arouses noble desires in noble minds, alone able to distinguish between true and false beauty, and stirs up sensual desire in base minds because they are blinded by lust; second, that the false Florimel, representing false beauty, mere physical beauty--beauty which does not have its source in a beautiful soul--appeals to base minds only and therefore never begets virtuous love or true friendship." Reprinted: 1935.65.

58   _____. "Spenser's Theory of Friendship." <u>PMLA</u> 49:490-500.
    Endeavors to show "that in the Fourth Book Spenser conceives of friendship as the operation in the world of man of a principle of cosmic love, a conception which he bases on the Hymn to Venus taken from Lucretius; and that there is a striking correspondence between the concord-discord antithesis in the Fourth Book and the conflict in <u>Mutabilitie</u>, a correspondence which not only throws light on the poet's interests in the Fourth Book but also helps to date <u>Mutabilitie</u> shortly after 1590. Finds influence of Lucretius in conception of love in <u>Hymne in Honour of Love</u>: "the universe is regarded as a kind of organism, the World having been brought out of chaos and all its parts bound together by the synthesizing power of love, which continues to maintain concord." Reprinted: 1935.65.

59 SMITH, G.C. MOORE. "Printed Books with Gabriel Harvey's
    Autograph or MS. Notes." MLR 29:68-70.
        Supplements 1913.31; 1933.61. For additional supplement,
    see 1935.67.

60 SPENS, JANET. Spenser's 'Faerie Queene': An Interpretation.
    London: Edward Arnold, 144 pp.
        Posits an original eight-book, eight-canto structure for
    the poem, with the Faerie Queene representing the Good or Hea-
    venly Beauty and Prince Arthur representing the soul, seven
    books devoted to the hero's conquest of the seven deadly sins
    and the last to Arthur's realization of his vision. The major-
    ity of the first three books, much of the fourth and sixth books,
    fragments of the fifth book, and all of the Mutabilitie Cantos
    belong to this plan. Mutabilitie Cantos, intended as the last
    three of the final book, incorporate Spenser's basic philosophy:
    "The philosophy of Plotinus with its tripartite division of both
    man and the universe at large into body, soul, and spirit affords
    a key to much that has been held inconsistent in or at least dis-
    connected in Spenser's poetry." In succeeding chapters compares
    and contrasts Spenser's symbolic artistry and habit of thinking
    with Wordsworth, Shakespeare, and Milton; considers Spenser's
    physical poetry and nature allegory and his ability to trans-
    figure intensely sensuous material; discusses love and love theme
    in Spenser's works as his "symbol for the unifying and dynamic
    forces in existence;" suggests that the world of The Faerie
    Queene is "the invisible world of the mind" and that the hero
    and focus of the poem is "the poet's own inner experience, made
    available for the uses of poetry by release from its relation to
    his external circumstances, which is the stuff of all the more
    vital parts." Reprinted: New York: Russell & Russell, 1967;
    Folcroft, Pa.: Folcroft Press, 1969.

61 STEIN, HAROLD. Studies in Spenser's Complaints. New York:
    Oxford University Press, 205 pp.
        Treats Complaints collectively and individually from per-
    spectives of Spenserian biography, bibliography, chronology,
    allegory, and versification; generally excludes study of paral-
    lels, analogues, and sources because Renwick (1928.38) covered
    these in his Complaints edition. Discusses in Part 1 "The
    Complaints Volume" publishing history and textual problems.
    Concludes in Part 2 "Dating and Composition" that "the signif-
    icant part of the Complaints is the product of Spenser's activity
    during his trip to England. . . . Its prevailing tone reflects
    all too clearly the checks and disappointments of his visit,
    deepened by his natural propensity for melancholy." Discusses
    allegory of Virgils Gnat, Mother Hubberds Tale, and Muiopotmos
    in Part 3. Makes case for Mother Hubberds Tale being attack on
    both Burghley (Fox) and James VI of Scotland (Ape); Lion repre-
    sents the English people as in The Faerie Queene. Rejects all
    interpretations of Muiopotmos for lack of evidence: "Muiopotmos

must be interpreted only in the same vague way that its counter-
part <u>Virgils Gnat</u> is to be read. All that the poem yields are
these few facts: two important men, one young and charming, the
other treacherous and cruel, had a disagreement, personal or
political; the unpleasant character won. From the depths of
ignorance we tend to assume that the only great men Spenser
admired were Sidney and Ralegh, and that the only ones he hated
were Burghley and Alençon." Part 4 "Early Verse and Revision"
is close study of <u>Epigrams</u>, <u>Sonnets</u>, and <u>Visions</u>. Notes
Spenser's use of blank verse to be mainly accidental. Part 5
includes collations, variants, and bibliography. Reprinted:
Folcroft, Pa.: Folcroft Press, 1969.

*62   STIRLING, BRENTS. "Spenser's Garden of Adonis and <u>Cantos of</u>
       <u>Mutabilitie</u>: A Reinterpretation." Ph.D. diss., University
       of Washington.
            Partially published: 1934.63.

63   _____. "The Philosophy of Spenser's 'Garden of Adonis."
       <u>PMLA</u> 49:501-38.
            Challenges several interpretations of Garden of Adonis:
       Greenlaw (1920.9-10; 1930.14), Levinson (1928.31), Albright
       (1929.4), Saurat (1930.42), Cumming (1931.11), and Bennett
       (1932.4). Interprets Spenser's philosophy as conventional
       Platonic doctrine at base, "with the union of Platonism and
       Ovid's 'Philosophy of turned shaped' found in Golding's trans-
       lation, as the probable immediate inspiration."

64   TAYLOR, GEORGE COFFIN. <u>Milton's Use of Du Bartas</u>.
       Cambridge, Mass.: Harvard University Press, 129 pp., passim.
            Notes Spenser's use of Du Bartas and how Spenser, in turn,
       influenced Milton.

65   TILLYARD, E.M.W. <u>Poetry Direct and Oblique</u>. London:
       Chatto & Windus, 28-32, 36, 57-58.
            Discusses <u>The Faerie Queene</u> in context of great common-
       place themes of literature. The great commonplace of <u>The Faerie</u>
       <u>Queene</u> is that Spenser's music and pageantry express his dis-
       satisfaction with life: the idealist creates an imaginary world
       which transcends the mundane. Comments on allegory of youth and
       old age in "February" eclogue of <u>The Shepheards Calender</u>. Re-
       vised: 1945. Reprinted: 1948; 1956; 1959.

66   Van PATTEN, NATHAN. <u>An Index to Bibliographies and Biblio-</u>
       <u>graphical Contributions Relating to the Work of American and</u>
       <u>British Authors, 1923-32</u>. Stanford: Stanford University
       Press; Oxford: Oxford University Press, p. 237.
            Brief Spenser bibliography.

67   WEBSTER, C.M. "A Note on Alexander Nowell." <u>NQ</u> 167:58-59,
       116.

Contends that Nowell as patron of Spenser was of little help, but may have introduced poet to the Dudleys. For related study, see 1934.68.

68   WELPLY, W.H. "Robert Nowell and Edmund Spenser." NQ 167:373.
     Presents evidence to show Webster (1934.67) is in error on Nowell as Spenser's patron and link to Dudleys.

69   WILLCOCK, G.D. "Passing Pitefull Hexameters: A Study of Quantity and Accent in English Renaissance Verse." MLR 29: 1-19.
     Comments on Spenser's and Harvey's adaptations of Drant's rules, as discussed in Spenser-Harvey correspondence. Notes innovations in The Shepheardes Calender.

70   WILSON, ELKIN CALHOUN. "The Idealization of Queen Elizabeth in the Poetry of Her Age." Ph.D. diss., Harvard University, pp. 531-611, passim.
     Relies on Spenser's treatments and praise of Elizabeth in The Shepheardes Calender, The Faerie Queene, and Colin Clouts Come Home Againe as points of reference to other tributes of the age. Thus, Spenser discussed generally in Chapters 4-6. Chapter 7, "Gloriana and Belphoebe," focuses on The Faerie Queene to show how Gloriana and Belphoebe "epitomize the familiar Judith, Deborah, Eliza, Elisa, Diana, Laura, Idea, and Cynthia." Concludes that "the idealization of Elizabeth was the inevitable result of the imaginative needs of the age, which made her an adequate symbol of the good and beautiful in sovereignty and womanhood."

*71 WOOD, RUTH. "Ovid's Metamorphoses and Spenser's Faerie Queene." Master's thesis, University of Colorado.
     Cited in Atkinson, 1937.

72   YATES, FRANCES A. John Florio. The Life of an Italian in Shakespeare's England. Cambridge: Cambridge University Press, pp. 48-50.
     Considers Spenser's acquaintance with Florio to be amicable; thus, questions identification of Rosalind (The Shepheardes Calender) with Florio's wife ("Rose Daniel").

                                1935

*1   ALLEN, WILLIE. "Spenser, Lucretius, and the New Science." Master's thesis, University of Texas.
     Cited in Stephens, 1950.

2   ANDREWS, CHARLES M. "Note on Copy of the 1611 Folio Edition of Spenser." Publications of the Colonial Society of Massachusetts. 28:357-59.

Suggests that Chauncy (1935.38) had a variant copy of 1611
edition (one without The Faerie Queene) or had one of the 1617
folios. Concludes that if the latter is so, there may have been
two editions of Spenser's poems in Massachusetts Bay Colony before 1654.

*3   AYFERS, RUTH JANE. "A Study of Parallels in Spenser and
      Dante." Master's thesis, Ohio University.
           Cited in Stephens, 1950.

*4   BAROWAY, ISRAEL. Studies in the Bible as Poetry in the
      English Renaissance. Baltimore: Johns Hopkins Press.
           Cited in Atkinson, 1937. Published version of 1930.2.

5   BENNETT, JOSEPHINE WATERS. "Spenser's Fowre Hymnes: Addenda."
      SP 32:131-57.
           Answers Padelford (1932.52). Argues that Christian Neo-
      platonism permeates all four hymns, that Pico and Benivieni in-
      fluenced Spenser, and that Hymnes comprise one unified structure.
      Concludes that "if there were two hymns in honor of love and
      beauty, belonging to the 1578-80 period of composition, they
      were thoroughly revised to fit the scheme of four hymns in the
      publication of 1596."

6   BENSLY, EDWARD. "The Name 'Hudibras.'" NQ 168:160.
           Suggests Spenser as possible source for name of Samuel
      Butler's hero.

7   BHATTĀCHĀRYA, MOHINĪMOHANA (BHATTĀCHERJE, MOHINĪMOHAN).
      Platonic Ideas in Spenser. London: Longmans, Green, 200 pp.
           Considers the influence of Platonism and Neoplatonism on
      Spenser's works. Reprinted: Westport, Conn.: Greenwood Press,
      1970.

8   BOTTING, ROLAND B. "The Composition of the Shepheardes
      Calender." PMLA 50:423-34.
           Argues that The Shepheardes Calender resulted from "a some-
      what hasty gathering together" and revision of earlier poems at
      a time when The Faerie Queene preoccupied Spenser. Maintains
      that lack of thematic unity between eclogues (but not within
      eclogues) and inaccuracies in the gloss suggest inattentive,
      hurried preparation of poem for publication.

9   BRADNER, LEICESTER. "The Latin Translation of Spenser's
      Shepheardes Calender." MP 33:21-26.
           Observations on the Dove and the Bathurst translations,
      which show changing attitudes toward Spenser (and English Poetry)
      between 1584 and 1610.

10   CAIN, H. EDWARD. "Spenser's 'Shield of Faith.'" SAB 10:
      163-66.

Suggests that Elizabethans "would more readily have associated the phrase 'shield of faith' with a gold coin than with
the Epistle to the Ephesians,--with Elizabeth rather than with
Saint Paul" because a host of gold coins, prior to and during
her reign, bore the legend "Scutum Fidei Proteget Eam."

11   CAMPBELL, LILY B. "The Christian Muse." Huntington Library
     Bulletin, no. 8 (October):29-70.
          Spenser discussed in context of secular and divine literary
     traditions. Notes influence of Du Bartas on Spenser's conception
     of Urania (Teares of the Muses) and Sapience (Fowre Hymnes), also
     part of Urania tradition. Suggests that Fowre Hymnes illustrates
     Spenser's shift from secular to divine poetry, "that An Hymne of
     Heavenly Beautie rehearses the Christian story as Urania of The
     Teares of the Muses says that knowledge would reveal it," and
     "that Sapience resembles the Heavenly muse, who from being linked
     with the Holy Ghost as the inspirer of divine poetry gradually
     had bestowed upon her the attributes of the Holy Spirit."

*12 CONNELL, STELLA J. "The Literary Relationships of Edmund
     Spenser." Master's thesis, Baylor University.
          Cited in Stephens, 1950.

*13 CORRIGAN, MARIE C. "Spenser and the Geraldine Earls."
     Master's thesis, Western Reserve University.
          Cited in Stephens, 1950.

14   De SELINCOURT, E., ed. Introduction to The Poetical Works of
     Edmund Spenser. London, New York, and Toronto: Humphrey
     Milford, Oxford University Press, pp. vii-lxvii.
          Reprint of 1912.11.

15   EDWARDS, ROBERT DUDLEY. Church and State in Tudor Ireland:
     A History of Penal Laws Against Irish Catholics 1534-1603.
     Dublin: Talbot Press; London and New York: Longmans, Green
     & Co., pp. 206, 214, 236, 242, 260-61.
          Discusses how A Veue of the Present State of Ireland was
     used as source for weaknesses of Established Church in Ireland
     and poor quality of clergy. Notes Spenser's opposition to reli-
     gious persecution in Ireland, the work of Irish missionaries,
     and Spenser's account of Smerwick massacre. Includes bibliography.

*16 EKSTRAND, DORIS. "The Influences of Du Bartas on Spenser."
     Master's thesis, Stanford University.
          Cited in Stephens, 1950.

17   ERSKINE, JOHN. "The Faerie Queene." In The Delight of Great
     Books. Indianapolis: Bobbs Merrill Co., pp. 75-96.
          Reprint of 1928.12.

18   ESPINER, JANET G. "Les sonnets Élisabéthains." RLC 15:107-9.
      Notes Spenser's debt to Italian sources.

*19   FEARS, VELMA. "A Study of The Shepheardes Calender."
      Master's thesis, University of Texas.
      Cited in Stephens, 1950.

*20   FIFIELD, LOUISE D. "The Extent of Virgil's Influence upon
      Spenser as Revealed from a Study of The Shepheardes Calender
      and The Faerie Queene." Master's thesis, Boston University.
      Cited in Stephens, 1950.

21   FOWLER, EARLE B. Spenser and the System of Courtly Love.
      Louisville. Standard Printing Co., 91 pp.
          Reprint of 1934.22

22   FREYD, BERNARD. "Spenser or Anthony Munday?--A Note on the
      Axiochus." PMLA 50:903-8.
          Evidence (presented by F.M. Padelford, 1935.55) better
      supports Anthony Munday as translator of Axiochus than Spenser.

*23   GAERTNER, ADELHEID. Die englische Epithalamienliteratur im
      siebzehnten Jahrhundert und ihre Vorbidler. Ph.D. diss.,
      University of Erlangen. Coburg: A. Rossteutscher, passim.
          For published edition, see 1936.19; McNeir-Provost no. 2377.

24   GARNETT, RICHARD, and EDMUND GOSSE. English Literature An
      Illustrated Record. From the Age of Henry VIII to the Age
      of Milton. Vol. 2. New York: Macmillan Co., pp. 109-30.
          Reprint of 1904.12.

25   GOTTFRIED, RUDOLF B. A Veue of the Present State of Ireland.
      by Edmund Spenser. The Text of Bodleian MS Rawlinson B 478.
      Edited with Introduction and Notes by R.B. Gottfried. Ph.D.
      diss., Yale University, 1:362 pp.; 2:319 pp.
          Concludes that Spenser wrote A Veue of the Present State of
      Ireland on trip to England in 1596; that his purpose was not to
      defend Grey and to discuss Irish antiquities, but to flatter
      Essex, with whom he may have had a connection through Hugh and
      Henry Cuffe; that he "does not accuse Raleigh of having caused
      trouble between Grey and the Earl of Ormond; and that there is
      no reason to doubt his presence at the Smerwick massacre, which
      Grey performed in fulfillment of Elizabeth's own plans." Notes
      inaccuracies in Spenser's comments on Irish antiquities, due
      probably to his reliance on Buchanan, Holinshed, and Camden
      rather than on primary sources. Considers Spenser's proposals,
      recommendations, and opinions typical of those of his contempo-
      raries, but Spenser "surpasses all other Elizabethan writers on
      Ireland in the organized inclusiveness of his account." Traces
      influence of the work. Includes detailed Notes and Index.

26 GRAY, ARTHUR. "Spenser's Aëtion." TLS, 24 January, p. 48.
    Identifies Aëtion in Colin Clouts Come Home Againe as
Marlowe; finds considerable evidence. For related study, see
1935.58.

27 GRAY, F. CAMPBELL. "Milton's Counterpoint, Classicism and
    Romanticism in the Poetry of John Milton." SR 43:134-45.
    Shows Spenser to be most significant influence on Milton's
poetry.

28 GREEN, ZAIDEE E. "Observations on the Epic Similes in The
    Faerie Queene." PQ 14:217-28.
    Evaluates Spenser's similes apart from possible classical
sources and suggests that the poet created similes laboriously
and that as the poem progresses he became more interested in
similes than in the story.

29 GREENOUGH, JAMES BRADSTREET, and GEORGE LYMAN KITTREDGE.
    Words and Their Ways in English Speech. New York and London:
    Macmillan, pp. 118, 295, 354, 375.
    Reprint of 1901.11.

30 GRUBB, MARION. "A Brace of Villains." MLN 50:168-69.
    On the basis of "an odd parallel between the description
of the villain Malengin in the F.Q. and another villain in Arden
[of Feversham]," suggests that manuscript version of Book V of
The Faerie Queene must have existed at least as early as 1592,
the publication date of Arden of Feversham.

31 HEFFNER, RAY. "The Printing of John Hughes' Edition of
    Spenser, 1715." MLN 50:151-53.
    The Hughes edition was published in two sizes, the larger
being issued to subscribers. The text in the first volume of
the smaller size beginning with "A Letter of the Authors" and
continuing through part of The Faerie Queene is not from the
same type as the larger text. Throughout the first and second
volumes and to page 592 of the third "the initial letters, head-
pieces, tailpieces, other ornaments, swash letters, and the like
are all different." From page 593 to the end of the sixth volume
the large and small texts are from the same type. Concludes from
type differences and from variant readings and printer's errors
that the type for the smaller text was hastily reset and printed
without proofreading. Concludes that "the necessity for enlarg-
ing the edition indicates an unsuspected interest in Spenser in
the first quarter of the Eighteenth Century."

32 HINTZ, HOWARD W. "The Elizabethan Entertainment and The
    Faerie Queene." PQ 14:83-90.
    Spenser is "the direct link between the earlier court
entertainments and the Jacobean masques." Considers report of
Leicester's entertainment for Elizabeth on her "progress" to

Kenilworth Castle in 1575 in <u>Robert Laneham's Letter</u> typical in
its main features of the numerous entertainments provided for
Elizabeth on her frequent progresses through her realm. Studies
extent and nature of influence of these entertainments on first
three books of <u>The Faerie Queene</u>.

33   HUGHES, MERRITT Y. "Spenser's Palmer." <u>ELH</u> 2:151-64.
        Considers the Palmer in terms of classical and contemporary
literature, psychology, theology, and folklore, concluding: "it
was perhaps the classical influence which, in alliance with contemporary psychology, not popular and esoteric, confounded or
entangled the symbols of the guardian angel and of the old man,
whose ghostly benignity, when we meet him in <u>The Faerie Queene</u>,
makes us think of Hesiod's demons and heroes, the souls of good
men returned to help the living."

34   JENKINS, RAYMOND. "<u>Newes Out of Munster</u>, A Document in
     Spenser's Hand." <u>SP</u> 32:125-30.
        Cottonian MS (Titus B, xiii, 364; British Museum) appears
to be in Spenser's secretary hand and "appears to have been written at Dublin at a time when Spenser was in residence there."
Manuscript dated 23 March 1582.

35   JOHNSON, EDITH C. <u>Lamb Always Elia</u>. London: Methuen,
     pp. 81, 82, 134.
        Mentions Lamb's allusions to and comments on Spenser.
Reprinted: 1936.28.

36   JOHNSON, FRANCIS R. "The Progress of the Copernican Astronomy
     among English Scientists to 1645 and Its Reflection in Litera-
     ture from Spenser to Milton." Ph.D. diss., Johns Hopkins Uni-
     versity, pp. 324-30.
        Spenser's superficial knowledge of astronomy revealed in
loose and inaccurate astronomical references. "A brief recon-
sideration of Spenser's cosmological ideas in the light of the
progress of astronomy in sixteenth-century England leads quite
definitely to the conclusion that they were in no way indebted
to the new astronomy arising from the Copernican theory."

*37 JORDAN, ROSAMOND B. "The Heroic Simile in <u>The Faerie Queene</u>."
     Master's thesis, Marquette University.
        Cited in Stephens, 1950.

38   KITTREDGE, GEORGE LYMAN. "A Harvard Salutatory Oration of
     1662." <u>Publications of the Colonial Society of Massachusetts</u>
     28:1-24.
        Discusses commonplace Book of Elnathan Chauncy (A.B. Harvard
1661, A.M. 1664), which contains "more than a score of pages" of
quotations from Spenser's works, except <u>The Faerie Queene</u>. Speculates that Chauncy used edition that excluded <u>The Faerie Queene</u>.
For related study, see 1935.2.

39   KNOWLTON, E.C. "Spenser and Nature." JEGP 34:366-76.
          Outlines Spenser's conception of Nature and suggests a
     literary design for the Cantos of Mutabilitie: a brief and
     sudden ending--"Nature's almost laconic decision"--contrasted
     to the length of what precedes it--"the prolonged harangues of
     Mutabilitie." Compares Spenser's design to Luther's "Ein feste
     Burg ist under Gott," two pediments of the Temple of Zeus at
     Olympia, and Claudian's First Book against Rufinus.

40   KOLLER, KATHERINE. "Identifications in Colin Clout's Come
     Home Againe." SP 50:155-58.
          Identifications based on early sixteenth-century record:
     "scornful lass"--"delia"; Urania--Countess of Pembroke; Theana--
     Countess of Warwick; Mansilia--Marchioness of Northampton;
     Phyllis--Countess of Derby; Charyllis--Lady Comptom and Montegle;
     Amaryllis--Lady Hunsdon; Stella--Lady Riche.

41   KUERSTEINER, AGNES DUNCAN. "E.K. is Spenser." PMLA 50:140-55.
          Takes position that E.K. means Edmundus Kalendarius
     ("Edmund the Calenderer," i.e., Spenser); shows that use of
     initials was popular literary convention during Spenser's time.
     Considers gloss to be Spenser's work: "a philosophical, polem-
     ical, shrewd, whimsical, and altogether delightful accompaniment
     to the eclogues." Correspondence with Harvey supports view.

42   LEMMI, CHARLES W. "Astery's Transformation in Muiopotmos."
     PMLA 50:913-14.
          Notes possible source for Astery's transformation in
     Locantius's commentary on Statius.

43   _____. "The Serpent and the Eagle in Spenser and Shelley."
     MLN 50:165-68.
          Traces probable source of dragon-griffin simile which
     Spenser uses to describe the battle between Red Cross Knight
     and Sans Joy to the twelfth book of the Iliad, wherein a serpent
     and an eagle struggle in mid-air over the Trojan army. Suggests
     that Spenser changed eagle to griffin because the griffin is
     usually associated with righteous tenacity, as it is in Burke's
     Peerage, Physiologus, and Dante, in the last representing Christ.

44   _____. "Symbolism in Faerie Queene, II.12." MLN 50:161-65.
          Cites analogues for symbols in The Faerie Queene, II.xii in
     Fulgentius, Natalis Comes, and Kebes of Thebes.

*45 LITCHFIELD, FLORENCE LeDUC. "The Treatment of the Theme of
     Mutability in the Literature of the English Renaissance: A
     Study of the Problem of Change between 1558-1660." Ph.D.
     diss., University of Minnesota.
          Cited in National Union Catalog.

46   LOTSPEICH, H[ENRY] G. "Spenser's Urania." MLN 50:141-46.
          Traces religious aspects of Spenser's Urania (Teares of the
      Muses, lines 481-540) to Du Bartas' Urania. Regards Spenser's
      Urania as "the Spirit who leads men through the study of the
      works of nature to the contemplation of the Heavenly Hierarchy
      and of God himself."

47   LOTSPEICH, HENRY G. "Spenser's Virgils Gnat and its Latin
      Original." ELH 2:235-41.
          Identifies Spenser's text as Bembo's Dialogue on the Culex
      and Terence (1530), which was "found in the 1542 Antwerp edition
      of Virgil's Works published by A. Dumaeus." Considers poem an
      important early work.

48   MAYNADIER, HOWARD. "Spenser." In The Arthur of the English
      Poets. Boston: Houghton Mifflin & Co.; Cambridge, Mass.:
      Riverside Press, pp. 257-77.
          Reprint of 1907.22

*49   MICHIE, SARA. "Celtic Myth and Spenserian Romance." Ph.D.
      diss., University of Virginia.
          Cited in National Union Catalog.

50   MILLICAN, C. BOWIE. "Ralph Knevett's 'Supplement of the
      Faery Queene.'" TLS, 10 October, p. 631.
          Announces forthcoming article (1938) which shows that
      Ralph Knevett, and not Ralph Jegon, authored "A Supplement to
      the Faery Queene in three Bookes." See McNeir-Provost no. 1565.

*51   MORRELL, MINNIE C. "A Comparative Study of Spenser's Faerie
      Queene and Tennyson's The Idylls of the King." Master's
      thesis, University of Tennessee.
          Cited in Stephens, 1950.

52   NEILL, KERBY. "The Faerie Queene and the Mary Stuart Con-
      troversy." ELH 2:192-214.
          Sketches in "the background and main phases of the battle
      of the books that was waged over Mary Stuart" and relates "this
      material to the appearance of Duessa in Books IV and V of the
      Faerie Queene." Concludes that there is direct link between
      trial of Duessa and her appearance in Book IV; that one group
      of her sins is against temperance, the virtue of Book II; and
      that Spenser's view of Mary is in agreement with that of her
      enemies. Reprint of one chapter of 1935.53. Reprinted with
      summary of 1935.53: Baltimore: Johns Hopkins University, 1935.

53   _____. "Spenser and the Literature of Elizabethan Succession."
      Ph.D. diss., Johns Hopkins University.
          Discusses political background of Elizabeth's accession,
      the political background and interpretation of Gordoduc, the dis-
      cord over Elizabeth's succession, the battle of the books over

the succession, and Spenser's treatment of Mary Stuart in The
Faerie Queene. Published in part: 1935.52.

54   OSGOOD, CHARLES GROSVENOR. The Voice of England. A History
     of English Literature. New York and London: Harper &
     Brothers Publishers, pp. 163-70, passim.
          Surveys Spenser's achievement; identifies main influences
     on works.

55   PADELFORD, FREDERICK M. "Spenser or Anthony Munday?--A Note
     on the Axiochus." PMLA 50:908-13.
          Refutes Freyd (1935.22) by citing parallels between the
     Axiochus and The Shepheardes Calender (and other Spenser works)
     to show that Spenser is the translator.

56   PURCELL, J.M. "The Date of Spenser's Mutabilitie Cantos."
     PMLA 50:914-17.
          Frequency of color, light, and shade words in the Mutabilitie
     Cantos suggests that they were written during the period of com-
     position of first three books of The Faerie Queene. Concludes
     that "the counting of words in a partial analysis of vocabulary
     is not satisfactory evidence for determining the dates of compo-
     sition of portions of The Faerie Queene." For related studies,
     see 1928.1; 1929.3, 6; 1930.4, 36; 1932.1.

57   RENWICK, W.L. "Edmund Spenser." In The Great Tudors.
     Edited by Katharine Garvin. New York: E.P. Dutton & Co.,
     pp. 521-36.
          Introduction to the man and his works. Defends A Veue of
     the Present State of Ireland as practical proposal to solve
     problems in Ireland. Reads poetry on several levels: literal,
     topical, and anagogical or spiritual. Considers anagogical
     meaning in poems to be ethical, not mystical, drawn from Chris-
     tian ethics and contemporary social teachings, "that tried to
     combine the personal virtues of the mediaeval knight with the
     intellectual enlightenment of the cultivated mind, and the
     artistic sensitiveness of cultivated senses."

58   _____. "Spenser's 'Aëtion.'" TLS, 31 January, p. 62.
          Accepts Gray's identification in Colin Clouts Come Home
     Againe of Aëtion with Marlowe (1935.26), but finds supportive
     evidence weak.

*59 SARGENT, RALPH M. "At the Court of Queen Elizabeth. The
     Life and Lyrics of Sir Edward Dyer." Ph.D. diss., Yale
     University.
          For published edition, see 1935.60.

60   _____. At the Court of Queen Elizabeth. The Life and Lyrics
     of Sir Edward Dyer. London and New York: Oxford University
     Press, pp. 58-65, passim.

Concludes on Areopagus "that these people were ever gathered
together at the same time there is not the slightest evidence";
"it is more probable that Spenser . . . is speaking metaphorically
of his esteem for Dyer and Sidney." Notes that "when Spenser lik-
ens Dyer and Sidney to the Areopagites he is bearing witness to
the superiority of these courtiers over professional literary
men," both in social status and in their being in "closer com-
munion with the muses" due to their social rank. Published version of 1935.59.

61   SCHULZE, IVAN L. "Elizabethan Chivalry and the Faerie Queene's
     Annual Feast." MLN 50:158-61.
     Cites various festivals and celebrations at Elizabeth's
court to show that "although the feast motif must ultimately go
back to the romances, in all probability, it is also an allegorical treatment of some features of the revival of chivalry at
Elizabeth's court.

62   SEATON, ETHEL. Literary Relations of England and Scandinavia.
     Oxford: Clarendon Press, pp. 60-61, 235-36, passim.
     Discusses allusions and dedications to Helena Snakenborg,
wife of Marquess of Northampton, William Parr, and, later, wife
of Sir Thomas Gorges (note dedication of Daphnaida and Mansilia
in Colin Clouts Come Home Againe). Points out references in A
Veue of the Present State of Ireland to Irish "dane-rathes,"
and Danish forts, and Danish funeral monuments.

63   SELWYN, E.G. "Some Philosophies in English Poetry."
     Quarterly Review 264:224-37.
     Mentions Spenser as faithful to spirit of the Christian
Renaissance.

64   SMITH, CHARLES G. "Sententious Theory in Spenser's Legend
     of Friendship." ELH 2:165-91.
     "Examination of the various episodes in the Fourth Book of
the Faerie Queene reveals that Spenser's theory of friendship as
the operation in the world of man of a harmonizing and unifying
principle of cosmic love is based on certain ideas which seem to
satisfy the conditions required by such a conception. The purpose of this study is to point out where in the Fourth Book these
ideas are found and to show that they were widespread and even
considered proverbial in much of the literature with which Spenser
was probably acquainted." Reprinted: 1935.65.

65   _____. Spenser's Theory of Friendship. Baltimore: Johns
     Hopkins Press, 74 pp.
     Previously unpublished fifth chapter considers analogous
relationship between Alain's conception of Nature in The Complaint
of Nature and Spenser's conception of Venus, symbolized in Lady
Concord and figured forth throughout the fourth book of The Faerie
Queene. Published version of 1930.46. Reprint of 1934.57-58;
1935.64, 66; New York: AMS Press, 1972.

66   _____. "Spenser's Theory of Friendship: An Elizabethan
      Commonplace." <u>SP</u> 32:158-69.
          Shows parallels with Spenser's theory of concord in various
sixteenth-century texts and concludes that these parallels "must
be considered as a part of the provenience of the Fourth Book of
the <u>Faerie Queene</u> along with the data previously adduced by
scholars." Reprinted in 1935.65.

67   SMITH, G.C. MOORE. "Printed Book with Gabriel Harvey's
      Autograph or MS. Notes." <u>MLR</u> 30:209.
         Supplements 1913.31; 1933.61; 1934.59.

68   SMITH, ROLAND M. "Spenser's Irish River Stories." <u>PMLA</u>
      50:1047-56.
         Spenser did not invent his Irish river stories, as Judson
suggests (1933.38). "Even if Spenser's sources for his river
stories are unwritten or no longer extant, there can be little
doubt that he drew heavily on the topographical lore he picked
up in Ireland." Identifies sources for river stories in <u>Colin
Clouts Come Home Againe</u>, lines 92-155, and <u>Cantos of Mutabilitie</u>,
VI.xxxvii-lv.

69   _____. "Una and Duessa." <u>PMLA</u> 50:917-19.
         Suggestion for Una's name comes from Ireland where it is
common name, though Spenser uses the name's Latin implications.
Duessa also derives from the Irish compound of <u>Dub</u> (meaning black)
and <u>Esa</u> (a woman's name).

70   STIRLING, BRENTS. "Two Notes on the Philosophy of
      <u>Mutabilitie</u>." <u>MLN</u> 50:154-55.
         Notes evidence of Spenser's verbal borrowings from Arthur
Golden's translation of the Metamorphoses and clarifies Boethian
interpretation in 1933.63 "by pointing out that the concept of
things conquering change and achieving perfection by returning
'to themselves,' and that of change being transcended upon union
with God, can be considered as one and the same philosophical
doctrine."

71   STRATHMANN, ERNEST A. "Lady Carey and Spenser." <u>ELH</u> 2:33-57.
         Discusses Lady Carey as a literary patron. Minimizes sig-
nificance of literary references to Lady Carey in Spenser's works;
finds allusions only in several dedications, as Phyllis in <u>Colin
Clouts Come Home Againe</u>, and possibly to her handiwork in
<u>Muiopotmos</u> (rejects many earlier identifications). Explains
nature of Spenser's addresses by kinship, conventions of patronage, and friendship with the Careys. Partial reprint of 1930.48.

72   THALER, ALWIN. "Shakspere and Spenser." <u>SAB</u> 10:192-211.
         Explores general relations between Shakespeare and Spenser,
suggesting that Shakespeare was influenced by the <u>Epithalamion</u>
and <u>The Faerie Queene</u>.

73   THRALL, WILLIAM FLINT. "The Faerie Queene, 'First Part'--
     In Variorum." SP 32:245-58.
         Extensive review of first volumes of the Variorum Spenser,
     their reflection of twenty-five years of Spenser scholarship, and
     their suggestion of future lines of Spenser scholarship.

74   TILLOTSON, KATHLEEN. "Spenser's Aëtion.'" TLS, 7 February,
     p. 76.
         Identifies Aëtion in Colin Clouts Come Home Againe as
     Drayton; Spenser's praise similar to contemporary attitudes
     toward Drayton.

75   TUVE, ROSAMOND. "Spenser and the Zodiake of Life." JEGP
     34:1-19.
         Concludes that Spenser wrote in same tradition as
     Palingenius, who attempted to explain the mysteries of the
     world: God, Nature and Man; Man's "end on earth, his tempta-
     tions, his virtues, and his possible helps." The Zodiake of
     Life "presented these in ways which Spenser approved of and
     often used--astronomical framework, didactic allegory; quests,
     dream-visions, gardens-of-love, and all the familiar devices of
     Mediaeval romance." Spenser indebted to Googe's translation of
     Zodiake; evident in The Faerie Queene, Fowre Hymnes, Teares of
     the Muses, and Colin Clouts Come Home Againe. Reprinted: 1970;
     see McNeir-Provost no. 1155.

76   WEITZMANN, FRANCIS WHITE. "Notes on the Elizabethan Elegie."
     PMLA 50:335-43.
         Examines various meanings "elegy" had to Elizabethan
     writers. Daphnaida first "elegy" of personal grief prompted by
     death of beloved person.

77   WHITE, HAROLD O. Plagiarism and Imitation During the English
     Renaissance. Cambridge: Harvard University Press, pp. 96-97.
         Mentions Spenser's poetic techniques. Reprinted: New
     York: Octagon Books, 1965.

78   WILLIAMSON, GEORGE. "Mutability, Decay, and Seventeenth-
     Century Melancholy." ELH 2:121-50.
         Study of the "Decay of Nature" as powerful theme and mood
     from Spenser's Mutabilitie to Browne's Urn Burial.

79   WRINN, MARY J.J. The Hollow Reed. New York and London:
     Harper & Brothers, pp. 58-59, 469-70.
         Illustrates and describes Spenserian stanza.

80   WURTSBAUGH, JEWEL. "Digby's Criticism of Spenser." RES
     11:192-95.
         Reviews Digby's two early seventeenth-century commentaries
     on Spenser, Observation on the 22nd Stanza in the 9th Canto of
     the 2d. Book of Spencer's [sic] Faery Queen and Concerning Edmund
     Spencer [sic]. Considers Digby's criticism significant.

81 _____. "Thomas Edwards and the Editorship of the Faerie
Queene." MLN 50:146-51.
Considers Edwards's interest in producing a standard edition of The Faerie Queene and his contribution of the correction
of the text for Upton's 1751 edition. "Failure to make a satis-
factory arrangement with a publisher and distaste for the tedious
business of an editor had inhibited his own edition."

1936

1 ALLEN, DON CAMERON. "Symbolic Color in the Literature of the
English Renaissance." PQ 15:81-92.
Shows renaissance color symbolism (rooted in medieval folk
culture, art, blazonry, and church ritual) to be intentional and
patterned. Notes that Spenser observed tenets of this symbolism.

2 ATKINSON, DOROTHY F. "Edmund Spenser's Family and the
Church." NQ 170:172-75.
Questions poet's relationship to Thomas, Richard, and John
Spenser of Wroughton, Wiltshire. For related studies, see
1936.4, 21.

3 BENNETT, JOSEPHINE WATERS. "Renaissance Neoplatonism in the
Poetry of Edmund Spenser." Ph.D. diss., Ohio State Univer-
sity, 292 pp.
First chapter traces development of Platonism into Neo-
platonism, the Florentine Academy, the movement of this Neoplatonism to England. Sections include Philosophy and Allegory,
Reasoning from Analogy, The Antiquity of Truth, and the Poet as
Teacher. Second chapter identifies Clio as muse of The Faerie
Queene, and says her records of heroic deeds performed by
Gloriana's knights are preserved in Cleopolis, the city of fame,
the capitol of Fairyland, set apart from the earth as an ideal
realm. This city "is a sort of bright image of England, lacking
the material imperfections, and amplifying the virtues of the
island, yet 'shadowing forth' the ideals and the heroid deeds
of Spenser's age as they were stripped of their flaws by the
imagination of the poet and made part of those eternal ideas
which Plato conceived of as the only Realities." Four appendices consider Spenser and Lucretius, Lucretian parallels with
the Garden of Adonis, Gabriel Harvey and Louis le Roy, and the
date of composition of the first two Fowre Hymnes. Third, fourth,
and fifth chapters correspond to 1933.7; 1932.4; 1931.4, and
1935.5.

4 BENSLY, EDWARD. "Edmund Spenser's Family and the Church."
NQ 170:230-31.
Information on Thomas Spenser. For related studies, see
1936.2, 21.

5   BRADFORD, GAMALIEL. "The Women of The Faery Queen." In
     Elizabethan Women. Edited by Harold Ogden White. Boston:
     Houghton Mifflin; Cambridge, Mass.: Riverside Press,
     pp. 207-26.
          Blending strong moral sense with his Renaissance love of
     beauty, Spenser creates "ladies of a pure and almost unearthly
     loveliness" and scatters "an abundance of dubious and objection-
     able characters" throughout the poem as their foils.

6   BROOKS, PHILIP. "Notes on Rare Books." NYTBR, 26 April,
     p. 24.
          Notes that Spenser's "divine herb" in The Faerie Queene is
     the first poetical reference in English to tobacco.

7   BUYSSENS, E. "Aristotelianism and Anti-Puritanism in
     Spenser's Allegory of the Three Sisters (Faerie Queene II,
     ii)." English Studies 18:68-73.
          Concludes that Spenser owes nothing to Plato in II.ii,
     Medina's Castle, but is faithful to Aristotle; demonstrates
     through Elissa and her lover that Spenser was not a Puritan.

8   CASTELLI, ALBERTO. La "Gerusalemma Liberata" nella Inghil-
     terra di Spenser. Publicazione della Università Cattolice del
     Sacro Cuore. Serie quarta: Scienza Filologische, XX. Milan:
     Società Editrice "Vita e Pensiero," 139 pp.
          Considers The Faerie Queene to be La Gerusalemme Liberata
     of English literature: Spenser knew well Italian literature and
     culture and follows Tasso closely in Books I and II, which gives
     these parts of The Faerie Queene a more unified structure than
     rest of poem exhibits. Shows Spenser used Tasso in two ways:
     in creating situations analogous to those in Gerusalemme Liberata
     and in borrowing specific picturesque elements, incidents, and
     parts of episodes. Concludes that Spenser represents same ideals
     as Tasso: religion, chivalry, and love. Also discusses Tasso's
     influence on Spenser's contemporaries. Concludes "La grandezza
     dello Spenser fu compresa ed esaltata dai critici: alla sua
     luce essi videro tutti gli altri atristi, ed alla sua practica
     soluzione dei problemi misurarono anche il nostro Tasso. L'opera
     di Edmund Spenser fu, si piò dire, l'arbitro della gloria del
     Tasso nel primo mezzo secolo della sua vita in Inghilterra."
     Chapters include: "Il Rinasciemento Inglese e L'Italia," "La
     Gerusalemme Liberata e La Faerie Queene," "Contemporanei e
     Seguaci di Spenser," "La Traduzioni," and "La Critica Letteraria
     Del Periodo Elisabettiano e La Gerusalemme Liberata."

*9   CLARK, RUTH E. "Elizabethan Animal Lore and Its Sources,
     Illustrated from the Works of Spenser, Lyly, and Shakespeare."
     Master's thesis, University of Arizona.
          Cited in Stephens, 1950.

10   CRAIG, HARDIN. The Enchanted Glass: The Elizabethan Mind in
      Literature. New York: Oxford University Press, 293 pp.
          See McNeir-Provost no. 606.

*11   DeLONG, CARLOTTA D. "A Comparison of the Influence of Virgil
      on Milton and Spenser." Master's thesis, University of North
      Carolina.
          Cited in Stephens, 1950.

*12   DONNELLY, HENRY E. "The Influence of The Courtier of
      Baldassare Castiglione on Spenser's Fowre Hymnes." Master's
      thesis, University of Detroit.
          Cited in Stephens, 1950.

13   DRAPER, JOHN W. "Spenser's Talus Again." PQ 15:215-17.
          Concludes that Spenser's Talus, who represents the enforce-
      ment of the law, is a classical borrowing in name and conception
      of character, whether borrowed from Plato, Apollonius, or
      Apollodorus. For supplement, see 1936.26.

14   DRESSLER, GRAHAM McF. "A Study of Aphorisms in the Poetry of
      Edmund Spenser." Ph.D. diss., University of Washington,
      136 pp.
          Examines sources, characteristics, contexts, and consis-
      tency of use of Spenser's aphoristic language, mainly in The
      Faerie Queene. Concludes that "while the sententia is unques-
      tionably a stylistic embellishment, Spenser did not consider it
      primarily so, but also as a serious device in emphasizing a fun-
      damental moral concept and as a natural element in cultivated
      speech." Aphorisms in The Faerie Queene serve Spenser's moral
      purpose, yet consistently reflect particular character's points
      of view.

15   DUNN, ESTHER CLOUDMAN. The Literature of Shakespeare's
      England. New York: Scribner's, 326 pp.
          See McNeir-Provost no. 637.

16   FINNEY, CLAUDE LEE. The Evolution of Keats's Poetry. 2 vols.
      Cambridge, Mass.: Harvard University Press, pp. 24-33, 248-
      50, 469-71, 546-47, passim.
          Discusses influence of Spenser and of eighteenth-century
      schools of Spenser and Milton on Keats. Concludes that "Imita-
      tion of Spenser" was Keats's "imaginative reactions to Spenser's
      Bower of Bliss" and "as imaginative a poem as [Keats] could have
      composed out of his impressions of a natural landscape." Notes
      Spenser's influence on Keats's poetic theories and his poetic
      diction. Concludes that "Keats derived the theme of his Endymion,
      the neo-Platonic quest of essential or ideal beauty, from several
      sources, the chief of which were Spenser's Fowre Hymnes and
      Faerie Queene." Notes several other borrowings and influences
      from The Faerie Queene in Endymion and that in October 1818,

Keats composed Spenserian stanza in which he objected to the conservative political philosophy in Book V of The Faerie Queene.
Shows that The Eve of St. Agnes is written "in the sensuous,
romantic style" of The Faerie Queene, is "the quintessence of
Spenser's sensuous style," and is written in the "intricate
stanza of The Faerie Queene.

*17   FRAZIER, F.E. "Spenser's Arthur: A Study in Allegorical
       Significance." Master's thesis, University of Oregon.
          Cited in Stephens, 1950.

 18   FRIEDRICH, WALTER G. "The Stella of Astrophel." ELH 3:114-39.
          Some references to Astrophel to help determine the identity
       of Stella in Sidney's sonnet sequence, Astrophel and Stella.

 19   GAERTNER, ADELHEID. Die englische Epithalamienliteratur im
       siebzehnten Jahrhundert und ihre Vorbilder. Coburg:
       A. Rossteutscher, 100 pp.
          Published version of 1935.23.

 20   GLEISSNER, FRIEDRICH. Die Eklogendichtung von Barclay bis
       Pope in ihrer Abhängigkeit von griechischen, lateinischen,
       und heimischen Vorbilden. Ph.D. diss., University of Vienna,
       pp. 25-29, 32-52, 58-66, 67-75, 81-97.
          See McNeir-Provost no. 2233.

 21   GLENCROSS, R.M. "Edmund Spenser's Family and the Church."
       NQ 170:231.
          Note on Thomas Spenser. For related studies, see 1936.2, 4.

 22   GOTTFRIED, RUDOLF. "Spenser and Stanyhurst." TLS, 31 October,
       p. 887.
          Considers Spenser's attack on Stanyhurst in A Veue of the
       Present State of Ireland inaccurate and unfair due to hasty com-
       position at a time (1596) when Spenser was focusing on
       Prothalamion, Fowre Hymnes, and publishing The Faerie Queene.

 23   _____. "Spenser's Ireland Dialogue." TLS, 8 February, p. 116.
          Suggests that A Veue of the Present State of Ireland was
       used by some officials to note current state of Ireland--could
       account for large number of manuscript copies of Veue and lack
       of printed edition before 1663.

 24   HEFFNER, RAY. "Essex and Book Five of The Faerie Queene."
       ELH 3:67-82.
          The episode of Burbon in The Faerie Queene, V.x.43-65
       belongs to the 1590-1594 period. Artegall is Essex, Burbon is
       Henry IV of France, and Flourdelis is France, fulfilling his
       promise in the dedicatory sonnet to make famous Essex's
       "Heroicke Parts." The episode recounts Essex's military and
       diplomatic feats in securing France as an English ally.

25   HENLEY, PAULINE. "Spenser's 'Stony Aubrian.'" <u>TLS</u>,
     28 November, p. 996.
         Suggests Bray-Dangle River as identification of the Irish
     River which Spenser calls the "Stony Aubrian" in <u>The Faerie
     Queene</u>, IV.xi.41.

26   HULBERT, VIOLA B. "Spenser's Talus Again." <u>PQ</u> 15:413.
         Points out Draper's (1936.13) oversight of a note in
     Gough's edition of Book V of <u>The Faerie Queene</u> in writing that
     "Spenser's source for Talus has somewhat escaped the attention
     of the scholars."

*27 JACKSON, ELLEN P. "Monotony and Variety in <u>The Faerie Queene</u>."
     Master's thesis, University of Colorado.
         Cited in Stephens, 1950.

28   JOHNSON, EDITH C. <u>Lamb Always Elia</u>. Boston: Marshall Jones
     Co., pp. 81-82, 134.
         Reprint of 1935.35.

*29 KEITHLEY, LENORA T. "A Comparison of Spenser's <u>Faerie Queene</u>,
     Book VI, and Castiglione's <u>The Courtier</u>." Master's thesis,
     Oklahoma A and M University.
         Cited in Stephens, 1950.

*30 KNUDSON, ANNA E. "A Study of Spenser's Influence on Milton's
     <u>Comus</u>." Master's thesis, State College of Washington.
         Cited in Stephens, 1950.

31   LANDRUM, GRACE W. "Spenser's 'Clouded Heaven.'" <u>SAB</u> 11:
     142-48.
         On the basis of Spenser's images of sky and atmosphere,
     suggests that though Spenser both consciously and unconsciously
     remembered haunting passages of "olde books . . . he reveals a
     firsthand interest in discerning the face of the sky."

32   LARRABEE, STEPHEN. "Bydding Base ('October' 5)." <u>MLN</u>
     51:535-36.
         See McNeir-Provost no. 2258.

33   LEWIS, C.S. <u>The Allegory of Love: A Study in Medieval Tradi-
     tion</u>. Oxford: Clarendon Press, 378 pp.
         See McNeir-Provost no. 1513. Reprinted: London: Oxford
     University Press, 1946, 1959; New York: Oxford University Press,
     1958; Chapter 7 reprinted: <u>Essential Articles for the Study of
     Edmund Spenser</u>, ed. A.C. Hamilton (Hamden, Conn.: Archon Books,
     1972).

34   _____. "Genius and Genius." <u>RES</u> 12:189-94.
         Distinguishes two types of Genius in <u>The Faerie Queene</u>:
     (1) the god of generation--the Porter of the Garden of Adonis;
     (2) a type which can be either good or bad--the Porter of
     Arcasia's Bower exemplifies bad type.

*35   LIEVSAY, JOHN L. "Spenser and Guazzo: A Comparative Study
       of Renaissance Attitudes." Ph.D. diss., University of
       Washington.
            Cited in Atkinson, 1937.

*36   McCALIB, CLYTIE. "The Influence of Aristotle's <u>Nichomachean
       Ethics</u> upon the Fourth Book of Spenser's <u>Faerie Queene</u>."
       Master's thesis, Oklahoma A and M University.
            Cited in Stephens, 1950.

*37   McCLAIN, MARY E. "The Epithalamions of Spenser and of
       Jonson: A Comparative Study." Master's thesis, University
       of Arizona.
            Cited in Stephens, 1950.

 38   McPEEK, JAMES A.S. "The Major Sources of Spenser's
       <u>Epithalamion</u>." <u>JEGP</u> 35:183-213.
            Compares and contrasts <u>Epithalamion</u> with similar works of
       Catullus, Du Bellay, and Buttet, and concludes that "Spenser owes
       more to the obscure Marc-Claude de Buttet than to any other author
       in the composition of the <u>Epithalamion</u>." Influence evident
       largely in thematic structure of Spenser's poem.

 39   PARMENTER, MARY. "Spenser [sic] <u>Twelve Aeglogues Proportion-
       able to the Monethes</u>." <u>ELH</u> 3:190-217.
            See McNeir-Provost no. 2287.

 40   RATHBORNE, ISABEL E. "A New Source for Spenser's Faerie
       Queene, Book I." <u>SP</u> 33:166-81.
            Concludes: "1. The homily 'Against Disobedience and
       Wilful Rebellion' may well be a direct source for parts of the
       <u>Faerie Queene</u>, Book I, and throws considerable light on Spenser's
       probable attitude toward the virtue of holiness and the religious
       basis of his encomium on the queen. 2. The evidence of the
       homily supports the belief recently gaining ground among Spenser
       scholars that we are to look to Elizabethan conditions and habits
       of thought rather than to classical philosophy or even to con-
       tinental Renaissance literature for the interpretation of Spenser's
       allegory. 3. It reinforces the now generally accepted belief in
       Spenser's Anglican conservatism. 4. It points out a somewhat
       neglected field of study in the <u>Homilies</u>, which contained the
       official teachings of the English Church in Spenser's day."

*41   RUSSELL, RUTH W. "Spenser's Use of the Bible in the First
       Two Books of <u>The Faerie Queene</u>." Master's thesis, University
       of Oklahoma.
            Cited in Stephens, 1950.

 42   RUUTZ-REES, C. <u>Flower Garlands of the Poets: Milton,
       Shakespeare, Spenser, Marot, Sannazaro</u>. In <u>Mélanges offerts</u>
       a M. Abel Lefranc. Paris: E. Droz, pp. 75-90.
            See McNeir-Provost no. 1054.

*43   SNODGRASS, DOROTHY M. "Shakespeare's Sonnets: Their Relation
      to Other Sonnets of the Elizabethan Period." Master's thesis,
      Stanford University.
            Cited in Atkinson, 1937.

 44   STEIN, HAROLD. "Spenser and William Turner." MLN 51:345-51.
            See McNeir-Provost no. 2307.

 45   SUGDEN, HERBERT W. The Grammar of Spenser's "Faerie Queene."
      Language Dissertations, no. 22. Edited by George Melville
      Bolling et al. Philadelphia: Linguistic Society of America,
      228 pp.
            Spenser generally conforms to standard usage of Elizabethan
      writers, but he is distinguished from his contemporaries by his
      free use of archaic forms. Asks and answers three principal
      questions about Spenser's archaism: In what does it consist?
      How far is it authentic and accurate? What is its extent? The
      answers: it consists chiefly in vocabulary; to a high degree it
      is authentic and accurate in spelling; its extent is in inflec-
      tions and only slightly in syntax. His archaisms almost all have
      counterparts in Middle English, and their extent is greater than
      commonly supposed. Sets forth essentials of Spenser's grammar,
      at many points comparing Spenser's English with that of Chaucer,
      Malory, Shakespeare, and Milton. Systematically presents "the
      inflection and syntax of all the parts of speech, with the excep-
      tion of the interjection." Eight chapters deal in order with
      nouns, pronouns, articles, adjectives, verbs, adverbs, preposi-
      tions, and conjunctions. Published version of 1933.66. Re-
      printed: New York: Kraus Reprint Co., 1966.

 46   THALER, ALWIN. "Shakspeare and Spenser." SAB 11:33-40.
            Finds strong evidence to suggest influence of Epithalamion
      on parts of Romeo and Juliet (e.g., "the 'runawayes eyes' passage
      in Juliet's epithalamium") and A Midsummer Night's Dream. Notes
      other parallels between the two writers.

 47   THOMPSON, EDWARD. Sir Walter Ralegh: Last of the Elizabethans.
      New Haven: Yale University Press, pp. 69-71.
            Sketches Ralegh's visit to Ireland, Spenser's commemoration
      of that visit in Colin Clouts Come Home Againe, and Ralegh and
      Spenser's visit to the Queen in London, and her bestowal of a
      £50 pension on Spenser. See McNeir-Provost no. 216.

*48   TIDWELL, M. FRED. "Aristotle's Influence on Spenser's Treat-
      ment of Justice." Master's thesis, Oklahoma A and M
      University.
            Cited in Stephens, 1950.

 49   TRAVERSI, D.A. "Revaluations (X): The Vision of Piers
      Plowman." Scrutiny 5:276-91.

Compares Spenser to Langland to show latter to have more
depth, conviction, and unity of style and content in poetry.
Contends that Spenser speaks with "the voice of a new sophisti-
cation" and is "remote from the real soil . . . his words become
little more than pleasant decorative trimmings" (illustrates with
The Shepheardes Calender). Considers Spenser first great Puritan
poet, Milton the second: "No two men have done more, by their
very genius to crush the true poetic tradition of England."
Sees Spenser caricaturing Christian sanctity in his attempt to
escape the physical and live by the spiritual (Neoplatonism).
The Faerie Queene, Book V, typical of whole poem, "represents
a view of Justice coloured by the bitter Puritan melancholy so
typical of Spenser." Regards Red Cross Knight and Guyon as the
same: "This suggests that Puritanism, as embodied in Spenser,
is nothing else than the disembodied and destructive intellect
preying on the body to kill the soul."

50 TUVE, ROSAMOND. "Spenser's Reading: The De Claris Mulieribus."
    SP 33:147-65.
        Deals "with a small but fairly simple and clear example of
    the relationship between Spenser and Boccaccio: with what traces
    there are of Spenser's having read the De claris mulieribus,
    with the question of which form (and in fact which edition) he
    read it in, and (the most significant point to be made) with the
    way in which this reading, often betrayed by mere phrases which
    it is quite unimportant to remark upon as far as source study is
    concerned, affected his notion of the significance of his mate-
    rial, pointed and directed it, and gave extra values, emotional
    'loading,' to certain names, figures, or stories."

51 WATKINS, W.B.C. Johnson and English Poetry before 1660.
    Princeton Studies in English, 13, edited by G.H. Gerould.
    Princeton: Princeton University Press, pp. 66-69.
        Johnson knew Spenser's work thoroughly, quotes from the
    whole range of Spenser's works in the Dictionary, and criticizes
    Spenser's imitators. Reprinted: New York: Gordian Press, 1965.

52 WHITAKER, VIRGIL K. "DuBartas' Use of Lucretius." SP
    33:134-46.
        Suggests that Spenser, like DuBartas, borrowed ideas from
    Latin writers without embracing their philosophies as a whole.
    Seems more probable that Spenser borrowed from Lucretius than
    from Empedocles.

53 WURTSBAUGH, JEWEL. Two Centuries of Spenserian Scholarship
    (1609-1805). Baltimore: Johns Hopkins Press; London: Oxford
    University Press, 174 pp.
        Published version of 1932.71. Reprinted: New York: AMS
    Press, 1970; New York: Kennikat Press, 1970.

No Date

*1 BROADUS, ELEANOR H. "The Influence of Chaucer on Spenser's Poetry." Manuscript. Chicago: University of Chicago Library.
    Cited in Atkinson, 1937.

*2 CARPENTER, FREDERICK IVES. "Survey of the Renaissance Lecture on Spenser." Manuscript. Chicago: University of Chicago Library.
    Cited in Atkinson, 1937.

*3 KEYES, EVA B. "Spenser and His Political Philosophy." Manuscript. Chicago: University of Chicago Library.
    Cited in Atkinson, 1937.

*4 McVICKER, ALBERTA. "Spenser's Literary Reputation from 1579-1650." Manuscript. Chicago: University of Chicago Library.
    Cited in Atkinson, 1937.

*5 WURTSBAUGH, JEWEL. "Upton's Edition of the <u>Faerie Queene</u> (1758)." Proceedings of Dr. Greenlaw's Seminary "C," [no number]. Manuscript. Baltimore: Johns Hopkins University Library.
    Cited in Atkinson, 1937.

Index

Abbatt, Thomas K., 1900.1
Acheson, Arthur, 1922.1; 1933.1
Achilles Tatius, 1925.13
Adam, Robert B., 1929.1
Adams, R. Bingham, 1927.1
Addleshaw, Percy, 1909.1;
    1910.1
Agrippa, Cornelius, 1933.67
Ainsworth, Edward Gay, 1929.2
Alabaster, William, 1923.8
Alan of Lille (Alanus de
    Insulis), 1923.17; 1924.20;
    1929.6, 29; 1935.65
Albright, Evelyn May, 1926.1;
    1927.2; 1928.1; 1929.3-4;
    1932.1
Alden, Raymond M., 1903.1;
    1931.1
Allegory
-historical, topical, political,
    moral, 1900.15, 17; 1902.8;
    1903.4; 1904.2, 10, 14-15,
    18, 22, 24; 1905.19-20, 27;
    1906.13, 23; 1907.15, 25;
    1908.19; 1909.25, 29, 34-35;
    1910.7, 9, 19-20, 24-25;
    1911.4, 6, 9-10, 16, 31, 34,
    37; 1912.9, 11-12, 18-19,
    23, 31-33, 39, 42, 45;
    1913.2, 25-26, 40; 1914.10-
    11, 14-15, 19-20; 1915.3-4,
    7, 10, 13, 18; 1916.16,
    19, 21-22; 1917.15-17;
    1918.9, 12-14, 28; 1919.11-
    13; 1920.2, 4, 6, 10, 12,
    14, 21, 24-26; 1921.2-3,
    8, 14; 1923.1, 17, 21, 26,

28, 32, 37; 1924.15, 17, 19-
    20, 25, 30; 1925.9, 13, 24,
    26, 28, 30, 34; 1926.3, 5,
    14, 24, 30, 37, 45, 49;
    1927.2, 25, 36; 1928.1, 3,
    24, 28, 37, 39, 43, 49;
    1929.2, 4, 15, 18, 20, 23,
    24, 28, 35; 1930.5, 17, 20,
    26-27, 31, 34, 39, 42-43,
    47, 50, 55; 1931.3, 30, 33,
    37, 39, 46, 48, 52; 1932.3-4,
    7, 13, 14, 24, 38, 39, 43,
    47; 1933.4, 7, 17, 20, 35,
    50, 52, 64, 67, 70-71;
    1934.1, 3, 4, 11, 15, 22,
    31, 33, 38-39, 46-47, 54,
    57-58, 60-61, 63, 65, 70;
    1935.11, 33, 45, 52-53, 57,
    64-66, 70, 75; 1936.3, 5, 8,
    17, 24, 33, 40, 49-50,
    no date 3
-tradition, theory, and tech-
    nique of, 1902.8; 1904.10,
    14-15, 22, 24; 1905.19, 27;
    1906.13, 23; 1907.15;
    1908.7, 19; 1909.25, 29, 35;
    1910.9, 18-19; 1911.4, 9,
    16, 31, 34; 1912.9, 11, 18-
    19, 23, 31-32, 39, 42, 45;
    1913.15, 26, 37; 1914.11,
    19-20; 1915.2, 4, 10, 13,
    18; 1916.19, 22; 1917.17;
    1918.9, 13, 23, 28; 1919.8,
    11-12; 1920.2, 4, 6, 14, 24,
    26; 1921.2, 8, 14; 1923.1,
    26, 28, 32; 1924.15, 17, 25,
    30; 1925.13, 24, 28, 34;

Index

Axiochus (translation attributed
    to Spenser), 1934.48–49;
    1935.22, 55
Ayfers, Ruth Jane, 1935.3
Ayers, Harry Morgan, 1908.4

B., E.K., 1918.1
B., R.S., 1928.2
Bacon, Sir Francis, 1901.3, 7,
    10, 24–25; 1902.13, 32;
    1907.9, 25, 34; 1908.11;
    1911.11, 42; 1912.44;
    1913.8, 13; 1914.7;
    1919.16; 1923.19; 1928.56;
    1929.45–46; 1930.49; 1933.6
Baïf, Jean Antoine De,
    1910.15; 1929.23
Baldwin, T.W., 1924.1
Ball, Lewis F., 1931.3; 1934.4
Ballière, Paul, 1927.4
Bamber, Juretta V., 1927.5
Bannerman, W. Bruce, 1912.1
Barber, Cora Livingston, 1905.2
Baroway, Israel, 1930.2;
    1933.5; 1934.5–6; 1935.4
Barrington, Sybil, 1923.2
Barrow, Sarah Field, 1902.4
Barry, E., 1901.1
Bartholomaeus Anglicus, 1907.10
Baskerville, Charles Read,
    1910.2; 1913.2; 1920.1
Bateson, F.W., 1934.7
Batman vppon Bartholme, 1933.67
Bauer, R., 1924.2
Bayfield, M.A., 1921.1
Bayley, A.R., 1911.1; 1912.2–4
Bayley, M.F., 1933.5–6
Bayne, Thomas, 1908.5; 1911.2
Beach, Joseph Warren, 1903.3
Beale, Dorothea, 1902.5
Beatty, Elsie, 1925.2
Beaumont, Francis, 1924.1
Beer, N.A., 1929.5
Beers, Henry Augustus, 1901.2
Behler, Mally, 1923.3
Belden, H.M., 1929.6–7
Bell, Edna F., 1928.3
Bellamy, Charles H., 1928.4
Bembo, Pietro Cardinal, 1927.6;
    1931.40; 1935.47
Benchoff, Howard S., 1904.2

Benedetti, Anna, 1914.1
Benivieni, Girolamo, 1900.7;
    1911.13–14; 1929.4; 1931.6;
    1932.52; 1935.5
Bennett, Josephine Waters,
    1931.4–6; 1932.4–5; 1933.7;
    1935.5; 1936.3
Bense, J.F., 1916.1
Bensly, Edward, 1918.2–3;
    1930.3; 1935.6; 1936.4
Berdan, John M., 1920.2; 1924.3
Berli, Hans, 1913.3
Berry, Albert M., 1932.6
Berry, Henry F., 1905.3; 1906.2
Berkley, Frances C., 1904.3
Bestor, Arthur Eugene, Jr.,
    1934.8
Beutner, Sister Mary Louise,
    1933.8
Bhattacherje, Mohinimohan,
    1929.8; 1935.7
Biblical references, allusions,
    influences in Spenser's
    poetry, 1905.22; 1906.18;
    1907.25; 1919.6; 1925.28;
    1926.27, 33; 1929.4, 9, 38;
    1930.2, 8; 1933.5, 20;
    1934.5; 1935.4; 1936.41
Bibliographies and bibliograph-
    ical studies, 1920.8; 1923.6;
    1924.6, 12; 1928.33–34;
    1930.22–23; 1931.58; 1932.25,
    71–72; 1933.30, 58; 1934.61,
    66; 1936.53
Binkley, Harold C., 1926.2
Biographical studies of Spenser,
    1900.5, 11; 1901.1, 16, 19,
    21; 1902.15; 1903.6–7, 9, 25,
    32–33; 1904.1, 6, 11–13;
    1904.20, 27, 37; 1905.1, 3,
    6, 8, 11–12, 18, 26; 1906.2,
    7–9, 21, 23; 1907.17, 20, 24;
    1908.10, 13, 22, 28; 1909.10,
    15, 27, 30, 34; 1910.24, 31;
    1911.41; 1912.1–4, 11, 20,
    22, 25, 37, 38–39, 42, 45;
    1913.1, 7, 14, 39; 1914.7;
    1915.10, 14, 17; 1916.18, 26,
    28; 1917.13, 21, 1918.19;
    1919.2, 16; 1920.4, 14, 17,
    20, 26; 1921.4, 7, 22;

1922.5-6, 9, 27-28; 1923.13,
19, 24, 26, 29, 42; 1924.2,
5, 7-9, 16, 29, 40-41;
1926.11, 25, 30, 36, 52, 57;
1927.1, 16-17, 24, 26, 33,
35; 1928.2, 4, 9, 13, 22-23,
47, 61; 1929.45-46, 48;
1930.10, 19, 22, 49; 1931.4,
12, 14, 22, 25, 49; 1932.1,
26-31, 36-37, 46, 65, 67,
70; 1933.15-16, 20, 32, 35,
38, 46, 50, 68-69; 1934.23,
35, 53, 55, 61, 67-68;
1935.12-13, 15, 25, 34, 57;
1936.2, 4, 21, 47
Bion, 1905.15; 1909.28; 1911.30;
1913.30; 1921.10; 1923.21;
1934.28
Blachiston, H.E.D., 1908.6
Blackmore, Richard, 1931.7;
1934.4
Blair, Lawrence, 1932.7; 1933.9
Blanchard, Harold H., 1921.2;
1925.3-4
Boas, Mrs. Frederick (Henrietta
O'Brien), 1903.4; 1904.4
Boas, Frederick S., 1909.3;
1926.3
Boas, Guy, 1926.4
Boatwright, Evelyn, 1929.9
Boccaccio, Giovanni, 1905.14;
1911.5; 1929.29; 1931.40;
1932.43; 1934.27; 1936.50
Boddy, Margaret P., 1932.8
Bodin, Jean, 1919.8
Boehm, Kurt, 1909.4-5
Boethius, 1933.64, 67
Böhme, Traugott, 1911.3
Boiardo, Matteo Maria, 1921.2;
1924.3; 1925.4; 1931.31
Bolwell, Robert, 1916.2-3
Bompas, G.C., 1901.3
Bond, R. Warwick, 1902.6;
1908.7
Borghesi, Peter, 1906.3
Borland, Lois, 1913.4
Botta, Anne C. Lynch, 1902.7;
1922.3; 1923.4
Botting, Roland B., 1935.8
Boughner, Daniel C., 1932.9

Boyle, Elizabeth, 1903.9, 25;
1904.37; 1905.3; 1907.14;
1908.26; 1910.27; 1911.26;
1916.15; 1922.27; 1923.13,
42; 1924.40; 1927.26;
1931.22; 1932.29; 1933.25
Boys, H. Ward, 1908.8
Bradford, Gamaliel, 1936.5
Bradley, Henry, 1904.5
Bradner, Leicester, 1928.5;
1934.9; 1935.9
Breslar, M.L.R., 1911.4
Breton, Nicholas, 1919.9
Brie, Friedrich, 1914.2; 1917.2;
1918.4; 1928.6
Briggs, William Dinsmore, 1911.5
Bright, James Wilson, 1910.3;
1913.5; 1921.3
Brinkley, Robert Florence,
1929.10; 1931.7
Brittain's Ida, 1909.3; 1923.40
Broadus, Edmund Kemper, 1903.5;
1921.4; 1932.10
Broadus, Eleanor H., no date 1
Broadribb, C.W., 1912.5
Brooke, C.F. Tucker, 1922.4;
1933.10
Brooks, Philip, 1936.6
Brown, L.A., 1914.3
Brown, Peter Franklin, 1905.4
Browne, William, 1904.38;
1905.2; 1911.7
Bruce, J. Douglas, 1912.6;
1928.7
Brunner, K., 1914.4
Bruno, Giordano, 1902.3;
1903.20; 1907.33; 1911.13;
1913.31; 1928.31; 1929.8;
1930.14
Bryan, Charleyne, 1932.11
Bryce, J.C., 1933.11
Bryskett, Lodowick, 1906.2, 13;
1914.13; 1915.17; 1918.9;
1924.8; 1927.24; 1932.36
Buchanan, George, 1924.8;
1935.25
Buck, Philo M., Jr., 1904.6;
1906.4; 1907.3; 1908.9;
1911.6
Buckley, George T., 1932.12
Bullock, Walter L., 1927.6;
1931.8

1916.10-11; 1917.12;
1918.13; 1920.9-10; 1923.16-
17; 1925.9-10; 1926.18;
1927.15; 1929.18; 1930.14;
1932.24-25
Greenough, James Bradstreet,
1901.11; 1902.16; 1906.11;
1908.17; 1911.18; 1914.6;
1916.12; 1920.11; 1926.19;
1929.19; 1931.21; 1933.27;
1935.29
Greenslet, Ferris, 1900.7
Greenwood, Granville G.,
1908.18; 1916.13
Greg, Walter Wilson, 1903.14;
1905.15; 1906.12; 1932.26
Greville, Fulke, 1908.37-38;
1928.39
Grey, Arthur, Baron de Wilton,
1909.14, 34; 1910.32;
1913.10; 1916.28; 1919.8;
1921.5; 1924.8; 1926.23;
1927.24; 1928.22; 1932.36;
1933.35; 1934.35; 1935.25
Grierson, Herbert John Clifford,
1922.12; 1929.20
Grindal, Edmund, 1934.33
Grismer, Frank A., 1934.25
Grolier Club, The, 1901.12
Grosseteste, Robert, 1919.14
Grubb, Marion, 1935.30
Guazzo, Stefano, 1910.11;
1936.35
Gummere, Francis B., 1908.22
Gurney, Thomas, 1909.30
Gwin, H.H., 1928.16
Gwynn, Stephen Lucius, 1904.17

H., A.C., 1912.20
Haggett, Dorothy Gene, 1928.17
Haines, C.R., 1924.18
Hales, John W., 1909.15;
1922.13; 1923.18
Hall, Edgar A., 1913.16
Hall, Joseph, 1910.25; 1932.24
Hall, William C., 1929.21
Hamer, Douglas, 1931.22;
1932.27-31
Hamer, Enid, 1930.15
Hanford, J. Holly, 1910.8
Hankins, John E., 1929.22

Haraszti, Zoltan, 1933.28
Hard, Frederick, 1926.20;
1928.18; 1930.16; 1931.23-24;
1933.29; 1934.26
Harington, Sir John, 1907.7
Harman, Edward George, 1914.7;
1923.19; 1925.11
Harper, Carrie A., 1908.19;
1910.9-10; 1913.17
Harris, Rendel, 1919.6
Harris, Robert Bruce, 1930.17
Harrison, Charles T., 1932.32
Harrison, John S., 1903.15-16;
1919.7
Harrison, T.P., Jr., 1930.18-19;
1933.30-31; 1934.27-28
Harvey, Gabriel, 1901.18, 25;
1902.26; 1905.25; 1907.14;
1908.36-37; 1910.7; 1912.42,
44; 1913.3, 31; 1915.16;
1918.27; 1923.24; 1926.11;
1927.26; 1928.1; 1929.16;
1931.4, 50; 1932.12; 1933.50,
61; 1934.59, 69; 1935.67;
1936.3
Harvey-Spenser Correspondence,
treatments of, 1902.26;
1904.35-36; 1905.25; 1906.4;
1908.36-37; 1910.7; 1912.44;
1913.3, 31; 1914.9, 12;
1915.16; 1922.5; 1926.2, 6,
11; 1927.16; 1928.15;
1930.22; 1931.4; 1932.1, 57;
1933.50; 1934.23, 69; 1935.41
Hawes, Stephen, 1905.28-29;
1922.17
Hawthorne, Nathaniel, 1933.63
Hayes, John R., 1908.20
Hazlitt, William Carew, 1902.17-
18; 1908.21; 1912.21
Heffner, Hubert C., 1922.14
Heffner, Ray, 1925.12; 1928.19;
1930.20; 1931.25; 1933.32;
1934.29; 1935.31; 1936.24
Heffner, Roy, 1933.18
Heinemann, Elfriede, 1928.20-21
Heise, Wilhelm, 1901.13; 1902.19
Heliodorus, 1925.13
Hendricks, Ira K., 1926.21
Henley, Pauline, 1928.22; 1933.33;
1936.25

Kilcolman Castle, 1900.11;
    1901.16; 1902.11; 1903.33;
    1905.26; 1908.28; 1909.27;
    1912.4, 15; 1915.14, 17;
    1917.3; 1920.17; 1924.8;
    1928.22; 1929.48; 1931.25;
    1933.38
Kindon, J., 1904.22
King, Emma C., 1912.27
King, R.W., 1920.15
Kingsford, C.L., 1923.24
Kirke, Edward, 1907.15; 1912.23,
    42; 1926.11
Kite, Edward, 1907.17
Kittredge, George Lyman,
    1902.16; 1920.11; 1935.38
Kliem, Hans, 1915.8
Knapp, Charles, 1934.40
Knolles, Lettice, 1930.27
Knowlton, E.C., 1924.20;
    1928.28; 1935.39
Knudson, Anna E., 1936.30
Koeppel, E., 1900.10; 1901.17;
    1905.16; 1906.15; 1910.14
Kohler, Karl, 1923.25
Koller, Katherine, 1932.41;
    1934.35; 1935.40
Krans, Horatio S., 1905.17
Kreb, Valentin, 1902.21
Kuersteiner, Agnes Duncan,
    1935.41
Kuhns, Oscar, 1904.23
Kurtz, Benjamin Putnam, 1920.8

L., H.P., 1902.22-23
Lamb, Charles (1775-1834),
    1925.27; 1931.23; 1933.24,
    29; 1935.35
Lamb, Charles, 1933.39
Landino, Cristoforo, 1929.24
Landrum, Grace Warren, 1926.27;
    1936.31
Langdon, Ida, 1911.23-24;
    1912.28; 1924.21
Langland, William, 1936.49
Language and Style, 1900.3;
    1901.11; 1902.4; 1903.2;
    1904.5, 26, 38; 1905.15;
    1906.15, 23; 1907.15;
    1908.30, 33-34; 1909.4-5, 13,
    17-18, 29, 33; 1910.25, 29;

1911.20, 28, 34, 36; 1912.7,
    11-12, 14, 18, 23, 27, 35-36,
    42, 45; 1913.29; 1914.4, 17,
    19; 1915.9, 11, 13, 15;
    1916.2, 13; 1917.8, 13;
    1918.3, 12; 1919.1, 3;
    1920.14-15, 19, 24; 1921.1-3,
    10, 13, 16; 1922.5, 7-8, 19-
    21; 1923.21, 26, 30, 36;
    1924.11-12, 25, 29; 1925.17-
    18, 23, 25, 28; 1926.12, 32,
    39, 42, 44; 1927.12, 19, 25;
    1928.3, 17, 42; 1929.23;
    1930.1, 22, 36, 51-52, 55;
    1931.45, 55; 1932.2, 20, 44,
    57; 1933.4, 19-20, 22, 66,
    72; 1934.7, 21, 45, 50;
    1935.10, 56, 69; 1936.14, 45
Lanz, Henry, 1931.29
Larrabee, Stephen, 1936.32
Latham, Minor White, 1930.24
Laureate, Poet, 1901.12; 1904.9;
    1913.1; 1921.4; 1928.4
Law, Robert Adger, 1924.22;
    1934.36
Lawrence, C.E., 1927.17-18
Lawson, Charles F., 1904.24
Lay of Clorinda, The, 1916.17;
    1920.19; 1930.22; 1933.30;
    1934.23
Lea, Kathleen M., 1925.14
Le Bel, Eugene C., 1931.30
Lee, Renselaer W., 1926.28;
    1928.29
Lee, Sidney, 1904.25-27; 1905.18;
    1907.18; 1908.25; 1909.15;
    1925.15; 1932.42; 1934.37
Leeming, Edith Mary, 1916.15
Lefrance, Abel, 1918.15
Legends (lost work of Spenser),
    1931.53
Legouis, Émile, 1921.11; 1923.26;
    1926.29-31; 1930.25; 1933.40-
    41
Leible, Arthur B., 1925.16;
    1930.26
Leicester, Robert Dudley, Earl of,
    1902.32; 1908.9, 11; 1910.7;
    1911.11, 42; 1912.19; 1913.14;
    1916.16; 1920.1; 1922.12;
    1923.26; 1926.6; 1928.37, 45;
    1931.48; 1935.32

--Roffyn, 1912.23; 1913.24
--Rosalind, 1904.7; 1907.9, 12,
    21; 1908.27; 1911.11, 17;
    1912.23; 1922.8; 1924.18;
    1927.22, 35; 1934.72
--"September," 1911.29;
    1912.23; 1924.34; 1930.17;
    1931.39; 1934.33
--Thomalin, 1912.23; 1913.13;
    1925.26
--Tityrus, 1923.41
--Willie, 1913.13; 1920.16
--Wrenock, 1913.33
Sheppard, S., 1923.41
Sherer, Gertrude R., 1917.20
Sherrick, Hazel L., 1925.30
Shipley, Joseph T., 1924.34
Shull, Virginia M., 1932.58
Sidney, Ambrosia, 1907.30
Sidney, Mary, 1912.23; 1933.25
Sidney, Sir Philip, 1901.18;
    1904.3, 26; 1906.4, 9;
    1907.4, 20, 30; 1908.36-37;
    1909.1, 26; 1910.6; 1912.23,
    42; 1913.15, 31; 1914.7, 9;
    1915.10, 16; 1916.8, 11;
    1917.2; 1918.4; 1920.12;
    1921.12; 1923.3, 16, 24;
    1928.24, 57; 1930.19, 27,
    40; 1931.12, 41-42, 49, 56;
    1932.36, 51, 55; 1934.23,
    53, 61; 1935.59-60; 1936.18
Sills, Kenneth, C.M., 1910.26
Simier, Jean de, Baron de
    St. Marc, 1910.7; 1930.27
Singleton, Hugh, 1925.26;
    1933.14
Sisson, Charles J., 1930.45
Skelton, John, 1910.2
Skinner, Robert, 1928.42
Smit, Johan, 1929.44
Smith, Charles G., 1926.49;
    1930.46; 1934.57-58;
    1935.64-66
Smith, D. Nichol, 1916.28;
    1932.59
Smith, George Charles Moore,
    1905.25; 1906.22; 1907.30;
    1913.31-33; 1933.61;
    1934.59; 1935.67
Smith, G. Gregory, 1904.36

Smith, J.C., 1910.27
Smith, L. Toulmin, 1909.20;
    1932.33
Smith, Reed, 1909.35; 1913.34
Smith, Roland, 1935.68-69.
Smythe-Palmer, A., 1908.35
Snodgrass, Dorothy A., 1936.43
Snyder, Edward D., 1920.25
Socrates, 1920.10; 1924.36
Sohr, Ludwig, 1921.16
Southey, Robert, 1911.38;
    1928.14
Sparke, Archibald, 1915.1
Spencer, Rosamund, 1906.8
Spencers of Althorp, 1906.21
Spens, Janet, 1934.60
Spenser, Catherine, 1924.40-41;
    1933.46
Spenser, Edmond, 1901.1
Spenser, Edmund, biography.
    See Biographical studies of
    Spenser
Spenser, James, 1921.22; 1933.69
Spenser, John, 1903.6
Spenser, Peregrine, 1924.40;
    1931.22
Spenser, Sarah, 1912.1
Spenser, Sylvanus, 1901.1;
    1924.40
Spenser, Thomas, 1936.4
Spenser, William, 1901.1
Spenser-Harvey Correspondence.
    See Harvey-Spenser
    Correspondence, treatments of
Spenserians (Seventeenth Century),
    1900.7; 1911.8; 1916.25
Spenser's influence. See Imita-
    tations of Spenser and
    Spenser's influence
Spenser's literary reputation.
    See Literary reputation
Speroni, Sperone, 1927.6;
    1929.24; 1931.40
Sprague, Arthur Colby, 1933.62
Spruill, Mary J., 1922.23
Spurgeon, Caroline F.E., 1911.36;
    1913.35; 1914.17; 1918.26;
    1921.17; 1922.24; 1924.35;
    1925.31
Squire, John Collings, 1919.16

Winstanley, Lilian, 1900.17;
1907.33; 1914.20; 1915.18;
1920.28; 1924.42; 1928.59-
60; 1932.69
Wither George, 1904.38
Wollerman, Ira D., 1927.36
Women, treatment of in Spenser's
works, 1901.14; 1902.5;
1905.27; 1916.23; 1917.16;
1928.20-21; 1934.70; 1936.5
Wood, Herbert, 1929.48
Wood, Ruth, 1934.71
Woodberry, George Edward,
1905.27; 1906.24; 1912.43;
1920.29
Woodford, Samuel, 1912.8
Woodward, Parker, 1901.24-25;
1907.34; 1911.42; 1912.44
Wordsworth, William, 1908.8;
1927.18; 1932.53; 1934.60

Wormell, Helen E., 1932.70
Wrinn, Mary J.J., 1935.79
Wurtsbaugh, Jewel, 1932.71;
1933.73; 1935.80-81;
1936.53, no date 5
Wyld, Henry Cecil, 1930.55
Wyllie, J.W., 1931.58; 1932.72

Yardley, E., 1907.35
Yates, Frances A., 1934.72
Yeats, William Butler, 1912.45;
1919.18
Young, John, Bishop of Rochester,
1912.23; 1913.24; 1916.16;
1934.9, 33

Zander, Friedrich, 1905.28-29
Zeitler, W.I., 1928.61
Zocco, Irene, 1906.25